UNSETTLED PASTS

unsettled pasts

RECONCEIVING THE WEST

THROUGH WOMEN'S HISTORY

edited by Sarah Carter, Lesley Erickson,

Patricia Roome, *&* Char Smith

UNIVERSITY *of* CALGARY PRESS

© 2005 Sarah Carter, Lesley Erickson, Patricia Roome, Char Smith

Published by the
University of Calgary Press
2500 University Drive NW
Calgary, Alberta, Canada T2N 1N4
www.uofcpress.com

We acknowledge the financial support of the Government of Canada, through the Book Publishing Industry Development Program (BPIDP), and the Alberta Foundation for the Arts for our publishing activities. We acknowledge the support of the Canada Council for the Arts for our publishing program.

Library and Archives Canada Cataloguing in Publication

Unsettled pasts : reconceiving the west through women's history / edited by Sarah Carter ... [et al.].

Papers presented at a conference held at the University of Calgary, June 2002.
Includes bibliographical references and index.
ISBN 1-55238-177-3

1. Women – Canada, Western – History – Congresses. 2. Women – Canada, Western – Social conditions – Congresses.   I. Carter, Sarah, 1954–

HQ1459.P6U57 2005   305.4'09712
C2005-906219-3

Cover design, Mieka West.
Cover photograph, Glenbow Archives, ND-3-5849D.
Internal design & typesetting, Garet Markvoort, zijn digital.

dedicated to

ELIANE LESLAU SILVERMAN

Feminist Activist, Educator, & Historian

table of contents

acknowledgments

This book emerged out of the "Unsettled Pasts: Reconceiving the West through Women's History" conference, held at the University of Calgary in June 2002. The event would not have been possible without the dedication and enthusiasm of a diverse group of women – activists, feminists, historians, and writers – who worked in concert with numerous funding agencies and departments to make the conference a success. We extend our thanks to the following members of the conference organizing committee: Jennifer Bobrovitz, Geertje Boschma, Cristine Bye, Catherine Cavanaugh, Laurel Halladay, Jennifer Hamblin, Elizabeth Jameson, Sheila Johnston, Nadine Kozak, Margaret McCready, Grit McCreath, Nancy Millar, Gayle Thrift, Cora Voyageur, and Anne White. Special thanks are extended to Brenda Oslawsky, Susan Austen, Roland Longpré, and Mark White.

We are grateful to the following organizations that helped fund the event: the Social Sciences and Humanities Research Council of Canada, the University of Calgary Special Projects Grant Committee, the University of Calgary Research Grants Committee, the Alberta Historical Resources Foundation, and the University of Calgary Planning Initiatives Fund:

Offices of the President and Vice-Presidents. At the University of Calgary, the following faculties, departments, institutes, and associations likewise provided invaluable financial support: Communications and Culture, English, the Graduate Students' Association, Graduate Studies, History, Humanities, Information Resources, the Institute for Gender Research, Nursing; the Nursing, Philosophy, and History Group; Political Science, Religious Studies, Social Science, and the University of Calgary Press. Finally, we extend our thanks to following sponsors: Athabasca University; Pat Burke, Remax/Landa; the Calgary Public Library; the Coalition for Western Women's History; Barb Dacks, *Legacy Magazine*; Detselig Press; Dr. N. A. Earl, D.M.D.; the Famous Five Foundation; Glenbow Museum and Archives; the Historical Society of Alberta; Kris Matthews, The Matthews Group; Scott McCreath; BMO Nesbitt Burns; Mount Royal College; University of Oklahoma Press; and University Printing Services.

We have had the good fortune to work with an excellent group of editors and designers. Special credit is due to Lesley Erickson for her work on the introductions to each of the articles and special thanks is extended to Walter Hildebrandt, John King, Scott Anderson, and Mieka West at University of Calgary Press for shepherding the manuscript through all stages of the publishing process. Finally, we would like to thank the anonymous reviewers for their helpful comments and questions.

one

INTRODUCTION

Sarah Carter, Lesley Erickson,

& Patricia Roome

On 19 June 1871, Sara Riel, who was sister to Louis Riel and a Grey Nun, began her sixty-eight-day journey by Red River cart from St. Boniface, Manitoba, to Île-à-la-Crosse in the Canadian subarctic. Riel kept a journal and corresponded with friends and family during the arduous journey; in both mediums, she revealed a woman in the process of becoming the first Métis missionary in the North American west. Describing her encounters with the land and the landscape, she wrote home, "The hardships of this trip are incredible. To avoid lying down in the water

... we cut spruce branches for ourselves to serve as bedsteads.... The mad mosquitoes supplied us with music every night – an orchestra all day long."[1] Forty-five years later, in 1916, Inga Fimrite, a recent immigrant and single mother with three children, began a similar journey when she joined a group of Scandinavian settlers on the Edson Trail who were planning to establish a Norwegian Lutheran settlement in Peace River Country, northern Alberta. Twenty-one years later, in 1937, Clare Sheridan, an upper-class British sculptor and writer, engaged in her own artistic and cultural odyssey when her world travels took her to Montana and Alberta, where she spent six months among the Blackfoot of the Great Plains. In the published account of her experiences, Sheridan commented that the land and the people "had a salutary effect upon me, they brought me back to earth."[2]

These women's stories hint at the complicated historical relationship that lies at the heart of this book: the connection between gender, place, and the processes that shaped the diversity of women's experiences in the Canadian west.[3] These women's narratives were told at a conference, held at the University of Calgary in the summer of 2002, that drew together ninety-five presenters in dialogue with seventy-five delegates to discuss, debate, and explore the history of the region from the vantage point of women and with an awareness of gender as a category of historical analysis.[4] We were and are fully cognizant that "the West" is a cultural construction that was shaped historically by diverse groups and competing interests over time. As an Aboriginal woman, Sara Riel understood the region known to central Canadians as "the West," simply as "home"; her "West" would have been the "West beyond the West," British Columbia.[5] To Inga Fimrite, a Norwegian immigrant who settled in Alberta via the United States, her eventual home was, perhaps, the "North"; to an international traveler like Sheridan, "the West" was one of many "frontier" outposts in the far reaches of the British Empire that she visited on her journeys. Place, as historical geographers argue, is a spatial reality constructed by people.[6]

We sought to challenge imposed definitions of "the West" by bringing together scholars from across the Pacific Northwest and the Prairies, from the North and the Great Plains, and from both sides of the Canadian-American border.[7]

Historians Elizabeth Jameson and Sheila McManus are currently editing a volume of articles that will introduce the work of conference participants engaged in studying western women's cross-border and

PLACES, BORDERS, & BOUNDARIES

provincial borders

pre 1905 territorial boundaries

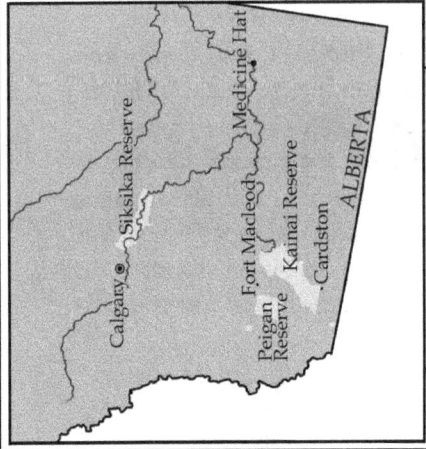

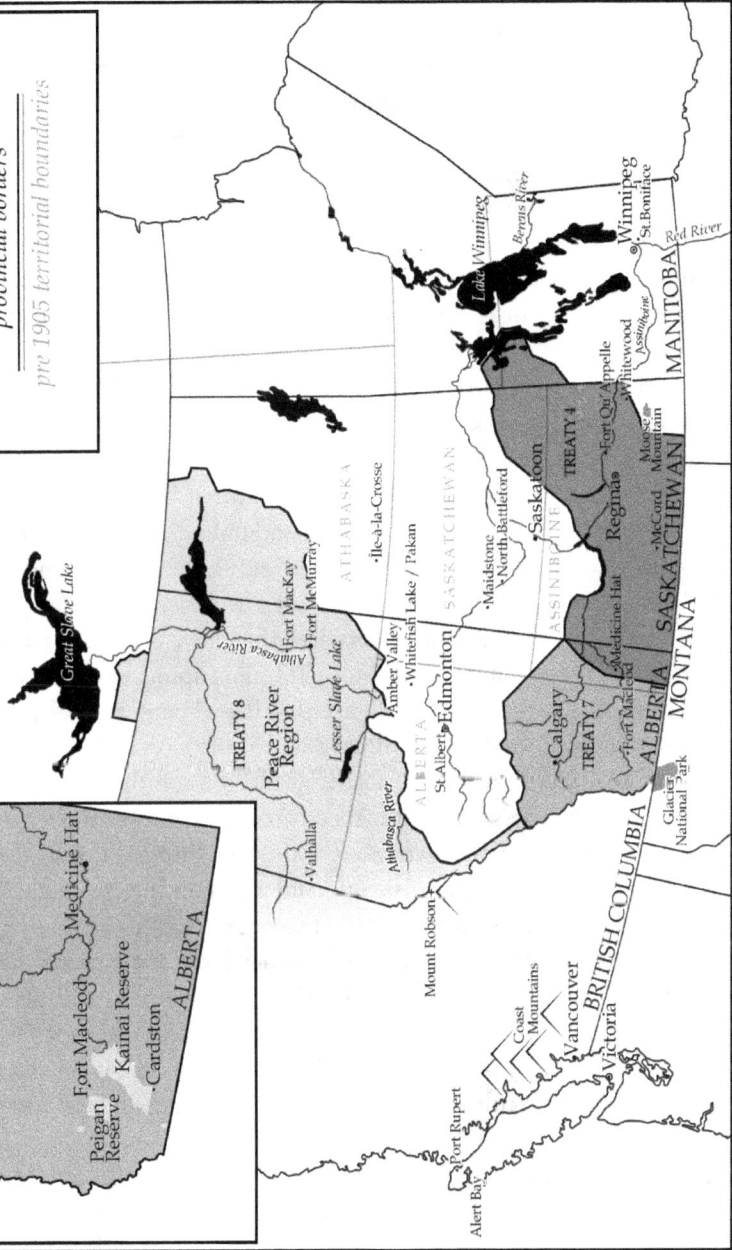

Courtesy: Roland Longpre

transnational experiences within a comparative historical framework.[8] Our volume introduces the work of scholars, activists, artists, and writers who are engaged in exploring how women negotiated their lives and identities within the imposed and resisted structures of colonialism and nation-building in what would become the three Prairie provinces (Manitoba, Saskatchewan, and Alberta) and British Columbia.[9] These essays and articles explore, from diverse perspectives and vantage points, how Native and newcomer women navigated constraints within a region that was sold in the late nineteenth century as a land of opportunity and freedom, but was envisaged by the builders of nation and empire as a "frontier" for a reinvigorated masculinity and a "reinstituted patriarchy."[10]

After nearly three decades of increasingly sophisticated work in women's and gender history, popular and academic narratives of the West continue to privilege the masculine and to be dominated by the powerful images of the whisky trader, Indian chief, cowboy, Mountie, missionary, stalwart pioneer, farmer, and politician.[11] This volume builds upon past research, not simply by bringing new stories and narratives about women and gender to light, but also by creating dialogues across the cultural and geographic borders that have shaped how historians approach the region and its history. It builds upon the conversations and dialogues that began at the "Unsettled Pasts" conference, conversations that sought to bridge disciplinary and professional boundaries and to create dialogue between the academy and the community.[12] Because the contributors represent a broad spectrum of the public (university faculty and graduate students, activists within the Aboriginal community and archivists, museum professionals and independent researchers, novelists, politicians, and filmmakers), the book includes a variety of modes of expression, analysis, and narration: academic articles and interviews, ficto-critical monologue and reminiscences, speeches and performance pieces, post-structural discourse analysis, and life writing.[13] The result is a nuanced history of the West, one that presents the region as a place "in which different cultures met, sometimes conflicted, but also compromised and intermingled."[14]

Part 1, "Complicating Categories: Women as Cultural Mediators," and Part 2, "Colonial Projects and their Legacies," include articles that assess the complicated role that women and gender played in Canada's colonial and nation-building projects to create a White settler society in the West following its entry into Canadian Confederation.[15] The articles and interviews by Lesley Erickson, Patricia Roome, Graham MacDonald, and Cora Voyageur, for instance, highlight the degree to which women's experiences and gender as a category of historical analysis can complicate traditional narratives of Native-newcomer relations.[16] Erickson builds upon feminist histories of the fur trade and Catholic sisterhoods by using the experiences of Louis Riel and his sister, Sara, as a case study to explore how gender intersected with race and class to shape Métis men and women's divergent responses to colonization and Catholicism. In its exploration of the siblings' role as cultural mediators, her work challenges, or complicates, simplistic historical categorizations that depict Euro-Canadians as colonizers and Aboriginal peoples as victims. Patricia Roome builds upon this theme by exploring how Henrietta Muir Edwards, one of Alberta's "Famous Five," far from being an "infamous racist," tried to negotiate or challenge many of the constraints imposed upon middle-class White women on colonial frontiers when she developed personal relationships with Aboriginal men and women and spoke on their behalf. Clare Sheridan, the subject of Graham MacDonald's research, likewise became an outspoken critic of the Canadian government's Indian policy; she provides a fascinating example of a European traveler and newcomer who was determined to learn about Aboriginal culture and society.

Cora Voyageur's conversation with Senator Thelma Chalifoux, a Métis activist, spokesperson, and politician from Alberta, however, reminds us of the barriers, hardships, and challenges that many women and children faced growing up Aboriginal in the region. Kristin Burnett, in fact, examines the process by which Indigenous women were constructed negatively as racialised "others" in opposition to White newcomer women. Burnett focuses on the writings of three male Methodist missionaries, John Maclean, Egerton Ryerson Young, and John McDougall, in order to examine the complex role that women and gender played in British-Canadian identity construction at the turn of the twentieth century. Muriel Stanley Venne's speech, "The 'S' Word: Reclaiming 'Esquao' for Aboriginal Women," offers an anti-racist feminist critique of race relations in the West by disclosing how negative stereotypes of Aboriginal women have adversely affected the women in her family. As the first Métis woman appointed to the Alberta Human Rights Commission and the founder and president of the Institute for the Advancement of Aboriginal Women, Stanley Venne has dedicated her life to correcting and challenging the legacies of conquest. Drawing extensively upon (post)colonial theory, Mary Leah de Zwart examines another aspect of these legacies by deconstructing recipes that appeared in domestic science handbooks on the Prairies and in British Columbia and interpreting them as metaphors for the aspirations and racial assumptions of White, urban, and middle-class British-Canadians.

The extent to which "expert" advice and opinion, contained in advice to wives and mothers, often diverged from the everyday realities of Native and newcomer women's lives is a theme that runs throughout Part 3, "Family, Region, Nation." The essays by Sarah Carter, Nadine Kozak, and Cristine Bye contribute to an expanding body of scholarship that explores how the management of domestic and sexual relationships was integral to colonial and nation-building projects in the late nineteenth and early twentieth centuries.[17] Carter focuses on the federal administration of marriage law among Aboriginal peoples in the key decades between 1887 and 1906. She examines how Department of Indian Affairs and judicial officials sought to impose Western gender norms and monogamous, Christian unions on Aboriginal peoples, and how individual men and women resisted, evaded, or were unable to conform to these legal rules and regulations. This discrepancy between advice ideals and regional prairie realities lies at the heart of Nadine Kozak's discussion of the scientific motherhood advice literature that proliferated in the 1920s. Kozak questions whether women in rural, geographically marginalized communities aspired to the urban and middle-class ideals regarding marriage and motherhood that were promulgated in dominant, national advice literature. Cristine Bye's study of one farm family in Depression-era Saskatchewan continues the dialogue by suggesting that some rural women did normalize the ideal: they favoured their first-born sons over their daughters and other children, thereby contributing to women's further oppression.

Cristine Bye's exploration of the Graves family's dynamics speaks to a debate that has raged since scholars first began to rewrite the West through women's eyes in the 1970s. Although agents of empire and nation envisaged the settlement "frontiers" of the late-nineteenth century as a promised land for a reinstated patriarchy, one of the central debates in the field of western women's history addresses whether the West, particularly the Prairies, offered women equal opportunity with men – a "flannel shirt and liberty."[18] Historian Kathryn McPherson examines the debate and questions its utility in her article "Was the

'Frontier' Good for Women?" She urges scholars to shift their focus to women's activities in the market economy, and their experiences with race, racism, and colonialism, in order to "move outside the heterosexual matrix, in which women's status is elevated only in terms of their male peers."[19] As the contributions to this volume attest, women's relationships with other women, with their families and their neighbours, and with capital and the state played a powerful role in shaping their experiences and identities.

In the final two parts of the volume, contributors use a variety of narrative forms and strategies, sources and modes of expression, to explore the complex historical interplay between femininity and the "frontier." The authors of Part 4, "From the Inside Looking Out," build their narratives upon oral testimonies, personal reminiscences, and material possessions. Novelist and poet Aritha Van Herk's "Washtub Westerns" provides a ficto-critical monologue (an imaginative yet informed feminist reading of texts, photographs, and material culture) to capture the attention of a wider audience, and to draw its gaze to an overlooked and undervalued side of the settlement process. The late Olive Stickney and writer/filmmaker Cheryl Foggo likewise recount the experiences of Scandinavian and Black "pioneer" women who suffered the hardships of cross-border migration and discriminatory immigration and homestead laws, but were sustained and inspired by their faith and their families to devote themselves to community-building and development.[20]

Florence Melchior's article on the history of nursing education at Medicine Hat General Hospital enhances the discussion and provides a segue to Part 5, "Negotiating Constraints: On Leaders and Leadership." Both she and Siri Louie explore the exceptional activities of middle-class, Protestant women who moved beyond domestic spaces in the first half of the twentieth century to engage in the nursing profession and the sport of mountaineering. Both authors highlight how middle-class, imperial, and medical notions of masculinity and femininity inhibited these relatively privileged women from achieving their peak leadership potentials. By contrast, the section closes with writings by two scholars, Eliane Leslau Silverman and Cora Voyageur, who are engaged actively in writing the life stories of women who have taken on strong leadership positions in the community, business, and political sectors in the latter half of the twentieth century. Using oral interviews and business directories, Silverman writes one of the possible narratives detailing the life of Lena Hanen, the daughter of Jewish immigrants to Calgary, who went on to establish a chain of women's clothing stores, the Betty Shops. Voyageur's tribute to Dorothy McDonald, the first woman chief of the Fort MacKay First Nation, not only addresses the activist role played by women in contemporary Aboriginal communities, it stresses the degree to which spiritualism and environmentalism shaped McDonald's political and community-development agendas. Both articles draw attention to religion, culture, and community as potential sources of strength for women; both suggest the sacrifices that women may have to make to assume leadership roles in societies where systemic inequalities continue to prevail.

At the beginning of the twenty-first century, western and women's history remains a contested, or unsettled, terrain. Indeed, the greatest strength of historical analyses that take sex and gender into account is their ability to complicate and, consequently, transcend traditional narratives and regional myths that emerged out of imperial and masculine priorities and perspectives. The contributors to this volume seek to overcome those legacies by documenting and telling the stories of women's diverse activities as community builders, cultural liaisons, and political and cultural activists. Several themes and debates reoccur throughout: the inappropriateness of the "frontier" as an analytical category and the complexity of colonialism as a process; the degree to which western women's experiences were diverse, yet unexceptional in a global, comparative perspective; and the importance of spirituality and the complexity of religious belief.[21] Some authors embrace "the cultural turn" and demonstrate how discursive practices and cultural representations of women and gender norms hastened the colonial and nation-building projects, others focus on women's experiences as related through oral and written memory, material culture, and life writing.[22] Although historians have debated these dichotomous trends in history writing in recent years, this volume demonstrates that, when both approaches are brought to bear on the past, a more nuanced history of the West results, one that moves it beyond the exceptional assumptions of the "frontier" myth.[23] The diverse subjects and methodologies represented in *Unsettled Pasts* continue the fruitful conversations that the conference generated, and the articles explore the debates that characterized western women's history for the past three decades. Although women's and gender history as a field has come a long way since the 1970s, Eliane Leslau Silverman, to whom this book is dedicated, ends the volume by expressing her fear that western women's historic role, as activists and feminists leaders in Canada, will be forgotten. Her fears are particularly germane, given the current political climate and the ongoing economic and social marginalization of parts of the region.[24]

ENDNOTES

1   Quoted and translated in Mary V. Jordan, *To Louis from your sister who loves you, Sara Riel* (Toronto: Griffin House, 1974), 49.

2   Clare Sheridan, *Redskin Interlude* (London: Nicolson and Watson, 1938), 209.

3   For a discussions of the concepts of space, place, and process in western historiography, see: Michael Lansing, "Different Methods, Different Places: Feminist Geography and New Directions in US Western History," *Journal of Historical Geography* 29 (April 2003): 230–47.

4   The conference introduced some of the most recent research in western women's and gender history to a wider audience and generated new scholarship that has since been published elsewhere. An article in the *Calgary Herald* announced "Missing Voice of Women in History Now Loud and Clear," while the Winter 2002 issue of *Legacy: Alberta's Heritage Magazine* featured three articles by presenters, two of which appear in this volume: Cora Voyageur, "They Called Her Chief: A Tribute to Fort MacKay's Indomitable Leader Dorothy McDonald," Cheryl Foggo, "Black Faces in Unexpected Places: The Unfolding Story of Alberta's Black Pioneers," and "Heritage to the Next Generation: Linda Goyette Searches for Missing Stories." See also, Debbie Culbertson, "The other vote goes to the sister," *Beaver: Exploring Canada's History* 83 (December 2002): 28–34; Dianna Birchall, *Onoto Watanna: The Story of Winnifred Eaton* (Chicago: University of Illinois Press, 2001) and Brian Bergman's article about her, "A Flamboyant, Flirtatious Fraud: Winnifred Eaton used a fake Japanese identity to become a successful novelist," *Maclean's* 3 (March 2003): 40–41; Sylvia Larson, Sharon Aney, and Razia Jaffer, *Women of Aspenland: Images from Central Alberta*: <http://www.albertasource.ca/aspenland/eng/index.html>; Reinhold Kramer and Tom Mitchell, *Walk Towards the Gallows: The Tragedy of Hilda Blake, Hanged 1899* (Oxford: Oxford University Press, 2002); David Bright, "'Go Home. Straighten Up. Live Decent Lives': Female Vagrancy and Social Respectability in Alberta," *Prairie Forum* 28 (Fall 2003): 161–72.

5   Within this volume, the terms "Aboriginal," and "Native peoples" are used, depending upon the preference of individual authors and specific historical contexts, as all-encompassing terms that refer to the Métis, to those defined statutorily as "Indian" under the Indian Act, and to those Aboriginal peoples who are not statutorily defined as "Indians" (formerly known as "Non-Status Indians"). Section 35 of the Constitution Act, 1982, recognized and affirmed the rights derived from original occupancy, and it used the generic term "aboriginal" to

refer to the Indian, Inuit, and Métis peoples. "First Nation" is a political term and refers to a political body authorized to represent a First Nation community. A First Nation community is a band of First Nation persons who reside together on a reserve as defined under the Indian Act.

6 Richard White and John M. Findlay, "Introduction," *Power and Place in the North American West*, ed. White and Findlay (Seattle and London: Centre for the Study of the Pacific Northwest and University of Washington Press, 1999), x.

7 For recent books and historiographical discussions that reassess the West as an imagined community, see: John Herd Thompson, *Forging the Prairie West* (Toronto: Oxford University Press, 1998); Bill Waiser, "Introduction: Place, Process, and the New Prairie Realities," *Canadian Historical Review* 84 (December 2003): 509–17.

8 The book is titled tentatively *One Step over the Line: Toward a History of Women in the North American West*. For recent examples of books and articles that adopt a cross-border, transnational approach, see Carol L. Higham and Bob Thacker, eds., *One West, Two Myths: A Comparative Reader* (Calgary: University of Calgary Press, 2004). See also, Sheila McManus, "'Their own country': Race, Gender, Landscape, and Colonization around the 49th Parallel, 1862–1900," *Agricultural History* 73 (Spring 1999): 168–83, and Sarah Carter, "Transnational Perspectives on the History of Great Plains Women: Gender, Race, Nations, and the Forty-ninth Parallel," *American Review of Canadian Studies* 33 (Winter 2003): 565–96.

9 Gerald Friesen argues that the Prairies, "as a defined community, are far less relevant than they were in earlier days": the old, formal region of three Prairie provinces has been displaced by a single West, consisting of four western provinces, each with its own distinctive political society. See Gerald Friesen, "Defining the Prairies: or, Why the Prairies Don't Exist," in Robert Wardhaugh, ed., *Toward Defining the Prairies: Region, Culture, and History* (Winnipeg: University of Manitoba Press, 2001), 19, 21–22. Friesen's evolving conceptualization of the West is reflected in the field of women's history. Prior to the publication of Catherine A. Cavanaugh and Randi R. Warne's edited volume, *Telling Tales: Essays in Western Women's History* (Vancouver: UBC Press, 2000), which treated the Prairie provinces and British Columbia together, western women's and gender history tended to be explored within a provincial framework. For a discussion of these historiographical trends, see: Deborah Gorham, "From Bonavista to Vancouver Island: Canadian Women's History as Regional History in the 1990s," *Acadiensis* 28 (Spring 1999): 119–25; Adele Perry, "Feminism, History, and Writing British Columbia's Past," and Kathryn McPherson, "Was the 'Frontier' Good for Women? Historical Approaches to Women and Agricultural Settlement in the Prairie West, 1870–1925," *Atlantis: A Women's Studies Journal* 25 (Fall/Winter 2000): 69–86; Ann Leger-Anderson, "Canadian Prairie Women's History: An Uncertain Enterprise," *Journal of the West* 37 (January 1998): 47–59. For edited volumes that centre on the province, see: Barbara K. Latham and Roberta J. Pazdro, eds., *Not Just Pin Money: Selected Essays on the History of Women's Work in British Columbia* (Victoria: Camosun College, 1984); Gillian Creese and Veronica Strong-Boag, eds., *British Columbia Reconsidered: Essays on Women* (Vancouver: Press Gang Publishers, 1992); Catherine A. Cavanaugh and Randi R. Warne, eds., *Standing on New Ground: Women in Alberta* (Edmonton: University of Alberta Press, 1993); David De Brou and Aileen Moffatt, eds., *"Other" Voices:*

Historical Essays on Saskatchewan Women (Regina: Canadian Plains Research Center, 1995); Mary Kinnear, ed., *First Days, Fighting Days: Women in Manitoba History* (Regina: Canadian Plains Research Center, 1987).

10   Howard I. Kushner, "The Persistence of the Frontier Thesis: Gender, Myth, and Self-Destruction," *Canadian Review of American Studies* 23 (1992), special issue, Part 1, *Reinterpreting the American Experience: Women, Gender, and American Studies*, 53; Sandra Rollings-Magnusson, "Hidden Homesteaders: Women, the State and Patriarchy in the Saskatchewan Wheat Economy, 1870–1930," *Prairie Forum* 24 (Fall 1999): 171–83.

11   Catherine Cavanaugh addresses specifically how the Canadian prairies were imagined in masculine terms in "'No Place for a Woman': Engendering Western Canadian Settlement," *Western Historical Quarterly* 28 (Winter 1997): 493–518, as does Sarah Carter in *Capturing Women: The Manipulation of Cultural Imagery in Canada's Prairie West* (Montreal and Kingston: McGill-Queen's University Press, 1997). For a brief discussion of the American context, see: Richard W. Slatta, "Taking Our Myths Seriously," *Journal of the West* 40 (2001): 3–5.

12   For useful discussions that explore and decry the boundaries between the academy, the community, and public history, see David B. Danbom, "'Cast Down Your Bucket Where You Are': Professional Historians and Local History," *South Dakota History* 33 (Fall 2003): 263–73; Greg Marquis, "Going Public: Atlantic Canadian Academics and Popular History," *Acadiensis* 31 (Autumn 2001): 146–51. For an excellent discussion of the evolving relationship between Aboriginal women and feminist scholarship, see Jo-Anne Fiske, "By, For, or About? Shifting Directions in the Representations of Aboriginal Women," *Atlantis* 25 (Fall/Winter 2000): 11–27.

13   Franca Iacovetta, "Post-Modern Ethnography, Historical Materialism, and De-centring the (Male) Authorial Voice: A Feminist Conversation," *Histoire sociale/ Social History* 32 (Nov. 2000): 275–93; Sarah Barbour, "Diverse Patterns of Relationalities: Expanding Theories of Women's Personal Narratives," *National Women's Studies Association Journal* 14, no. 2 (2002): 181–91; Helen Buss, *Mapping Our Selves: Canadian Women's Autobiography* (Montreal and Kingston: McGill-Queen's University Press, 1992); Veronica Strong-Boag and Michelle Lynn Rosa, "Introduction: 'Some Small Legacy of Truth,'" *Nellie McClung: The Complete Autobiography; Clearing in the West and The Streams Runs Fast*, ed. Veronica Strong-Boag and Michelle Lynn Rosa (Peterborough, ON: Broadview Press, 2003) provides an excellent discussion of the complicated nature of texts and the ambiguity and performance constructed by authors.

14   Richard W. Etulain, "Meeting Places, Intersections, Crossroads, and Borders: Toward a Complex Western Cultural History," *Historian* 66 (Fall 2004): 509.

15   Historians of women and gender in Canada, as elsewhere, have fostered a heightened awareness of their nation's contradictory and conflicted role as a White settler society that came to embrace "multiculturalism," with its history as a colonizer of Aboriginal peoples. As Catherine Cavanaugh, Randi Warne, and Ann Leger-Anderson have argued, the traditional focus on the White pioneer immigrant women in the Canadian West became particularly problematical once historians addressed their contradictory position as both colonized and colonizer: Catherine Cavanaugh and Randi R. Warne, "Introduction," *Telling Tales*, 3–31. For collections that take a global approach to these issues, see in particular, Daiva

Stasiulis and Nira Yuval-Davis, eds., *Unsettling Settler Societies: Articulations of Gender, Race, Ethnicity, and Class* (London: Sage, 1995) and Ruth Roach Pierson and Nupur Chaudhuri, eds., *Nation, Empire, Colony: Historicizing Gender and Race* (Bloomington: Indiana University Press, 1998). At the national level, this recent trend is reflected in Veronica Strong-Boag et al., eds., *Painting the Maple: Essays on Race, Gender and the Construction of Canada* (Vancouver: UBC Press, 1998) and in Marlene Epp, Franca Iacovetta, and Frances Swyripa, eds., *Sisters or Strangers? Immigrant, Ethnic, and Racialized Women in Canadian History* (Toronto: University of Toronto Press, 2004). Throughout the text, we capitalize "White" to signal its status as a constructed racialized identity.

16   For examples of this literature in the Canadian West, see Carter, *Capturing Women*; Sylvia Van Kirk, *"Many Tender Ties": Women in Fur Trade Society in Western Canada, 1670–1870* (Winnipeg: Watson and Dwyer, 1980); Adele Perry, *On the Edge of Empire: Gender, Race, and the Making of British Columbia* (Toronto: University of Toronto Press, 2001); Myra Rutherdale, *Women and the White Man's God: Gender and Race in the Canadian Mission Field* (Vancouver: UBC Press, 2002). For further examples of studies that address White women's conflicted positions as both colonized and colonizers, see: Antoinette Burton, *Burdens of History: British Feminists, Indian Women, and Imperial Culture* (Chapel Hill: University of North Carolina Press, 1994); Fiona Paisley, *Loving Protection? Australian Feminism and Aboriginal Women's Rights 1919–1939* (Carlton South, Australia: Melbourne University Press, 2000); Jennifer Henderson, *Settler Feminism and Race Making in Canada* (Toronto: University of Toronto Press, 2003).

17   For western Canada, see Terry L. Chapman, "Sex Crimes in the West, 1890–1920," *Alberta History* 35 (Autumn 1987): 6–21, and "'Till Death do us Part': Wife Beating in Alberta, 1905–1920," *Alberta History* 36 (Autumn 1988): 13–22; Catherine A. Cavanaugh, "The Limitations of the Pioneering Partnership: The Alberta Campaign for Homestead Dower, 1909–25," *Canadian Historical Review* 74 (June 1993): 198–225; Margaret E. McCallum, "Prairie Women and the Struggle for a Dower Law, 1905–1920," *Prairie Forum* 18 (Spring 1993): 19–33; Lesley Erickson, "'A Very Garden of the Lord'? Hired Hands, Farm Women, and Sex Crime Prosecutions on the Prairies, 1914–1929," *Journal of the Canadian Historical Association*, new series 12 (2001): 115–35, and "The Unsettling West: Gender, Crime, and Culture on the Canadian Prairies, 1886–1940" (Ph.D. diss., University of Calgary, 2003). For the international context, see Ann Laura Stoler, "Tense and Tender Ties: The Politics of Comparison in North American History and (Post)Colonial Studies," *Journal of American History* 88 (December 2001): 829–64; Nancy F. Cott, *Public Vows: A History of Marriage and the Nation* (Cambridge, MA: Harvard University Press, 2000); Julie Ann Clancy-Smith and Frances Gouda, eds., *Domesticating the Empire: Race, Gender, and Family Life in French and Dutch Colonialism* (Charlottesville: University of Virginia Press, 1998); Anne McClintock, *Imperial Leather: Race, Gender, and Sexuality in the Colonial Contest* (New York: Routledge, 1995); Anne Laura Stoler, *Carnal Knowledge and Imperial Power: Race and the Intimate in Colonial Rule* (Berkeley: University of California Press, 2002).

18   As Susan Jackel demonstrates, British "pioneer" gentlewomen themselves promoted this ideal in their correspondence, journalism, and published writing, *A*

Flannel Shirt and Liberty: English Emigrant Gentlewomen in the Canadian West, 1880–1914 (Vancouver: UBC Press, 1982).

19   McPherson, "Was the 'Frontier' Good for Women?" 79.

20   For other studies that explore ethnic and racialised women's experiences as community builders, see: Ellenor Ranghild Merriken, *Looking for Country: A Norwegian Immigrant's Alberta Memoir*, introduction by Janice Dickin (Calgary: University of Calgary Press, 1999); Shirley J. Yee, "Gender Ideology and Black Women as Community-Builders in Ontario, 1850–1870," in *Rethinking Canada: The Promise of Women's History*, 4 ed., ed. Veronica Strong-Boag, Mona Gleason, and Adele Perry (Oxford: Oxford University Press, 2002), 87–102.

21   Ruth Compton Brouwer, "Transcending the 'unacknowledged quarantine': Putting Religion into English-Canadian Women's History," *Journal of Canadian Studies* 27 (Autumn 1992): 47–61; McPherson, "Was the 'Frontier' Good for Women?" 75–86; David M. Wrobel, "Introduction: What on Earth Has Happened to the New Western History?" *Historian* 66 (Fall 2004): 437–42; Glenda Riley, "The Future of Western Women's History," *Historian* (Fall 2004): 539–45.

22   For historiographical discussions of these trends and debates, see the discussion between Joan Sangster, Karen Dubinsky, Franca Iacovetta, Linda Kealey, and Lynne Marks in *left history* 3 (Spring/Summer 1995): 109–21, 221–37 and 3 (Fall/Spring 1995/96): 109–21, 205–20, 238–48. Kara Flynn discusses why she feels the shift towards cultural and gender history has had a negative impact on women of colour in "Bridging the Gap: Women's Studies, Women's History, Gender History, and Lost Subjects," *Atlantis* 25 (Fall 2000): 130–32.

23   For a similar position, see Kathryn McPherson, Cecilia Morgan, and Nancy Forestell, "Introduction: Conceptualizing Canada's Gendered Pasts," in *Gendered Pasts: Historical Essays in Femininity and Masculinity in Canada*, ed. McPherson, Morgan, and Forestell (Toronto: University of Toronto Press, 1999), 1–11. See also Antoinette Burton, "Thinking Beyond the Boundaries: Empire, Feminism, and the Domains of History," *Social History* 26 (January 2001): 60–71.

24   See Kathleen Cairns and Eliane Leslau Silverman, *Possessions: The Stories Women Tell About the Things They Keep* (Calgary: University of Calgary Press, 2004).

part one

COMPLICATING CATEGORIES

Women *as* Cultural Mediators

two

"Bury Our Sorrows in the Sacred Heart":

Gender and the Métis Response to Colonialism

– The Case of Sara and Louis Riel, 1848–83

LESLEY A. ERICKSON

In A Room of One's Own *(1929), British novelist Virginia Woolf posed the question: What had happened to Shake-speare's sister and why had her life been overshadowed by that of her brother? The feminist impulse to search for women's past underpins Lesley Erickson's interpretation of Louis Riel's sister, Sara. As the first Métis Grey Nun and missionary in the Canadian northwest, Riel's experiences are worthy of study in their own right; yet, scholarly works that address her life fall neatly into a biographical genre identified by literary critic Carolyn G. Heilbrun as "women celebrated as events in the lives of great men."*

Erickson rescues Sara Riel from the historical margins by illustrating how she, like her brother, occupied a liminal space where she was uniquely situated to serve as a cultural mediator – between the Catholic Church, the Métis, Aboriginal peoples, government officials, and the Hudson's Bay Company.

Like Graham MacDonald and Patricia Roome's articles that follow, Erickson's exploration of Sara Riel's conflicted identity as both missionized and missionary, colonized and colonizer, shows how rewriting the West through women's eyes can complicate historical narratives that depict missionaries as conquerors, White women as auxiliaries to evangelization, and Aboriginal peoples as victims. Build-ing upon feminist histories of the fur trade, Catholic sisterhoods, and missions, the author concludes that, with the recession of the fur trade in the 1840s and 1850s, a religious vocation became an outlet for the aspirations of multilingual mixed-blood women (like Riel) living within the constraints of an increasingly patriarchal culture. Consequently, by the end of their short lives, being "Métis" meant dramatically different things to Sara and Louis Riel. The siblings' parallel, yet divergent, experiences highlight how gender shaped Métis men and women's diverse responses to Christianity and colonialism.

In early September 1868, on the eve of the Red River Resistance, Sara Riel, a Sister of Charity or Grey Nun, wrote her brother Louis with these words of comfort: "Louis, chase away the sad and troubling thoughts to which our last meeting gave birth. With time and the Grace of God, the darkness of the present will disappear. Be confident! Until then, we must do our duty; you as a fervent Christian and me as a Sister of Charity."[1] Born in 1844 and 1848, respectively, Louis and Sara Riel came to adult-hood during a period when political and economic power was shifting progressively away from Indian and Métis economies and cultures in favour of British-Canadian institutions.[2] Following the Resistance, how-ever, Louis fled Red River to the United States in full confidence that he had fulfilled his mission to preserve and protect Métis, French, and Catholic cultural rights in the newly created province of Manitoba.[3] His confidence was misplaced. As early as September 1870, Sara wrote him to describe Métis hardships and advised, "Louis, let us Bury our Sorrows in the Wound of His Sacred Heart…. [T]o love and pray, these are the arms with which we must fight to vanquish the conqueror."[4]

As members of the Métis elite at Red River, the Riel siblings had enjoyed a relatively privileged childhood enhanced by their family's close relationship to the Catholic clergy. The transfer of Rupert's Land to Canada, however, coincided with an influx of Anglo-Canadian settlers and the collapse of the Métis buffalo-robe trade. While many Métis chose to move west in search of new land and new opportunities, others remained at Red River where they increasingly suffered poverty and discrimination. By early 1871, Lieutenant-Governor Adams G. Archibald reported to Prime Minister John A. Macdonald, "Many of them actually have been so beaten and outraged that they feel as if they were living in a state of slavery. They say that the bitter hatred of these people is a yoke so intolerable that they would gladly escape it by any sacrifice."[5]

Following the Resistance, Louis and Sara Riel's letters to each other were replete with references to suffering, sacrifice, and exile as a means to achieve both personal salvation and collective redemption for the emerging "Métis nation."[6] Although Louis Riel's religious beliefs and response to shifting power relationships in Canada have been the subject of countless books, articles, documentaries, and plays that address his contributions to Canadian history, identity, and culture, Sara Riel's life has received little attention from popular or academic historians.[7] Since the 1970s, however, feminist historians have reconceived the North American west by moving women from the margins to the centre of historical scholarship, giving birth to a more inclusive history of the region that addresses how variables like race, class, gender, and religion shaped cultural interactions, familial relationships, and individual experience.[8] More recently, historians have drawn upon anthropological and ethnohistorical models of cultural contact to highlight the historical role that Indian and mixed-blood women – as wives, missionaries, health-care providers, and educators – played as cultural brokers or mediators in specific colonial contexts.[9]

As members of the Métis elite who were educated in Catholic and European traditions and cultures, Louis and Sara Riel were situated uniquely to serve as intercultural brokers between Native peoples and newcomers in the Canadian West. Although the clergy at Red River groomed Louis for a leadership position in the Catholic Church, he instead became a political and cultural spokesperson for the Métis. He chose the path of negotiation and, as that failed, resisted both church and government when he led the Métis and their non-Native allies during the 1885 Rebellion and then proclaimed himself "prophet of the New World." Sara, by contrast, chose the path of accommodation. She became the region's first Métis Grey Nun in 1868 and, three years later, made what she referred to as the ultimate "sacrifice" when she volunteered to become a missionary in exile at Île-à-la-Crosse in present-day northern Saskatchewan.[10] For the remainder of her short life (she died from tuberculosis in 1883), Riel distanced herself increasingly from the Red River Métis and dedicated herself to "Christianizing" and "civilizing" the Métis, Cree, and Dene of the North.

Sara and Louis Riel's similar, yet divergent, experiences were gendered responses to cultural contact that paralleled men and women's reactions to Catholicism and colonization within the larger Métis and Mixed-Blood communities. Although the Oblates of Mary Immaculate tried to foster an Indigenous priesthood that would hasten Indian and mixed-blood people's transition to a sedentary and Christian lifestyle, Louis Riel was their most famous failure. The Grey Nuns, by contrast, successfully recruited mixed-blood women into their congregation; Sara Riel was their most famous success story. Like other mixed-blood women who joined the Grey Nuns, Sara Riel adapted women's traditional role as cultural mediators in the fur trade to the Catholic tradition of female congregations and community service. Her knowledge of French, English, Michif, and Cree enhanced her career as a teacher and missionary and enabled her to broker relations between male clergy and female converts, between the Catholic Church and the Hudson's Bay Company (HBC), and between the Métis community and Anglo-Canadian politicians. Evidence suggests, however, that Sara Riel's life decisions did not come easily: she suffered repeated crises of faith and, at one point, contemplated taking her own life. Although she has been overshadowed by her more famous brother, an examination of Sara Riel's life highlights, not only women's contributions to the Catholic mission field, but also the ambiguities, contradictions, and complexities of Native-newcomer relations in the early settlement period.

"Teach them to live well and to become good mothers": The Riel Family and Catholic Missionary Strategies among the Métis, 1840–68

Unlike their counterparts in eastern Canada and the United States, historians of prairie Canada have tended to either overlook or underplay the central role played by women and gender in the Catholic mission field.[11] As Kristin Burnett illustrates in chapter 6, historians of Protestant missions in the Canadian northwest have likewise only recently addressed this oversight. Sara and Louis Riel's births, however, coincided with the

The Grey Nuns Convent is located on the banks of the Red River in St. Boniface.
Archives of Manitoba, St. Boniface – Grey Nuns Home 3.

arrival of the Sisters of Charity of Montreal and the Oblates of Mary
Immaculate at Red River. The siblings were among a select group of
Métis and Mixed-Blood children upon which the Catholic clergy hung
its aspirations. In 1841, Joseph-Norbert Provencher, bishop of Juliopolis,
wrote to his eastern superiors to express what he felt was the urgent need
for a Catholic and French-Canadian sisterhood at Red River: "Our
inhabitants' daughters do not need an advanced education. Rather, our
principal goal will be to teach them to live well and to become good
mothers. This process will raise the country's civilization level in accordance with the times."[12] Provencher's request was part of a two-pronged
missionary strategy that he developed to extend and consolidate Catholic
influence throughout the Prairies and the Canadian North. On the one
hand, Provencher looked to the Oblates to staff missions and nurture
an Indigenous male clergy; on the other, he hoped to hasten the conversion process by singling out for special attention those Métis women
of the merchant-trader and farming class who appeared most receptive
to Catholicism. To that end, four Grey Nuns arrived at Red River on
21 June 1844. They quickly established a day school that fell under the
supervision of two Oblate fathers, Pierre Aubert and Alexandre-Antonin
Taché, who arrived at Red River one year later.[13]

The Riel family's intense religiosity and high standing within the Métis merchant-trader and farming class made its members ideal candidates for Catholic missionary endeavours. Although the family's economic fortunes declined progressively throughout the 1840s and 1850s, Sara and Louis's parents, Jean-Louis and Julie (née Lagimodière), continued to hold a central place among the Métis social and political elite due to his political activism and her family's wealth and influence.[14] Politically, Jean-Louis distinguished himself by leading, at certain stages, Métis resistance against the HBC's monopoly over the fur trade. The struggle culminated in the 1849 Sayer Trial, which granted the Métis political representation to the Council of Assiniboia and the right to independent trade. Over the next two decades, members of Métis merchant-trading families, who resided at St. Boniface and profited from trade with American companies, came to share common interests with British, Anglo-Canadian, and Mixed-blood HBC officials. Families like the Lagimodières, Riels, Marions, and Hamelins sought further distinction by fostering close ties with the Catholic clergy, which often involved embracing European systems of morality and education. Consequently, they increasingly divorced themselves from the unlettered and unpropertied *engagés*, tripmen, hunters, petty traders, and small farmers who made up the majority of the Métis communities at St. Francis-Xavier and Pembina. Métis hunters and their families were only nominally Catholic, they organized their lives around the seasons of the hunt, and they engaged freely in social activities like drinking and dancing, which the clergy deplored.[15]

By contrast, Jean-Louis and Julie Riel's intense faith and devotionalism shaped the rhythms of the Riel household.[16] Prior to marriage, Jean-Louis and Julie had both aspired to the religious life; their eldest son and daughter absorbed their faith. Unlike most Métis men, Jean-Louis played an active role in transmitting faith in the home.[17] He and Julie used religious icons and devotional aids – rosaries, crucifixes, figures of Jesus and Mary, images of the Sacred Heart of Jesus, and portraits of the Virgin and Child – to foster devotion and teach Catholic doctrine to their children.[18] When Louis reminisced about his youth in a letter to Archbishop Taché in 1885, he recalled, "My earliest years were scented with the sweet perfume of faith, for my beloved father permitted no one to speak evil in my presence. Family prayer and the rosary were always before my eyes. They were part of my nature like the air I breathe."[19] Julie likewise inspired her daughter: "It is on your lap that I learned to listen to the voice of God. It is you, beloved Mama, who has made me a Sister of Charity. Your motherly voice speaking to me of God made me a true religious and a better missionary."[20]

Jean-Louis and Julie Riel, however, entrusted their children's formal education to the Catholic clergy. By the time that Sarah and Louis were of school age, the Catholic school system at Red River had evolved to reflect race, class, and gender hierarchies that governed cultural relations in the local community and the Church. Two years before Louis began to attend the Grey Nuns' day school in 1853, for instance, Bishop Taché had requested permission to establish a separate boys' school in the parish. He wrote to Bishop Bourget in Montreal to justify his request, "The education of boys has been badly neglected among our Catholics at Red River.... The Métis do not like to be governed by women, and this probably explains why their children do not go to school."[21] When the Christian Brothers, a teaching order, arrived at Red River in 1854, Louis's parents immediately enrolled him in their school where he received the foundations of a classical education that would, Taché hoped, prepare him for the priesthood. Four years later, Louis, along with two other Métis boys, began training in the seminaries of Quebec.[22]

The same year that Louis enrolled with the Christian Brothers, the Grey Nuns opened a boarding school for girls. Taché explained the underlying rational for the school in a letter to Bishop Bourget, "If the Sisters could conduct an English school they would probably attract more bourgeois children. Their reputation will bring in the rest."[23] Recognizing that wealthy, influential, and Catholic HBC officials did not want to send their daughters to the Grey Nuns' day school, where they would rub shoulders with Métis, Mixed-blood, and Saulteaux girls of the hunting class, Taché and the Grey Nuns created a curriculum for their boarders that was on par with European finishing schools. Unlike the Grey Nuns' day school students, who learned the rudiments of reading, writing, religion, and sewing, boarding school students prepared for their role as wives to future HBC officers. Bishops Provencher and Taché hoped, however, that the boarding school's pious and strict atmosphere would also foster religious vocations among Mixed-blood girls, binding the company more intimately to the church.[24]

Although Sara Riel was Métis, her family's wealth and status permitted her to attend the boarding school between 1858 and 1865. Already conversant in French, Cree, and Michif, Sara also learned English under the Grey Nuns' tutelage and through her daily interactions with Mixed-

A Grey Nun with students from the day school. Undated. Archives of Manitoba, Stovel Advocate 283 (N10202).

blood students. In addition to spinning, knitting, sewing, and embroidery, the boarding school's curriculum also included the "advanced" arts. Father Ritchot, curé of St. Norbert, attended the Grey Nuns' annual public examinations in August 1862 and noted that the Sisters taught their twenty charges French, English, history, mathematics, painting, and music.[25] Under the guidance of Sister L'Esperance, Riel demonstrated marked talent in the fine arts; her renderings of the Catholic mission at Île-à-la-Crosse have since distinguished her as the first artist in the European tradition born in the Northwest.[26]

Although Riel's training would later prove to be a tremendous asset in her teaching and missionary career, her notebooks, along with references in the Grey Nuns' chronicles, suggest that the Grey Nuns sought primarily to prepare their charges to become good wives and mothers to distinguished Catholic families. Despite their advanced curriculum, the spirit of nineteenth-century devotional Catholicism, which sought to promote and preserve patriarchy and paternalism in French-Canadian society, infused the Grey Nuns' pedagogy. As part of their cultural

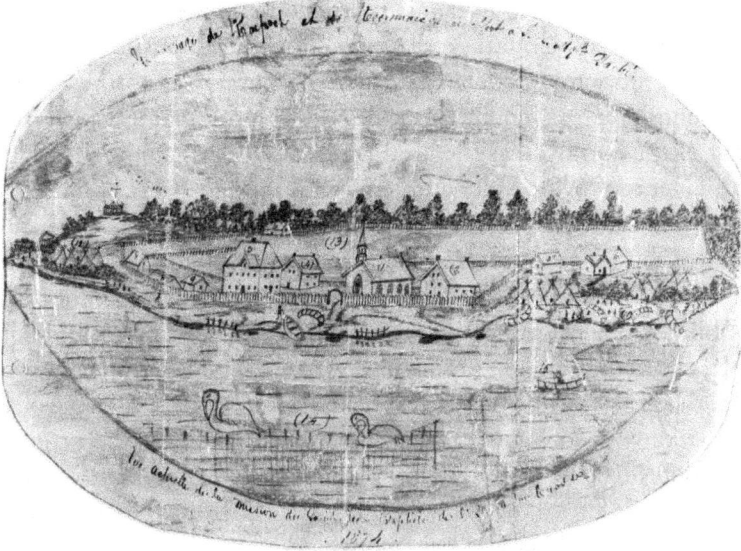

The Catholic Mission at Île-à-la-Crosse as sketched by Sara Riel, 1874. Saint-Boniface Historical Society Archives, Corporation archiépiscopale catholique romaine de Saint-Boniface fonds.

baggage, the Grey Nuns and the Oblates had brought the ultramontane devotional revolution to the Prairies. Ultramontanism, or clerical nationalism, was a reactionary ideology that swept Europe in the wake of the French Revolution. Following the 1837–38 Rebellions in Quebec, Bishops Bourget and Laflèche blamed secularization and liberalism for socio-economic and cultural dislocations in French-Canadian society. As a remedy, they declared patriarchal principles, medieval devotionalism, and rural living as necessary to the survival of the French-speaking, Catholic family.[27] In *Quelque considérations sur les rapports de la société civile avec la religion et la familee* (1866), for instance, Abbé Laflèche outlined three divinely ordained patriarchs that, he argued, emerged from natural principals of authority: pope over king, king over man, and man over woman.[28] When Joseph Royal, superintendent of education, visited the St. Boniface convent school in 1871, he reported, "The [students] are a testimony to their teacher who devotes herself not only to teaching them to read and to write, but also to show them propriety and modesty: virtues that are so precious and natural in Christian women."[29]

The Grey Nuns used sermons, translation exercises, and parables to teach their mixed-blood students ultramontane devotionalism and Euro-Catholic gender roles. Dictated sermons, for example, portrayed Jesus, Mary, and Joseph as models of the perfect European family. Joseph, the "head of the family," was the ideal father and breadwinner, working as a carpenter to provide Mary and Jesus with the necessities of life.[30] Sara Riel's notebooks likewise included a sermon entitled *La Sainte Famille* that depicted Mary as the perfect Catholic wife and mother: "Mary was Jesus' mother and she fulfilled her role as Saint Joseph's wife to the best of her abilities. She placed Joseph before her own desires and she did nothing to displease him. She was, as always, in her home doing housework when the Lord sent the angel Gabriel to tell her of the mystery of the Incarnation."[31] More subtly, the Grey Nuns encouraged their students to develop filial devotion to Bishop Taché and his mother, Henriette. Writing to the latter on behalf of St. Boniface boarding school students, Sara Riel expressed her and her companions' love, devotion, and admiration for Henriette and their veneration of her son who, Riel claimed, was like a father to them. In her personal correspondence to friends, Sara elaborated upon the influential role that the bishop played at the boarding school: "We were happy to hear our first Pastor's voice encouraging us in the practice of goodness and the love of virtue. His Grace extolled the advantages of a Christian education. I realize I am happy to have spent the best years of my life in a house of education, living under the same roof as God."[32]

Although the Grey Nuns sought ultimately to prepare their boarding school students to become ideal Catholic wives and mothers, the Sisters' example – along with certain aspects of devotional Catholicism – contrarily promoted the religious life as being more pleasing to God. Ultramontane Catholicism's emotional and romantic spirit particularly appealed to women. Renewed devotions to the Virgin Mary and the female saints, for instance, enhanced women's interest in Catholicism since these women's lives provided examples of and justifications for female independence and participation in the Church. The feminization of Catholicism that took place in the last half of the nineteenth century offset the paternalistic and patriarchal foundations of French-Catholic, and later Métis, nationalist ideology. Mary was the ideal mother, yet she was also the ideal virgin.[33] Unlike the wives of Protestant missionaries described by Burnett, the Grey Nuns themselves served as role models of chaste unmarried women who pursued independent lives and careers within a patriarchal and hierarchical institution. Riel's notebooks, for instance, contain biographies of female saints like Catherine of Sienna, Theresa of Avila, and Marguerite-Marie of Alocoque that were designed to appeal to young impressionable girls seeking wealthy, beautiful, and noble role models. By contrast, marriage and motherhood may have appeared less than heroic – particularly when canon ten of the Council of Trent's twenty-fourth session declared, "Virginity and celibacy are better and more blessed than the bond of matrimony."[34] The Oblates and the Grey Nuns enhanced this belief by fostering within their students and converts veneration of the Cult of the Sacred Heart of Jesus. By the time that Louis and Sara Riel completed their formal education, they firmly believed that suffering and self-sacrifice were the true paths to salvation.[35]

"An Ardent Christian and a Sister of Charity": Louis and Sara Riel's Response to Catholicism and Colonization, 1864–71

The gendered assumptions that underpinned Catholic missionary strategies and devotionalism, combined with changing class and race relations on the eve of the Red River Resistance, influenced Sara Riel's decision to enter the Grey Nuns' novitiate in 1865 and to become a professed nun three years later. These developments also shaped her brother's decision to withdraw from the seminary. Louis Riel's rejection of the priesthood remains a matter of historical debate. George F. G. Stanley, for instance, argues that the familial responsibilities that fell to Riel upon his father's death in 1864 left him little choice. Thomas Flanagan and Maggie Siggins, however, place more weight upon Riel's failed love affair with Montrealer Marie Geurnon.[36] Although both arguments have merit, given how masculine and feminine ideals were constructed in Catholic and Métis culture, Stanley's argument is more convincing. Contrary to Bishops Provencher and Taché's highest expectations, no Métis men chose the religious life over marriage and family. In 1823, for instance, Provencher personally groomed two boys, one Métis and one Indian, for the priesthood: they both discontinued their studies after one year. Provencher's failure motivated him to recruit the Oblates to the Northwest mission field. The Oblates, however, also met with little success. When Louis Riel traveled to Quebec to attend the College of Montreal, two mixed-blood men, Daniel McDougall and Louis Schmidt, accompanied him. McDougall, suffering from homesickness, soon returned home, while Schmidt, the Métis son of a HBC fur trader, returned to Red River in 1860.[37]

The patriarchal nature of Catholic and Métis culture and the feminization of devotional Catholicism influenced Métis men's responses to Catholic missionary strategies. Historian Brian P. Clarke, for instance, discovered that ultramontane piety ran counter to the masculine ideals of Irish working-class culture in nineteenth-century Toronto. Contrary to the clergy's expectations, women rather than men sought involvement in the St. Vincent de Paul Society in that city.[38] In the Northwest, Euro-Canadian and Catholic gender ideals had come to permeate all levels of Métis society by the latter half of the nineteenth century. In her study of the Métis at Batoche, Saskatchewan, historian Diane Payment argues that, although the Métis had leaned towards egalitarianism in the eighteenth century, the arrival of Catholic missionaries signalled a growing adherence to patriarchal norms that relegated women to the domestic sphere.[39] Changing gender roles also reflected the demise of fur-trade culture, which had historically provided Indian and mixed-blood women (as country wives, provisioners, translators, and intermediaries) an accepted and respected role in politics and commerce.[40] By 1873, however, the editors of *Le Métis* frequently published articles like "Women's Vocation," which praised Métis women's role in the private sphere because it better enabled their husbands to engage in public affairs.[41]

When Jean-Louis Riel died in 1864, Louis became *pater familias* to his mother and seven brothers and sisters. For the remainder of his life, his brothers and sisters referred to him as "our eldest" or "Papa's replacement" and looked to him for spiritual guidance and financial support.[42] By the eve of the Resistance, the family's precarious financial situation had taken a drastic turn for the worse. Plagued by drought and famine, the Riel family had planted no crops since 1863, they possessed only a few head of livestock, and they had difficulty procuring bread. To alleviate the situation, the youngest Riel children withdrew from school to save the cost of tuition and the eldest children engaged in waged labour: Marie sought and gained employment at the Grey Nuns' convent at St. Charles, while Charles worked as a day labourer.[43]

The Riel children's sacrifices were necessary because racial discrimination and the emergence of racial boundaries to success at Red River limited Louis Riel's ability to financially support his mother and siblings. In Quebec, for instance, Guernon's parents had rejected Riel's marriage proposal because he was Métis. When Riel returned to the Prairies in 1868, he likewise discovered that his advanced education prepared him little for the career options that were then available to Métis men. Lacking the funds to set himself up in free trade, Riel also came up against racial barriers to socio-economic advancement in the HBC. Following the Sayer Trial, HBC officials sought to keep the Métis at the bottom rungs of the labour force by limiting their participation in the company to less than two hundred seasonal contracts and only eight apprenticeships in skilled trades. Historian Gerald Ens argues that, when the Métis gathered in October 1869 to resist the transfer of Rupert's Land from the HBC to Canada, the group consisted primarily of men – like Louis Riel, Louis Schmidt, and Ambroise Lépine – who were middle-aged and economically marginalized.[44]

By contrast, the Grey Nuns welcomed Sara Riel into their congregation. Although Riel's religious vocation alleviated her family's financial situation, the appeal of ultramontane piety to women and the fluidity of race and class relations within the Grey Nuns' congregation influenced her decision. When Riel entered the novitiate in 1865, the Grey Nuns had a well-established tradition of accepting members, students, and boarders from diverse socio-economic and cultural backgrounds. Bound by vows of poverty, obedience, chastity, and service to the poor, the congregation had, from its inception in Quebec, catered to those less favoured. When Bishop Provencher approached the Grey Nuns of Montreal to staff the missions of the Northwest, they selected Mother Valade to found the Red River convent because she was one-quarter Aboriginal.[45] By 1869, the Red River congregation numbered twenty-six Sisters. Although the majority originated from Quebec, the community also included four English-Canadian and four Mixed-Blood Sisters. In terms of socio-economic background, the congregation's membership was likewise diverse, ranging from Sister Vitaline Royal who was born into a wealthy French-Canadian family from Repentigny, Quebec, to Sister Mary O'Brien who hailed from a modest Irish-American and working-class background.[46]

Unlike the Oblates, the Grey Nuns at Red River immediately re-cruited mixed-blood women into their community. Although Bishop Provencher predicted that these women had little hope of rising to the "first ranks," Métis and Mixed-blood nuns who preceded or accompanied Sara Riel into the congregation found that their linguistic abilities allowed them to pursue prestigious teaching and administrative careers.

When Marguerite Connolly, the daughter of HBC Chief Factor William Connolly and *MiyoNipiy*, a Cree woman, entered the novitiate in 1845, for instance, she immediately began to teach catechism at the Saulteaux lodges near Red River. Marie-Jane McDougall, the daughter of a Scottish-Protestant trader and a Salish woman, spoke her perpetual vows in 1865 and likewise began to teach at the Grey Nuns' convent school at St. Norbert. McDougall later established St. Mary's English school at Fort Garry and, in 1890, became the superior of the St. Boniface community. Annie Goulet, a Métis boarding-school student who entered the novitiate one year after Riel, became a teacher at the Oblate's residential school in the Qu'Appelle Valley, where she demonstrated a marked proficiency in both Saulteaux and Cree.[47] A religious vocation, therefore, remained one of the few remaining avenues by which Métis and Mixed-Blood women could achieve social status independent from a husband or father during the declining decades of the fur trade.[48]

The Red River Resistance proved to be not only a turning point for Louis Riel, but also for his eldest sister. After Sara Riel made her perpetual vows in 1868, she began teaching at the Grey Nuns' day school at St. Norbert. Because she had demonstrated some musical talent as a student, the Grey Nuns also placed Riel in charge of teaching the students the chant. Sara's ties to the Riel family and the Métis community, however, threatened and challenged her vocation and career as the events of the Resistance began to unfold. Fearing for her physical safety, the Grey Nuns recalled Riel to St. Boniface in 1869, where she took charge of the sacristan and taught classes at the congregation's day school. Over the next two years, the turn of events forced Riel to relocate twice to St. Vital and St. Francis-Xavier parishes.[49]

Throughout the Resistance and its aftermath, Sara Riel and the Grey Nuns struggled to reconcile their private sympathies for the Métis with their status as women religious within the Catholic Church. Following Louis Riel's declaration of a provisional government on 8 December 1869, and the execution of Thomas Scott three months later, the Red River colony fell into a state of mob rule that persisted throughout negotiations of the Manitoba Act. The arrival of Colonel Garnet Joseph Wolseley's "peace mission" and Anglo-Protestant settlers from Ontario only enhanced Anglo-Canadian hostility towards the Métis. To avoid persecution, Louis Riel fled to the United States. Although Bishop Taché supported Canada's annexation of the West, and tried to ease tensions by counselling the Métis towards a more moderate position, the Grey Nuns privately sympathized with the Métis cause. When Sara Riel wrote to her brother from St. Norbert on 7 September 1868, she assured him of her superiors' support and disclosed that Sisters Laurent, O'Brien, and Connolly prayed for the "perfect accomplishment of all [his] wishes."[50] As the political situation at Red River worsened, the Grey Nuns continued to support the Métis and they justified their stance to the Montreal motherhouse by interpreting the conflict as deriving exclusively from Riel's desire to protect the Catholic faith. Sister Mary A. Curran, secretary to Bishop Taché, for instance, wrote to Montreal in 1869, arguing that resistance had become the only option for Riel once it became clear that the persecution of Catholics would commence under the new regime.[51]

Despite their private sympathies, Bishop Taché and the Grey Nuns placed Sara Riel in an awkward position when, in November 1870, they designated her as an ambassador of good will to Sir Adams George Archibald, the new lieutenant-governor of Manitoba and the North-West Territories. Two months after Archibald arrived at Red River, he, his daughter, and his private secretary visited the Grey Nuns' St. Boniface convent. With the exception of the mother superior, Sara Riel and Annie Goulet were the only members of the congregation who personally met the party. In an outward demonstration of allegiance, the Grey Nuns hastily mounted photographs of the Archibald family on the convent walls and had their boarding-school students prepare an address. Sara Riel later described the event to her brother: "Afterwards, everyone began to talk. I found myself close to Miss Archibald. I tried to entertain her as well as I could. I tried to forget the past – I kept silent and thought only of the present. I spoke to Mademoiselle for close to a quarter of an hour. Every time that I looked at his Excellency, I found his eyes on me."[52] Although the Grey Nuns appeared publicly reconciled to the new political realities, Riel found the situation untenable.

One month after the Archibald incident, Riel asked that she be allowed to join the Grey Nuns at Île-à-la-Crosse. The northern mission held a special place in the hearts of the Riel family because Jean-Louis's parents had met and married there. Sister Charlebois, who would later accompany Riel to the mission, presented Riel's request to the Montreal motherhouse. Riel, Charlebois explained, risked losing her faith in Red River's hostile environment. Although Charlebois believed that Riel's missionary impulse came to her only after Louis took refuge in the United States, she felt that the impulse should be encouraged because

Riel had displayed suicidal tendencies that year. In Sara Riel's personal letters to her brother, however, she explained that she hoped to derive spiritual benefit from the trials of exile.[53]

Although Mary Jordan argues that Sara Riel's decision stemmed from a misguided belief that self-sacrifice was in order if Louis was to be returned to his people, Riel's motivations were more complex. The Grey Nuns and Oblates had fostered devotion to the Cult of the Sacred Heart at Red River and taught their students that suffering and sacrifice were the truest paths to salvation. Drawing upon Christ's example, they depicted the life of the missionary, or exile, as the ultimate sacrifice. In the 1860s, the Grey Nuns' chronicler wrote, "To be a missionary does not necessarily mean that one wants to expatriate herself. Jesus, the missionary ideal, did not leave his homeland.... Jesus' life is an example to the Grey Nun missionary who labours in the immense country of Canada."[54] Educated in ultramontane Catholicism, Louis Riel subsequently advised his mother that sacrifice and suffering were the true Christian's lot in life: "If our real suffering can be compared to the heaviness of a yoke, we can console ourselves. God has said: 'Happy are those who have carried the yoke since their youth.'"[55]

In addition, unlike her brother, who increasingly distanced himself from orthodox Catholicism and the Catholic Church, Sara Riel also embraced the Oblate and Grey Nuns' belief that Aboriginal and Métis people's future survival depended on their adoption of a Christian, sedentary lifestyle. When Bishop Vital-Justin Grandin arrived at Red River in June 1871 to recruit personnel for the northern missions, Sara Riel eagerly accepted his invitation. The editors of *Le Métis* believed that Riel's decision symbolized a new day for the Métis nation in Canada: "[Sara Riel] is, believe us, the first missionary from the Métis Nation of Red River given to this great Apostolic work, and one could not find a more dignified person. A kindly heart, keen intelligence, and inexhaustible charity distinguish this new missionary. Her departure is a sacrifice for her family and the entire population, but at the same time it is an honour and a blessing for us."[56] Riel likewise took pride in her missionary status and assured her family that she would continue to work and pray for Louis and "the cause."[57] During her arduous journey to Île-à-la-Crosse, she wrote her mother from Green Lake, "I find myself more and more happy to have been chosen, me, Sara Riel, as the first Métis missionary in the North."[58]

"True Missionary of the North": Île-à-la-Crosse, 1871–83

Between her arrival at Île-à-la-Crosse on 25 August 1871 and her death in 1883, Riel lost touch with the trials and tribulations of the Riel family and the Métis at Red River. Located in the subarctic region, the area – called originally *Sa Key Ta Waow*, or "Mouth of the River" – was a traditional rendezvous site for nearly two thousand Dene and Cree who continued to make seasonal sojourns to the site after fur traders established a post in 1799 and the Oblates a Catholic mission in 1846. By the 1870s, Île-à-la-Crosse had evolved into a complex multicultural community. The Oblates used the mission as a base from which they engaged in "flying" or itinerant preaching journeys; they also hosted lengthier biannual missions when Dene and Cree bands came to trade with the HBC. Everyday life at the mission revolved around the Grey Nuns' relief and education work and regular Catholic services performed by a resident Oblate priest. Upon their arrival in 1860, the Grey Nuns became the only non-Aboriginal women in an evolving community that consisted of English-speaking and Protestant HBC officials, Métis families in service to the Bay, Dene and Wood Cree converts and non-Christians, and French-speaking Oblates. Because the Oblates' *Rules and Regulations* prohibited priests from interacting personally with lay Native women, male missionaries relied on the Grey Nuns to staff their schools and serve as role models for and liaisons with female converts.[59] By 1871, the Grey Nuns' convent, school, and hospital was staffed by four Sisters – Agnès, Pépin, Dandurand, and Riel – one Métis *fille donnée*, and one *fille engagé*. In addition to the ten male and sixteen female students who attended the Grey Nuns' boarding school, the congregation also cared for five orphaned children.[60]

Although Sara Riel immediately took up a position as Sister Pépin's teaching assistant, physical illness disrupted her teaching career. Her letters to family and friends relate, in exhausting detail, the misery, poverty, and isolation she and her companions experienced on a daily basis. In November 1872, Riel's physical misery and emotional turmoil culminated in a near-death experience that reinforced her faith, mysticism, and commitment to the mission. Fearing that Riel would soon die from tuberculosis, the resident Oblate priest, Father Prosper Légéard, administered the Last Rites. Riel, however, prayed to the Blessed Marguerite-Marie of Alocoque for divine intervention and promised, in return, to rededicate her life to God and to renounce the Riel name. Later, when Légéard and the Grey Nuns deemed Riel's rapid recovery a genuine miracle, Riel held true to her promise and became Sister Marguerite-Marie. She believed that her sacrifice would prove to God that she now truly placed her faith before her family. In letters to her family, however, she downplayed the significance of her decision, "Do not worry! I have never blushed at my name and God knows that it is dear to me. But it was a time of sacrifice, a time to do all I could to prove my gratitude to the Blessed. This name, I hope, will bring me happiness."[61]

Available evidence suggests that Sara Riel's renewed dedication to the mission was not embraced wholeheartedly by either the Riel family or the Métis at Île-à-la-Crosse. Throughout the 1870s, Riel's letters are replete with references to the unhappiness she experienced upon receiving few or no letters from her family in the biannual mail.[62] Although Riel cherished her Métis identity, life at the mission and her status as a missionary dislocated and disassociated her from the Red River Métis and their troubles.[63] In 1876, she wrote her family: "I hear often that Red River has changed; that I would not recognize it. It is good that big tall buildings are being built; that Red River grows affluent. But, what I ask of God, for my daily sacrifices, for my deprivation, suffering, and separation, is that the hearts of the Métis remain with God. That they remain fervent Christians and that drunkenness cease. If you only knew how I fear learning that my dear brothers have taken up this terrible passion."[64]

Following her recovery, Riel became intensely involved in missionary work. As a Métis woman and Grey Nun, she became an important liaison between the Catholic mission, the HBC, Métis labourers, and the Dene and Cree. As the only English-speaking missionary, she took it upon herself to establish the first English class at Île-à-la-Crosse. Légéard, who remained her Oblate superior until 1879, felt that the class would enhance the mission's prestige in the eyes of the Canadian government and ensure the goodwill of the HBC. The Oblates and Grey Nuns also entrusted Riel with presenting annual New Year's greetings and gifts to Bay officials on behalf of the Catholic mission. Although Riel fostered more intimate ties between the mission and the HBC, the Métis response to her efforts was less than encouraging. Writing to Louis in 1874, she lamented, "You understand the care and solicitude that is required to teach children. Here in the North our people, the Métis, do not appreciate the benefits of instruction.... We are required to fight against the indifference and caprice of children as well as against the weaknesses of their parents."[65] By 1875, the situation had deteriorated to the point where Métis labourers with the HBC were demanding the school's closure because Riel "forced" their children to speak English. One year earlier, for instance, Riel had encouraged her students to participate in an English recital to honour the birthday of the Chief Factor's son. Writing to Louis of her efforts, Sara explained that HBC officials had been enchanted "because our children bore little resemblance to Indians."[66] Métis resistance, however, forced the Grey Nuns to eliminate English from their curriculum until the next visitation by Bishop Grandin.[67]

Sara Riel's conflict with the Métis at Île-à-la-Crosse reflected changes that were occurring within the HBC. After 1872, for instance, the directors decided that the company would no longer provide Indian and Métis hunters with credit. Father Légéard feared that the company's new policy would force the Métis to leave the mission. Seven years later, Riel wrote Taché and informed him that the Catholic Métis at the fort suffered because the HBC bourgeois, Ewen M. McDonald, openly expressed his contempt for Catholicism.[68] Métis resistance to Riel's overtures, however, also derived from cultural differences that Riel was either unable, or unwilling, to acknowledge. The majority of the Métis at Île-à-la-Crosse consisted of itinerant hunters and trappers who spoke Cree or Chipewyan exclusively; their families formed part of the Native kinship and social systems of the region.[69] Much like the hunter-trader class at Red River, the subarctic Métis may have rejected the utility of a European and Christian education; Riel, however, hoped to raise the northern Métis to her own level of "civilization." In 1880, for instance, she wrote to Louis of the Cree mission at Canoe Lake, explaining that the families who lived there "are a little more civilized. They dress in the French or Canadian fashion, or perhaps it would be better to say 'Métis.'"[70]

The degree to which Sara Riel had ceased to identify with Métis aspirations became apparent in the 1870s and 1880s when she attempted to use the land she received as a Métis under the Manitoba Act to fund an orphanage at Île-à-la-Crosse. Riel's efforts met with resistance at all levels. Her superiors at the Montreal motherhouse felt that, because individual Grey Nuns could not own personal property, Archbishop Taché and the Grey Nuns at Red River should decide the best use for the funds. Both Taché and the Grey Nuns' Council agreed that the Riel family's financial need outweighed the mission's for an orphanage. Sara Riel disagreed and expressed her objections in a letter to Archbishop Taché:

I have a greater need for money than my relatives do, because I must care for my orphans and others who are needy. Monsignor, if I had remained at St. Boniface I would naturally feel the needs of my family whom I love with all my heart. But I have suffered at Île-à-la-Crosse for nine and a half years. During this time I have cried upon witnessing the misery of so many small abandoned children. For nine years I have felt the necessity of having more money. Our work depends upon it. I have always counted on my rights as a Métis child in order to found our orphanage.[71]

When Sara Riel had the opportunity to return to Red River one year later for a family reunion, she advised her mother that, given the choice between sacrifice and joy, she would always choose the former.[72]

By the end of her life, Sara Riel's sacrifices earned her respect and admiration at the mission. Although her plans for an orphanage did not go forward, she successfully created a lay organization for female students and elders who had contributed to Catholic missionary endeavours by working as teachers, translators, and cultural liaisons. Marie-Rose Piwapiskus, for instance, began to teach with the Grey Nuns following her husband's death. As the daughter-in-law of *Oppikakiw*, a well-respected storyteller, Piwapiskus drew students to the mission school, where she taught catechism and Cree syllabus with Sara Riel. Isabelle Bekatta, a Dene orphan raised by the Grey Nuns, likewise taught alongside the Grey Nuns. In 1880, Bishop Grandin sanctioned Riel's initiative by creating "Notre Dames des Victoires" for women, girls, and boys.[73] When Sara Riel died on Christmas Day in 1883, her funeral was a multicultural event attended by the bourgeois of the HBC, Métis labourers and students, Grey Nuns and Oblates, and Dene and Wood Cree converts.[74]

"She Was Loved and Respected as a Métisse": Reconciling Gender, Identity, and Culture

Sara Riel was much more than a pale imitation of her more famous brother. Her life and career as the first Métis Grey Nun and missionary in the Canadian northwest highlights the integral role that gender, race, and class played in shaping Métis men and women's responses to Catholicism and colonialism. As a Métis woman, student, and Grey Nun, Riel was uniquely situated to be both missionized and missionary, colonized and colonizer.[75] Her life belies simple historical categories – like conquered and conqueror, victim and oppressor – that often govern analyses of cultural contact.[76] Although Riel's career as a Grey Nun and missionary caused her to suffer repeated crises of faith, to weaken ties with her family and friends at Red River, and to contemplate suicide, it also allowed her to attain a position of influence among women and men from diverse socio-economic and cultural backgrounds. Both chronologically and geographically, Riel stood at a cultural crossroads in the history of the Canadian west, serving as a mediator between the Métis, Indian peoples, Catholic clergy, politicians, and HBC officials. As a consequence, her definition of what it meant to be "Métis" increasingly differed from her brother's. Although the Oblates and Grey Nuns had originally singled out Sara and Louis Riel as ideal candidates to enhance their missionary endeavours in the Northwest, the nature of gender, race, and class relations within the Red River community and the Catholic Church forced them onto divergent paths. While Louis eventually resisted cultural and political colonization, Sara Riel, as a Grey Nun, chose the path of accommodation as the truest means to ensure her people's survival under a new cultural and political regime.

Unlike Louis Riel, who earned for himself a place in the annals of Canadian history by championing French, Catholic, and Métis rights and freedoms in the political realm, Sara Riel has been relegated to the margins of historical scholarship on Métis and Canadian identity. Historian David Lee, who has studied the complex and diverse nature of Métis communities on the South Saskatchewan River, however, advocates using a flexible definition of "Métis" in order to account for diverse variations in culture, language, degree of acculturation, and expectations for the future.[77] The complexities and ambiguities of Sara Riel's life and experiences point to the need for more studies of Métis and Aboriginal women that broaden our conception of Native-newcomer relations by exploring how gender shaped individual and cultural responses to Christianity, contact, and conquest. As this examination of one Métis woman's life has revealed, women – as mothers, students, educators, missionaries, and converts – played a complex role in the Catholic mission field. Although Sara Riel's missionary efforts met with some resistance, she earned for herself an honoured place in the collective memories of the Grey Nuns and the Métis and Indian communities at Île-à-la-Crosse. Upon her death in 1883, her superior, Sister Agnes, wrote Julie Riel, "Her death was a summary of her life: the passage from a life of misery to a life of happiness…. people from everywhere came to pray by her body. She was loved and respected as a 'Métisse.' She used to say, 'show them love, and they will do the same in return.'"[78]

ENDNOTES

1   Sara Riel to Louis Riel, St. Norbert, 7 September 1868, Riel Papers, Provincial Archives of Manitoba (PAM). Approximately 150 of Sara Riel's letters to family, friends, and Archbishop Alexander-Antonin Taché have been preserved and are housed at the Provincial Archives of Manitoba and the Archbishop's Archives of St. Boniface, Manitoba (AASB). In addition, a small number of Louis Riel's letters to Sara have been collected, edited, and published in George F. G. Stanley, ed., *The Collected Writings of Louis Riel/Les Écrits Complets de Louis Riel* (Edmonton: University of Alberta Press, 1985). The majority of the analysis for this paper is based upon my master's thesis entitled, "At the Cultural and Religious Crossroads: Sara Riel and the Grey Nuns in the Canadian Northwest, 1848–1883" (University of Calgary, 1997).

2   In "'No Place for a Woman': Engendering Western Canadian Settlement," Catherine A. Cavanaugh contends that this transformation took place as early 1850, when the Foss-Pelly scandal erupted in the colony, *Western Historical Quarterly* 28 (Winter 1997): 501.

3   George F. G. Stanley, *Louis Riel* (Toronto: Ryerson Press, 1963), 156.

4   Sara Riel to Louis Riel, 21 September 1870, quoted and translated in Mary V. Jordan, *To Louis from your sister who loves you, Sara Riel* (Toronto: Griffin House, 1974), 23. Unless stated otherwise, all translations are the author's own.

5   Lieutenant-Governor George Adams Archibald to John A. Macdonald, 1871, quoted in Gerhard J. Ens, *Homeland to Hinterland: The Changing Worlds of the Red River Metis in the Nineteenth Century* (Toronto: University of Toronto Press, 1996), 161.

6   The term "Métis" is used as it would have been in the nineteenth century. At that time, "Métis" referred to the children of Indian and White parentage, but more specifically to French-speaking descendants at Red River. The appellation is used in contradistinction to "Mixed-Blood," which refers to those persons at Red River who were the children of Indian and Anglo-Celtic Canadians. The term "mixed-blood" refers to both Métis and Mixed-blood peoples. For an introduction to the controversy surrounding outside naming, see John E. Foster, "The Métis: The People and the Term," *Prairie Forum* 3 (March 1978): 79–90; Paul Chartrand, "'Terms of Division': Problems of 'Outside-Naming' for Aboriginal People in Canada," *Journal of Indigenous Studies* 2 (Summer 1991): 1–22; and Jennifer S. H. Brown, "Métis, Halfbreeds, and Other Real People: Challenging Cultures and Categories," *The History Teacher* 27 (November 1993): 19–26.

7   See in particular Doug Owram, "The Myth of Louis Riel," *Canadian Historical Review* 63 (September 1982): 315–36, for the evolving historiography pertaining to Riel. In his biography *Louis "David" Riel: Prophet of the New World* (1979), for instance, political scientist Thomas Flanagan argued that Sara Riel's religious vocation and faith inspired Louis to break progressively away from the Catholic Church as he developed a "new religion" for the Métis in prairie Canada. Although Mary V. Jordan dedicated a book-length study to Sara Riel, Riel emerges as a mere shadow of her brother. Based largely on Sara's letter to Louis, Jordan wrote little of Sara Riel's experiences with the Grey Nuns or her life as a missionary at Île-à-la-Crosse, but instead interpreted her life as an extension of Louis's: Sara Riel chose to become a Grey Nun only after Louis forsook the priesthood; she became a missionary in exile only after Louis fled Red River in the aftermath of the Resistance; and, she too felt she had a divine mission to carry out on earth. Sara Riel, Jordan concluded, was Louis's "conscience." In both Flanagan and Jordan's studies, Sara's life and experiences are deemed valuable only to the extent that they can shed light on her more famous brother: see, Jordan, *To Louis from your sister who loves you, Sara Riel*, xi, and Thomas Flanagan, *Louis 'David' Riel: Prophet of the New World* (Halifax: Goodread Biographies, 1983). The only other academic study of Sara Riel is Rossel Vein's, "La Correspondance de Sara Riel," *Écrits de Canada Français* 22 (1966): 243–76.

8   For excellent historiographical treatments of women's history and gender history that address how these methodological approaches have contributed to a more inclusive history of the American and Canadian wests, see the introductions to, and articles in, Elizabeth Jameson and Susan Armitage, eds., *The Women's West* (Norman and London: University of Oklahoma Press, 1987) and *Writing the Range: Race, Class, and Culture in the Women's West* (Norman and London: University of Oklahoma Press, 1997); Elizabeth Jameson, "Toward a Multicultural History of Women in the Western United States," *Signs* 13 (1988): 761–91; Susan Johnson, "'A Memory Sweet to Soldiers': The Significance of Gender in the American West," *Western Historical Quarterly* 24 (November 1993): 495–518; Aileen Moffat, "Great Women, Separate Spheres, and Diversity: Comments on Saskatchewan Women's Historiography," in *"Other" Voices: Historical Essays on Saskatchewan Women*, ed. David de Brou and Aileen Moffatt, 10–26 (Regina: Canadian Plains Research Centre, 1995); Ann Leger-Anderson, "Canadian Prairie Women's History: An Uncertain Enterprise," *Journal of the West* 37 (January 1998): 47–59; and the introduction to Catherine A. Cavanaugh and Randi R. Warne, eds., *Telling Tales: Essays in Western Women's History* (Vancouver: UBC Press, 2000).

9   Since historian Silvia Van Kirk wrote her pioneer study, *"Many Tender Ties": Women in Fur Trade Society in Western Canada, 1670–1870* (Winnipeg: Watson and Dwyer, 1980), which turned the traditional historical narrative of the fur trade on its head by revealing the fundamental role that marriages between Indian and mixed-blood women and White fur traders played in creating a distinct fur-trade culture, historical assessments of women's role as cultural mediators have blossomed on both sides of the Canadian-American border. See in particular: Peggy Pascoe, "Western Women at the Cultural Crossroads," in *Trails: Toward a New Western History*, ed. Patricia Nelson Limerick, Clyde A. Milner II, and Charles E. Rankin (Lawrence: University of Kansas Press, 1991) and "Race, Gender, and Intercultural Relations: The Case of Interracial Marriage,"

in *Writing the Range*, 69–80; Clara Sue Kidwell, "Indian Women as Cultural Mediators," *Ethnohistory* 39 (1992): 97–107; Margaret Connell Szasz, ed., *Between Indian and White Worlds: The Cultural Broker* (Norman: University of Oklahoma Press, 1994); Nancy Shoemaker, ed., *Negotiators of Change: Historical Perspectives on Native American Women* (New York: Routledge, 1995); Sarah Carter, *Capturing Women: The Manipulation of Cultural Imagery in Canada's Prairie West* (Montreal and Kingston: McGill-Queen's University Press, 1997), 169–82; Susan Sleeper-Smith, *Indian Women and French Men: Rethinking Cultural Encounter in the Western Great Lakes* (Amherst: University of Massachusetts Press, 2001); Adele Perry, *On the Edge of Empire: Gender, Race, and the Making of British Columbia, 1849–1871* (Toronto: University of Toronto Press, 2001); Lucy Eldersveld Murphy, "Public Mothers: Native American and Métis Women as Creole Mediators in the Nineteenth-Century Midwest," *Journal of Women's History* 14 (Winter 2003): 142–66. Historians have also turned increasingly to biography to explore Native cultural adaptation and responses to colonization: Ingo W. Shröder, "From Parkman to Postcolonial Theory: What's New in the Ethnohistory of Missions?" *Ethnohistory* 46 (1999): 809–15, and Bernd Peyer, *The Tutor'd Mind: Indian Missionary-Writers in Antebellum America* (Amherst: University of Massachusetts Press, 1997). For examples of studies of individual female cultural brokers that have particularly influenced my interpretation of Sara Riel, see: Lisa E. Emmerich, "Marguerite LaFleshe Diddock, Office of Indian Affairs Field Matron," *Great Plains Quarterly* 13 (1993): 162–71; Nancy Shoemaker, "Kateri Tekakwitha's Tortuous Path to Sainthood," in *Negotiators of Change*, 49–71; and Susan Sleeper-Smith, "Entre Catholique et Devenir Indienne: Souer Cecelia, Une Femme Odawaise," *Recherches Amérindienne au Quebec* 32 (2002): 53–61.

10   Sara Riel was not the first mixed-blood woman to take the veil – Marguerite Connolly entered the Grey Nuns' congregation in 1846. Riel was, however, the first *Métis* woman to take her final vows.

11   Robert Choquette, for instance, barely mentions women or the work of women religious in *The Oblate Assault on Canada's Northwest* (Ottawa: University of Ottawa Press, 1995). Martha McCarthy and Raymond J. Huel, by contrast, address the role of the Grey Nuns in the Northwest, but present the congregation as "auxiliaries to evangelization" rather than missionaries in their own right. See McCarthy's, *From the Great River to the Ends of the Earth: Oblate Missions to the Dene, 1847–1921* (Edmonton: University of Alberta Press, 1995) and Huel's, *Proclaiming the Gospel to the Indians and the Métis: The Missionary Oblates of Mary Immaculate in Western Canada, 1845–1945* (Edmonton: University of Alberta Press, 1996). Despite this oversight, the role played by Native women in either accommodating or resisting Christian missionary endeavours has become central to modern anthropological and ethnohistorical debates in North America. For an excellent review of the literature – along with recent articles that address the issue – see Michael Harkin and Sergei Kan, eds., *Special Issue: Native American Women's Responses to Christianity, Ethnohistory* 43 (1996), particularly 563–71.

12   Bishop Provencher to Bishop Signay, 8 August 1841, quoted in Diane Payment, "'*La vie en rose*': Métis Women at Batoche, 1870–1920," in *Women of the First Nations: Power, Wisdom, Strength*, ed. Christine Miller and Patricia Chuchryk (Winnipeg: University of Manitoba Press, 1996), 22. Provencher became bishop of St. Boniface in 1845.

13   In 1829, Provencher had urged two Métis women, Angelique and Marguerite Nolin, to open a girls' school. The school, however, closed in the 1830s: Huel, *Proclaiming the Gospel to the Indians and the Métis*, 14–17; Choquette, *The Oblate Assault*, 9–11. For the establishment of the Grey Nuns in the West, see: P. Duchaussois, o.m.i., *The Grey Nuns in the Far North, 1867–1917* (Toronto: McClelland and Stewart, 1919); G. Dugas, "Établissement des Soeurs de Charité à la Rivière Rouge," *Revue Canadienne* (1890), 20–27 and (1891), 719–25; Donald Chaput, "The 'Misses Nolin' of Red River," *The Beaver* (Winter 1975): 14–17; George Barclay, "Grey Nuns Voyage to Red River," *The Beaver*, outfit 297 (Winter 1966): 15–18.

14   During their childhood, Sara and Louis Riel lived at the forks of the Red and Seine Rivers on land owned by the Lagimodières who, by then, were among the wealthiest farming families at Red River. Although the Lagimodières were French-Canadian, they acculturated to the norms and values of the Métis majority at Red River. Julie Lagimodière's marriage to Jean-Louis Riel, the son of a voyageur with the North West Company and a French-Dene woman he met at Île-à-la-Crosse, symbolized the acculturation process.

15   Robert Gosman, *The Riel and Lagimodière Families in Métis Society, 1840–1860* (Ottawa: Parks Canada, manuscript no. 171, 1977), 4, 6, 24, 58–59. "Class" here refers to inequalities in the distribution of wealth, status, and power that existed at Red River prior to Confederation. In Rupert's Land, the presence of the HBC, the arrival of missionaries, the growth of the buffalo-robe trade, and the development of a sedentary, agricultural, and proto-industrial population at Red River created diverse segments within the mixed-blood population. Historians disagree, however, as to whether social status derived from familial and social connections, degree of acculturation, or wealth. While Frits Pannekoek, in *A Snug Little Flock*, argues that sectarian divisions cut deep into Red River's past, causing hostile and mutually exclusive divisions between the Catholic and French-speaking Métis and the Protestant and English-speaking Mixed-blood, historians Irene Spry and Gerhard Ens argue that Red River society was divided along socio-economic, not ethnic or religious lines. For the controversy, see: Frits Pannekoek, *A Snug Little Flock: The Social Origins of the Riel Resistance, 1869–70* (Winnipeg: Watson and Dwyer Publishing, 1991); Irene Spry, "The Métis and Mixed-bloods of Rupert's Land before 1870," in *The New Peoples: Being and Becoming Métis in North America*, ed. Jacqueline Peterson and Jennifer S. H. Brown, 98–118 (Winnipeg: University of Manitoba Press,1985); Ens, *Homeland to Hinterland*, 4–8.

16   Gosman, *The Riel and Lagimodière Families in Métis Society*, 79–85; Flanagan, *Louis "David" Riel*, 3–4.

17   Diane Payment, "Une Aperçu des Relations entre les Missionaires Catholique et le Métisses Pendant le Premier Siècle de Contact (1813–1918) dans l'Ouest Canadien," *Études Oblates de l'Ouest* 3 (1994): 151.

18   Sarah Carter, "The Woman's Sphere: Domestic Life at Riel House and Dalnavert," *Manitoba History* 11 (1986): 57.

19   Louis Riel to A.-A. Taché, 24 July 1885, quoted and translated in Thomas Flanagan, "Louis Riel's Religious Beliefs: A Letter to Bishop Taché," *Saskatchewan History* 27 (1974): 15–28.

20   Sara Riel to Julie Riel, Île-à-la-Crosse, 6 March 1882, Riel Papers, PAM.

21 A.-A. Taché to Bourget, 22 May 1851, quoted and translated in Stanley, *Louis Riel*, 20.

22 Ronald P. Zimmer, "Early Oblate Attempts for Indian and Métis Priests in Canada," *Études Oblates* (October-December 1973): 277–78.

23 Quoted in Elizabeth de Moissac, s.g.m., "La femme de l'Ouest: Leur rôle dans le histoire," (master's thesis, University of Ottawa, 1945), 63.

24 Estelle Mitchell, *The Grey Nuns of Montreal and the Red River Settlement, 1844– 1984* (Montreal: Éditions du Méridien, 1987), 75; Elizabeth de Moissac, s.g.m., "The Grey Nuns in Red River: Educational Institutions, 1844–1874," unpublished manuscript, translated by Sister Hedwidge Neuman, typescript, 9, Grey Nuns' Archives, St. Boniface (GNASB); Ibid., chronicles, 31 December 1860 and 1871. The GNASB is now closed; its collection has been transferred to the Grey Nuns' motherhouse in Montreal.

25 Chronicles, 1 August 1862; Sara Riel to Octavie, Eulalie, and Henriette Riel, St. Boniface, 13 October 1870 and 29 January 1871, Riel Papers, PAM. These letters likewise mention the subjects that Sara Riel's sisters learned at the convent school.

26 David Karel, "Sara Riel," *Dictionnaire des Artistes de Langue Française en Amerique de Nord*, 694.

27 Choquette, *The Oblate Assault on the Northwest*, 2–4.

28 Discussed in McCarthy and Anne Gagnon, "The *Pensionnat Assomption*: Religious Nationalism in a Franco-Albertan Boarding School for Girls, 1926–1960," *Historical Studies in Education* 1 (Spring 1989): 96–97.

29 Chronicles, 1871, GNASB.

30 Sara Riel, notebook, 1861–1863, 274–75, PAM. For another example of the missionary use of the Holy Family as role model, see Laura Peers, "'The Guardian of All': Jesuit Missionary and Salish Perceptions of the Virgin Mary," in *Reading Beyond Words: Contexts for Native History*, ed. Jennifer S. H. Brown and Elizabeth Vibert (Peterborough, ON: Broadview Press, 1996), 288.

31 Sara Riel, notebook, 276, PAM.

32 Sara Riel to Henriette Taché, 31 December 1863, Taché papers, AASB, no. 1465; Sara Riel to Azoline (?), 12 October 1862, St. Boniface Pensionnat, notebook, PAM.

33 Marta Danylewycz, *Taking the Veil: An Alternative to Marriage, Motherhood, and Spinsterhood in Quebec, 1840–1920* (Toronto: McClelland and Stewart, 1987), 39– 41.

34 Aileen Mary Brewer, *Nuns and the Education of American Catholic Women, 1860– 1920* (Chicago: Loyola University Press, 1987), 92–98; Marina Warner, *Alone of All Her Sex: The Myth and the Cult of the Virgin Mary* (London: Picador, 1990), 336–37.

35 The official cult of the Sacred Heart was established in the seventeenth century, but became popular only after Marguerite-Marie of Alocoque, a French nun, announced that the Lord had revealed the true nature of the devotion to her at Paray-le-Monial between 1673 and 1675. Mother d'Youville, foundress of the Grey Nuns, became one of Canada's first proponents of the cult. She asked that her disciples foster the devotion in their own communities and wherever they engaged in missionary work. P. Duchaussois, an Oblate priest, elaborated: "The Heart of Jesus, represented on the Cross which they wear, sets their own heart

on fire with the spirit of self-sacrifice, and most closely unites their life with that of their Divine model, the victim of atoning Love": Duchaussois, *Grey Nuns in the Far North*, 206; C. J. Moell, "Devotion to the Sacred Heart," *New Catholic Encyclopedia*, vol. 12 (San Francisco: The Catholic University of America, 1967), 818–20; Jeanne Weber, "Devotion to the Sacred Heart: History, Theology, and Liturgical Celebration," *Worship* 72 (May 1988): 244–45; Raymond Jonas, *France and the Cult of the Sacred Heart: An Epic Tale for Modern Times* (Berkeley: The University of California Press, 2000).

36 Stanley, *Louis Riel*, 29–30; Flanagan, *Louis "David" Riel*, 17–19; Maggie Siggins, *Riel: A Life of Revolution* (Toronto: Harper Collins, 1994), 59–62.

37 Zimmer, "Early Oblate Attempts for Indian and Métis Priests in Canada," 277–80; Stanley, *Louis Riel*, 21–27; Siggins, *Riel*, 25–29.

38 Brian P. Clark, "The Parish and the Hearth: Women's Confraternities and the Devotional Revolution among the Irish Catholics of Toronto, 1850–1885," in *Age of Transition: Readings in Canadian Social History, 1800–1900*, ed. Norman Knowles (Toronto: Harcourt Brace, 1998), 357–69. Ollivier Hubert and Enrico Cumbo likewise explore the complexities of French-Canadian and Italian men's responses to Catholicism in central Canada. See their contributions in Nancy Christie, ed., *Households of Faith: Family, Gender, and Community in Canada, 1760–1969* (Montreal and Kingston: McGill-Queen's University Press, 2001).

39 Payment, *"La vie en rose?"* 19–37, and *"The Free People-Otipemisiwak": Batoche, Saskatchewan, 1870–1930* (Ottawa: Minister of Supply and Services, 1990).

40 Van Kirk, *Many Tender Ties*, particularly chapters 7, 8, and 9; Cavanaugh, "No Place for a Woman," 501; Erica Smith, "'Gentlemen, This is no Ordinary Trial': Sexual Narratives and the Trial of the Reverend Corbett, Red River, 1863," in *Reading Beyond Words*, 375.

41 "Vocation des Femmes," *Le Métis*, vol. 3, no. 19, 4 October 1873.

42 Sara Riel to Marie, Octavie, and Eulalie Riel, Île-à-la-Crosse, 19 July 1871, Riel Papers, PAM.

43 Diane Payment, *Riel Family: Home and Lifestyle at St. Vital, 1860–1910* (Ottawa: Parks Canada, report no. 379, 1980), 71–72.

44 Ens, *Homeland to Hinterland*, 72–73, 134–38.

45 Mitchell, *The Grey Nuns and the Red River Settlement*, 11.

46 Elizabeth de Moissac, "The Grey Nuns in Red River: Educational Institutions, 1844–1974," 45; necrologies, GNASB.

47 Necrologies, GNASB; Mitchell, *The Grey Nuns of Montreal*, 37, 40, 42–44, 77; Van Kirk, *Many Tender Ties*, 188–89; de Moissac, "The Grey Nuns in Red River: Educational Institutions," 10.

48 Whether Catholicism, or a religious vocation, was an outlet for women's aspirations has been debated since the publication of Marta Danylewycz's study, *Taking the Veil*. For studies that emphasize Catholicism as a force of oppression in Aboriginal and White women's lives, see: Bernard Denault and Benoit Levesque, *Eléments pour une sociologie des communautés religieuses au Québec* (Montreal: Les Presses de l'Université de Montréal, 1975); Eleanor Leacock, "Montagnais Women and the Jesuit Program for Colonization," *Myths of Male Dominance: Collected Articles on Women Cross-Culturally* (New York: Monthly Review Press, 1981), 43–62; Karen Anderson, *Chain Her by One Foot: The Subjugation of Women in Seventeenth-Century New France* (New York: Routledge, 1991); Carol Devens,

Countering-Colonization: Native American Women and Great Lakes Missions, 1630–1900 (Berkeley: University of California Press, 1992). Those historians that tend to support Danylewycz's thesis include: Micheline Dumont-Johnson, "Une perspective féministe dans l'histoire des congregations de femmes," *Études d'histoire religieuse* (1990): 29–35; Barbara J. Cooper, "The Convent: An Option for Quebecoises, 1930–1950," *Canadian Women Studies* 7 (Winter 1986): 31–34; Natalie Zemon Davis, "Iroquois Women, European Women," in *Women, "Race," and Writing in the Early Modern Period*, ed. Margo Hendricks and Patricia Parker (New York: Routledge, 1994), 243–58; Nancy Shoemaker, "Kateri Tekakwitha's Tortuous Path," 49–71.

49   Irene Drouin, "La Qualité de l'esprit de Sara Riel," *La Liberté*, 72 November 1985; Anonymous, "Connaissez-vous Sara Riel, Soeur de Louis Riel?" typescript, revised by Gilberte Guibord, s.g.m., GNASB.

50   Sara Riel to Louis Riel, St. Norbert, 7 September 1868, Riel Papers, PAM.

51   Quoted in Elizabeth de Moissac, "Les Soeurs Grises et les événements de 1869–70," La Société Canadiene d'Histoire de l'Église Catholique, *Sessions d'Étude* (1970): 215; Chronicles, October 1869, GNASB.

52   Sara Riel to Louis Riel, St. Boniface, 25 November 1870, Riel Papers, PAM.

53   Jordan, *To Louis from your sister who loves you, Sara Riel*, 23–27.

54   Annals, Vol. 3, 1862–1863, 102, GNASB.

55   Stanley, ed., *The Collected Writings of Louis Riel*, Louis Riel to Julie Riel, St. Paul, 10 August 1867, 1–1007.

56   "Depart de Mgr. Grandin," *Le Métis* 1, no. 4 (22 June 1871): 2.

57   Sara Riel to Alexander Riel, 2 July 1871, Riel Papers, PAM.

58   Sara Riel to Julie Riel, Green Lake, 10 August 1871, Riel Papers, PAM. For an excellent study that addresses the conflicts faced by other Native missionaries in prairie Canada, see: Winona Stevenson, "The Journals and Voices of a Church of England Native Catechist: Askenootow (Charles Pratt), 1851–1884," in *Reading Beyond Words*, 304–29.

59   Germain Lesage, *Capitale d'une Solitude* (Ottawa: Editions des Etudes Oblates, 1946), 110; Barbara Benoit, "The Mission at Île-à-la-Crosse," *The Beaver* (Winter 1980): 40–42; HBC Archives (HBCA), mission history; Philip Taft Spalding, "The Métis at Île-à-la-Crosse" (Ph.D. diss., University of Washington, 1970), 55–56; Chronicles, 23 July 1859 and 9 July 1860, GNASB; Adrien-Gabriel Morice, *Histoire de l'Église Catholique dans l'Ouest canadien* (1659–1915), Vol. 2 (St. Boniface and Montreal: Author and Granger Frères, 1921), 391; Payment, "Une Aperçu des Relations entre les Missionaires Catholiques et les Métisses," 145–46.

60   Chronicles, Ste. Famille Convent, Île-à-la-Crosse, 1872; "Île-à-la-Crosse: Historique, 1860–1892"; and Annals, 1882, Grey Nuns' Archives, Province of Alberta and Saskatchewan (GNAAS). Beginning in 1846, the Grey Nuns began to accept *filles données* as regular sisters within the order. They were women with little or no formal education who were accepted with limited privileges. More often than not, they performed manual labour for the Grey Nuns.

61   Sara Riel to Joseph, Charles, and Alexandre Riel, 26 December 1872; Sara Riel to Julie and Louis Riel, 1872, Riel Papers, PAM.

62   Ibid., Sara Riel to Julie and Louis Riel, 1872; Sara Riel to Octavie Riel, 14 January 1875.

63 Between 1871 and 1875 it became difficult for Sara to write to Louis because his location was unknown to her. Throughout the period, she wrote frequently to her long-time spiritual advisor, Archbishop Taché, asking him if her sacrifice was in vain. When Louis went into official exile in February 1875, the Grey Nuns kept the news from his sister. Upon hearing of it from Taché, however, she felt betrayed by her superiors and discontinued her correspondence with her advisor for two years. Louis's troubles continued to disrupt Sara Riel's peace of mind. In late 1876, for example, Riel learned through correspondence that Louis had been admitted to an asylum. She wrote to Taché and explained to him that, although her faith had suffered upon hearing the news, she sought solace and resignation in the Sacred Heart of Jesus: Mary Jordan, *De ta soeur, Sara Riel* (St. Boniface: Editions des Plaines, 1980), 131–33; Sara Riel to A.-A Taché, Île-à-la-Crosse, 9 January 1877, Taché Papers, AASB.

64 Sara Riel to Riel Family, c. January 1876, Riel Papers PAM. Perhaps because her work stood for everything her brother had resisted, Riel related only a few details of her career to her family. The Grey Nuns' chronicles and Riel's letters to Archbishop Taché and Joseph Dubuc, founder of *Le Métis* and member of the Manitoba Legislative Assembly, however, reveal her commitment to converting the Métis and Native populations of the North. In 1876, for instance, she stood as godmother to Louis Jourdain, a recent convert. She wrote home to her family: "This conversion is a conquest for the Sacred Heart of Jesus. What a consolation to see this soul on the right path." Ibid., 24 June 1876.

65 Ibid., Sara Riel to Louis Riel, 6 August 1874.

66 Ibid., Sara Riel to the Riel Family, 24 June 1876.

67 Sara Riel to A.-A. Taché, 20 January 1876, AASB.

68 Ibid., Sara Riel to A.-A. Taché, c. 1879.

69 Richard Slobodin, "The Subarctic Métis as Products and Agents of Cultural Contact," *Arctic Anthropology* 2 (1964): 50.

70 Sara Riel to Louis Riel, 4 January 1880, Riel Papers, PAM.

71 Sara Riel to A.-A. Taché, 17 November 1879 and 26 September 1880, AASB.

72 Sara Riel to Julie Riel, 6 March 1882, Riel Papers, PAM.

73 Robert Longpré, *Île-à-la-Crosse, 1776–1976: Sakitawak Bi-Centennial* (Île-à-la-Crosse: Île-à-la-Crosse Bi-Centennial Committee, 1977), 26; Prosper Légéard to Martinet, Île-à-la-Crosse, 17 January 1875, *Missions* 13 (1875); Chronicles, 17 January 1874, GNAAS; Sara Riel to A.-A Taché, 12 July 1880, AASB.

74 Chronicles, 29 December 1883 and Annals, Vol. 3, 1884–1887, 21, GNASB; Ste. Famille Convent, Île-à-la-Crosse, chronicles, 26 December 1883, GNAAS.

75 Sara Riel's cultural heritage shaped her liminality. As a liminal being, she was "neither here nor there; [she was] betwixt and between the position assigned and arrayed by law, custom, convention, and ceremonial": Victor Turner, *The Ritual Process: Structure and Anti-Structure* (Ithaca: Cornell University Press, 1969), 95. For an article that draws upon the concept of liminality to interpret a "frontier" woman's life, the life of a woman who lived on the borderlands between two cultures, see Noreen Groover Lape, "'I Would Rather Be with My People, but Not to Live as They Live': Cultural Liminality and Double Consciousness in Sarah Winnemucca Hopkins's *Life Among the Piutes: Their Wrongs and Claims*," *American Indian Quarterly* 22 (1998): 259–79.

76   For the historical debate on this issue, see in particular Sarah Carter, *Aboriginal Peoples and the Colonizers of Western Canada to 1900* (Toronto: University of Toronto Press, 1999), 73–78; Robin Brownlie and Mary-Ellen Kelm, "'Desperately Seeking Absolution': Native Agency as Colonialist Alibi?" *Canadian Historical Review* 75 (1994): 543–56; J. R. Miller, "'Owen Glendower, Hotspur and Canadian Indian Policy," in *Sweet Promises: A Reader on Indian-White Relations in Canada*, ed. J. R. Miller, 323–52 (Toronto: University of Toronto Press, 1991).

77   David Lee, "The Métis Militant Rebels of 1885," in *Readings in Canadian History: Post Confederation*, 4th ed., ed. R. Douglas Francis and Donald B. Smith (Toronto: Harcourt Brace and Company, 1994), 80.

78   Sister Agnes to Julie Riel, Île-à-la-Crosse, 29 December 1883, quoted and translated in Jordan, *To Louis from your sister who loves you*, 101–2.

three

"From One Whose Home Is among the Indians":

Henrietta Muir Edwards and Aboriginal Peoples

PATRICIA A. ROOME

Rewriting the West through women's history means return-ing to traditional sources and reading them through femi-nist eyes; yet, as Patricia Roome illustrates, it also entails returning to, and revising, earlier feminist scholarship. Roome's interpretation of Henrietta Muir Edwards's attitudes and experiences reminds us that scholarship on first-wave feminism remains unsettled. As one of Alberta's "Famous Five," Edwards played a celebrated role in early histories of social reform and the women's suffrage move-ment. As feminist scholars became attuned to the issues of gender and imperialism, however, the "Famous Five" emerged anew as "Infamous Racists" who championed reform to enhance and consolidate their own privileged position. Roome joins a growing list of scholars who acknowledge the importance of race and class to first-wave feminist thought, without portraying its members as uncomplicated racists. She moves beyond simplistic categorizations by exploring how Edwards's intimate, long-term encounters with Aboriginal men and women shaped her feminist outlook and perceptions of racialized "others." She argues that Edwards's interaction with Aboriginal peoples was constrained by the limitations placed on British-Canadian, middle-class women. Within these imposed structures, however, there existed a common women's culture that allowed Edwards to transcend racial boundaries in order to become one of the few advocates for Aboriginal women's rights in early twentieth-century Canada. Edwards's life, much like Sara Riel's and Clare Sheridan's (whose life story follows), reminds us to take gender and individual experience into account when we address the issue of Canadian cultural identity and power.

Henrietta Muir Edwards is remembered as one of the Alberta "Famous Five" whose successful legal challenge in the 1920s established women's personhood and eligibility for senate appointment in Canada. This chapter explores a lesser-known side of Edwards: her relationship with Aboriginal peoples and the cross-cultural friendships she developed during the early settlement era in western Canada. From 1882 until her death in 1931, Edwards travelled and lived among the Cree, Assiniboine, Blackfoot, Blood, and Peigan. In the early years, she photographed, collected and sent Aboriginal artwork to her family in eastern Canada. Her mother, in particular, admired the "very beautiful Indian curiosity," remarking: "How very clever the squaws are in beadwork and in choice of colors."[1] Few Euro-Canadian feminists shared Edwards's experiences or possessed enough knowledge of Aboriginal peoples to critique what historians describe as the "centrality of racism in first-wave feminist thought." However, living at the cultural crossroads challenged Edwards to examine her privileged position as a White feminist and a colonizer.[2]

Women's role in the colonization of western Canada and the United States in the mid-nineteenth and early twentieth centuries demonstrates the importance of gender and race to imperial and nation-building projects.[3] Early studies of Canadian fur-trade society document how White women in the Northwest after 1830 challenged fur trade marriage alliances between European and Canadian-born men and Aboriginal and Métis women. As Lesley Erickson recounts in chapter 2, further political events exaggerated the racial tensions created by the arrival of White women. Aboriginal and Métis anger at the expansion of the new Dominion of Canada produced two major conflicts, the 1869–70 Red River Resistance and the 1885 Northwest Rebellion, and a series of treaties. As an intrinsic part of the empire-building process, White women on the Canadian frontier displaced Aboriginal women. And, as Kristin Burnett demonstrates in chapter 6, symbolic representations of Aboriginal women also changed. Increasingly, missionaries, the Canadian press, and government officials portrayed Aboriginal women as dissolute, dangerous, and sinister. In contrast, White women on the Canadian frontier carried the banner of purity and spirituality as civilizers and reproducers of the race. Along with fur trade histories, studies of gender relations in colonial British Columbia demonstrate the importance of sexuality to race relations and document attempts to control Aboriginal women's sexuality.[4]

Complementing this scholarship on race, reproduction, and sexuality are studies of first-wave Canadian feminism and feminists.[5] Prominent writers and activists, like Emily Murphy and Nellie McClung, receive the most attention, especially from literary critics. Janice Henderson's study of settler feminism places Murphy at the heart of the Canadian race-making project by exploring "the paradoxical *combination* of the settler woman's functions as an emblem of sexual vulnerability and an agent of the government."[6] As she concludes, "from the perspective of gender" Murphy was "at a maximal distance from the state; from the perspective of race, she was the very embodiment of its liberal 'essence.'"[7] Race and gender contradictions permeated Murphy's work as writer, feminist, and judge of the Edmonton Women's Court. A confident Murphy advanced a racist ideology, which she articulated in conspiratorial tones in *The Black Candle*. Although Henderson examines only three writers including Murphy, her analysis extends these assumptions to other first-wave feminists.

Using post-colonial and critical race theory, Janice Fiamengo explores the racial ideas of Nellie McClung, Sara Jeanette Duncan, Agnes Maule Machar, and Flora MacDonald Denison, charting the "difference between and within early White feminist writers." McClung's fair deal, Machar's liberal ecumenism, and Denison's Theosophy "enabled antihegemonic thinking about race" and demonstrated that first-wave feminism did not necessarily produce "monolithic racism." As Homi

Bhabha argues, "the ambivalence of colonial discourse" left space for dissent, difference and ambiguity. Following his analysis, Fiamengo further distinguishes racialism from racism.[8] McClung's writings demonstrated racialism by attributing racial characteristics, both cultural and biological, to certain groups. In contrast to Murphy, McClung's work does not advocate a racial hierarchy of privilege and pain. Drawing on McClung's private papers and unpublished work in addition to her famous texts, Fiamengo documents McClung's challenge to racial hierarchy, White exclusiveness, and conspiracy theories. In the 1930s and 1940s, she became one of the few commentators "naming and deploring the racism of Whites," and defending Doukhobors, European Jews, and Chinese- and Japanese-Canadians.

If Fiamengo presents McClung as a complicated modern subject, journalists see her simply as one of "a squad of racist, elitist bigots." A *Calgary Sun* reporter, in denouncing the October 2004 *Bank of Canada* release of a new $50 bill that featured a statue of the Famous Five, told readers that "modern-day revisionists have tried to whitewash the dark doctrine of the group"; however, "it's a well-documented truth that the Five consisted of upper-class women who promoted Canada as a racially-superior society of wealthy, educated Anglo-Saxons. No blacks, Asians or East Europeans need apply." A *Globe and Mail* editorial, while more moderate, drew similar conclusions.[9] Few commentators knew their history well enough to discuss McClung's critique of the racist politics of the Mackenzie King government in the 1930s, a government led, ironically, by the prime minister profiled on the front of the $50 bill. Motivated more by contemporary anti-feminist sentiments than a serious concern for racial justice and historical accuracy, such negative press tells us little about first-wave feminism. Instead we learn about Canada's attachment to a "mythology of racelessness," which attributes early-twentieth-century racism to a few individuals.[10] Journalists concluded that Murphy's well-publicized racism represented the group – an assumption that is problematic since Irene Parlby, according to her biographer, remained silent on issues related to Aboriginal peoples, race, and citizenship. A scholarly biography of Louise McKinney, if and when it is written, will probably establish that the Dominion Women's Christian Temperance Union president likewise made few public statements. Henrietta Muir Edwards's life experiences positioned her differently: they unsettled her bourgeois upbringing, privileging speech over silence and commitment over indifference.[11]

The Persons Case created a significant partnership; however, disagreements and conflict characterized the group. Comparative study shows significant differences in age, personality, family background, religious beliefs, tolerance for cultural difference, and exposure to Aboriginal peoples. Nineteen years separated Henrietta Muir Edwards (1849–1931) from Emily Murphy (1868–1933), Irene Parlby (1868–1965) and Louise McKinney (1868–1931). The youngest member, Nellie McClung (1873–1951), was a contemporary of Henrietta's eldest daughter. As authors and publicists, McClung and Murphy created fictional identities, but Edwards (who disliked Murphy) never enjoyed writing, detested interviews with journalists, and preferred research, organizing, and lobbying. If Edwards had been born later, she could have enjoyed a successful law career. Denied the opportunity, she spent fifty years as an unpaid advocate seeking stronger legal rights for women. Unlike Murphy, Edwards never wrote or spoke in public using racially charged language. Nor could she ignore Aboriginal peoples, as did Parlby and McKinney. Closer to McClung in religious views, temperament, and beliefs, Edwards maintained contradictory views on the question of race.

In reconstructing Edwards's relationship with Aboriginal peoples, especially women, her extensive collection of Aboriginal artifacts and photographs, family letters, and public reports are useful, although the record is often fragmented and confused. Political issues such as suffrage, temperance, and property rights dominate her extensive public correspondence and, like her colleagues, Edwards seldom mentions Aboriginal women, until after her husband's death in 1915. Prior to the 1920s, Edwards did not enter the public debate on Aboriginal women's sexuality, a field occupied by male missionaries, medical doctors, Indian Affairs officials, and politicians (see, for instance, Sarah Carter's discussion of official attitudes in chapter 9).[12] Similar to feminists in other colonial contexts, Edwards occupied an ambiguous position between colonized and colonizer, one riddled with contradictions.[13]

Henrietta Muir Edwards's story begins in Montreal in December 1849 with her birth to William and Jane Muir, an important Baptist merchant-tailor family. After her radical and charismatic Scottish grandfather immigrated to Montreal in 1820, he established the first Baptist chapel then, along with his many sons, created schools, newspapers, churches, and the Montreal Baptist College.[14] Henrietta spent a privileged bourgeois childhood, haphazardly educated at home and in small Montreal private schools, whose religious basis fostered a passionate evangelical

Henrietta Muir
Edwards, Montreal,
1876, age 26. Wedding
photograph. Glenbow
Archives, NA-4035-162.

activism and unhappiness with the gender restrictions imposed on
women in Victorian Canada. After travelling throughout Europe and
attending art school in New York, she created the Montreal Working
Women's Association in 1875, a charitable organization that also housed
the offices of the Montreal Women's Printing Office. Here, Henrietta and
her sister trained women as compositors and launched *Women's Work for
Women*, a newspaper publicizing evangelical Christian women's activities. She became a founding member of the Baptist Women's Missionary
Society of Montreal, sending female missionaries to India. These years
witnessed the development of her Christian feminism; one grounded in
the Christian language of duty and service, and captured in the phrase
"A Women's Commission." To support her work, Henrietta also opened

Edwards family, Ottawa, 1890. *L-R*: William Muir, Henrietta, Margaret, Oliver Cromwell, Alice. Glenbow Archives, NA-4035-164.

an art studio in Montreal and accepted painting commissions. Although these were unusual activities for a Canadian female philanthropist, they were characteristic of her independent spirit.[15]

  Henrietta Muir never became a model society matron. Marriage in 1876 to Oliver Cromwell Edwards, a medical doctor, son of a Baptist Ottawa Valley timber merchant, and kindred spirit, did little to tame the ambitious young woman. In 1883, her restless husband abandoned his Montreal medical practice and moved to Fort Qu'Appelle where he worked as a medical officer for Aboriginal peoples who had signed Treaty 4 with the Canadian government in 1874. Dr. Edwards invited his wife and their two small children to join him. Over the next seven years, while Henrietta lived in the North-West Territories, she gave birth to a third child and used her energies to establish new frontier communities; in 1890, however, her husband decided abruptly that they should return to central Canada to advance his career and seek further education for their children.

Living in Ottawa, the national capital, opened many doors for Henrietta: her art studio provided lessons for young artists, established her reputation, and allowed her to submit paintings to numerous exhibitions. The city also welcomed Lady Ishbel Aberdeen, wife of Canada's governor general and founder of the National Council of Women of Canada (NCWC). Edwards accepted executive positions on the NCWC and its local affiliate, the Ottawa Local Council of Women. Soon Edwards became president of the Ottawa Young Women's Christian Association, superintendent of its building project, and an executive member of the Ontario Women's Christian Temperance Union. A successful public life concealed private difficulties, however, as Dr. Edwards's medical practice floundered and debts and impending bankruptcy forced Henrietta to accept many painting commissions in a desperate attempt to salvage their reputation. In the end, they sold their Ottawa residence in 1896. Still deeply in debt, the couple reluctantly separated for the next decade.[16]

The Edwards's financial problems seemed endless and were rooted in a combination of Dr. Edwards's career and the restrictions imposed upon married women. During post-graduate training in Scotland, Dr. Edwards studied homeopathy, an approach popular within the British medical profession in the 1870s. When Dr. Edwards returned to Canada, he entered battles between doctors and homeopaths and, within medical professional associations, debated the "scientific" merits of homeopathy. A stubborn individualist, Dr. Edwards refused to abandon his use of homeopathy because he was convinced it represented a safer treatment approach.[17] This decision, combined with his personality, caused problems throughout his career; his wife, unable to accept paid employment without bringing shame to their marriage, often faced difficult decisions. In 1896, Henrietta saw no other alternative but to return to her Montreal family where she supervised her children's education, re-established her art studio, and started working in Quebec women's organizations. Dr. Edwards again became a medical officer with the Department of Indian Affairs. Although he was posted in Regina, the position did not provide his family with financial security. In 1900, he accepted a new assignment as medical officer for the Treaty 8 Commission in charge of vaccinating Aboriginal peoples throughout northern Alberta and the Yukon district. Two years later, tired and in poor health, he accepted a final move to the isolated Blood Reserve in southern Alberta where Henrietta joined him in 1904. Oliver's unexpected death in 1915 left Henrietta financially destitute. Her son, who was now a professor at the University of Alberta, loaned her enough money to buy a small house in nearby Macleod, where she lived until her death in 1931.

Dr. Edwards's treks across Canada and his career upheavals challenged, but did not dampen, Henrietta's spirit or commitment to the women's movement. For over thirty years, she served as the Convener of Laws for the NCWC, lobbied for legal reforms, and wrote books on women and the laws of Canada and Alberta. Nothing deterred Henrietta from this project: neither her frequent moves, her isolation on the Blood Reserve, her residence in a small southern Alberta town, her family's chronic financial difficulties, nor the premature deaths of her husband, her daughter, and her son.[18] Throughout her life, Edwards juggled contradictory roles that were created as much by circumstances as by her own desires. Like many settler women, she never chose to live in western Canada: marriage and her husband's fortunes dictated place of residence and her association with Aboriginal peoples.[19] When thrust into a new environment Edwards showed flexibility, compassion and determination, important assets in cross-cultural experiences. Blessed with a cheerful disposition, she adjusted easily to new situations. Numerous letters, personal reflections and tributes reflected on Edwards's gentle nature, sense of humour, wit and energy. A niece lamented Henrietta's death, recalling, "her joyous living, and outlook gave one such an uplift." A younger National Council executive member commented on Edwards's reputation and expressed gratitude that she had "an opportunity of learning something of the tenderness and sweetness of her nature."[20]

The following pages explore Edwards as an artist and collector of "Indian curios," an employer of Aboriginal women, a medical doctor's wife, a Christian advocate, and a feminist activist. Like the female missionaries in Canada and the British activists in India, her relationship with Aboriginal women often situated her as cultural mediator and missionary, sometimes as maternal imperialist; only occasionally, after the death of her husband, did she act as a feminist ally.[21]

The Muir family and the city of Montreal, Canada's premiere centre for art and culture, nurtured Henrietta's artistic ambitions and developed her collecting passion. Typical of bourgeois travellers, the Edwards became avid collectors of Indian "curios," a Victorian term for rare or unusual objects. Before leaving Montreal, they studied Aboriginal culture under the supervision of Henrietta's father, who was a member of the Montreal Natural History Society and curator of McGill

University's new Redpath Museum. In 1882, he wrote to advise the couple to keep notes on "the aborigines" and collect specimens and curios.[22] Family friends included George Mercer Dawson, the prominent Canadian geologist and ethnographer whose McGill University exhibition of Northwest photographs the Edwards attended. In *Sketches of the past and present condition of the Indians of Canada*, Dawson advocated education and assimilation as the moral approach to Native social evolution and opposed segregation on reserves and government paternalism.[23] The Edwards did not necessarily endorse Dawson's views although they shared the common belief that Aboriginal peoples in North America were a "vanishing race." As collectors, the Edwards hoped ironically to preserve Aboriginal artifacts for future generations of White Canadians; as ardent nationalists, they agreed with Dawson that these cultural artifacts should remain in Canadian museums regardless of the extravagant prices that could be earned in Europe and the United States.[24]

Between 1882 and 1915, the Edwards built an impressive collection of Aboriginal artifacts from the districts of Assiniboia, the Yukon, and northern and southern Alberta. For many years, few Canadians questioned such cultural appropriation.[25] Quite the reverse. Henrietta and Oliver earned praise for their work throughout the twentieth century. When Henrietta sold her collection to the University of Alberta in 1920, the university newspaper wrote:

The day of the Indian in Western Canada is fast passing and with him are disappearing the customs, utensils, and ornaments emblematic of his customs, beliefs, and institutions. There is still much of this material available, but each year it is becoming more and more difficult to obtain such articles as will form a lasting record of the craft and pomp of these past monarchs of the prairies. That much of this material, which is usually referred to as 'Indian curios,' should be collected and preserved on native soil for the education benefit of future generations, is a matter of vital national importance, and needs no argument.[26]

Paying Henrietta $5,000 for the collection of 250 items, the University explained it was especially valuable "'because Mrs. Edwards has been able to obtain details regarding the use, purpose, and legendary beliefs connected with many of the articles."[27] Such notes, if they ever existed, have disappeared, making it impossible to assess Edwards's skill as an ethnographer. The University of Alberta collection is eclectic: it includes women and children's dresses, head-dresses, belts, moccasins, leggings, jackets as well as a painted steer hide, catlinite pipes, gun cases, par fleches, sweet grass bags, and blanket strips. As late as 1985, curators for an exhibition *Buffalo 'these Beasts on ye Barren ground,'* drawing heavily upon the Edwards collection, praised the "foresight and generosity of the original collectors." Only in the last fifteen years have Canadian museums shifted their focus toward celebrating Aboriginal artistry and creativity.[28]

The Edwards collection provides a window into cultural relationships in this era. Correspondence indicates that the couple acquired some of the artifacts as gifts, purchased others, and commissioned drawings. Family members, especially their grandchildren, recalled that Henrietta was "all mixed up with the Indians," an unintended ironic statement.

When I was a little girl I can remember my grandmother in the house on the reserve. It had a big sun parlour and the walls of that sun parlour were hung with all these Indian things. There were bags with quill embroidery on them and… she had lots of things in boxes. When the Duke and Duchess … came the Indians dressed up in clothing from the collection because they didn't have their own ceremonial robes anymore. My grandmother frequently lent the stuff out. Then the Indians would bring it back to her.[29]

Following her father's Montreal example, Henrietta acted as a resident museum curator; an occupation reinforced by Victorian and Edwardian Canadians' passion for trinkets and tourist items. Although modern scholars view such collectors as insensitive and exploitative, the Edwards probably did not question the ethics of this practice, especially since they acquired these important cultural items from Aboriginal peoples during periods of intense poverty and cultural displacement.[30]

The context of the Edwards's collecting is important to this question. During their early years on the Prairies, Henrietta travelled with Oliver to the Assiniboine Agency where he attended to Aboriginal health problems. When the couple selected artifacts, Oliver relied upon Henrietta's artistic training and appreciation for women's workmanship. Many objects from this region are dated 1884–5: a beaded moose hide needle case and pouch, a buffalo horn head dress, a set of shaved and polished buffalo horns, and variety of catlinite pipe bowls and stems. We do not know if the destitute and starving Assiniboine were offered clothes, food, tools, or money as payment for these artifacts. Certainly, Dr. Edwards and Henrietta felt compassion for their situation. As a staunch Liberal, Dr. Edwards's criticism of Indian Affairs policy made him an unpopular employee and a liability, which hastened his return to Ottawa.

The following example illustrates Dr. Edwards's blunt approach. In the spring of 1884, angry and starving Cree, along with Saulteaux and Assiniboine chiefs and their respective bands, demanded a council with Indian Affairs Commissioner Edgar Dewdney after they gathered for a Thirst Dance.[31] After an official visit, Dr. Edwards reported that "Jack's people" were suffering from "land scurvy" that was "due entirely to the exclusive use of salt food," in his opinion an unnecessary and dangerous diet. Several months later, the Indian Affairs Department again sent Dr. Edwards to investigate since the assistant commissioner angrily refused to accept the legitimacy of these Aboriginal grievances: Dr. Edwards's "strongly-worded report" again condemned government policy and supported Aboriginal grievances. "The only proper treatment of this disease," explained the doctor, "is fresh food and vegetables and unless this policy is pursued in the case of these Indians the disease will spread."[32] Dr. Edwards could barely concealed his dismay at the "death toll" of forty-two Crees and thirty-three Assiniboines, which he felt "out of 873 souls is a very large proportion." He predicted, "the number will increase unless fresh food was supplied in large quantities."[33] The parsimonious Department partially implemented the doctor's recommendations although his partisan criticism of the Conservative federal government's policy in the Northwest prevented him from receiving patronage positions from government officials in Regina or Ottawa, which was already suspicious of his support for the Liberal Party. At home, Henrietta defended Oliver, quietly endorsing and supporting his campaign.

During these troubled years, the couple commissioned numerous drawings, called ledger art, from an Assiniboine artist named Hongeeyeesa. As artist and art teacher Henrietta influenced Hongeeyeesa's work and valued his drawings, refusing to sell them to the University of Alberta. They remained in the Edwards family for several generations and, although descendants no longer knew the artist's identity, they recognized their rarity as chronicles of early reserve life and creative expressions charting the impact of Western materials and Euro-Canadian perceptions on Aboriginal people.[34] After the Glenbow Museum purchased the forty-four ledger drawings from the family, curator Valerie Robertson, with the aid of Charlotte Nahbixie and residents of Carry the Kettle First Nation, re-established the artist's identity.

Hongeeyeesa's earliest drawing in 1885, which used paper from Indian agents' ledger books and pencils and watercolours supplied by Henrietta, bore a dedication to "Pearle Edwards," the youngest daughter born that year. In these drawings, "the representation of images is straight forward, using a singular outline and flat 'filling in' with colour washes or graphite." The later drawings, Robertson explained, "are distinguished by the expressive and loose application of various media, increased scale of images, the use of foreshortening and the mixing and layering of media." Hongeeyeesa's evolution as an artist, encouraged by the Edwards, documents his experience of profound cultural change.[35]

Art, cultural artifacts, and Aboriginal women dominated the family's domestic life in the North-West Territories and later in Alberta. Whether as servants, handicraft workers, patients of Dr. Edwards, or neighbours, contact with Aboriginal women formed an integral part of Henrietta's life. Little remains of the texture of these daily relationships except Henrietta's photographs, their artifact collection, family stories, and the occasional letter. In these fragments, we catch glimpses of daily interactions, but these need to be interpreted with discretion. Aboriginal women, when they appear in these letters, are most often described by others, rarely by Henrietta.

One early reference obliquely refers to a Lakota woman employed by Henrietta. When daughter Alice, seven years of age, later recalled the birth of her sister on 24 April 1885 during the Battle of Cut Knife Creek, she inadvertently commented on their servant:

My father was away at Qu'Appelle Station serving with the troops & the telegram that my mother sent to him calling him home was delayed. She was alone in the house with a young maid servant only & kept looking to the west for some sign of my father & finally went upstairs to bed to prepare as well as she could for the event. But then she heard the sound of the clip clop of my father's high stepping horse coming across the prairie & he got there just in time to wash up & looked after her. The baby was very small but survived and grew to be a lively child with blue eyes & curly red hair & was her father's pet & delight.[36]

Patience, the "young maid servant" who cared for Alice and her brother William, helped Henrietta prepare for childbirth and may have served as midwife, just as Aboriginal women did for other White settler women. Patience came from the Standing Buffalo Reserve north of Indian Head. Her husband may have worked for the Qu'Appelle Valley Farming

Company, an employer of Sioux labourers, and she may have attended Qu'Appelle Industrial School.[37] During the Northwest Rebellion of 1885, Cree and Métis messengers pressured these Sioux to support their rebellion; although some joined the rebellion, Patience and her family did not. According to Indian agents, the Sioux enjoyed an excellent reputation as "good workers" and commanded high wages from the residents. Dr. Edwards agreed with this assessment. In 1882 and 1883, he visited the Lakota, "the remnant of the once mighty Sioux nation," and recorded favourable impressions of their ceremonial dances, especially "the bragging dance."[38]

Henrietta likely gave Patience her Christian name while she worked for the family in Qu'Appelle. Although an indifferent housekeeper, Henrietta supervised her servant's domestic education, gave cooking lessons, and taught English phrases in the hope that Patience would establish a Christian home. During her employment with the Edwards, Patience brought her family to live nearby and Henrietta welcomed her young children, which allowed Patience to serve both families. Our picture of their relationship is one-sided, based solely upon a letter Oliver wrote to Henrietta in Montreal when he was working at the Regina Industrial School in 1898. Patience, her husband and five children arrived having "journeyed all the way from Saskatoon to see you thinking you were here with me." Patience "was disappointed," Oliver reported, to learn Henrietta lived thousands of miles away in Montreal.[39]

Patience's remarks, as translated by her eldest son, revealed the Christian domestic education she received from Henrietta. Patience "remembered Pearl's name and it was amusing to hear her come out with it in the midst of some Sioux," wrote Oliver who was surprised at her memory after the ten-year interlude. Henrietta taught Patience middle-class manners just as she had done with Irish servants in eastern Canada. "I asked her if she could say 'Good morning Mrs. Edwards.'" Oliver added, "how she doubled up and laughed and how she explained it all to the other women." His letter proudly chronicled the family's success, noting:

Her eldest daughter is a good looking young squaw about 14 ... they got the package of clothes you sent them from Ottawa – they have 30 cattle and garden stuff. I asked her if she remembered how to make the plum pudding – then you ought to have seen her laugh and tell the others – oh yes she could make and had made it and taught her daughter how to make it. I told her I expected to go down and eat a pudding just like we had at Qu'Appelle.[40]

Oliver's letter concluded with, "poor simple children of the prairie how pleased they seemed to be to see me again." Such language often appeared in the northern journal and weekly letters written by Dr. Edwards, reflecting a patronizing view that civilized Aboriginals were almost the same as Whites but not quite.[41] Unfortunately, we will never know Henrietta's reactions to Patience's story since Dr. Edwards did not keep his wife's weekly letters.

The family's experiences with women like Patience did not fit prevailing stereotypes that depicted Aboriginal women simply as "Indian Princess" or immoral "Squaw." Nor did Henrietta and Oliver believe the negative propaganda generated by government officials, missionaries and journalists. Canadian government policies became increasingly segregationist, blaming women for reserve problems, placing responsibility on them for everything from ill health and poverty, to lack of clothing and crop failures.[42] As Sarah Carter argues, government policy targeted Aboriginal women as key "civilizers" and attempted to restructure the domestic sphere. Assimilation focused on making women bearers of White values and culture to their children and husbands.[43] As was the case with a few male missionaries who laboured in the Protestant mission field (described by Kristin Burnett in chapter 6), Henrietta appreciated Aboriginal women's traditional role within their community while simultaneously endorsing "progress" and "civilization," which dictated the adoption of Christian and Canadian values.[44]

Henrietta and Oliver never became a medical missionary team; nor did Canadian Baptists establish Northwest missions until well after other Protestant and Catholic organizations. In settler communities, many opportunities for Christian service greeted the couple and, as a medical doctor, Edwards enjoyed greater prestige and earned more money.[45] Throughout the nineteenth century, missionaries in the Northwest faced extremely difficult circumstances. Only the hardiest survived. Oliver and Henrietta show little enthusiasm for such heroism or martyrdom, in contrast to some of the Methodist and Anglican missionaries they met in the Northwest.[46] Many believed their Christian duty lay in civilizing Aboriginal people, "a feeble, backward race, living in a world of ignorance, superstition and cruelty." They preached the superiority of Western agriculture, education, science, technology, and Christianity.[47]

In the early years, Henrietta tried unsuccessfully to generate support for Aboriginal women from family and friends in Montreal. In 1884, she addressed the Olivet Baptist Church's Women's Mission Circle "on the manners and customs of the North West Indians." Henrietta drew "a parallel to the Telugu," their Baptist mission in India. Although reluctant "to distract our attention from the Telugu field," explained the secretary, "she thought something might be done to enlighten them," by teaching literacy, domestic education, and Christian values.[48] Amelia Muir, Henrietta's elder sister, visited Indian Head but could not persuade her wealthy Montreal friends to support her as a missionary teacher. Amelia shared their doubts since her Northwest visit did not inspire a single essay for the *Canadian Missionary Link*, the Baptist women's paper. Instead, Amelia's column continued to feature the Baptist project in India. The romance of writing about exotic India appealed to Amelia's central Canadian audience more than the starving and poverty-stricken Plains Cree.[49]

A Christian perspective, nevertheless, framed all aspects of Henrietta's life. At fifty-six years of age, she received the name "Otter Woman" from the Blood Indians. This symbolic title reveals her reputation as a strong spiritual leader. The otter, a sacred animal, was placed on top of a tipi and used to make medicine bags for powerful women, representing female energy. According to early anthropologist Walter McClintock, next to the beaver, the otter was the most sacred animal; its spirit "inspired more designs than any other spiritual power."[50] Blood neighbours recognized the central place Christian commitment occupied for Henrietta in her daily life. Since she was the doctor's wife, Blood Indians gathered at her home at the Indian agency seeking medicine from the dispensary, food, and conversation. Grandchildren remember that Henrietta kept a pot of soup on the stove, never locked her door, welcomed many visitors and fed everyone. Doubtless she held many conversations exchanging information on the similarities and differences between Christian beliefs and rituals and Aboriginal ceremonies and spiritual practices.

Not surprisingly, communication and languages fascinated Henrietta, who learned Esperanto, perhaps by attending one of the clubs that were popular in Montreal around 1905. It seemed a logical solution to the bitter linguistic battles she witnessed in Quebec and the Northwest, and the communication problems she experienced living among the Cree, Sioux and Blackfoot. Edwards shared the optimistic vision of Esperanto's creator, a Polish-Jewish doctor named Dr. L.L. Zamenhof, who published a small book in 1887 called *Doktoro Esperanto* (*Doctor Hopeful*) in which he outlined the new language and expressed his dream that people of different ethnicity could live together peacefully, abandoning hatred and prejudice. In creating a new language, Zamenhof believed that he was giving people an opportunity for cross-cultural communication without fear of lost identity or language.[51] His egalitarian vision impressed Henrietta. Whether she tried to teach Esperanto to Aboriginal peoples is impossible to say. She never became fluent in Blackfoot, nor did Dr. Edwards, who struggled with Native languages and relied upon interpreters to assist him with patients. Somehow, Henrietta communicated with her visitors and servants, likely using younger, English-speaking Aboriginals.

On the Blood Reserve, Henrietta rarely provided nursing care for sick patients or accompanied Dr. Edwards to visit women in childbirth. The francophone Grey Nuns of Nicolet, who staffed Notre-Dame des Sept Douleurs, the first hospital build for Aboriginal peoples by the Department of Indian Affairs, assisted Dr. Edwards. Pregnant women stayed away from the hospital with its many tuberculosis patients. Over the years, Dr. Edwards lobbied unsuccessfully for a separate maternity home to offset the maternal mortality on the large reserve. Like her husband, Henrietta embraced modern medical practices including the homeopathy practised by Dr. Edwards, although the latter did not represent the mainstream of Canadian medicine.[52]

Henrietta's relatives and neighbours, especially the women of southern Alberta's conservative British ranching community, disliked her feminist politics, and criticized her tolerant and benevolent approach to Blood women. Following her daughter's wedding party in 1907 at their reserve home, Henrietta's English visitors complained loudly. In an unusual reversal of roles, Henrietta sent her servants to bed, worked late into the night, and "washed dishes while those savages slept."[53] Henrietta enjoyed training Aboriginal women like Patience and the numerous Blood women who worked for her: she spent many hours talking with them, learning their culture. Such relationships were not common among the ranching community. "I have tried to make use of a squaw who is the nominal wife of a White man near us to do the washing but had to give it up," wrote Mary Inderwick. After finding her fine linen ruined, she hired "a dignified coloured lady in Pincher Creek" who did not require either training or supervision.[54]

In the absence of extensive correspondence and diaries, reconstructing Henrietta's life on the reserve is challenging, even though other women (like Clare Sheridan, discussed by Graham MacDonald in the following chapter) penned biographical pieces. In *Life on an Indian Reserve*, for instance, Winifred A. Tims recalls her experiences as the daughter of Archdeacon J. W. Tims, an Anglican missionary who worked at the Sarcee Reserve near Calgary for thirty-five years.[55] Life for the Edwards family on the isolated Blood Reserve took a different path: they never achieved the stability, respectability, or status of the Tims family. After a ten-year separation, Dr. Edwards briefly enjoyed the company of his wife and adult daughters, who were ready for marriage and popular within the local ranching community. In 1907, Alice married a local rancher, while Pearl left to train as a nurse in Ottawa. At the time, the latter wrote to Alice, "poor darling Mum, I am afraid she will be very, very lonely for her daughters after you leave too."[56]

As sophisticated Montrealers, and supporters of the Liberal Party, the temperance movement, and the suffrage campaign, the Edwards family (and Henrietta in particular) ruffled many feathers and experienced difficulties with the Indian agency staff. When Henrietta wrote a letter to her sister describing Pearl's wedding, Amelia responded:

What a pity that the Reserve people should act so at such a time. They are a great mystery. If anyone has tried to be pleasant with them you have. It can only be jealousy but it is very unpleasant to have people among whom you must live so unfriendly. However in this world there are always people who don't like us and with people who have had no social training they show their dislike.[57]

Aware that Henrietta often faced loneliness and ostracism because of her feminist politics, Amelia ends her letter affectionately: "I wish that I could transport myself tonight… and sit by you and see your dear face." Shortly after, Amelia joined the Edwards family on the reserve and spent the remainder of her life with Henrietta, helping raise each new grandchild. In 1915, the sisters cared for Pearl's infant son following her death in childbirth and they mourned Oliver's passing.

Too busy in these years to write long letters, Henrietta also abandoned her painting and, instead, came to rely on her camera, a cherished possession, to frame Aboriginal peoples' lives and complement the artifact collection she acquired. Her earliest photograph, dated 1884, shows the Cree Chief Pasqua posed in regal dress outside his tipi.[58] In 1900, a photographic postcard that she never mailed, which was titled "Chief Joe Healy and Brave," served as her Christmas greeting to family in England. Edwards enjoyed the status she received from her exotic situation and signed her card "from one whose home is among the Indians." Her duty, she believed, lay in providing Aboriginal peoples an example

Cree Chief Pasqua, 1884. Photograph by Henrietta Muir
Edwards. Glenbow Archives, NA-4035-86.

of a Christian home, one that modelled "civilized" habits, although this
was interpreted loosely. Christian beliefs came first, cooking and sewing followed in importance. Edwards did not place equivalent value
on housekeeping nor did she hold Aboriginal women to exacting standards.[59]

A few individuals, especially those employed by the Edwards, stand
out in the surviving correspondence and documentation. A 1904 picture
of Julia Iron Pipe in traditional dress taken by Henrietta outside her
reserve home conceals a complex family relationship, one that is revealed

Julia Iron Pipe, 1904. Photograph by Henrietta Muir Edwards.
Glenbow Archives, NA-4035-66.

somewhat in a letter written three years later.[60] While visiting Calgary, Edwards travelled to the nearby Blackfoot Reserve at Gleichen. She carried a letter to Julia's brother, Paul Puk-a-pinni (Little Eyes) from his sister Julia (Kapa Kis-taka), which Edwards translated as "the woman who makes a sacrifice at home." After reading the letter to Paul, Edwards acted as his scribe, conveying his response to Julia with messages for their elder brother, Big Rib. Puk-a-pinni agreed to Julia's request for a new blanket and encouraged her upcoming visit. More importantly, in Henrietta's words, he expressed his Christian faith to his family:

My wife and I are very well and happy. There is never a day that I am sad. I have told you that why we are so happy. Our Heavenly Father's Life which he gives us is a very happy one. I always think of you, Big Rib (her brother) as not yet looking at the ways of our Father. You have been to church and know a little of the teaching – go always – I am your own brother and I urge you to take my words. Don't be in doubt as to this – but do it.[61]

When Henrietta reframed Puk-a-pinni's message, whatever its content, into familiar Christian language, she assumed the role of cultural mediator. Julia's response is unknown, although she probably attended the segregated Native service at St. Paul's Anglican Church. Her son, Ernest, became a pupil at the Anglican Mission School and, in 1920, the farm instructor on the Blood Reserve. Daughter Susie, however, moved back and forth between the reserve and the town of Macleod, between Aboriginal and White men, confirming Henrietta's worst fears about the precarious future for Aboriginal girls raised on the reserve.

Aboriginal women and men continued to visit Henrietta's home in Macleod where she maintained her role as hostess, cultural mediator, and confidante. Grandchildren remembered with fascination an older Blood woman who worked on the reserve for Henrietta: the "fierce looking" Quioto whose traditional dress intrigued the children.[62] In 1917 Henrietta described one of Quioto's frequent visits to daughter Alice:

Quioto and her daughter turned up on Sunday about 2 pm and spent the afternoon. I had finished my dinner but I was very glad to cook them theirs, there was plenty of meat and potatoes left over from Saturday so it was not much trouble. Clara, Quioto's daughter who was here with her on Saturday when you saw her is married to Joe Heavyhead who is the Indian scout at the Barracks so she and Quioto are living in town.

The women's conversation centered on the war in Europe and the recruitment of soldiers from the Blood Reserve. Henrietta patiently explained the war to Quioto:

Joe (her own son) and Nick King also his son are both at the war in France. The poor Mother pulled out the little bag the Catholics wear around their neck and told me she prayed many times during the night and in the day to God to bring them home safe. Clara can speak English very well so interpreted for me – when I told them what the English were fighting for, and also about some of the dreadful things the Germans did to the women and children of Belgium and France.[63]

Ambiguity permeates Henrietta's report. On the one hand, she sympathizes with the "poor Mother" worrying about the safety of her son; on the other, she positions herself as privileged with knowledge of the war and its importance. Her focus is motherhood and religion, the two pillars of Christian feminism.[64]

Henrietta's Christian feminism flourished while she lived on the reserve. She attended the tiny Anglican Church attached to St. Paul's Mission on the Blood Reserve, the only Protestant community for many miles. Henrietta also befriended and encouraged Christian Bloods trained by friend Jennie Wells, an Anglican missionary. A resident of the Blood Reserve since 1897, Wells used an abandoned church to teach girls sewing skills, hoping they would be self-supporting. Blood historians have paid tribute to Wells as "something of a miracle worker." Oral tradition maintains that Wells "became utterly devoted to the girls in her charge and they in turn adored her."[65] Blood writer Beverly Hungry Wolf remembered the impact that Jennie Wells left on her Grandmother AnadaAki:

Miss Wells wanted her young students to learn how to become ladies in the proper British style of the day. She taught them fancy ways of cooking, dressing, and wearing their hair. She got them into habits like dainty tea drinking, careful table setting, and wearing brooches to close up the fronts of their blouses. She taught them not only about agriculture but also about flower gardens and surrounding their homes with rows of bushes. They even picked up her British accent. These students became known as "Miss Wells's girls," and practically all of them became successful wives in charge of progressive farm households among the Blood people.

As Henrietta's relationship with Patience and Julia demonstrated, benevolence, education, and renaming were important colonial symbols.[66] Blood women learned to imitate or mimic the homes, clothing, and social graces of the White community. Willing to treat Aboriginal women with respect, Wells and Edwards established reciprocal and affectionate relationships in contrast to other Anglican missionaries. When Henrietta arrived in 1904, young rebellious girls set fire to their dormitory at St. Paul's Mission School and were arrested and convicted of arson.[67]

Underneath such respect and tolerance lay an enthusiasm for Christian marriages among St. Paul's graduates. When Joe Mountain Horse married Lizzie Acres, ex-pupils of St. Paul's Home, Lizzie wore a white lace wedding dress, carried a bouquet of flowers, and looked like a "proper" Euro-Canadian bride. For their wedding photograph, re-printed in the Diocese of Calgary's *Report on Indian Missions*, the couple posed for the camera looking "White." Joe wore the compulsory white shirt, vest, jacket, and pants of a gentleman.[68] Like Christian missionaries, Henrietta disapproved of traditional marriages involving very young women to older men, although such arrangements remained common as Beverly Hungry Wolf's oral history documents. Brown Woman's parents, for example, gave their seven-year-old daughter in marriage to William Wadsworth, an eighteen-year-old who had just graduated from the boarding school. Instead of Western dress, "Brown Woman," now called Annie Wadsworth, "wore a buckskin dress. My leggings were beaded, and I wore a fancy blanket with a safety pin in the front."[69] While Henrietta favoured the mission-educated Christian Bloods, traditional women who still "wore the blanket" found a welcome in her home if only because, as an artist and a seamstress, she appreciated their skills and traditional dress.

Henrietta believed Christianity could elevate the status of Aboriginal women as it had White women, a viewed shared by many missionaries. "Christianity has destroyed the hideous immorality of the camps, and introduced a noble standard in the life and person of Christ," wrote Reverend John Maclean; Christian teachings, he claimed "helped suppress many of the tribal laws which were injurious to the best interest of the people." Evangelicals argued that the gospel message could liberate Aboriginal women from hard labour and sexual oppression. "Civilization without the Gospel changes the position power and intelligence of Indian manhood, but to a very great degree the division of labour, as it touches womanhood, is slightly affected," concluded Maclean. As Burnett argues in chapter 6, Maclean believed that Christianity emancipated woman from their subservient status. In the transition to reserve life, he feared that without Christian values "the morality of the camps is very materially injured, indeed, is almost totally destroyed."[70] Critical of male sexuality in her own society, Henrietta viewed Aboriginal women's sexual independence with ambivalence, fearing the growth of prostitution. As a Christian feminist, Henrietta considered marriage sacred, supported monogamy, and insisted upon a single sexual standard for both men and women.

Controversy over Aboriginal women's sexuality surfaced during the annual Blood Sun Dance. An impressive ceremony, the Sun Dance drew many visitors, including Oliver and Henrietta who attended and took photographs. However, her voice is absent in the correspondence and public debate over sexuality and the Sun Dance. The Ontario Huron Anglican Women's Auxiliary, led by Harriet Boomer who had lived in the Canadian Northwest before 1860, urged the Department of Indian Affairs to ban the dances because they encouraged immorality.[71] Stories circulated that Christian Bloods asked the missionaries to keep their daughters in school during the Sun Dance because they feared they would be raped.[72] Henrietta refrained from making public statements on Aboriginal women. Her silence likely reflected her cautious temperament, combined with Dr. Edwards's precarious position as a medical doctor working for the Department of Indian Affairs. Just as in the earlier days, Dr. Oliver Edwards waged war with his superiors, forcing his wife to use her Liberal Party connections in Ottawa and the patronage system to keep her husband employed on the Blood Reserve.[73]

By overlooking Aboriginal women's spiritual power within their own communities, which the Sun Dance demonstrated, Henrietta and the missionaries pitied what they perceived to be the more difficult life of Aboriginal women, especially when compared to their husbands. Such condescension exaggerated Euro-Canadian women's importance as positive role models.[74] In this context, Henrietta, a modest woman, nevertheless emphasized her own significance, proud of her "valuable Indian collection." Although Blood women sometimes appeared to her as childlike and dependent, Henrietta also viewed them as unique individuals, whose impressive culture was being destroyed, a process she fatalistically accepted as inevitable. She never attacked Christianity or blamed the colonial process: she was optimistic that her "reformed" Canada could provide a welcoming home for everyone, regardless of race or gender.

In later years, Henrietta moved into the public arena to defend and interpret Aboriginal women to the Canadian public with twin publications. *Legal Status of Canadian Women* (1908) and *Legal Status of Women of Alberta* (1917) were studies meant as educational tools to inform women, rally interest in the suffrage campaign, and map future political battles. In preparing these books, Henrietta used extracts from dominion and provincial laws to discuss women's status in "marriage, property, dower, divorce, descent of land, franchise and other subjects." Indian women appear in the 1908 document under Chapter XI, "Extracts from the Criminal Code," and the section concerning "Seduction." Here, Henrietta reproduces Section 220 of the Criminal Code concerning penalties for an Indian woman who "prostitutes herself," and for persons who maintain a house of prostitution with "unfranchised Indian women," that is one who is a ward of the Canadian government by virtue of the treaties signed by their people. The Blood women Henrietta knew fell into this category. The later Alberta publication cites Chapter XV, Extracts from the Criminal Code, but under the heading "Seduction," Henrietta added the phrase "Additional Protection for Indian Women, Irrespective of Age."[75]

During the First World War, after Dr. Edwards died, Henrietta made public statements on Aboriginal women and continued to lobby the government privately. Her campaign followed themes raised in 1910 by the NCWC. As convener of the law committee of the NCWC she sponsored a resolution in 1917: "That the National Council seek such legislation as will raise the social status of our Indian women and afford her equal legal protection with our White women." Such a simplistic and vague resolution gathered support from council women. When the NCWC federated with the Dominion Social Service Council, they appointed Henrietta to their committee on "Indian Affairs."[76] In her capacity as convener for the NCWC's law committee, Edwards requested interviews with senior government officials. In June 1925, Edwards arranged meetings with officials in the Department of Indian Affairs to discuss Indian marriage laws. The superintendent's private secretary reported: "She is very anxious that the marriage laws of the Indians should be submitted to the Department of Justice for a discussion as to whether they are legal." Her further correspondence suggests that Edwards and some Blood elders felt that younger Blood men were taking advantage of Native "custom" in order to abandon their first wives and remarry.[77]

As a liberal feminist working to ensure that the law advanced women's status, Henrietta believed implicitly in universal access to justice and the importance of democratic legislation. On the one hand, she seemed tolerant of racial difference; on the other, her advocacy of equality often implied sameness. It is doubtful that Edwards resolved the paradox of equal but different. Her concept of equality in its assumption of universality never addressed White privilege adequately. When Euro-Canadians of her generation discussed racism, they often overlooked its systemic and institutionalized nature. But, as second-wave feminists later discovered, legal systems paradoxically advance women's status while simultaneously limiting their campaigns for social justice. For Aboriginal women, legal protection proved to be a double-edged sword.[78]

On a personal level, Henrietta participated in a women's culture that allowed her to make friendships and treat Aboriginal peoples with respect. However, just as the western Canadian judiciary was unable to conceive of "marriage" as anything outside of monogamy and life-long union (see Sarah Carter's discussion in chapter 9), Edwards's religious-based feminism prevented her from embracing cultural difference and understanding Aboriginal spiritual traditions. She entered Aboriginal women's lives, meeting them as domestic servants, pupils, Christians, and medical patients. While Henrietta spent many hours studying Aboriginal art and culture and examining women's lives as mothers and wives, she left mission work to her friends, devoting her energy and organizational talents to the middle-class women's movement. Like the more sensitive missionaries in Africa and Asia, living among Indigenous peoples caused Henrietta to question Western superiority. Although a few British women in Africa and Asia went further and became feminist allies of Indigenous women, race and class prejudices seriously constrained Henrietta's feminism. While her conflicting views on Aboriginal peoples grew stronger as she aged, Henrietta never resolved her ambiguous position. Nor did her advocacy of Aboriginal women in the 1920s seriously challenge her culture's race and gender hierarchy.

ENDNOTES

1   Glenbow Archives (GA), Edwards Gardiner Family Fonds (EG Fonds), 1 October 1883, Jane Muir to Hettie Edwards. For a biographical study see Patricia Roome, "Henrietta Muir Edwards: The Journey of a Canadian Feminist" (Ph.D. diss., Simon Fraser University, 1996).

2   Editors' introduction, Janice Fiamengo, "A Legacy of Ambivalence: Responses to Nellie McClung," in *Rethinking Canada: The Promise of Women's History*, 4th ed., ed. Veronica Strong-Boag, Mona Gleason, and Adele Perry (Don Mills, ON: Oxford University Press, 2002), 149. For a recent study of Anglican woman missionaries see Myra Rutherdale, *Women and the White Man's God: Gender and*

Race in the Canadian Mission Field (Vancouver: UBC Press, 2002). See also Fiona Paisley, *Loving Protection? Australian Feminism and Aboriginal Women's Rights 1919–1939* (Carlton, Victoria: Melbourne University Press, 2000).

3   Jennifer Henderson, *Settler Feminism and Race Making in Canada* (Toronto: University of Toronto Press, 2003). Adele Perry, *On the Edge of Empire: Gender, Race and the Making of British Columbia, 1849–1871* (Toronto: University of Toronto Press, 2001); Elizabeth Jameson and Susan Armitage, eds., *Writing the Range: Race, Class, and Culture in the Women's West* (Norman: University of Oklahoma Press, 1997).

4   For early, 1980s fur trade studies see Sylvia Van Kirk, *"Many Tender Ties": Women in Fur Trade Society, 1670–1870* (Winnipeg: Watson & Dwyer, 1980) and "What If Mama is an Indian?: The Cultural Ambivalence of the Alexander Ross Family," in *The Developing West: Essays on Canadian History in Honour of Lewis H. Thomas*, ed. John E. Foster (Edmonton: University of Alberta, 1983), 123–36. For later, 1990s studies, see Sarah Carter, "Categories and Terrains of Exclusion: Constructing the 'Indian Woman' in the Early Settlement Era in Western Canada," *Great Plains Quarterly* 13 (Summer 1993): 47–61; "First Nations Women and Colonization on the Canadian Prairies, 1870–1920," in *Rethinking Canada: The Promise of Women's History*, 135–48; and *Capturing Women: The Manipulation of Cultural Imagery in Canada's Prairie West* (Montreal and Kingston: McGill-Queen's University Press, 1997), 8, 156. For the Pacific region see Jean Barman, "Taming Aboriginal Sexuality: Gender, Power and Race in BC, 1895–1900," *BC Studies* 115–16 (Fall-Winter 1997–98): 237–66. Also useful is Antoinette Burton, *Gender, Sexuality and Colonial Modernities* (London and New York: Routledge, 1999).

5   For an early analysis, later reprinted, see Mariana Valverde, "'When the Mother of the Race is Free': Race, Reproduction, and Sexuality in First-Wave Feminism," in Franca Iacovetta and Mariana Valverde, *Gender Conflicts: New Essays in Women's History* (Toronto: University of Toronto Press, 1992). For a critique of Valverde, see Fiamengo, "A Legacy of Ambivalence," 148–63. On the famous Mohawk feminist, see Veronica Strong-Boag and Carol Gerson, *Paddling Her Own Canoe: The Times and Texts of E. Pauline Johnson, Tekahienwake* (Toronto: University of Toronto Press, 2000).

6   Henderson, *Settler Feminism and Race Making in Canada*, 43.

7   Ibid., 204.

8   Janice Fiamengo, "Rediscovering Our Foremothers Again: The Racial Ideas of Canada's Early Feminists, 1885–1945," *Essays on Canadian Writing* 75 (Winter 2002): 86–117. See Homi Bhabba, "Of Mimicry and Man: The Ambivalence of Colonial Discourse," in *Tensions of Empire: Colonial Discourse in a Bourgeois World*, ed. Frederick Cooper and Ann Laura Stoler (Berkeley: University of California Press, 1997), 152–60.

9   Michael Platt, "Famous Five aren't worth a plug nickel," *Calgary Sun*, 19 August 2004; Deborah Yedlin, "To some, it's the Infamous Five," *Globe and Mail*, 19 October 2004.

10 See Daniel Coleman and Donald Goellnicht, "Introduction: 'Race' into the Twenty-First Century," *Essays on Canadian Writing*, 74 (Winter 2002): 3. Constance Backhouse, *Colour-Coded: A Legal History of Racism in Canada, 1900–1950* (Toronto: University of Toronto Press, 1999).

11   Catherine Cavanaugh, "Irene Marryat Parlby: An 'Imperial Daughter' in the Canadian West, 1896–1934," in *Telling Tales: Essays in Western Women's History*, ed. Catherine A. Cavanaugh and Randi R. Warne (Vancouver: UBC Press, 1990), 112–13. Louise McKinney remains to be studied. See Valverde's analysis of the WCTU in "When the Mother of the Race is Free," 15–19.

12   Barman, "Taming Aboriginal Sexuality," 249. See also Rutherdale, *Women and the White Man's God.*

13   See Anne McClintock, *Imperial Leather: Race, Gender and Sexuality in the Colonial Contest* (New York: Routledge, 1995), chapter 7, "Olive Schreiner: Limits of Feminism."

14   Roome, "Daughter of the Montreal Muirs, an Evangelical Family," chap. 1 in "Henrietta Muir Edwards: The Journey of a Canadian Feminist".

15   Roome, "'Woman's Commission' the Missionary Impulse, 1868–1883," chap. 2 in "Henrietta Muir Edwards: The Journey of a Canadian Feminist".

16   See Colin D. Howell, "Elite Doctors and the Development of Scientific Medicine: The Halifax Medical Establishment and 19th Century Medical Professionalism," and S.E.D. Shortt, "'Before the Age of Miracles': The Rise, Fall and Rebirth of General Practise in Canada, 1890–1940," in *Health, Disease and Medicine: Essays in Canadian History: Proceedings of the First Hannah Conference on the History of Medicine, McMaster University, June 3–5, 1982*, ed. Charles G. Roland (Toronto: Clark Irwin for the Hannah Institute for the History of Medicine, 1984).

17   On homeopathy in America see the four-volume study by Harris Coulter, *Divided Legacy* (Berkeley: North Atlantic, 1975) and Paul Starr, *The Social Transformation of American Medicine* (New York: Basic Books, 1982).

18   Roome, "A Woman's West: Political Success and Personal Tragedy, 1910–1915," chap. 7 in "Henrietta Muir Edwards: The Journey of a Canadian Feminist".

19   See Eliane Silverman, *The Last Best West: Women on the Alberta Frontier, 1880–1930* (Montreal: Eden Press: 1984); Susan Armitage and Elizabeth Jameson, eds., *The Women's West* (Norman: University of Okalahoma Press, 1987).

20   Patricia Roome Collection, 15 November 1931, Lucy Edwards to Alice Edwards Gardiner; 3 November 1931, Margaret Roberts to Mrs. Muir Edwards.

21   Barbara N. Ramusack, "Cultural Missionaries, Maternal Imperialists, Feminist Allies: British Women Activists in India, 1865–1945," *Women's Studies International Forum* 13 (1990): 309–21. Also Vron Ware, *Beyond the Pale: White Women, Racism and History* (London: Verso, 1992); Antoinette M. Burton, "The White Woman's Burden: British Feminists and the Indian Woman, 1865–1915," in *Western Women and Imperialism: Complicity and Resistance*, ed. Nupur Chaudhuri and Margaret Strobel (Bloomington: Indiana University Press, 1992).

22   *Montreal Natural History Society Proceedings* (1881): 4.

23   F. J. Alcock, *A Century in the History of the Geological Survey of Canada* (Ottawa: King's Printer, 1947); Suzanne Zeller and Gale Avrith-Wakeam, "George Mercer Dawson," *Dictionary of Canadian Biography (DCB)*, vol. 13, 259; Douglas Cole and Bradley Lockner, eds., *The Journals of George M. Dawson: British Columbia, 1875–1878* (2 vol., Vancouver: UBC Press, 1989).

24   Curtis M. Hinsley, Jr., *Savages and Scientists* (Washington: Smithsonian Institution Press, 1981). Zeller and Avrith-Wakeam, "George Mercer Dawson," 259.

25   Maureen K. Lux, for instance, questions the Edwards's motives for collecting and selling Aboriginal artifacts in *Medicine that Walks: Disease, Medicine, and*

Canadian Plains Native People, 1880–1940 (Toronto: University of Toronto Press, 2001), 166–68.

26 "Valuable Indian Collection Purchased by the University of Alberta," *University of Alberta Press Bulletin* 5 (2 April 1920).

27 Laurie Hart "Collecting and curating objects of ethnology: an ethnohistorical case study of the O. C. Edwards Collection" (master's thesis, University of Alberta, 1998).

28 *Buffalo 'these Beasts on ye Barren ground.'* Ring House Gallery, June 21–October 6, 1985. University of Alberta Collections, 1985. For a critical assessment see Douglas Cole, *Captured Heritage: The Scramble for Northwest Coast Artifacts* (Seattle: University of Washington Press, 1985).

29 Quoted in "Dr. and Mrs. O. C. Edwards: Pioneer Collectors," *Buffalo 'these Beasts on ye barren Ground.'*

30 For a later British artist who lived on the Blood Reserve see Clare Sheridan, *Redskin Interlude* (London: Nicolson and Watson, 1938).

31 L. L. Dobbin, *A History of the Assiniboine Indian Reserve, Sintaluta, Saskatchewan: 1877–1940* (Regina: Legislative Library, Archives Division, 1963); John Tobias, "Payipwat," *DCB*, vol. 13, 815–18. Kenneth Tyler, "Paskwaw," *DCB*, vol. 11, 674–75.

32 Quoted in Bob Beal and Rod Macleod, *Prairie Fire: The 1885 North West Rebellion* (Edmonton: Hurtig, 1984), 88–89.

33 National Archives of Canada (NAC), RG 10, vol. 3745, file 29506-4, part 1, 13 May 1884, Dr. O. C. Edwards to Col. MacDonald. See also Beal and Macleod, *Prairie Fire*, 86.

34 Valerie Robertson, "Plains Ledger Art: The Documentation of a Way of Life through the Nineteenth-Century Pictorial Account of an Unknown Assiniboine Artist," *Prairie Forum* 17 (Fall 1992): 263–74; Howard D. Rodee, "The Stylistic Development of Plains Indian Paintings and its Relationship to Ledger Drawings," *Plains Anthropologist* 10 (November 1956): 218–32.

35 In January 1994, Glenbow mounted an exhibition of the forty-four drawings. *Reclaiming History: Ledger Drawings by the Assiniboine Artist Hongeeyeesa* (Calgary: Glenbow, 1993), 36.

36 GA, EG Fonds, handwritten notes by Alice Edwards Gardiner, n.d.

37 Peter Douglas Elias, *The Dakota of the Canadian Northwest: Lessons for Survival* (Winnipeg: University of Manitoba Press, 1988); James H. Howard, *The Canadian Sioux: Studies in the Anthropology of North American Indians* (Lincoln: University of Nebraska Press, 1984); Jacqueline Judith Kennedy, "Qu'Appelle Industrial School: 'White Rites for the Old North-West'" (master's thesis, Institute for Canadian Studies, Carleton, 1970).

38 GA, EG Fonds, 25 July 1898, Oliver Edwards to Alice Edwards. Nellie McClung, a young school girl in 1885, remembers taking her teachers' side, blaming the Canadian government and defending Riel and the Cree to her parents. See Nellie McClung, *Clearing in the West* and *The Stream Runs Fast*, ed. Veronica Strong-Boag and Michelle Lynn Rosa (Peterborough, ON: Broadview Press, 2003), 159–68.

39 GA, EG Fonds, 27 June 1898. Oliver Edwards to Henrietta Muir Edwards.

40 Ibid.

41 See David Leonard and Beverly Whalen, eds., *On the North Trail: The Treaty 8 Diary of O.C. Edwards* (Calgary: Historical Society of Alberta, 1998).

42 Carter, "Categories and Terrains of Exclusion," 147–61; Rayna Green, "The Pocahontas Perplex: The Image of Indian Women in American Culture," in *Unequal Sisters*, ed. Ellen Carol DuBois and Vicki L. Ruiz (New York: Routledge, 1990), 15–21.

43 Pamela Margaret White, "Restructuring the Domestic Sphere—Prairie Indian Women on Reserves: Image, Ideology and State Policy, 1880–1930," (Ph.D. diss., McGill University, 1987). See Anna Davin, "Imperialism and Motherhood," *History Workshop Journal*, 5 (1978): 9–65; Sarah Carter, "First Nations Women of Prairie Canada in the Early Reserve Years, the 1870s to the 1920s: A Preliminary Inquiry," in *Women of the First Nations: Power, Wisdom and Strength*, ed. Christine Miller and Patricia Chuchryk, with Marie Smallface Marule, Brenda Manyfingers, and Cherly Deering (Winnipeg: University of Manitoba Press, 1996).

44 See Henriette Forget, "Indian Women of the Western Provinces," in *Women of Canada: Their Life and Work*, compiled by the National Council of Women of Canada (Ottawa: 1900), 435–37.

45 See Robert Jefferson, *Fifty Years on the Saskatchewan* (vol. 1, Battleford: Canadian North-West Historical Society Publications, 1929), 31. Provincial Archives of British Columbia, "Notes and Observations 1882–1885." For an explanation of Oliver's appointment, see NAC, Laurier Papers, 14 February 1910, Dr. O. C. Edwards to Sir Wilfrid Laurier.

46 For the Anglican missions, see Ian A. L. Getty, "The Failure of the Native Church Policy of the CMS in the North-West," in *Religion and Society in the Prairie West*, ed. Richard Allen (University of Regina: Canadian Plains Research Center, 1974), 19–34; Jean Usher, "Apostles and Aborigines: The Social Theory of the Church Missionary Society," in *Prophets, Priests, and Prodigals: Readings in Canadian Religious History, 1608 to the Present*, ed. Mark G. McGowan and David Marshall (Toronto: McGraw Hill, 1992), 15–43. On women, see Rutherdale and Margaret Whitehead, "A Useful Christian Woman: First Nations Women and Protestant Missionary Work in British Columbia," *Atlantis* 18 (1992–93): 142–66.

47 Sarah Carter, "The Missionaries' Indian: The Publications of John McDougall, John Maclean and Egerton Ryerson Young," *Prairie Forum* 9 (1984): 28; "Man's Mission of Subjugation: The Publications of John Maclean, John McDougall and Egerton R. Young, Nineteenth-Century Methodist Missionaries in Western Canada" (master's thesis, University of Saskatchewan, 1981); J. R. Miller, *Skyscrapers Hide the Heavens: A History of Indian-White Relations in Canada* (Toronto: University of Toronto Press, 1989), 189.

48 Canadian Baptist Archives, McMaster University, Minute Book, 14 January 1884. "Qu'Appelle Northwest Territories," *The Baptist Visitor*, November 1893.

49 Rosemary Gagan, *A Sensitive Independence: Canadian Methodist Missionaries in Canada and the Orient, 1881–1925* (Montreal and Kingston: McGill-Queen's University Press, 1992), 189–90. See *Canadian Missionary Link*, June-December 1884.

50 Walter McClintock, *Painted Tipis and Picture Writing of the Blackfoot Indians* (Los Angeles: Southwest Museum Leaflet, No. 6).

51 See Marjorie Boulton, *Zamenhof: Creator of Esperanto* (London: Routledge and Kegan Paul, 1960).

52 See Roome, chapter 7. See also Mary-Ellen Kelm, *Colonizing Bodies: Aboriginal Health and Healing in British Columbia, 1900–1950* (Vancouver: UBC Press, 1998).

53 GA, EG Fonds, 26 January 1907, Barbara Gardiner to Miss Statham.

54 Mary E. Inderwick, "A Lady and her Ranch," in *The Best from Alberta History*, ed. Hugh Dempsey (Saskatoon: Historical Society of Alberta, 1981), 70.

55 GA, Archdeacon J.M. Tims Family Fonds, M1234/32. Winifred A. Tims, "Life on an Indian Reserve." (My thanks to Sarah Carter for sharing this reference.)

56 Roome collection, 14 January 1907, Pearl Edwards to Alice Edwards.

57 GA, EG Fonds, M8896, File 38, 3 February 1907, Amelia (Millie) Muir to Henrietta Muir Edwards.

58 GA, NA 4035-86.

59 GA, EG Fonds, M7283 File 22, Henrietta Muir Edwards, Miscellaneous Correspondence, 1897–1918. For recent studies of colonization, photography and Aboriginal people see Carol J. Williams, "Framing the West: Race, Gender and the Photographic 'Frontier,' on the Northwest Coast, 1858–1940" (Ph.D. diss., Rutgers University, 1999) and Daniel Francis, *Copying People: Photographing British Columbia's First Nations, 1860–1940* (Saskatoon and Calgary: Fifth House, 1996).

60 GA, Edwards-Gardiner Photographic Collection. See Kim Greenwell, "'Picturing Civilization': Missionary Narratives on the Margins of Mimicry," *BC Studies*, no. 135 (Autumn 2002): 3–45.

61 Roome collection, 31 January 1907, Paul Puk-a-pinni (little eyes) to Julia (Kapa Kis-taka) – the woman who makes a sacrifice at home.

62 Interview, Patricia Roome with Claudia Gardiner Whipple, Calgary, 3 September 1995.

63 GA, EG Fonds, 15 August 1917, Henrietta Muir Edwards to Alice Gardiner.

64 For western Canadian women's views on World War I, see Nellie McClung, *In Times like These* (Toronto: 1915).

65 NAC, RG10, vol. 1544, 10 October 1904, R. N. Wilson to Assistant Secretary S. Stuart. Hugh Dempsey, *The Gentle Persuader: A Biography of James Gladstone Indian Senator* (Saskatoon: Western Prairie Producer, 1986), 20.

66 Beverly Hungry Wolf, *The Ways of My Grandmothers* (New York: Quill, 1982), 21–22. See Diocese of Calgary, *Report of Indian Missions for 1903* (Toronto: Oxford Press, 1904), 608. Myra Rutherdale, "Revisiting Colonization through Gender: Anglican Missionary Women in the Pacific North-West and the Arctic, 1860–1945," *BC Studies* 104 (Winter 1994–95): 3–23.

67 NAC, RG10, vol. 1544, 7 December 1904, R. N. Wilson to Mr. Gale; 9 December 1904 and 23 January 1905, R. N. Wilson to Indian Commissioner. See Jean Barman, "Separate and Unequal: The Indian and White Girls at All Hallows School, 1884–1920," in *Rethinking Canada: The Promise of Women's History*, ed. Veronica Strong-Boag and Anita Clair Fellman (Toronto: Copp Clark Pitman, 1991), 11–27.

68 Diocese of Calgary, *Report of Indian Missions for 1904* (Toronto: Oxford Press, 1905), 4. For an analysis of missionaries' use of photographs, see Greenwell, "Picturing Civilization." On the Mountain Horse family see Mike Mountain Horse,

My People the Bloods (Standoff, AB: Glenbow-Alberta Institute and Blood Tribal Council, 1979).

69   Hungry Wolf, *The Ways of My Grandmothers*, 29.

70   John Maclean, *The Indians: Their Manners and Customs* (Toronto: William Briggs, 1889; Coles Reprint 1970), 290.

71   *Letter Leaflet* 12, no. 1 (November 1900): 21.

72   See J. R. Miller, "Owen Glendower, Hotspur, and Canadian Indian Policy," in *Sweet Promises: A Reader on Indian-White Relations in Canada*, ed. J. R. Miller (Toronto: University of Toronto Press, 1991), 330–33.

73   Roome, 218–20.

74   See S. A. Archer, comp., *Heroine of the North Pacific: Memoirs of Charlotte Selina Bompas (1830–1917)* (London: Society for Promoting Christian Knowledge, 1929). See Mary Louise Pratt, *Imperial Eyes: Travel Writing and Transculturation* (London: Routledge, 1992); Jean and John Comaroff, *Of Revelation and Revolution: Christianity, Colonialism and Consciousness in South Africa*, vol. 1 (Chicago: University of Chicago Press, 1991).

75   Henrietta Muir Edwards, *Legal Status of Canadian Women* (Ottawa: National Council of Women of Canada, 1908), 56–67; and *Legal Status of Women of Alberta* (Edmonton: Attorney-General, 1921, 2nd ed.), 63.

76   NCWC, *Report of the Proceedings of the Annual Meeting and Conference 31 May– June 1917*; NCWC, *Report 15 June 1921*.

77   NAC, RG 10, vol. 6816, file 486-2-8, Correspondence Regarding Indian Marriage and Divorce Law, 15 June 1925, W. G. Pratt, Private Secretary to the Superintendent of Department of Indian Affairs to Dr. Scott. (I wish to thank Lesley Erickson for bringing this correspondence to my attention.)

78   Mary Jane Mossman, "The Paradox of Feminist Engagement with the Law,' in *Feminist Issues: Race, Class and Sexuality*, ed. Nancy Mandell (Toronto: Prentice Hall, 1995).

four

Clare Sheridan's Western Interlude:

The Importance of Being Well-Connected

GRAHAM A. MACDONALD

The study of western women artists on both sides of the Canadian-American border is of recent vintage. The first major exhibition and critical study of the topic, Independent Spirits: Women Painters of the American West, *was not mounted until 1995. At the time, the catalogue's author argued, "Attention and focus have been directed only toward nineteenth-century art created by men and toward stereotypical imagery of the Old West conveyed in their work." Although this observation also held true for Canada, the "Unsettled Pasts" conference brought to light numerous women involved in regional artistic traditions:*

French-Canadian Grey Nuns who taught their mixed-blood pupils European arts and crafts; Sara Riel, one of their pupils, who is credited with being the first painter in the European manner born in the region; Métis and immigrant women's skilled domestic sewing, which literally "dressed the West"; and Henrietta Muir Edwards's work as an artist, collector, and painting instructor among the peoples of the Great Plains (see chapter 3). In this article, Graham A. MacDonald describes the artistic and cultural odyssey of British sculptor and writer, Clare Sheridan, who traveled the world and spent six months among the Blackfoot of Montana and Alberta in 1937. She worked alongside others to foster the growth of Aboriginal artistic traditions and, like Edwards, she collected artifacts that found their way into museum collections. The published account of her experiences, Redskin Interlude, *includes rare photographs of her sculptures of Aboriginal men and women. As MacDonald argues, Sheridan's cross-cultural, cross-border, and transnational experiences infused her art, her philosophy, and her spirituality, causing her to transcend the narrow cultural and imperial vision of British upper-class society to become an outspoken critic of North American Indian policy.*

In the spring of 1937, the British sculptor and writer, Clare Sheridan (1885–1970), fresh from personal tragedy, arrived in America destined for Glacier National Park, Montana. Her objective was to join and teach with Weinold Reiss at his "art colony," an enterprise that sought to rekindle artistic traditions among the Native peoples of the area. This was merely one of several in-depth encounters that Sheridan would have with "others" foreign to her own cultural tradition; the sojourn, however, was also a personal rediscovery of a region where she had family roots. Typically, a remarkable book issued out of this episode: the now largely forgotten *Redskin Interlude* (1938). In it, her association with and observations of the Blackfeet of Montana and the related Bloods of southern Alberta are set forth in a striking and instructive way.

Sheridan's name is no longer familiar to scholars of arts and letters, not even in her native England. This was less the case in the 1920s, when she gained a reputation in Europe, America, and England as something of an *enfant terrible*. Sculptor, journalist, diarist, novelist, painter, and adventurer, her many achievements illustrate the extreme watershed that the First World War represented for social expectations in general, and for women in particular. Her background and upper-class connections were every bit as interesting as those of her more famous contemporary, Virginia Woolf, but what a different route each took towards defining a room of her own.

On her mother's side, Sheridan descended from Leonard Jerome and Clara Hall, an enterprising American family. The family contended that the Hall line had been supplemented by Indian blood.[1] Their marriage in 1847 produced three daughters: Clara, Leonie, and Jennie. Leonard Jerome's diplomatic postings in Europe became the vehicle by which all three daughters married back into the English upper class – Jennie most famously through her match with Lord Randolph Churchill. In 1881, Jennie's sister, Clara, married Moreton Frewen, who was of old Sussex Puritan stock. Four years later, Clare was born.[2]

Clare's father cut an intriguing and romantic figure; one need look no further for the model of Clare's own considerable eccentricity. In 1878, he and his brother Edward took up cattle ranching in Wyoming, thus joining the many British "remittance men" active on the high plains of the North American west.[3] Their home, "Frewen Castle" in the Powder River country, was well known: "life in this wilderness mansion was one long houseparty."[4] When, under pressures of settlement and inflation, the ranching industry and Frewen's Powder River Cattle Company started to come apart in 1884, Moreton drove his herd north to Calgary where he wound up his operation and returned to England in 1886. The limited financial success of his past and future schemes gained him the nickname "mortal ruin."[5] The ranching episode of the father would become, nevertheless, a source of stimulus for the daughter in the 1930s.

Young Clare had little interest in the late Edwardian London scene or pursuing the life of a debutante. By marrying Wilfred Sheridan in 1910, however, she managed to please both herself and her extended family. Wilfred was not only a direct descendant of the great eighteenth-century playwright, Richard Sheridan, he also had an eye for business. Their marriage, however, was soon marred by all too common tragedies: the passing of their second daughter Elizabeth, in 1913, was followed by Wilfred's death at the front in 1915. His death coincided with the birth of a third child, a son; both events set Clare firmly on course towards the life of an artist. On the strength of a war widow's pension, she set off determinedly to get training, but enjoyed little family support in the process. Upon completing night classes in Aldwych, she arranged for lessons with John Tweed, a student of Rodin, and Eduard Lantéri, a Royal Academician.[6]

In 1919, Sheridan mounted a successful show in London. Her first major commission, from Canadian flying ace Billy Bishop, was later sold to the Canadian War Museum.[7] She then produced one of her most original works, *Victory – 1918*.[8] Notoriety came in 1920 when she went to Russia in the company of a few of the new Soviet leaders, who had recently been in England on business. She prepared sculptures of the leadership's upper echelon, including Lenin, Trotsky, Kamaneff, and several others in the hierarchy.[9] This adventure led to her first success as a writer, *Russian Portraits* (1921); her cousin, Winston, however, was far from amused.[10] As secretary of war, Churchill was trying to put the revolution down, not encourage it, and there, in Moscow, was his scatter-brained, pacifist cousin dancing with the leadership! Single-minded in his opposition to the revolution, Churchill referred to it as "the plague bacillus of Bolshevism."[11] The cousins barely spoke for two years.

Sheridan remained unapologetic. *Russian Portraits* revealed her talents to a wider audience. She went to America on a speaking tour and, on the strength of her family's connections, entered upon a career in journalism.[12] In the early 1920s, "roving commissions" took her across Mexico, the United States, southern and eastern Europe, and through the lands of the old Ottoman Empire. In 1923, she observed closely the emergence of the Turkish nation, an event that sparked her personal interest in Muslim countries, which she and her children then visited between 1925 and 1936.[13] Daughter Margaret's marriage in 1935 was a happy event, but the death of her son Richard in 1936 nearly unhinged the artist. In response, she set out on another pilgrimage of discovery, this time to the Rocky Mountains, to pursue art and give instruction with Reiss in Glacier National Park.[14] En route, she had her father's memoirs in hand.

The half year that Sheridan spent in Montana and southern Alberta in 1937 was creative and restorative. When the engaging and insightful *Redskin Interlude* appeared the following year, it included impressive photographs of personalities, and many of Sheridan's own sculptures of Blackfoot men, women, and children.[15] As was the case with her earlier work, *Arab Interlude*, this book did not reveal an inclination towards systematic anthropology. Sheridan would have certainly rejected such an impulse. The idea that one might "live in" with an unfamiliar group, while consciously remaining an "objective" outsider, would have appalled her for the simple reason that it would have been an intense bore. Such a posture would have defeated any effort to become meaningfully connected with those same people. Her reasons for "going native" were to learn about the values of those she was joining, test them out in a personal sense, learn from them, and make a few new friends. Years later, she would – rather romantically – admit that her sojourn to western North America was at least partially therapeutic: "I little knew that I was cauterizing my wound; that out on the great plains among those beloved Indians whose blood flowed in my veins I was to find my 'medicine.'"[16]

At the time, the therapeutic benefits of her journey were less than clear to Sheridan; she appeared to approach the new adventure with a variety of motives. First, it provided a way to visit the theatre of her father's youth, a locale that had always been a source of interest to Moreton Frewen's children. Second, she was interested in the current experiment going on in the United State's Bureau of Indian Affairs under the new policy initiatives of John Collier who, among other things, was attempting to mitigate the longstanding effects of the 1887 Dawes Act.[17] Collier hoped to restore a sense of dignity to American Native peoples by rediscovering and fostering the growth of their artistic traditions. The initiative was modeled on non-governmental initiatives underway in the southwest since 1900; in 1932, the Bureau of Indian Affairs finally caught up and established the Sante Fe Art Studio.[18] Characteristically, before heading for Montana, Sheridan first stopped in Washington, D.C., where she met the man in charge, John Collier.[19]

Sheridan then embarked by automobile for the high plains and the Powder River country. She noted the increasing visibility of Native peoples as she went, but also the obvious signs that they were being systematically excluded from national communal life.[20] Upon arrival, she experienced a moment of empathy for her father, with whom her relations had been far from smooth: "From infancy I had heard my father's fantastic tales about his ranch on Powder River. He was financially a ruined man for the rest of his life, but I always had the impression that he considered it was worth while to be ruined for the experience of those years."[21]

At Cody, Wyoming, she was met by Winold Reiss's brother, Hans, who toured her about Yellowstone before taking her to Glacier National Park. She was quick to notice that, despite the harshness of the environment, there were forces favourable to art. She commented, "Prairie life is apt to make poets of sensitive men."[22] She was also quick to note that, in an age of corporate hotel tourism, authentic images of the Native past

Clare Sheridan sawing a cotton-wood tree preparatory to carving it at the St. Mary's Art Colony, Montana, 1937 (From Clare Sheridan's book *Redskin Interlude* [between pp. 132–33]).

were often trivialized. She compared the shoddy imitation Blackfoot tents built by the proprietors of Great Northern Hotels with traditional construction methods to prove her point.[23]

At the colony, Sheridan was soon introduced to the aged writer, James Willard Schultz, and to his wife, Jessie, who helped run the craft store at Browning.[24] The couple arranged for her to attend a Sun Dance and other ceremonies. This had the desirable result of putting her in touch with tribal members, several of whom became subjects for her sculpture work.[25]

The natural materials available in the mountain country influenced Sheridan's approach. She moved away from her normal routines of modeling sculpture towards woodcarving. In a letter to Anita Leslie, she stated, "How strange that through losing one child I discovered myself as modeler, through losing another I found myself a carver. It seemed to me that I hadn't been a sculptor until now, for modeling is not sculpting. To tackle wood is a great sensation. Wood lives, comes to life under one's hand, one wrestles with it, humours it, coaxes it, argues with it. The grain gives fight."[26]

Big Bull (Pikanni or Peigan) beside the carving of him by Clare Sheridan, St. Mary's Art Colony, Montana, 1937 (From Clare Sheridan's book *Redskin Interlude* [between pp. 144 and 145]).

Although many of the students at the St. Mary's Art Colony were from the Blackfeet Reservation on the Montana side, Gerald Tailfeathers, of the Blood Reserve in southern Alberta, attended that summer. His parents, Sakoyena and Estomachi Tailfeathers, were also there to watch over Gerald and his brother, Alan. Sheridan soon became close to the family. She was impressed with young Gerald's efforts and purchased his charcoal sketch of Big Bull, later recording a prophetic compliment in *Redskin Interlude*: "Alone he did it...there was no teacher who touched it ... the first picture he ever sold and not likely to be his last." Gerald Tailfeathers (1925–1975) did indeed go on to a remarkable career as an artist, becoming one of the main representatives of the mid- and late-twentieth-century Native art revival.[27] The Tailfeathers family, by taking Gerald to the art colony, helped to further an earlier tradition on the Blood Reserve by which the self-taught artist, Two Gun (Percy Plainwoman) had sold his artwork to passers-by at Standoff, Alberta.[28] To Sheridan's delight, before August had ended, "Esto Tailfeathers invited me to come north and stay with the family on the Blood Reservation."[29]

As a mother who had always, if somewhat chaotically, looked to the education of her own children, she was shocked and saddened by the effect of residential schools on family life at the Blood Reserve. She referred to the "unspeakable anguish" that Native peoples experienced upon having their children taken from them. Unlike other parts of Canada, Blood children remained close to home where their parents could visit them regularly; nevertheless, the effects were, in Sheridan's view, still very serious.[30] She recorded her argument with Canon Middleton, the muscular, and certainly always proper, Anglican clergyman in charge of the school at Cardston. In a passage, which resonates with the contemporary situation in Canada, Sheridan wrote: "On the way back I argued a good deal with the Canon, who boasts of being progressive and *is* really an excellent soul, jovial and kind. We did not, of course, see alike on any Indian subject; we saw in fact, exactly opposite. How one can argue when one side is convinced a thing is absolutely right, and the other that it is absolutely wrong."[31]

Several weeks later, Sheridan visited St. Paul's School with Middleton, who wanted to give her a first-hand tour of the facility. "It was rather like an artist showing his work to a friend who doesn't admire it, but tries to hide his feelings."[32] In her view, there was nothing to be said: "Dormitories are dormitories." They are "always white, always bare, always there are many windows and a great glare. There were the usual rows of white beds, and not so much as a night table upon which to place the childish treasures and reminders of home." At St. Paul's, she observed a "small square room like a well, with a top-light and some stiff chairs round a central table"; this "was the meeting place for parents and children."[33] Everything was "just as I expected it to be only infinitely more dreary": ten years of life "to be lived in this prison-reformatory." The visit brought back memories of her own youth: "Ten years is a long time for a child. I remember being ill-treated by a governess for five years that seemed an unending lifetime."[34]

Sheridan worked conscientiously on her photography and sculpting, the latter worked both in wood and in the round. She thus added a substantial body of artistic work to the inheritance, some of which is now in the Glenbow Museum in Calgary. Sheridan also purchased a good number of artifacts and some of these, along with some of the sculptures, worked their way into the Blackmore Collection in the Hastings Museum.[35] During her working time, she met many others in the Native community besides the Tailfeathers family: Shot-on-Both-Sides, Big Bull, the Gladstones, Rough Hair, Crazy Crow, the Blackplumes, Mountain Horse, and the venerable Heavy Head. All the while, she compiled notes and observations that became the basis for *Redskin Interlude*.

Consider, for instance, her recollection of the traditional medical aid that Crazy Crow's wife gave to her aged husband. The account illustrates the sympathetic, documentary style of Sheridan's writing, one that had served her well in her journalism days. Following a conversation with Crazy Crow, Sheridan wrote that he went off, "smiling and cheerful as ever," but "before he reached his tent he collapsed in the snow and was carried into his tent in a dying condition." All attempts to help were interrupted by his wife, Conquered-by-Night, who had suddenly "shaken herself out of her deaf and blind inertia" and was now "transformed into an active and authoritative person." She had her own methods that "were those of a Medicine-woman":

A handful of seeds thrown on the fire filled the tent with a sweet scent of aromatic herbs. Kneeling at her husband's side, she produced out of a bag a "black weasel" skin (summer ermine) that had belonged to her famous father and brought him safely through his war-paths. With prayers and incantations she passed it several times round the sick man's head, his neck and wrists, and across his chest. Then she took red earth powder, which is the war-paint of the Indians, and with a rhythmic shout rubbed it into his chest, repeating this several times. She would blow into his open mouth, giving him her breath when his failed.

In his unconscious agony he called for smoke, for the sacred precious tobacco; she lit a cigarette and blew the smoke into his face, then removed one of his moccasins and painted the sole of his foot. At intervals she beat his bare breast with an eagle wing.

Their daughter, young, beautiful, sphinx-like, stood by, taking no part. The final scene was when, all her ministrations having failed, Conquered-by-Night took the old man's head in her lap and began to sing. He had told her, far back, that if ever he were in danger of dying, she was to sing his Medicine-song to him, and if he were able to sing it with her, he would live.[36]

If Sheridan did not record her observations in the format of an anthropologist or ethnologist, she certainly had that artistic eye for detail, which recommended her work to later readers and scholars. For example, her impressions of a contemporary pow-wow and her observations and interviews dealing with Sun Dance ceremonies of the 1930s are full of intelligence and interest. There is a lack of rigidity about her observations. While predictions of the demise and passing of Native culture had long been common in colonial and official government literature, Sheridan was aware of the survival capacities and strategies of Native peoples; she viewed their contemporary problems as simply a difficult phase, arguing that they survive because "they have an inner life."[37]

Sheridan's artistic endeavours and interactions with Native peoples contributed to her own well-being. The Tailfeathers family "had a salutary effect upon me, they brought me back to earth"; just as "the Sahara awakens in one's soul a deep spiritual consciousness, so too the prairie in the stillness of its immensity filled one with a realization of the Great Spirit."[38] Years later, she would recall, "As one renewed, reborn, strengthened, I finally returned to England."[39] She would not return to western North America, but her experiences exercised an important influence on her subsequent work.

The Second World War found Clare Sheridan back in the British Isles where her work came to be inspired by the artistic outlook of the Middle Ages. Upon her conversion from the Anglican Church to Catholicism in 1946, she traveled to Assisi where, with customary flamboyance, she took her instruction and vows.[40] She then sought out a more cloistered atmosphere at a convent in County Cork, Ireland, where she was determined to live communally by contributing sculptures to the church and gaining commissions for larger works. *To the Four Winds* (1957), provides many insights into her late quest for peaceful accommodation with the world.

Sheridan's writings, taken as a whole, raise questions about the motivations that underpinned her travels and her place in twentieth-century art and culture. Her lived experiences pushed her towards mysticism and an expansive vision of social connectedness; they distanced her from intellectual presuppositions held by members of the governing elite, like the Bloomsbury Group, with which she appears to have had no links. It is certainly natural enough to wonder about her relationship with that great haven of British iconoclasm, of whom Virginia Woolf was such a famous member. Sheridan's pacifism was as genuine as Bloomsbury's, growing out of the emotional horrors of war and loss. While accustomed to moving in the company of the well-connected, she refused to respect those in power unless they proved their worth. By contrast, Bloomsbury tended to express a faith in intellectual and economic aristocracy; indeed, Virginia Woolf recognized the irony of this position. In reviewing Clive Bell's Bloomsbury tract, *Civilization*, in which Bell tried to define its elusive quality, Woolf noted, "He has great fun in the opening chapters, but in the end it turns out that civilization is a lunch party at No. 50 Gordon Square."[41] *That* idea would seem to be the one upon which Clare Sheridan had taken her leave in 1916, finding the confines of inward-looking, nationalist, upper-class circles remarkably suffocating and narrow-minded. If Sheridan demonstrated an affinity with any of the intellectuals of her day, it was probably (implicitly at least) with Herbert Read. She liked to think of herself as an anarchist: anarchism, with its lack of precision as a concept, appealed to both her psychological and practical side. In Read's formulation, anarchism preserves the importance of individual action and religious conviction and sensibility.[42]

What then, was the importance of being well-connected for Clare Sheridan? To be well-connected was to be authentically involved in a moral and supportive relationship that was existential in nature, rather than merely inherited. Details of a person's origins or background were of factual interest, but no more than that. If one's connections were in a position to open doors for you on occasion, or give you a room to stay in, so be it, provided such gestures were made unconditionally. The object of life was not to confine oneself to a circle of the like-minded, Bloomsbury-style, but to be part of an ever-expanding constellation. If these ideas needed any confirmation in the mid-1930s, Sheridan found them during her time in Montana and Alberta.

In her final years, there was still a twinkle in Clare Sheridan's eye. Having put her tools down for good in 1960, she lived in an Irish convent in County Monaghan. As was long her custom, she had a room of her own. Her formal Catholicism still did little to conceal her own brand of latitudinarian inclinations. To her cousin and biographer, Anita Leslie, she put the question: "What must the nuns think of me? In my room I have a Madonna and a Buddha."[43]

ENDNOTES

1   Anita Leslie, *The Fabulous Leonard Jerome* (London: Hutchinson, 1954), 19–36.

2   See Shane Leslie, *Long Shadows* (London: John Murray, 1966). Clare Sheridan's biographer, Anita Leslie, was a daughter of Shane Leslie. Illustrations of many of the prominent Frewens are contained in Mary Frewen, *Catherine's Ring: A Romance of Brickwall House* (Seaview: Angel Design, 1995).

3   Anita Leslie, *Clare Sheridan* (London: Hutchinson, 1977), 19; Anita Leslie, *Mr. Frewen of England: A Victorian Adventurer* (London: Hutchinson, 1966), 53–55; John L. Merritt, *Baronets and Buffalo: The British Sportsman in the American West, 1833–1881* (Missoula: Mountain Press, 1985), 154; Helen Huntington Smith, *The War on Powder River* (New York: McGraw-Hill, 1966), 7–21. On the "remittance men," see L.G. Thomas, "Privileged Settlers," in *Ranchers' Legacy: Alberta Essays*, ed. Patrick A. Dunae (Edmonton: University of Alberta Press, 1986), 159–62.

4   Smith, *The War on Powder River*, 15.

5   Ibid.; Ernest Staples Osgood, *The Day of the Cattleman* (Minneapolis: University of Minnesota Press, 1954), 110–12, and note 222. Frewen left his own account of this period in his *Melton Mowbray and Other Memories* (London: Herbert Jenkins, 1924), chapters 10 to 20.

6   Clare Sheridan, *To the Four Winds* (London: Andre Deutsch, 1957), 77–80.

7   Ibid., 80.

8   Ibid.; Clare Sheridan, *Russian Portraits* (London: Jonathan Cape, 1921). A slightly different, American version was published as *Mayfair to Moscow* (New York: Boni and Liveright, 1921). For a more recent edition, see, *Russian Portraits*, ed. Mark Almond (Cambridge: Ian Faulkner Publishing, 1992). Lenin found this work "too beautiful": see Christopher Hill, *Lenin and the Russian Revolution* (Harmondsworth: Penguin, 1971), 158–59.

9   See Sheridan, *Russian Portraits*.

10   Ibid., 9; see John Pearson, *The Private Lives of Winston Churchill* (Toronto: Viking, 1991), 177; Sheridan, *To the Four Winds*, 149.

11   See Piers Brandon, *Winston Churchill: A Brief Life* (Toronto: Stoddart, 1984), 90–95.

12   Leslie, *Clare Sheridan*, 159; Sheridan, *To the Four Winds*, 161; Ralph G. Martin, *Jennie: The Life of Lady Randolph Churchill*, Vol. 2, *The Dramatic Years, 1895–1921* (Englewood Cliffs: Prentice-Hall, 1971), 394–95.

13   See Clare Sheridan, *My American Diary* (New York: Boni and Liveright, 1922); *West to East* (New York: Boni and Liveright, 1923); *Across Europe with Satanella* (London: Duckworth, 1925); *A Turkish Kaleidoscope* (London: Duckworth, 1926). *Arab Interlude* (London: Ivor Nicholson and Watson, 1936). See also, Leslie, *Clare Sheridan*, 159–64.

14   John C. Ewers, "Winold Reiss: His Portraits and Protégés," *Montana: The Magazine of Western History* 21 (1971): 44–55.

15   Her achievements were of great interest to the Hastings collector and promoter of Indian culture, Edward Blackmore. See *Edward Blackmore and the American Indians*. Fact Sheet no. 5 (Hastings: Hastings Museum and Art Gallery, n.d); and Betty Taylor, *Clare Sheridan* (Hastings: 1984).

16   Sheridan, *To the Four Winds*, 318.

17 See Francis Paul Prucha, ed. *Documents of United States Indian Policy*, 2nd ed. (Lincoln: University of Nebraska Press, 1975), 171–74.

18 See Graham MacDonald, *Where the Mountains Meet the Prairies: A History of Waterton Country* (Calgary: University of Calgary Press, 2000), 126.

19 Clare Sheridan, *Redskin Interlude* (London: Nicolson and Watson, 1938), 22.

20 Ibid., 38, 50–51, 70–71.

21 Ibid., 41. Moreton Frewen, *Melton Mowbray*, unfinished, but published in the year of his death in 1924. See Leslie, *Long Shadows*, author's note.

22 Ibid., 56.

23 Ibid., 146.

24 Schultz was the author of many books on Blackfoot lore. See also Annie Banks, "Jessie Donaldson Schutlz and Blackfeet Crafts" *Montana: The Magazine of Western History* 33 (1983): 18–25.

25 Sheridan, *Redskin Interlude*, 79–84.

26 Leslie, *Clare Sheridan*, 278.

27 Hugh Dempsey, *Tailfeathers: Indian Artist* (Calgary: Glenbow-Alberta Institute, 1970).

28 Sheridan, *Redskin Interlude*, 169, and Dempsey, *Tailfeathers*.

29 Ibid., *Redskin Interlude*, 149.

30 Ibid., 161–63.

31 Ibid., 164–65.

32 Ibid., 175.

33 Ibid.

34 Ibid., 175–76.

35 See Taylor, *Clare Sheridan*.

36 Sheridan, *Redskin Interlude*, 225–26.

37 Ibid., 196.

38 Ibid., 209.

39 Sheridan, *To the Four Winds*, 319.

40 Ibid., 334.

41 Cited in Quentin Bell, *Bloomsbury*, 2nd ed. (London: Phoenix/Giant, 1986), 88.

42 Herbert Read, "The Philosophy of Anarchism," in *Selected Writings: Poetry and Criticism*, with a foreword by Allen Tate (London: Faber and Faber, 1963), 319.

43 Leslie, *Clare Sheridan*, 306.

five

A Conversation with Senator Thelma Chalifoux

CORA J. VOYAGEUR

In 1980, historian Sylvia Van Kirk turned the traditional narrative of Canadian history on its head by demonstrating the integral role that Indian and Métis women played as cultural liaisons and mediators in the fur trade. While Lesley Erickson demonstrates how Métis women, like Sara Riel, continued to act as cultural mediators after the fur trade waned, sociologist Cora Voyageur's conversation with Senator Thelma Chalifoux explores how they continue to do so in the present. On 26 November 1997, Chalifoux became the first Aboriginal woman and Métis person appointed to the Senate of Canada. The appointment recognized

Chalifoux's long-term status as a spokesperson in Alberta for "those without a voice": Aboriginal peoples, women and children, new immigrants, low-income families, and Canadians in isolated areas. Born on 8 February 1929 into a traditional Métis family in Calgary, Alberta, Senator Chalifoux's social activism emerged out of her childhood experiences with the Salvation Army, her struggles as a single mother with seven children, and her fieldwork with the Métis Association of Alberta. In this conversation with the senator, Voyageur constructs an engaging narrative of the events, experiences, and hardships that culminated, in the 1990s, with Chalifoux's appointment to the University of Alberta's Senate and a National Aboriginal Achievement Award.

As a senator representing Alberta, Chalifoux was the first Métis woman to chair the National Métis Senate, the Senate Constitution Commission, and the Senate Standing Committee on Aboriginal Peoples; to co-chair the Alberta Métis Senate; to serve as an appeal panel member with Alberta Child Welfare and Alberta Social Allowance; and to be appointed Métis Elder for Nechi Institute. Like Muriel Stanley Venne (who discusses negative stereotypes of Aboriginal women in chapter 7) Chalifoux is an ardent advocate for the maintenance of Métis culture, identity, and history. Following her retirement from the senate in February 2004, she remains committed to alleviating and drawing public attention to issues confronting Aboriginal and Métis women in Canada, serving alongside Venne as a board member to the National Aboriginal Women's Association. Voyageur's interview and Chalifoux's reminiscences draw attention to women's past and present role as community builders and cultural mediators.

In June 2002, Senator Thelma Chalifoux delivered the luncheon keynote address at the "Unsettled Pasts: Reconceiving the West through Women's History" conference in Calgary, Alberta. Senator Chalifoux, the first Métis woman appointed to the Senate of Canada, regaled listeners with her life story. She told of being born in Calgary's Ramsey District in 1929, and described the community as it existed at that time.

Many conference goers expressed an interest in learning more about Senator Chalifoux. Since I have known her for many years, conference organizers asked me to interview her. I interviewed her in Edmonton, Alberta, and gathered more details of her life to include in this chapter.

Her story is one of perseverance and survival. She was born during a snowstorm; her father prophesized that she would have to be strong to survive. His words could not have been more true. Here is my interview.

CV: Senator Chalifoux, can you tell me a bit about your upbringing?

SC: My father was Paul Michel Villeneuve. He was born in St. Albert, Alberta, in either 1892 or 1895 (we are not sure which). My mother, Helene Margarite Ingerson, was born to wealthy Danish ranchers in Iowa in 1902. She immigrated to Alberta with her father and stepmother in 1905 – the year our province was created. I was born the second of five children. We were all born in Calgary. My older sister, Irene Shirley was born in 1927. I was born at the Grace Hospital in 1929 – the year the stock market crashed. My brother George was born in 1931, but died just before his fourteenth birthday of spinal meningitis. Ralph was born in 1933. He joined the Royal Canadian Navy when he was eighteen and went on to be a career Navy man. My youngest sister, Mary, was born with a heart defect in 1936 and passed away in 1978. My brother Ralph and I are the only surviving siblings.

I grew up in a very strong traditional Métis family. We were taught to look after not only the family but also the extended family. My role was to look after the old people and my brothers and sister. Each of us in the family unit had a very special role, and if we did not do our jobs it really affected the entire family. The responsibility was a very good learning experience.

My parents dedicated all of us to the Salvation Army. My father said that, when he was a World War I soldier, the Salvation Army gave out what were called Lonely Soldier parcels. According to my father, the Salvation Army members also went into the trenches and provided free food and drinks to soldiers. In gratitude, my father promised that if he ever had children he would dedicate them to the Salvation Army. As Salvation Army members, my siblings and I did a tremendous amount of volunteer work. I was a member of the League of Mercy, which visited nursing homes. I also worked in the Thrift Stores and taught Sunday School.

CV: Can you tell me about your own family?

SC: I got married at eighteen. I was raised to believe that if you were not married by the time you were eighteen, then you were an old maid. I married a Princess Patricia Canadian Light Infantry soldier, Robert Coulter, in 1947. This was a very hectic and traumatic time in my life. It seems that as soon as I got pregnant my husband left town. When my first child Robert Jr. was born in 1948, my husband was away at the floods in Manitoba. When my next son Scott was born in 1949, Robert was at the floods in British Columbia. When Cliff was born in 1950, his father was part of the Canadian contingent fighting in the Korean conflict that ran from 1950 to 1953. Then he came back and I got pregnant with Debbie. When she was born in 1953, he was back in Korea. He returned to his family for good after being wounded in combat. By the time I gave birth to my fifth child Orlean in 1956, he was off with another woman. The hospital staff would not help me very much because in those days you were nothing if your husband was not with you.

At twenty-six, I was a single mother with five children to feed and a ninth grade education. I went on to have two more children. If you were single and if you had children, especially if you were Aboriginal, you suffered discrimination. I created a little world of our own for the children and me. I was lonely, homesick, and flat broke but I never thought about going to welfare. I had five babies to support, so I just went to work. I did waitress work but kept looking for something else. I started working in a furniture store and ended up getting an interior design certificate. I became a construction estimator and colour formulator for Bapco Paints in Calgary.

cv: Can you tell me how you started your community advocacy work?

sc: I moved to Duffield and was hired as a field worker by the Métis Association office in Edmonton. There, I formed the welfare department and the land department. I have always been a strong advocate for women, children, and families. I think I was an effective agency worker because I had been poor and a single parent. I could empathize with the people I worked with.

I was later sent to work in Slave Lake in central Alberta by the Métis Association. I started to organize members of the Aboriginal community to deal with local governance issues and trained them in negotiation skills. I established the Isolated Communities Advisory Board with representatives from seven communities: Loon Lake, Peerless Lake, Wabasca, Chipewyan Lakes, Little Buffalo, Cadotte Lake, and Trout Lake. My group of volunteers and I established the Slave Lake Native Friendship Centre and the MITTA Detoxification Center in High Prairie; we had the Cree language taught in the local schools and founded an adult upgrading program in Grouard. The funny thing is that most of this community work was done while I was receiving unemployment insurance benefits because I had been fired from my job. Our group eventually secured a federal government grant to support our service and advocacy work. This money allowed us to hire a court worker, social worker, health care worker, recreation director, bookkeeper, and cottage industry coordinator.

While working in the community, I found women to be the most dedicated. We came up against a lot of resistance from local people who did not want to see change, and from some husbands who said their wives were spending too much time working outside the home. At times, people who did not like what we were doing challenged us on the street. We were told that women belonged at home.

I moved back to Edmonton and hosted a weekly, half-hour television series for ITV called *Our Aboriginal People*. This program dealt with issues concerning the Aboriginal community. I think my contract was not renewed because the topics I tackled were deemed too controversial. I think the station simply wanted feathers and beads but they got a lot more than that from me.

I have always been a strong advocate of making sure our people, and others for that matter, know about our history and culture because that is our identity. It seems that nobody seemed to know about our proud Canadian history. I started teaching Métis culture and Métis history in Edmonton areas schools. I am adamant that our children know who they are and that they be proud of who they are. In 1985, I produced a Métis culture and history video and curriculum guide aimed at Grades 4 to 6 for the Métis Nation of Alberta. I also worked with Alberta Education on a Métis history and culture project. In addition, while serving on the board of directors of the Alberta Native Communications Society, we developed training programs in journalism and drama. I think these programs helped create a greater awareness of Aboriginal issues in both TV and radio stations around the Edmonton area.

CV: In conclusion, what message do you have for the Aboriginal community?

SC: We must teach our children how to respect each other and that the family unit is the most important unit of all. That is where our identity is. That is where our heart is. I think we need to appreciate and recognize Aboriginal women. We are the strong ones. We are the ones who get things done. I always say that if you want something done – ask a woman.

I have worked all of my adult life to help make conditions better in the Aboriginal community. If I have helped just one person to become a better person in my lifetime then I have done the best that I can. In conclusion, I would like to ask God to bless each and every one of you and the most important thing is never ever lose your faith and always stand up and be proud of who you are as a human being. Be proud of our history and our culture.

part two

COLONIAL PROJECTS

AND THEIR LEGACIES

six

Aboriginal and White Women in the Publications

of John Maclean, Egerton Ryerson Young, and

John McDougall

KRISTIN BURNETT

*Reconceiving the West through women's eyes often means
returning to traditional texts and reading them "against
the grain." Kristin Burnett does this by rereading the writings of three prominent late-nineteenth-century Methodist
missionaries. As feminist historians were quick to argue
in the 1970s, male missionaries, fur traders, and explorers
were the main actors in traditional narratives of western
exploration and settlement: they "conquered" the "wilderness" and brought "civilization" to the region's original
inhabitants. By contrast, Burnett builds upon the work
of feminist and postcolonial scholars, demonstrating that*

popular images of Aboriginal and non-Aboriginal women in missionary litera-
ture were critical to Euro-Canadian identity formation and the establishment
of a White settler society in western Canada.

   John Maclean, Egerton Ryerson Young, and John McDougall wrote accounts
of their experiences for popular consumption by potential settlers and contrib-
utors. As in other colonial settings, non-Aboriginal observers tended to rep-
resent White women as the "frail harbingers of civilization"; in opposition,
they constructed Aboriginal women as dark, sinister, and dangerous. The two
trends legitimized official policies of segregation and exclusion. Muriel Stanley
Venne's contribution to this volume, which follows, illustrates the damaging
effect that negative stereotypes continue to have on Aboriginal women. Yet, as
Burnett demonstrates, the imperial lens through which colonial agents viewed
Aboriginal women was not uniform: in order to justify their work, missionar-
ies had to allow for Aboriginal people's redeemability. Sustained contact with
Aboriginal peoples could also lighten the "cultural baggage" that missionaries
carried west with them. Venne and Burnett's work highlights the importance of
creating intercultural dialogues to overcome the legacy of our patriarchal and
colonial pasts.

Protestant missionaries in western Canada during the late-nineteenth
and early-twentieth centuries produced an enormous volume of records
regarding their work among First Nations people. These records ranged
in form from institutional reports and correspondence, to personal
letters and diaries, to autobiographies and monographs. Regardless of
form, missionaries tailored many of their texts for their audiences, using
stereotypical images that were easily identified and recognized in Euro-
Canadian popular culture.[1] The latter half of the nineteenth century had
witnessed a proliferation of literature by artists, writers, travelers, sur-
veyors, amateur anthropologists, ethnographers, and missionaries who
observed and wrote about Aboriginal people. Such works were popular
in central and eastern Canada because audiences wanted to "know" how
Aboriginal people "really lived." These images were highly gendered,
relying on narrowly constructed stereotypes of First Nations people
and, more specifically, women. This chapter provides an examination of
the images of Aboriginal and non-Aboriginal women in the writings of
three well-known western Canadian male missionaries: John Maclean,
Egerton Ryerson Young, and John Chantler McDougall. Such images,
although they were not expressed in precisely the same manner by each

missionary, produced a set of social understandings about First Nations women that helped to both socially and physically marginalize them within Canadian society, while at the same time alleviating the federal government of responsibility for its actions.

Missionary texts in no way provide accurate and objective accounts of First Nations people, but they do offer an opportunity to examine how stereotypes of Aboriginal people were created and manipulated. Much of the knowledge about Indigenous cultures that the average middle-class, Protestant Euro-Canadian received during the nineteenth and early twentieth centuries was provided through the publications of missionaries.[2] Not only were eastern Canadian perceptions of the missionary experience influenced by the published works of people in the field, but Euro-Canadian understandings of First Nations people were shaped by them as well. In these ways, we can see the dual effects of missionary narratives. Missionary texts were used to not only attract public attention to and encourage the financial and spiritual support of mission work, but to serve the broader colonial project, which sought to design and build a White settler society by physically and socially marginalizing First Nations people.[3]

Following the termination of their careers as missionaries in the West, both Egerton Ryerson Young and John Maclean spent a great deal of time writing books and promoting them on lecture tours throughout North America and Britain. John McDougall had a much longer, active career in the mission field but, like Young and Maclean, he also wrote books and lectured on his experiences as a missionary. All three missionaries were regarded as authorities on First Nations people and were often cited in newspapers or asked for advice by the federal government.[4] For example, John McDougall worked as a liaison and interpreter for the federal government in the negotiation of Treaty 7, encouraging First Nations people to accept the government's offer and to settle on reserves.[5] Likewise, the *Macleod Gazette* in 1889 commended John Maclean for his work among First Nations people and lauded his "tireless efforts to encourage the white settlement of Western Canada" during his promotional tour of eastern Canada.[6]

Building on the published works of retired missionaries like Young, Maclean, and McDougall, historians of mission work in Canada initially emphasized the heroic and masculine nature of the mission enterprise, applauding these exceptional men who traveled west to bring Christianity and "civilization" to Indigenous peoples.[7] In early histories, male missionaries were depicted as administering circuits that covered thousands of miles; in the tradition of muscular Christianity, they braved the dangers of a harsh land to seek out First Nations people.[8] Such studies implied that contact between First Nations and White people in western Canada occurred primarily between men, and that the presence of women, both Aboriginal and non-Aboriginal, was essential neither to the success of missionary work nor to the well-being of Aboriginal families and communities.

More recent scholarship has challenged this earlier interpretation by emphasizing the coercive dimension of mission work and the vital presence of women in the mission field.[9] Feminist scholars like Rosemary Gagan and Ruth Compton Brouwer argue that mission work presented educated middle-class White women with a socially acceptable alternative to marriage and an opportunity to work in spheres previously prohibited to them. In her recent work, Myra Rutherdale has extended the analysis of Anglican missionary women in northern British Columbia, the Yukon, and Canada's Arctic to include race, drawing connections between the work of women missionaries and colonization.[10] Rutherdale argues that the mission field represented a contested terrain of shifting identities where preconceived attitudes and beliefs, with a few exceptions, were used to understand new environments and human conditions.[11]

As the scope of research on missionary work has expanded, historians have begun to examine mission work, immigration, and the settlement of the West as part of an internal colonial project that involved the displacement of First Nations people and the creation of settler colonies that were premised upon privileging notions of "whiteness."[12] Missionaries were deeply involved in the production of images and stereotypes of First Nations people; these images not only legitimized the dispossession of First Nations people, they also served as sites of production for Euro-Canadian identity and power.[13] In settings where Aboriginal populations outnumbered missionaries, colonial discourses were as much about creating and reinforcing Euro-Canadian identity, as they were about denigrating First Nations people and justifying mission work.

One of the most thorough examinations of missionary images of Aboriginal peoples is Carol Higham's work *Noble, Wretched, and Redeemable*, which provides a comparative analysis of the images produced by Protestant missionaries in Canada and the United States between 1820 and 1900. Higham identifies three ongoing images within missionary literature: the "noble savage," the "wretched Indian," and the "redeemable savage." The "noble savage" represented the free, natural man, unhindered by the rules of society, who would ultimately become extinct through the inevitable march of "progress."[14] The image of the "wretched Indian," according to Higham, was a direct response to the growth of missionary endeavours in the North American west throughout the 1840s and 1850s.[15] Increasing contact between Protestant missionaries and various First Nations groups created an image, the "wretched Indian," that emphasized the perceived degraded and savage state of First Nations people. In turn, the image of the "redeemable Indian" combined missionaries' belief in the redeemability of the "noble savage," with the acceptable flaws of the "wretched Indian," justifying the missionary project and emphasizing the necessity of its "civilizing" agenda.[16]

Higham's work demonstrates that the representations produced about Aboriginal people had more to do with non-Aboriginal people's political, economic, and social interests than the realities of Aboriginal people's lives. What Higham's work does not address is how the publications of missionaries also conveyed contemporary perceptions of gender norms and roles. Adele Perry's work on White settler colonies in British Columbia clearly shows that "notions and practices of womanhood and manhood were central to the twinned businesses of marginalizing Aboriginal people and designing and building a white society."[17] Consequently, it is necessary to include gender as a category of analysis when examining representations of First Nations people. Fortunately, key works like Rayna Green's study "The Pocahontas Perplex" provide a context for studying the gendered aspects of missionary narratives. Green contends that non-Aboriginal observers in colonial America represented Aboriginal women in two oppositional categories: the "squaw," who was lustful and threatening to White men, and Pocahontas, who was pure and protective of White interests.[18] The image of the "squaw," as an overworked and abused drudge, also prevailed during the nineteenth century. It was used to exemplify the supposed brutality of contemporary First Nations culture, particularly its men, justifying assimilationist policies instituted by the Canadian government.[19]

Sarah Carter's work extends Green's analysis to include representations of White women on the Canadian Prairies who were constructed in relation and opposition to First Nations women.[20] Carter notes that the arrival of White women in the region did not introduce racial boundaries and categories; rather, their arrival coincided with treaties, settlement, and the growth and consolidation of Euro-Canadian institutions.[21] Carter argues that images of White women were manipulated to legitimize growing spatial and social segregation in the West. White women operated as signifiers of "western civilization" and Aboriginal women were constructed as dark, sinister, and dangerous; they were blamed for the ill health and poor living conditions on reserves, as well as the "failure" of First Nations people to assimilate and adopt Euro-Canadian norms.[22]

Adele Perry contends that the logical conclusion to depicting First Nations women as White women's mirror image was to exclude First Nations women from the category of "women" entirely.[23] This oppositional construction of Aboriginal and White women ensured that the dominant paradigm of Aboriginal women in western Canada would remain that of the "unwomanly squaw." While the negative image of the "squaw" was pervasive in popular literature in the West, representations of Aboriginal women in the publications of missionaries were more complex in the late-nineteenth and early-twentieth centuries. Missionaries themselves were slightly different from other colonizers because they needed to justify their work; in order to do so, they needed to allow for the redeemability of Aboriginal peoples. If Aboriginal peoples were merely "wretched Indians" or "squaws," then why would Euro-Canadians continue to support their mission work?

Throughout the nineteenth and early twentieth centuries, Protestant denominations, especially Methodists, had become increasingly involved in establishing missions among Indigenous peoples throughout the globe.[24] The Methodist Church, in particular, hoped to include everyone in its fellowship because its adherents believed that salvation was a conscious choice available to all.[25] Methodists perceived the world as divided between those who had converted and those who had not.[26] Thus, missions among First Nations people were an important step in transforming Canada into God's Kingdom on Earth, and missionary societies within the Methodist Church eagerly sought to participate in Protestantizing the nation.[27]

Missions to convert the "heathen" were largely supported by missionary societies and Protestant congregations. Interest in the North American west as a mission field did not occur until the 1830s; in particular, Methodists turned their attention to western Canada in 1839.[28] Early mission work was exceptionally challenging. Missionaries found that the mobility of First Nations people, the unfriendly physical environment, and the scarcity of Euro-Canadian settlements posed serious problems for their mission enterprise. As a result, the nature of missionary work prior to the reserve period (post-1870s) required the missionary to travel with First Nations peoples, learn their languages, and live in isolated areas.[29] In the post-reserve period, work among Aboriginal peoples assumed a new character and attracted a different type of missionary, one who would serve as a steady pastor to his congregation and as an able administrator capable of working closely with government agents and farm instructors.

John Maclean, Egerton Ryerson Young, and John McDougall possessed characteristics from the pre- and post-reserve periods. Young and McDougall worked among First Nations people prior to the negotiation of treaties and the creation of reserves. Young remained in western Canada less than ten years after his arrival in the late 1860s. Accompanied by his wife, he worked among the Swampy Cree on the north end of Lake Winnipeg, and among the Saulteaux at Berens River until he retired in 1876. Although Young had no contact with Plains people, particularly the Blackfoot, his monographs claimed knowledge and authority regarding their social and cultural customs. Young's books seem to be a mixture of fiction and autobiography.[30] Many of Young's stories were written as parables, illustrating the dangers of living without the benefits of Christianity. Young emphasized what he perceived to be the savage brutality of First Nations' culture and contrasted it to the goodness and light of Anglo-Saxon culture. In particular, he stressed the tremendous impact he had as a missionary – apparently converting thousands of Aboriginal people on his own.[31] Young's publications were intended obviously to garner public support for mission work, but also seem to be an attempt to give meaning and importance to his own life and work.

Scottish-born Maclean also spent ten years in the mission field, following his marriage to Sara Anne Barker of Guelph, Ontario, in 1880. He worked on the Blood Reserve in southern Alberta during the 1880s, and began publishing books on Aboriginal culture shortly after he retired in 1889. Like Young, Maclean also provided information about First Nations groups with which he had no contact, having only worked among the Blackfoot. Maclean's monographs describe groups as diverse as the Ojibwa, Cree, Inuit, Mi'kmaq, and Nez Perce. Where Maclean obtained information on these groups is unclear, but like many of his contemporaries in the United States, Maclean joined the ranks of missionaries who acted as amateur ethnographers, cataloguing what they believed to be the vestiges of dying cultures.[32] Of course, to legitimate their status as authoritative voices on Indigenous peoples, such commentators were obliged to offer insight into the daily lives and intimate relations that characterized the people under study.

In contrast to Maclean and Young, McDougall's experiences with First Nations peoples were quite intimate, and he expressed them through a slightly different genre. One of the best-known and controversial figures in Alberta history, McDougall spent thirty years of his life working in the western mission field among the Woodland Cree and Nakoda. Born in Owen Sound, Ontario, in 1842, McDougall followed his father, George McDougall, west in the early 1860s, helping him to establish missions at Pakan and Whitefish Lake, in present-day Alberta. His arrival in the early 1860s predated intensive Euro-Canadian settlement; therefore, his early missionary experience involved traveling with First Nations people, especially after he married Abigail Steinhauer in 1864. Born at Norway House in 1847, Steinhauer was the second child of Henry Bird Steinhauer, an Ojibwa Methodist missionary, and Seeseeb Mamanuwartum (Jessie Joyful), a Swampy Cree. The McDougall's first child, Flora, was born at Victoria in 1866; Ruth, their second child, was born at Pigeon Lake in 1867; and Augusta, their last child, was born in 1870. A year after Abigail's death in 1871, McDougall was ordained and he married Elizabeth Boyd, a woman he had met while on a trip to Ontario. The couple were first posted among the Woodland Cree at Pigeon Lake, Alberta, and then, in late 1873, relocated to Morley, Alberta, where they lived among the Nakoda until McDougall retired in 1905. Unlike Maclean and Young, McDougall was intimately involved in promoting the settlement and industrial development of the West; consequently, he was highly criticized for pursuing his own self-interests as a trader and landowner, particularly during the negotiation of Treaty 7.[33]

McDougall did not publish the first sustained account of his experiences until *Forest, Lake, and Prairie* appeared in 1895. The book was in response to what McDougall felt was Young's misrepresentation of Aboriginal peoples in *Stories from Indian Wigwams and Northern Campfires*. McDougall's criticisms indicate that missionaries' beliefs regarding Aboriginal peoples were not homogeneous. McDougall's monographs are different from the other authors because they are more autobiographical;

they were also written as exciting adventure stories that featured him as a hero who overcame great physical danger in order to accomplish his spiritual mission. Unlike the authoritative pseudo-scientific works of John Maclean, McDougall's works adhered to the conventions of nineteenth-century adventure stories that featured the exciting travel narratives of Europeans who had explored South America and West Africa.[34]

Despite these differences in genre, images of the "noble savage," the "wretched Indian," and the "redeemable Indian" are present in the works of all three missionaries. Their writings also include highly gendered images that complicate the framework established by Higham. Missionaries portrayed Aboriginal peoples as dirty, lazy, backward, and wretched because, as Albert Memmi argues, "nothing could better justify the colonizers privileged position than his industry and nothing could better justify the colonized's destitution than their indolence."[35] Both Maclean and Young relied heavily on the image of the "wretched Indian" in order to emphasize the current and desperate state of First Nations people. The image of the "squaw drudge" was juxtaposed against the former "primitive virtue" of First Nations culture, highlighting the supposedly wretched state of First Nations people in the present day and, by extension, the condition of Aboriginal women. However, Young also included a transitional image for women in his writings. This transitional representation was premised on a combination of the Pocahontas ideal and the "redeemable Indian," allowing Young to convey in his texts both the potential of the Christianized Indian and the imperial desire to remake First Nations people in his own image.[36] McDougall differed from both Maclean and Young in his representation of First Nations people because he did not depict Aboriginal women as "squaws." Rather, McDougall admired the hard work of Aboriginal women and their ability to survive and thrive in an environment as harsh as the West. Despite this admiration, McDougall still believed that White settlement and "progress" would bring about a lessening of Aboriginal women's work.[37]

Although no unanimity existed between Maclean, Young, and McDougall regarding the representations of Aboriginal women they used, all three agreed on the transformative power of Christianity and the imperative of First Nations people adopting Euro-Canadian values and beliefs to ensure their future survival. By contrast, their representations of Euro-Canadian women were infinitely more flattering. The arrival of the Euro-Canadian wives of Maclean, Young, and McDougall (Sara Anne, Eliza, and Elizabeth, respectively) in the 1870s and 1880s, coincided with other stabilizing forces: the North-West Mounted Police, the Dominion Lands Act, the Canadian Pacific Railway, the negotiation of treaties, the pass system, and increasing non-Aboriginal immigration.[38] White women were perceived as an imperial panacea. Just as the Catholic clergy had looked to the Grey Nuns to serve as cultural and moral examples for Métis women in the 1840s (describe by Lesley Erickson in chapter 2), Protestant missionaries believed that missionary wives would have an edifying influence on First Nations people. They would teach Aboriginal women to be "proper wives and mothers," thereby consolidating Euro-Canadian identity in the West.[39]

In their monographs, both Young and Maclean idealized the roles of Euro-Canadian women. In *Canadian Savage Folk* (1896), Maclean referred to female missionaries as the "saintly heroines of the lodges," who came to impart civilization upon the "poor red men."[40] White women were portrayed as representatives of Anglo-Saxon culture and labelled as "cultural gatekeepers."[41] The arrival of Euro-Canadian women in the West, as throughout the imperial world, was thought to bring the qualities of gentility, morality and piety: qualities Young and Maclean believed the "wretched Indian," especially the "squaw," lacked.[42] Maclean described Euro-Canadian women as follows: "The wise women from the east, the magi of modern times, who have traveled westward with their gifts of culture, grace, and love and laid them at the feet of the men and women who sit in loneliness and with depressed hearts in the lodges widely scattered on prairie and mountain, and in the cold and bleak regions of the northland."[43] Maclean was particularly lavish in his tributes to Euro-Canadian missionary women. He regarded White women as central to the development and settlement of the West; their arrival was presented as a prerequisite for the establishment of Euro-Canadian social and cultural institutions.

White women were regarded as essential to the "civilizing" project, both as purveyors of Euro-Canadian culture and as support systems or "helpmeets" for their husbands. John McDougall portrayed his mother, Elizabeth McDougall, as the perfect "helpmeet." In *Forest, Lake, and Prairie*, McDougall described her as a "strong Christian woman, content, patient, plodding, full of quiet restful assurance, pre-eminently qualified to be the companion and helper."[44] In *Oowikapun* (1896), Young likewise argued that missionary women were to serve as examples, showing Aboriginal women how to be good Christian wives and mothers because the home would be the vehicle through which First

Mrs. Elizabeth George McDougall. Glenbow Archives, NA-1010-22.

Nations' society would be transformed.[45] Such discourses emphasized the unwomanliness of Aboriginal women, assuming that the abilities of First Nations women were somehow not an essential element to their families' survival, while at the same time denigrating First Nations culture.

Despite the perceived utility of White women in the mission field, Young, Maclean, and McDougall worried about the material, familial, and social deprivations that their wives experienced living in the West. In *Canadian Savage Folk*, Maclean lamented that the wives of missionaries faced hardship without protest, and that not one biography had been written about these "saintly heroines."[46] Furthermore, Maclean, Young, and McDougall commiserated over their wives lack of feminine company, ignoring the presence of Aboriginal women, thus implying Aboriginal women were somehow unfeminine.

By contrast, when the missionaries did portray the suffering and deprivation of Aboriginal women, they interpreted it as deriving from Native culture, not as a facet of life in western Canada. Like his contemporaries, Maclean perceived the amount of work that Native women performed as an indication of their poor status rather than important work performed to ensure their families' survival. Maclean failed to recognize that the work of Aboriginal women had always been essential, and had only become more so in the early reserve period during years of low resources and morale.[47] Relying on the image of the work-worn "squaw," Maclean believed that the lives of Aboriginal women were wretched and that little had improved even with the introduction of Christianity. The supposed degradation of Aboriginal culture, he argued, had led to immorality, particularly among the women.[48] In *The Indians: Their Manners and Customs* (1907), Maclean described Native women's lives as "idle, filthy, and painful – they were sold into marriage like property and treated like chattel."[49] As Perry argues, First Nations women were often represented in mission literature as overtly sexual, physical, and base: they were simultaneously monstrous forms of humanity and quintessential objects of desire.[50]

Although Maclean expressed concern over the degraded condition of Aboriginal women, he also eloquently described the beauty of Aboriginal motherhood in *Canadian Savage Folk*.[51] Aboriginal women, according to Maclean, were redeemable only through their roles as mothers.[52] Maclean juxtaposed the alleged low status of Aboriginal women with their potential as future Christian wives and mothers in order to justify the Church's "civilizing" mission among First Nations people. Apparently for Maclean, motherly love was a force powerful enough to transcend racial boundaries.[53]

In *Children of the Forest* (1902), Young similarly created two opposing images of Aboriginal women: the "squaw drudge" and the "beautiful Indian maiden."[54] The "squaw drudge" was timid, submissive, and work-worn. She was beaten for the smallest infraction and was forced to endure abject conditions. The second image, "the beautiful Indian maiden," was similar to the Pocahontas image identified in American literature by Green.[55] Like the mythical Pocahontas, Young's virtuous and good maiden was complicit in the colonization of her people because she provided help and succour to missionaries. The "beautiful

Mrs. Maggie Big Belly (Tsuu T'ina) drying saskatoon berries. Glenbow Archives, NA-667-346.

Indian maiden," in Young's version, was also dissatisfied and restless because she was repulsed by the brutality of her own culture. The "beautiful Indian maiden" allowed Young to draw upon both the "redeemable Indian" and "noble savage" images. As a potential Christian convert, the Indian maiden became beautiful, possessing qualities that would allow her to easily assimilate to Euro-Canadian culture. On the other hand, the "squaw" was not a Christian convert, nor likely to be one; therefore, she was unattractive and unappealing. Through Christianity, the beautiful "Indian maiden" and the "squaw drudge" would find freedom from their hard work and poor treatment. In Young's works, Aboriginal women were redeemable; their wretched condition existed only because of the alleged superstition and ignorance of traditional First Nations culture.[56] Young used what he regarded as the elevated status of Aboriginal women through Christianity as evidence that his work among Aboriginal people was successful.

At the same time, however, Young did not approve of the freedom women exercised in First Nations society. As a result, there emerged a third type of Aboriginal woman in his book *By Canoe and Dog Train Among the Cree and Saulteaux Indians* (1890). This woman was exemplified by the bold "Saulteaux Chieftainess, Ookemasis," who was portrayed as unfeminine because of her position of authority and the initiative she took in seeking Young out.[57] Ookemasis had heard about Young's work and had traveled to the mission station to learn about Christianity and to persuade Young to return with her and preach to her people. Young disapproved of this figure, despite Ookemasis's status as a potential convert. The authority Aboriginal women possessed made Young uncomfortable with Ookemasis; as a result, she was not characterized as a "beautiful Indian maiden," despite her desire to become a Christian. Aboriginal women, according to Young, should not exercise authority and privilege; they should occupy the same domestic role that bound Euro-Canadian women. Yet, because of their "Indianness," Aboriginal women would never have access to the same privilege and space as Euro-Canadian women. In her article, "Nobler Savages: Representations of Native Women in the Writings of Susanna Moodie and Catherine Parr Traill," Carole Gerson argues that authors often used literary representations of Aboriginal women to express their unspoken concerns and fears.[58] The creation of a strong female political figure, like Ookemasis, was perhaps a reflection of Young's discomfort regarding the position of women in First Nations society and the growing emergence of a women's rights movement among middle-class, Euro-Canadian women.

Both Young and Maclean believed that, once Aboriginal women converted to Christianity and adopted the precepts of Euro-Canadian culture, their lives would be transformed. The transformative power of Christianity would not only reduce and alter the work Aboriginal women had to perform, it would change the way Aboriginal women were treated by their male counterparts. Young used Aboriginal men's supposed poor treatment of women to exemplify the necessity of conversion and assimilation. The superiority of Euro-Canadian culture, according to Young and Maclean, was evident through its treatment of women.[59] Apparently, without the benefits of Christianity, Aboriginal men were savage, regularly beating their women and children. This perception is particularly apparent in Young's monograph *When the Blackfeet Went South*, in which he created two types of Aboriginal men: potential Christian converts and those who were not.[60] This dichotomy was exemplified through his story of Hard Hand and Shining Arrow.[61] Shining Arrow was the potential Christian convert and served as the foil for Hard Hand. Hard Hand was a cruel and violent man who forced his wife to work like a slave, beat her for the smallest infraction, and tried to murder Shining Arrow because he was jealous of him. Shining Arrow, in contrast, was a kind person who loved his family and treated his wife in a benevolent and gentle manner.

In her monograph *Women and the White Man's God*, Myra Rutherdale identifies declining incidents of Aboriginal violence as the standard by which missionaries measured their success.[62] To justify their work and highlight its necessity, missionaries included stories of such behaviour, particularly murder and violence against women and children in their descriptions of First Nations' societies. Young used examples of men like Hard Hand in order to present a portrait of the degraded state of First Nations' culture. A critique of Aboriginal masculinity was implicit in Young's representations of Aboriginal domestic violence. Hard Hand, through his ill treatment of women, operated outside the bounds of proper behaviour, while Shining Arrow was a non-threatening domesticated figure. According to Young, the redeemability of Aboriginal women and men were connected. Aboriginal women could not be "saved" without their male counterparts.

Unlike Maclean and Young, McDougall seemed to possess a degree of respect for First Nations people and culture. In *Pathfinding on Plain and Prairie* (1898), McDougall rejected the notion of the violent and savage "wretched Indian" and embraced elements of the "noble savage." He showed a great deal of appreciation for the work ethic of Aboriginal people, noting that western Canada's harsh environment forced Aboriginal people to work hard in order to survive.[63] McDougall often complained about other missionaries, referring to them derisively as "tenderfeet" because of their lack of "outdoorsmanship."[64] According to McDougall, the environment was a challenge only the hardiest of people could survive. The depiction of Aboriginal women in McDougall's writings also differed from that of Maclean and Young. McDougall did not refer to Native women as "squaw drudges"; in 1895, he went so far as to criticize Young's writings: "In the name of decency and civilization and Christianity, why call one person a woman and another a squaw?"[65] McDougall believed that the lives of First Nations women were difficult, but the difficulties were a result of their environment rather than a function of race.

Kainai woman, southern Alberta. Glenbow Archives, NA-2313-23.

Nor did McDougall portray Aboriginal women as unfeminine. McDougall noted that Aboriginal women accomplished their tasks with "efficiency, contentment, and happiness." In fact, McDougall observed that Native women performed such hard work and still had time to "practice all the mysterious arts which have charmed and magnetized the other sex."[66] Hard work, according to McDougall, did not undermine a woman's femininity. In fact, unlike Maclean and Young, who found their wives' hard work a regrettable result of their environment, McDougall applauded his second wife, Elizabeth, for her labour, referring to her as a "heroine of the frontier."[67] Perhaps McDougall's first marriage to an Ojibwa-Cree woman altered his perception of Aboriginal women. Unlike, Maclean and Young, McDougall did not regard Aboriginal women as a separate and inferior category. According to McDougall, the only failure of First Nations culture was that it was not Christian; their lifestyle was an impediment to the settlement and industrial development of the West. McDougall believed in the transformative power of Christianity to uplift and improve Native people, particularly women. According to McDougall, when Native people gave up "communalism and adopted the precepts of Christianity they would be transformed."[68] McDougall thought that Christianity, and the example set by missionaries and their wives, would enable Aboriginal people to adopt notions of individualism and private property, which would eventually improve the status of Native women.[69]

While McDougall understood (and may have even admired) the hard work of Aboriginal women, he nonetheless regarded their key role in the mobile economy as lamentable and destined to be eclipsed. Aboriginal women's roles would be improved through settlement and agricultural development: Aboriginal men would be farmers or ranchers and women would work and live in permanent houses. McDougall believed that First Nations people had a natural physical strength, which made Native people aptly suited for their "traditional" environment. Yet, this environment was changing and progress was inevitable. In order to survive and prosper, Native people needed to assimilate. McDougall regarded Aboriginal people as an impediment to Euro-Canadian settlement because they did not own private property, participate in western-style agriculture, or build large cities.[70] In order to open up the West for White settlement, First Nations people needed to be segregated on reserves and their land freed up for agriculture.[71] To further this agenda, McDougall worked for the federal government, persuading Plains groups to accept Treaty 7.[72]

McDougall's representation of Aboriginal women illustrates that unanimity did not exist among missionaries. As colonial agents, missionaries had a vested interest, both in promoting their work and justifying its utility. The images of the "noble savage," the "wretched Indian," and the "redeemable savage" identified by Higham, were clearly used in all three of these authors' works. Obviously, the three images Higham examines were pervasive and important within missionary texts; however, these representations ignored the powerful and influential images of women that missionaries used to promote their work and criticize Aboriginal culture. As Stanley Venne argues in chapter 7, missionaries like Young and Maclean relied strongly on the image of the "squaw" to emphasize the superiority of Euro-Canadian culture at the expense of Aboriginal peoples. McDougall – who depicted Aboriginal women as both feminine and redeemable, and criticized other missionaries for calling Aboriginal women "squaws" – continued to believe that Christianity would ameliorate the lives of Aboriginal women.

The dominant paradigm of Aboriginal women in western Canada remained the "squaw drudge" in both missionary texts and popular literature because it legitimized the spatial and social segregation of First Nations women and the appropriation of Aboriginal land, while undermining and undervaluing Aboriginal culture. Analyzing three western Canadian missionaries' representations of Aboriginal and White women in the mission field clearly shows that their missionary narratives were more than an individual recording his experiences. An examination of these texts reveals that gender is central to the colonial project. Gender was used by the authors to establish their authority as witnesses to the social organization or disorganization of a people believed to be in need of salvation and, thus, of conquest. Indeed, although the authors claimed to be reflecting on their individual experience, by writing and lecturing to a wider audience, their works transcended the local mission field and missionary institutions and spoke to a wider colonial imperative.

Aboriginal women in western Canada throughout the late-nineteenth and twentieth centuries faced growing discrimination and marginalization. Representations that constructed Aboriginal women as "threats" to White society were reinforced and legitimized in more formal ways through local bylaws, which restricted the movement of Aboriginal women in urban areas, and federal government legislation under the Indian Act. Thus, the texts of missionaries and the images they constructed about Aboriginal women served to legitimize the confinement of Aboriginal women both physically and socially to the reserve by informing the government and the general public of, not only the potential danger posed by Aboriginal women, but also the necessity of "civilizing" First Nations people.[73]

ENDNOTES

1   C.L. Higham, *Noble, Wretched, and Redeemable: Protestant Missionaries to the Indians in Canada and the United States, 1820–1900* (Calgary: University of Calgary Press, 2000). During the nineteenth century, Protestant missionaries produced reports, studies, and works of fiction about First Nations people and the West. They wrote for the benefit of missionary societies, church groups, government officials, the general public, and future missionaries. Higham's study examines the works of over eighty nineteenth-century missionaries, newsletters and publications of numerous missionary societies, and approximately one hundred works of fiction and non-fiction published by Protestant missionaries and their children.

2   Daniel Francis, *The Imaginary Indian: The Image of the Indian in Canadian Culture* (Vancouver: Arsenal Pulp Press, 1992), 16–60. See also Higham, *Noble, Wretched, and Redeemable*, 31–60.

3   Nicholas Thomas, *Colonialism's Culture: Anthropology, Travel and Government* (Princeton: Princeton University Press, 1994), 104. Thomas defines a colonial project as "a socially transformative endeavour that is localized, politicized, and partial, yet also engendered by larger historical developments and ways of narrating them." See also: Anne McClintock, *Imperial Leather: Race, Gender, and Sexuality in the Colonial Contest* (New York: Routledge, 1995); Julie Evans et al., *Equal Subjects, Unequal Rights: Indigenous Peoples in British Settler Colonies, 1830–1910* (Manchester: Manchester University Press, 2003); Philippa Levine, *Prostitution, Race, and Politics: Policing Venereal Disease in the British Empire* (New York: Routledge, 2003); and Adele Perry, *On the Edge of Empire: Gender, Race, and Making of British Columbia, 1849–1871* (Toronto: University of Toronto Press, 2001), 19.

4   "Mr. Maclean's Work," *The Macleod Gazette*, 21 March 1889. See also Higham, *Noble, Wretched, and Redeemable*, 111–17.

5   Treaty 7 Elders and Tribal Council et al., *The True Spirit and Original Intent of Treaty 7* (Montreal: McGill-Queen's University Press, 1996), 267–69.

6   "Mr. Maclean's Work," *The Macleod Gazette*, 21 March 1889.

7   The following authors discuss this earlier approach, which portrayed the mission field as heroic and masculine: George Neil Emery, "Methodism on the Canadian Prairies, 1896–1914: The Dynamic of an Institution in a New Environment" (Ph.D. diss., University of British Columbia, 1970). See also, William Howard Brooks, "Methodism in the Canadian West in the Nineteenth Century" (Ph.D. diss., University of Manitoba, 1972); John Webster Grant, *Moon of Wintertime: Missionaries and the Indians of Canada in Encounter Since 1534* (Toronto: University of Toronto Press, 1984).

8   Emery, "Methodism on the Canadian Prairies," 12.

9   Rosemary Gagan, *A Sensitive Independence: Canadian Methodist Women Missionaries in Canada and the Orient, 1881–1925* (Montreal: McGill-Queen's University Press, 1992) and Ruth Compton Brouwer, *New Women for God: Canadian Presbyterian Women and Indian Missions, 1876–1914* (Toronto: University of Toronto Press, 1990).

10   Myra Rutherdale, *Women and the White Man's God: Gender and Race in the Canadian Mission Field* (Vancouver: UBC Press, 2002).

11   Ibid., 152–53.

12   Perry, *On the Edge of Empire*, 19.

13   Ibid., 48–57. See also Ann Laura Stoler, *Carnal Knowledge and Imperial Power: Race and the Intimate in Colonial Rule* (Berkeley: University of California Press, 2002), 13.

14   Higham, *Noble, Wretched, and Redeemable*, 31–33.

15   Ibid., 56–60.

16   Ibid., 179–83.

17   Perry, *On the Edge of Empire*, 19.

18   Rayna Green "The Pocahontas Perplex: The Image of the Indian Woman in American Culture," in *Unequal Sisters: A Multicultural Reader in U.S. Women's History*, ed. Ellen Carol Dubois and Vicki Ruiz (New York: Routledge, 1990), 15–21.

19   Sarah Carter, "Categories and Terrains of Exclusion: Constructing the 'Indian Woman' in the Early Settlement Era in Western Canada," *Great Plains Quarterly* 13 (Summer 1993): 148; Kim Greenwell, "Picturing 'Civilization': Missionary Narratives on the Margins of Mimicry," *BC Studies* 135 (Autumn 2002): 3–45.

20   Sarah Carter, *Capturing Women: The Manipulation of Cultural Imagery in Canada's Prairie West* (Montreal: McGill-Queen's University Press, 1997).

21   Carter, "Categories and Terrains of Exclusion," 147.

22   Ibid., 148.

23   Perry, *On the Edge of Empire*, 56.

24   The experience of being a Methodist was firmly grounded in both revivalism and their "mission" to convert the heathen world. John Webster Grant, *A Profusion of Spires: Religion in Nineteenth Century Ontario* (Toronto: University of Toronto Press, 1988), 34, 107.

25   Neil Semple, *The Lord's Dominion: The History of Canadian Methodism* (Montreal: McGill-Queen's University Press, 1996), 3–4.

26   Ibid., 3.

27   Ibid., 276–77.

28   Higham, *Noble, Wretched, and Redeemable*, 14.

29   Grant, *Moon of Wintertime*, 162.

30   Higham, *Noble, Wretched, and Redeemable*, 19. See also Carol Gerson, "Nobler Savages: Representations of Native Women in the Writings of Susanna Moodie and Catherine Parr Traill," in *Rethinking Canada: The Promise of Women's History*, ed. Veronica Strong-Boag et al. (Don Mills, ON: Oxford Press, 2002), 79–84.

31   Sarah Carter, "Man's Mission of Subjugation: The Publications of John Maclean, John McDougall, and Egerton Ryerson Young, Nineteenth Century Methodist Missionaries in Western Canada" (master's thesis, University of Saskatchewan, 1981), 29. See also Sarah Carter, "The Missionaries' Indian: The Publications of John McDougall, John Maclean and Egerton Ryerson Young," *Prairie Forum* 9, no. 1 (1984): 27–44.

32   Higham, *Noble, Wretched, and Redeemable*, 181–84.

33   Treaty Seven Elders, *The True Spirit and Original Intent of Treaty 7*, 157–58.

34   Higham, *Noble, Wretched, and Redeemable*, 19 and 181–84. See also Mary Louise Pratt, *Imperial Eyes: Travel Writing and Transculturation* (London: Routledge, 1992), 201–4.

35   Albert Memmi, *The Colonizer and the Colonized* (Boston: Beacon Press, 1965), 79. See also Edward Said, *Orientalism* (New York: Random House, 1978).

36   Hayden White, *Tropics of Discourse: Essays in Cultural Criticism* (Baltimore: Johns Hopkins University Press, 1978), 194.

37   John McDougall, *Pathfinding on Plain and Prairie*, 12.

38   Stoler, *Carnal Knowledge*, 32–33. The term 'stabilization' ambiguously expressed either as securing of empire or a response to its vulnerability. In India, after the Great Rebellion of 1857, "stabilization" meant further segregation from contact with local Indian groups.

39   Perry, *On the Edge of Empire*, 139.

40   John Maclean, *Canadian Savage Folk: The Native Tribes of Canada* (Toronto: William Briggs, 1896), 34.

41   Ibid., 348.

42   Perry, *On the Edge of Empire*, 139.

43   Maclean, *Canadian Savage Folk*, 348.

44   John McDougall, *Forest, Lake, and Prairie: Twenty years of Frontier Life in Western Canada, 1842–1902* (Toronto: Ryerson Press, 1895), 12.

45   Egerton R. Young, *Oowikapun: Or How the Gospel Reached the Nelson River Indians* (New York: Eaton and Mains, 1896), 236–37.

46   Maclean, *Canadian Savage Folk*, 344.

47   Sarah Carter, "First Nations Women and Colonization on the Canadian Prairies, 1870s-1920s," in *Rethinking Canada: The Promise of Women's History*, 139.

48   John Maclean, *The Indians: Their Manners and Customs* (Toronto: William Briggs, 1907), 26.

49   Ibid.

50   Rutherdale, *Women and the White Man's God*, 30. See also Perry, *On the Edge of Empire*, 51.

51   Maclean, *Canadian Savage Folk*, 193.

52   Ibid., 190.

53   Perry, *On the Edge of Empire*, 54.

54   Egerton R. Young, *Children of the Forest: A Story of Indian Love* (Toronto: Musson, 1902), 15–34.

55   Green, "The Pocahontas Perplex," 15–21.

56   Egerton R. Young, *Indian Life in the Great North-West* (Toronto: Musson, Led., 1902), 12.

57   Egerton R. Young, *By Canoe and Dog Train Among the Cree and Saulteaux Indians* (London: Hazell, Watson, and Viney, 1890), 262–64.

58   Gerson, "Nobler Savages," 79–84.

59   Egerton R. Young, "Life among the Red Men of America," *The Missionary Review of the World* 18 (July 1895): 485.

60   Young never worked among the Blackfoot.

61   Egerton R. Young, *When the Blackfeet Went South: And Other Stories* (London: Wyman and Sons, n.d.), 9.

62   Rutherdale, *Women and the White Man's God*, 36–37.

63   John McDougall, *Pathfinding on Plain and Prairie: Stirring Scenes of Life in the Canadian North-West* (Toronto: William Briggs, 1898), 16.

64   John McDougall, *In the Days of the Red River Rebellion*, ed. Susan Jackel (Edmonton: University of Alberta Press, 1983), 270.

65 John McDougall, *A Criticism: Indian Wigwams and Northern Campfires* (Toronto: William Briggs, 1895) 12–13.

66 McDougall, *Pathfinding on Plain and Prairie*, 13.

67 McDougall, *In the Days of the Red River Rebellion*, 302.

68 McDougall, *Pathfinding on Plain and Prairie*, 12–13.

69 Ibid., 12.

70 Treaty 7 Elders, *The True Spirit and Original Intent of Treaty 7*, 267.

71 Ibid., 266–68.

72 Ibid., 263.

73 Carter, *Capturing Women*, 201.

seven

The "S " Word: Reclaiming "Esquao"

for Aboriginal Women

MURIEL STANLEY VENNE

As Kristin Burnett demonstrates in the previous chapter, over the past decade, anti-racist feminists and (post)-colonial historians have highlighted how negative stereotypes of Aboriginal women helped to construct White settler societies in the late nineteenth century. In this speech, which is an updated version of the one presented at the "Unsettled Pasts" conference, Muriel Stanley Venne recounts the ways that the "S" word continues to have a negative impact on Aboriginal women in their daily lives and interactions with non-Aboriginal peoples, the police, and the state. She advocates reclaiming a stylized version of the Cree word for "woman" – "Esquao" – in order to overcome the legacy of racism in western Canada and to foster pride among Aboriginal women and their communities.

Born at Lamont, Alberta, Muriel Stanley Venne has dedicated herself as an activist and spokesperson for Métis and, more generally, Aboriginal peoples' rights in provincial, national, and international forums. In 1973, Premier Lougheed appointed her as one of the first seven commissioners of the Alberta Human Rights Commission. Since then, she has worked tirelessly to inform Aboriginal peoples of their human and legal rights, and to draw public and official attention to contemporary violations. As the president and founder of the Institute for the Advancement of Aboriginal Women, she played a leading role in the creation of the Annual Esquao Awards, which recognize Aboriginal women's achievements. Through the organization, she has also lent her expertise on issues confronting First Nations and Métis women in contemporary settings. "The 'S' Word: Reclaiming Esquao for Aboriginal Women," highlights the necessity of confronting negative stereotypes and racism by fostering cross-cultural dialogues among the diverse segments of the feminist and activist community, and between Indigenous peoples and government agencies.

Before I begin, I want to tell you that I am not a historian, nor an academic; I'm an activist who has managed to survive throughout these years. I grew up at Whitford, Alberta, which was named after my mother's uncle, Andrew Whitford, for whom the two towns were named. I wanted to believe that he was my great-grandfather, but my great-grandfather's name was Philip Whitford; his second wife, Rachel Bangs, was my grandmother's mom.

This is coincidental to me because, without knowing my great-grandmother's name, I named my only daughter Rachelle. I mention this because, as was the case with many Métis or "half-breed" women, my grandmother's heritage and identity were hidden. My grandmother was not allowed to speak Cree in her home; so neither my mother nor I learned Cree. I consider that a great loss.

Background

My activist ideas sprang from wondering as a child why my beloved grandmother was not treated with the same respect as my grandfather. I could not understand why.

In 1980, after a televised interview, I was phoned and was threatened with a lawsuit by my Aunt Emma to keep quiet about my heritage; otherwise, she would sue me. She stated very emphatically that her father, Robert Littlechild, was an Englishman – which he was – and that was the end of it. She and her sisters denied their own mother. Needless to say, we ended up in a big argument, which continues to be an issue in my family and with my relatives to this day. The shame remains.

By the way, my Aunt Emma is the youngest of the five Littlechild girls. She achieved her high school diploma, went to one-year Normal School, and taught in various schools in Alberta for thirty-seven years.

So you can understand why the title of this piece is "Esquao," the beautiful stylized word that means "Woman" in Cree. In preparing my conference presentation, I reflected on the hurt and the injustice that Aunt Emma suffered; the need to redeem this word for my grandmother, and for me and all my sisters, my cousins, my mother, and all of the other beautiful women I know who have been called the word "Squaw," or thought of as a "Squaw." In my experience, and the experiences of my sisters, this word has never been used in anything but a derogatory manner. When my Ukrainian-Canadian brother-in-law tells me that there were a couple of "squaws" in the bar, or that the mother of the man who was wrongfully thrown in jail as a drunk (when he was actually a heart attack victim) was called "Squaw" on the street, I cringe.

So – what happened? How did "Esquao" come to be?

First of all, in my observation, when a person is called a "Squaw" she is no longer a human being who has the same feelings as other women. She is something less than other women. From the Hudson's Bay Company's record of my great Aunt's name, written "E-Squaw," it was evident that the colonists did not know how to pronounce the word "esquao" or "iskiwiw," as linguists have pointed out to me. I have always explained that the word "esquao" was meant to be a stylized version of the word, and besides, it was probably a priest that first wrote and spelled "iskiwiw."

What have we done?

We have taken this beautiful word and reclaimed it for our own. In fact, I was delighted and astonished that there is a mystery car driving around Calgary and surrounding area with "Esquao" licence plates!

The idea to stylize the word came to me when I was standing in front of the upscale fashion store "Escada" in Edmonton Centre and I said to myself, if they can have "Escada," then we can have "Esquao"!

After nine years of determination and promotion, we have just completed our ninth Annual Esquao Awards Gala, in which we honour Aboriginal women across the province who are nominated from their community. These awards are non-competitive, completely community-driven, and are refined into categories to which each nominee is placed. Almost a thousand people attended on 5 May 2004 at the Ramada Edmonton Inn. The Institute for the Advancement of Aboriginal Women was formed because of the dire need to have a support system and power base from which Aboriginal women could draw strength and know that other women would support them. The incident where a female Aboriginal law student was charged with assault and needed community support started it all: IAAW was created to help her.

IAAW basically does two things – we honour Aboriginal women and deal with the issues that confront them. To illustrate why I became so concerned, in December 1995, the *Globe and Mail* reported that 470 Aboriginal women had been reported missing. The Royal Canadian Mounted Police came up with this figure when they accessed computer databases in an attempt to find a missing Aboriginal woman. In their search, they found the bodies of two other Aboriginal women, who had not been reported missing, in a park outside of Saskatoon. In an attempt to find out what was going on, I phoned "K" Division in Edmonton and spoke to an officer. When I told him of the article, he replied, "I'm not surprised."

IAAW gained intervener standing in the Connie and Ty Jacobs fatality inquiry from 1 February to 16 December 1999. (I know this last date because I was the very last to testify). In another case, Jack Ramsay pleaded guilty to indecent assault in Melfort, Saskatchewan, after being accused of raping a fourteen-year-old girl from Pelican Narrows, where he was stationed and the officer in charge. We have this courageous woman as one of our members who can count on us for support and help. At one of our chapter meetings in Cold Lake, the organizer mentioned, "You are a hero." This case is still in the courts with a lawsuit against Ramsay for damages and redress. "Achieving Social Justice" has been our passion and our theme for all our events and activities. Everything we do has this objective in mind, as we honour our women and deal with the issues that we are confronted with.

In this regard, we have created the Social Justice Awards. In 2001, we honoured City of Edmonton Detective Freeman Taylor for solving the Joyce Cardinal murder case after eight years of pursuit and investigation. Joyce's name is one of the 110 we have of Aboriginal women in western Canada who have been murdered with no charges laid. We were able to help bring closure for the family and attention to the situation many of our women find themselves in. Unfortunately, or fortunately, the terrible murders in Vancouver have helped us in approaching the police forces and bringing this to the public's attention.

My thrill and reward is to see Aboriginal women accomplishing their goals and being accepted, as they should be. We present our bouquet of red roses to as many women as we know of who have been admitted to the Bar, who have graduated from their social-work class, or any other graduating class.

To add to my hope and optimism, the Amiskwaciy Academy, an Aboriginal high school, officially opened two years ago in Edmonton. This is so exciting because of the wonderful atmosphere of success, accomplishment, and respect that permeates the school, with Dr. Phyllis Cardinal as principal.

I would like you to join with me in saying the beautiful word "Esquao" so that never again will the other word be used.

eight

White Sauce and Chinese Chews:

Recipes as Postcolonial Metaphors

MARY LEAH DE ZWART

When feminist scholars first sought to demonstrate that the "personal is political," they drew attention to women's food production in the home as unpaid labour that was integral to the maintenance and persistence of ethnic identity. Drawing upon (post)colonial history and theory, however, Mary Leah de Zwart joins a growing list of scholars who are re-evaluating domestic spaces as sites for colonial agendas. Just as the domestic spaces and social arrangements of Aboriginal peoples came under the imperial eye of missionaries like Maclean, Young, and McDougall and the Department of Indian Affairs (see Sarah Carter's contribution in chapter 9), so too did food become a symbol and metaphor for imperial and nation-building projects at the turn of the twentieth century.

De Zwart places two domestic science manuals used in home economics public school classrooms across western Canada within a (post)colonial and international framework; she argues that ordinary recipes can be interpreted as metaphors, or cultural narratives, that represented (and reflected changes in) discourses that emerged out of race and class conflicts in colonial settings. While first-wave feminists initiated and promoted the Home Economics Movement in the first decades of the twentieth century, Nadine Kozak demonstrates in chapter 10 that these women also contributed to motherhood-advice literature that prevailed in the interwar decades. Both movements drew upon scientific management models that sought to reinforce the domestic sphere as women's primary vocation and to acculturate rural and immigrant women, and their children, to urban, middle-class, and British-Canadian citizenship ideals. From her reading of Chinese Chews and white sauce recipes, de Zwart concludes that home economics courses, which were directed at the future mothers of the nation, could have the same political impact as the discriminatory or restrictive legislation that emanated from governments.

[The white sauce] recipe is given first because it will be referred to so frequently. The children should be taught at the first to make a smooth white sauce.[1]

In 1916, Fannie Twiss, the first director of home economics education for the Province of Saskatchewan, informed public school teachers about the foregoing imperative to make white sauce a staple product for the hot school lunch program. She, along with others, believed that white sauce was a major civilizing influence in cooking: few foods could not be enriched or elevated by its addition.[2] I became aware of the educational impact of white sauce when I opened up the filing cabinets in my first home economics classroom and found a large number of recipes that included this bland, inoffensive sauce. As I studied the history of race and nation, I began to see white sauce as a metaphor for the ways in which early home economics education perpetuated White identity when it set the course for women's education in Canada.

In order to develop further the idea of recipes as metaphor, I examine two domestic manuals: *Girls' Home Manual*, which was written by Annie Juniper and published in 1913, and *Foods, Nutrition and Home*

Management Manual, which was authored by Jessie McLenaghen and published in British Columbia in 1931.[3] Both manuals were used widely in the public schools of British Columbia and the Canadian prairies. When placed in the context of contemporary postcolonial history and theory, these sources reveal how recipes acted as historical narratives of the relationships between daily life and political events. The name given to the recipe; the ingredients selected for inclusion; the quantities produced; the wording of the method; all of these details reflected prevailing class and race relations, assumptions, and biases. I locate my study as a colonial project within postcolonial theory, described by Nicholas Thomas as a "socially transformative endeavour located within a larger movement and bound politically and racially to it."[4] While Lisa Heldke proposes that recipes can be used to theorize about the use of power to oppress, Colleen Cotter argues that socio-cultural assumptions reveal themselves when recipes are viewed as cultural narratives.[5] Taken together, these two viewpoints support the application of postcolonial theory – which takes a basic position against imperialism and Eurocentricity – to home economics: a field of study that takes as its mission the improvement of daily life for families. This chapter asks, How did the domestic manuals exemplify and perpetuate colonialist viewpoints in the public school system? How do recipes act as micro-narratives of history?

Background to Home Economics in the School System

In order to view the role of domestic manuals in context, it is necessary to understand how home economics became part of the public school system. Home economics courses were added to curricula at the turn of the twentieth century, during decades when the structure of public education in Canada became firmly established. The purposes of education between 1900 and 1935 followed the principles of progressive education, which brought together child-centred and practical education.[6] Adherents of both approaches subscribed to the view that the whole child went to school and should be taught by hand and heart as well as by head.[7] This perspective opened the school door to manual training for boys and, by default, home economics for girls.

An educational phenomenon known as the Macdonald-Robertson education movement was responsible for the introduction of manual training in public schools.[8] This movement, linked to the New Education (the name given to progressive education in Canada), began in

1899 as a seed-growing contest concocted by James W. Robertson, the National Dairy Commissioner for Canada, and Sir William Macdonald, the tobacco merchant and philanthropist. Robertson was keenly interested in preserving the quality of rural life and convinced Macdonald to fund manual training schools for a period of three years, after which the schools would potentially carry on under their own steam. After Robertson visited British Columbia in 1900, manual training programs (for boys only) were set up in Vancouver and Victoria.

The resulting gap in girls' education was filled quickly and conveniently by the introduction of home economics in the schools. Adelaide Hoodless, the acknowledged founder of home economics in Canada, had attended the International Council of Women meeting at the 1893 Chicago World's Fair. Hoodless worked with other philanthropic-minded women to organize the first meeting of the National Council of Women of Canada in Toronto later that year. Prestige was added with the election of Lady Aberdeen, wife of the governor general of Canada, as first president of the National Council of Women. In 1894, Hoodless convinced the National Council of Women to pass a motion in support of manual training for girls because "such training will greatly conduce to the general welfare of Canadian homes."[9] Local Councils of Women across Canada took up the cause of domestic science with a passion, although not without controversy about its purposes. Would it limit women's opportunities rather than open them up? Was it intended to train servants or relegate women to the home? These questions were not satisfactorily answered; consequently, they contributed further to the conflicting purposes of the new education for women.

The entry of home economics into the British Columbia school system differed from other school subjects because it depended almost entirely on independent promotion by women's groups followed by the goodwill of the school boards. In 1903, after much lobbying by the Victoria Local Council of Women, the Victoria School Board agreed to provide a classroom and to pay for maintenance costs and half a year's salary for a home economics teacher. The Local Council raised four hundred dollars for the outfitting of the room, mostly from personal donations by its members.[10]

The history of the home economics movement has been studied from philosophical, global education, and feminist perspectives.[11] Its alignment with the promotion of White, northern European (usually British) culture has been mostly disregarded except for some research into African colonies, which supports the contention that early home economics practices were modeled on British norms. For example, Deborah Gaitskell relates how early mission education in Africa before 1910 "set great store by Christian home-making and the schooling of future wives."[12] Judith Waudo remarks that, even today, home economics in Kenya retains many British practices such as giving emphasis to potato cookery instead of indigenous foods like cassava or plantains.[13]

Education in the White settler colony of Canada had some similarities to colonies of occupation in the promulgation of British values.[14] In his study of twentieth-century childhood, Neil Sutherland proposed that an underlying motive of education was the desire to "Canadianize" all immigrants other than those of British origin.[15] Domestic science, according to George Tomkins, was seen as an important way to remedy the defects of the poor, who were thought to be deficient in moral fortitude, and New Canadians, who were seen as short on loyalty to their new country.[16] Much like missionaries who worked among Aboriginal peoples (described by Erickson and Burnett in chapters 2 and 6), early Canadian educators saw their non-British pupils as sadly lacking in proper habits of daily life. In 1918, a Saskatchewan school inspector reported on the labour of an itinerant home economics teacher, Mary Hiltz, who worked in schools populated by Ruthenian (or Ukrainian) immigrants:

Many Ruthenian schools are engaging in [home economics instruction] and others will follow as soon as Miss Hiltz has visited them. Wonderful possibilities lie before those engaged in this work. These children must be taught how to sew and cook as well as how to read and cipher. They must be taught concerning our home life – our modes of housekeeping. Politeness, table etiquette, cleanliness, hygiene, et. [sic], must be inculcated in these schools. The work being done by Miss Hiltz will assist materially in accomplishing this desired end.[17]

In many ways, homemaking education in Africa and public school home economics in Saskatchewan did not differ substantially in their aims. Both were intended to promote White cultural values, specifically British or northern European values, with groups that were considered inferior by virtue of their race, class, or both. The interesting point about White cultural values is that they appear to be culturally neutral unless they are examined in context.[18] Claire Pajaczowska and Lola Young label this phenomenon the "absent centre of White ethnicity."[19] The (mostly) White women who spread home economics education also spread White, northern European/North American imperial and cultural power. Examination of the domestic manuals in connection with contemporaneous events, however, points out historical discrepancies between the imposition of White culture and societal realities.

Girls' Home Manual

The 187-page *Girls' Home Manual of Cookery, Home Management, Home Nursing and Laundry*, published in 1913, was the first home economics textbook in British Columbia. The author, Annie Bessie Juniper, dedicated the book to Margaret Jenkins, a Victoria politician and Local Council of Women organizer. Juniper was British-born and had received her home economics training in England. She had also held home economics teaching positions in three other Canadian provinces before being appointed as the Supervisor of Household Science for the Victoria School Board in 1911.[20] David Wilson, officer in charge of the Free Text-Book Branch of the Department of Education proudly announced the addition of *Girls' Home Manual* to the free textbooks list in 1914, declaring that "Domestic or Household Science now justly holds a place in nearly every modern school curriculum."[21] The manual became part of Juniper's legacy. It was described in a 1926 Victoria newspaper article, ten years after she had left her teaching position in that city, as "an enduring souvenir of her connection with [the Education] department."[22]

In the introduction to *Girls' Home Manual*, Annie Juniper indicated that the book covered a three-year course in Household Science "in the hope that girls, not only at school, but in after life also, may find it helpful in making them more efficient in the noble art of 'home-making.'"[23] Almost half of the manual was comprised of recipes, with one-quarter of those being candies and desserts and two pages given over to white sauce. In addition to a table of weights and measures and a list of necessary kitchen equipment, Juniper listed essential spices for the kitchen: curry powder, cloves, mace, cinnamon, and celery salt. The choice of curry powder is worthy of note. It has a curious history with the word *curry* derived from the Tamil word *kari*, which refers to spicy vegetable dishes served with rice. According to Uma Narayan, the concept of curry powder was invented by British colonialists in India to describe a specific mixture of spices, which then became a fixture in British cooking.[24] Curry powder was appropriated as a standard condiment in Juniper's domestic manual, but it had no relationship to the actual status of East Indians in Canada: only five persons of East Indian origin were allowed to immigrate to Canada in 1913.[25]

Four pages were spent on combustion and management of the kitchen range, with the inclusion of two unusual ways to cook food: the fireless cooker (a type of thermos) and paper-bag cookery. Both of these cooking methods were intended to encourage thrift on the part of the poor, who might not have proper cooking ranges, but would have access to thermoses or expensive single-use paper bags. In the extensive list of recommended books and magazines at the end of *Girls' Home Manual*, Juniper listed *Paper Bag Cookery* by Alexis Soyer (1810–1858), known as the greatest chef of the nineteenth century in Britain and inventor of the soup kitchen.[26] The inclusion of paper-bag cookery was an example of Juniper's wholesale adaptation of British methods to colonial home economics education. However, paper-bag cookery, which involved steaming food in parchment or butcher paper, never became standard procedure in British Columbia home economics classrooms.

Further knowledge essential for the noble art of homemaking included: a chapter on table setting and etiquette, the duties of the waitress, how to clear a table, and how to wash up after a meal single-handed. Hygienic forms of floor and wall coverings were indicated, while a lift from the basement through the kitchen to the top floor of the house was recommended to save steps for the housewife. According to the author, cheap lace curtains should be avoided; one should buy the best linen possible, as it would prove to be cheapest in the end. Simplicity and sanitation in all respects was emphasized: furniture should have straight lines rather than curves and decorations, described by Juniper as "tawdry," because she thought they harboured dust and dirt.[27] The recommendations seemed to be far from the realities of pioneer life in British Columbia. On one hand, *Girls' Home Manual* seemed to reflect middle-class daily life in England; on the other, it provided glimpses of ways to elevate one's class position in future home life. Juniper did not use the word "family"; rather, she referred to the necessity of being efficient in the kitchen for the health of the "inmates." She used an industrial model as her example: "No workman can do good work without proper tools."[28] In this respect, she reflected the growing perspective – pioneered by women such as Christine Frederick – of the home as factory, rather than moral centre, with women as consumers rather than producers.[29]

The Political Agenda of Education

At least two significant political changes took place in the province of British Columbia between the publication of *Girls' Home Manual* in 1913 and *Foods, Nutrition and Home Management* in 1931 that influenced the contents chosen for inclusion in a domestic manual intended for use by girls at school and in their future families. One was the increasing racialization of British Columbia and the second was the societal move towards social efficiency that was expressed in curriculum reform.

Some blatant aspects of racism in British Columbia have been well documented, such as the anti-Asian riots in Vancouver in 1907 and the episode of the Komagata Maru in Vancouver Harbour in 1914.[30] Following these incidents, most racist occurrences were more subtle as the White population increased and power differentials based on race became institutionalized. Public statements made by home economics educators corresponded to Timothy Stanley's argument that White supremacy was becoming deeply-embedded in British Columbia society in the early years of the twentieth century.[31] For example, Alice Ravenhill, a highly respected British home economist who immigrated to Vancouver Island in 1911, clearly linked the empire, victory in battle, domestic science, and good breeding in an article she wrote for the *Women's Institute Quarterly* in 1915: the next soldiers of the empire, she wrote, were to be well-born thanks to eugenics, and well-bred thanks to domestic science.[32] Similarly, Rosalinde Esson Young, wife of Henry Esson Young, one-time minister of education, spoke to the Home Economics section of the Provincial Teachers' Institute in 1924, suggesting that the goal of domestic science was to imbue the young with high ideals of home life. This would only be possible, Young intoned, if every Anglo-Saxon woman gave birth to at least four children.[33] Such racialization of home economics did not necessarily coincide with racist practices, but did imply White privilege. Every home economics practice that reinforced British culture precluded the inclusion of other cultures.

Social efficiency was a catchword for the Survey of the British Columbia School System, conducted by J.H. Putman and George M. Weir in 1924–25.[34] The survey included a submission from the Victoria Local

Council of Women that emphasized the pressing need for home economics instruction. The Local Council reflected contemporary gender norms, declaring that the home was the "natural and rightful domain of women" and, therefore, home economics was a logical form of study. Women were the "keepers of the health of the nation"; the life of tomorrow depended on the education of future mothers and home economics should be given its rightful place in a national and international scheme of education.[35] Experts would tell women how to run their homes; the nation would be more efficient as a result. Home economics education overlapped with motherhood education in the first part of the twentieth century. As Katherine Arnup and Nadine Kozak (see chapter 10 for the latter) argue, women were asked to give up the power of their own knowledge and turn homemaking and family decision-making over to specialists.[36] Franca Iacovetta has likewise explored the role that "experts" played in instructing immigrant women in post-World War II Canada to be good citizens.[37] With poverty and regional disparities given no consideration, immigrants were criticized for insisting on their own ways and expected to conform to middle-class ideals of good housekeeping. Although *Foods, Nutrition and Home Management* was compiled well before the Second World War, it foregrounds Iacovetta's work, demonstrating the desire to use homemaking education to achieve a national identity based on White, middle-class, and British standards.

Foods, Nutrition, and Home Management Manual

The Putman-Weir School Survey made sixteen recommendations for change in the British Columbia school system, one of which was the appointment of a "thoroughly competent woman" to head home economics education. Although many of the recommendations were not implemented until a change in government in 1933, one immediate result was the 1926 appointment of Jessie McLenaghen as Director of Home Economics for the British Columbia Department of Education. McLenaghen was an experienced home economics teacher and supervisor who had taught grade school in Ontario and Manitoba, and worked as an itinerant home economics teacher at the Saskatoon Normal School in Saskatchewan and at the New York State Teachers College.[38]

In the foreword to *Foods, Nutrition, and Home Management Manual*, McLenaghen claimed that it would "prove that Home Economics is not an 'unprepared' subject" because students would be able to get

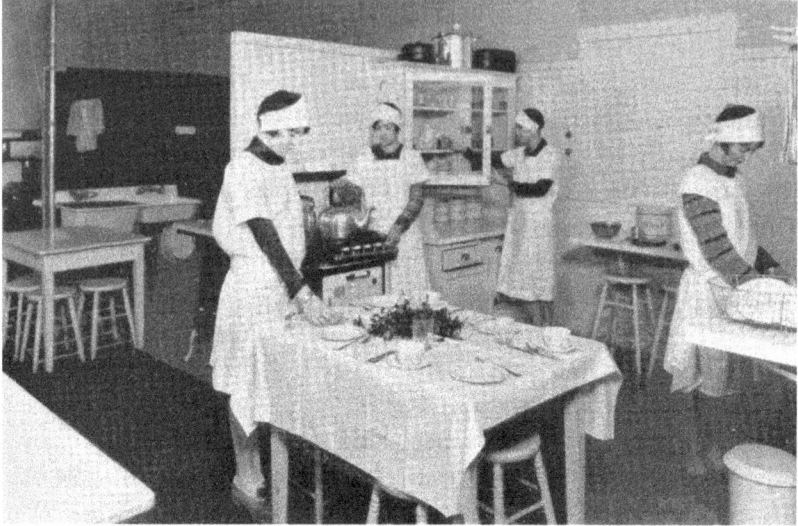

In the first junior high school in British Columbia, opened in 1927, the home economics classroom was set up to emulate a family, reflecting the increasing role of education in promoting social values. British Columbia Archives, G-00003

information from the printed page instead of copying out notes and recipes.[39] In particular, McLenaghen declared that ensuring that the book was family-oriented was essential; portion sizes in the recipes should be sufficient for the average family of six and lend themselves to preparation in the home. The move to family-sized recipes, accompanied by unit kitchens in which four students approximated family roles, was part of a major shift in home economics as curricula were adjusted to suit shifting ideals of domesticity and motherhood, ideals that increasingly in the 1930s represented wives and mothers as responsible for their family's happiness.[40] The table setting section was distinctly value- and class-oriented: "No amount of lavishness and perfection in the preparation of the food will compensate for poor arrangement and service in the dining-room.... *Paper flowers are not in good taste* [italics in original]."[41] Questions followed the information: "Which is preferable, coarse table-linen which is well laundered, or fine table-linen poorly laundered?"[42] This question drew class lines: it discriminated between the ignorant habits of newcomers and the educated, cultured Canadian.

The food preparation section was over one hundred pages long. Food was categorized into beverages, fruits, cereals, soups, vegetables, salads, eggs, flour mixtures, stiff doughs, desserts, candy, meat, fish, poultry, canning, jelly-making, sandwiches, lunch-box requirements, invalid cookery, and infant-feeding. There was certainly no pasta and only one rice recipe (for pudding). The recipes were traditional British ones: matrimonial cake, bread and butter pudding, blanc mange, Welsh rarebit, shepherd's pie, and kippered herring. Three pages were given up to white sauce and its variations. The only recipe in *Foods, Nutrition and Home Management* that did not have an English name was Chinese Chews (see appendix), a type of cookie made of white sugar, flour, dates, walnuts, and eggs.

The Genealogy of Chinese Chews

The scope of this chapter does not permit a detailed analysis of the various homemaking injunctions in the domestic manuals. However, the Chinese Chews recipe, viewed over time as an historical narrative, provides an intriguing way to trace societal changes. Dates were a common ingredient in pioneer cooking, imported not from China, but from North Africa and the Middle East. They usually came in enormous barrels to the local dry goods store and were the one fruit, other than home canning, available during the winter. They were used in popular recipes such as matrimonial cake and squares – but only in Chinese Chews did they reach their exotic potential. The original Chinese Chews recipe had a unique, complicated method: perhaps this was what allowed it to be labelled "Chinese." The Chinese descriptor signified difference that did not have to be culturally authentic or accurate, but simply not British.

A commercial version of Chinese Chews was published in 1932 in the *Purity Cook Book*.[43] This version specified Purity Flour over any other brand. The procedure was shortened to six steps and simplified to cutting into squares before rolling into balls. No specific baking time was given: the mixture was supposed to remain in the oven until baked, whatever that meant to the cook. The absence of this instruction indicates that the recipe book was directed towards cooks with a certain amount of baking experience, but not so much experience that the cook did not need to be reminded to use Purity Flour. Cooking was "no longer a democratic, feminine discourse" but a standardized, commercialized procedure.[44]

Three Web site recipes located in 2002 (see appendix) provide examples of cultural adaptations of Chinese Chews; not coincidentally, they indicate how recipes reflect changing community social values. *A Treasury of Jewish Holiday Baking* described Chinese Chews as a wonderful recipe that tasted rich, but was not, tasted buttery, but was kosher, seemed fancy, but was easy to make.[45] The directions for the Jewish Chinese Chews were concise and direct: three main steps with clear indications of what the batter would look like when cooked. Sifting of dry ingredients was eliminated, as was rolling the cooked dough into balls before dipping into powdered sugar. Use of a food processor was suggested, and the final product had become convenient squares rather than tedious hand-rolled balls.

Extreme alteration of Chinese Chews occurred in a 2002 newspaper advice column devoted to quick cooking tips. A mother had requested a treat for her son who had a sweet tooth, but only a hot plate to cook on in his university room. In the advice columnist's answer, she included a No Bake Chinese Chews recipe in which the original ingredients of dates, walnuts, sugar, flour, baking powder, and eggs had changed to a no-bake combination of chocolate chips, butterscotch chips, salted peanuts, and Chinese dry noodles.[46] Preparation time was cut from ten minutes of fiddling with dough and thirty minutes of baking, to one minute of popping open packages and five minutes in a double boiler, with the results plopped onto wax paper.

Chinese Chews finally became "Chinese" on a 2002 Chinese New Year Web site. The recipe was included as an example of the sweets that Chinese parents expected their children to eat "to get their bodies prepared for the sweetness that the New Year will bring."[47] A self-fulfilling prophecy came true: The cookies became part of Chinese tradition because they were labelled Chinese, not because they were linked to the culture.

Conclusion

In following the genealogy of Chinese Chews, both ingredients and name are significant. The first domestic manual that I examined, *Girls' Home Manual*, did not include any food outside British culture. The subject matter appeared to be lifted from the experiences of the manual's British author, Annie Juniper. The Putman-Weir School Survey asked for someone to take charge of home economics in British Columbia in order to promote social efficiency in training young women to be good homemakers. Implicitly, they aimed to produce good Canadian citizens. The inclusion of the Chinese Chews recipe could be considered as a small example of the need of White people to have an exotic "Other" to contrast with their own identity.[48] The use of the word "Chinese" initially made the recipe in *Foods, Nutrition and Home Management* seem more special, and the embedded British culture more natural.

Commercial elements in the recipe were introduced via the Purity Flour version, which changed the recipe to represent particular groups (i.e., *kosher* and *quick*). The inclusion of Chinese Chews on the Chinese New Year Web site confounds and confuses the concept of Othering; the recipe that might have initially been an example of culinary imperialism finally became absorbed by the culture to which it was originally (and falsely) attributed.[49] Jean Duruz has called this turnabout in food culture "eating back"; it is a way of handling differences without being patronizing or colonial.[50] While space does not permit discussion of this concept, further study may show that treating food preparation and recipes in an open manner is one small way to work toward an anti-colonial, anti-imperial society.

The purpose of this writing has been to demonstrate how humble recipes in mild-mannered domestic manuals offer ways of examining colonial power and cultural meanings and providing a window into the past that impinges on the present. The appearance of the Chinese Chews recipe in *Foods, Nutrition and Home Management* was important; it signified the initial stages by which Canadians grappled with the exotic and the unfamiliar in Canadian culture, which came to fruition in 2002 Internet versions of the recipes. The recipes used in the domestic manuals contributed to colonialism and the belief in White (British) cultural superiority in the same way, if not the same magnitude, as any discriminatory or restrictive laws imposed by government.

Appendix

FOODS, NUTRITION AND HOME MANAGEMENT MANUAL CHINESE CHEWS

¾ cup flour

1 tsp. baking powder

¼ tsp. salt

2 eggs

1 c. white sugar

1 c. walnuts

1 c. dates

1. Sift flour and measure. Add baking powder and salt and sift again.
2. Beat eggs until light.
3. Add sugar and dry ingredients.
4. Add walnuts and dates, chopped.
5. Press into a greased pan (8 by 8 inches).
6. Cook in a slow oven (300° F – 325° F.) for 20–25 min.
7. When a crust forms (after about 15 min.) it is advisable to mix the crust into the softer centre portion with a fork.
8. Replace in oven and cook 10–15 min. longer; then repeat No. 7.
9. When cooked, lift out in spoonfuls and roll in the palm of the hand.
10. Roll in powdered sugar and store in a covered tin box.

Foods, Nutrition and Home Management Manual. Victoria, BC: King's Printer, 1942.

PURITY CHINESE CHEWS
¾ cup sifted Purity Flour
1 teaspoon baking powder
1 cup white sugar
¼ teaspoon salt
1 cup stoned dates, chopped
1 cup walnuts, chopped
2 eggs

Sift flour with baking powder, sugar and salt. Add dates and nuts. To this mixture add the eggs, which have been beaten until light. Spread as thinly as possible in well-greased shallow pan, and bake in moderate oven (350° F) for 20 minutes. When baked, cut into small squares and roll into balls. Then roll in fine granulated sugar.

Purity Cook Book. Toronto: Purity Flour Mills, [1932] 1945, 67.

JEWISH CHINESE CHEWS
¾ cup all-purpose flour
1 teaspoon baking powder
¼ teaspoon salt
1 cup granulated sugar
1 cup coarsely chopped walnuts
1 cup coarsely chopped dates
2 eggs, beaten
confectioner's sugar, for topping

Preheat the oven to 325° F. Lightly grease an 8" square pan. In a mixing bowl, stir together the flour, baking powder, and salt. Stir in the sugar, walnuts, and dates. Mix well, then add the beaten eggs to bind the mixture. Spread the batter in the pan. Bake for about 25 minutes, or until the batter is set and dry-looking. Cool very slightly, then cut into squares and dip the tops in confectioner's sugar. [Can be made entirely in food processor.]

<http://www.jewishfood-list.com/recipes/cookies/bars_brownies/
barschinesechews01.html>
Retrieved 10 June 2002

NO BAKE CHINESE CHEWS
1 (6-oz) package semi-sweet chocolate chips
1 (6-oz) package butterscotch chips
1 cup salted peanuts
1 can (3 ½ oz) Chinese dry noodles

In top of double boiler combine chocolate and butterscotch chips. In bottom of double boiler put hot (not boiling) water (don't let it touch bottom of top part of double boiler). Heat the chips, stirring occasionally, until smooth. Stir in the peanuts and noodles. Drop by teaspoonfuls onto waxed paper and let cool until set.

<http://www.hamiltonspectator.com/bidwell/539040.html>
Retrieved 10 June 2002

CHINESE CHEWS
Made in a shallow cookie pan and cut into squares then rolled and tossed in confectioner's sugar. Chewy and wonderful!

1 ½ cups cake flour
½ teaspoon salt
½ cup confectioner's sugar
2 cups pureed dates
2 cups white sugar
2 teaspoons baking powder
4 eggs

1. Preheat oven to 350° F (180° C).
2. Mix dry ingredients except confectioner's sugar. Add nuts and dates.
3. Then add eggs which have been lightly beaten. Mix well.
4. Press mixture into ungreased cookie sheet as thin as possible. Bake for 15–20 minutes.
5. Cut into 1–2 inch squares while hot. Roll into balls as soon as the squares are cool enough to handle then roll in confectioner's sugar. Allow to cool completely before eating.

<http://cookie.allrecipes.com/AZ/ChineseChews.asp>

ENDNOTES

1   Fannie Twiss, *The Rural School Luncheon* (Regina: King's Printer, 1916), 22.

2   Laura Shapiro, *Perfection Salad: Women and Cooking at the Turn of the Century* (New York: Farrar, Straus and Giroux, 1986), 91.

3   Annie Juniper, *Girls' Home Manual of Cookery, Home Management, Home Nursing and Laundry* (Victoria: King's Printer, 1913); *Foods, Nutrition and Home Management Manual* (Victoria: King's Printer, 1931).

4   Nicholas Thomas, *Colonialism's Culture* (Princeton: Princeton University Press, 1994), 1.

5   Lisa Heldke, "Recipes for Theory Making" *Hypatia* 3 (1988): 27; Colleen Cotter, "Claiming a Piece of the Pie: How the Language of Recipes Defines Community," in *Recipes for Reading: Community Cookbooks, Stories, Histories*, ed. A. Bower (Amherst: University of Massachusetts Press, 1997), 62.

6   Neil Sutherland, *Children in English-Canadian Society: Framing the Twentieth Century Consensus*, 2d ed. (Waterloo: Wilfrid Laurier University Press, 2000), 156.

7   J. W. Robertson, "Education for the improvement of rural conditions," *Semi-Weekly Patriot*, 25 July 1907, Robertson papers, Special Collections Division, University of British Columbia Library.

8   Sutherland, *Children in English-Canadian Society*, 182–201.

9   Naomi Griffiths, *The Splendid Vision: Centennial History of the National Council of Women of Canada 1893–1993* (Ottawa: Carleton University Press, 1993), 42.

10   Elizabeth Berry Lightfoot and Margaret Maynard, *The introduction and progress of home economics in British Columbia* [1896–1941] (Centennial project of the Teachers of Home Economics Specialist Association, 1971), 1.

11   Mary Leah de Zwart, "Home Economics Education in British Columbia 1913–1936: Through Postcolonial Eyes" (Ph.D. diss., University of British Columbia, 2003), 16–26.

12   Deborah Gaitskell, "At home with hegemony? Coercion and consent in African girls' education for domesticity in South Africa before 1910," in *Contesting Colonial Hegemony: State and Society in Africa and India*, ed. D. Engels and S. Marks (London: British Academic Press, 1994), 128.

13   Judith Waudo, "Home Economics in Kenya: Challenges and Perspectives," *Curriculum Technology Quarterly* 12 (2002): <http://www.ascd.org/publications/ctq/2002fall/toc.html> (14 January 2004), ASCD Web site. Par. 2.

14   Anna Johnston and Alan Lawson, "Settler Colonies," in *A Companion to Postcolonial Studies*, ed. H. Schwarz and S. Ray (Malden: Blackwell, 2000), 360–76.

15   Sutherland, *Children in English-Canadian Society*, 156.

16   George S. Tomkins, *A Common Countenance: Stability and Change in the Canadian Curriculum* (Scarborough, ON: Prentice-Hall, 1986), 120.

17   J.T.M. Anderson, "Saskatchewan-Household Progress," *Agricultural Gazette* 5, no. 10 (1918): 1002–1003.

18   Ruth Frankenberg, *White Women, Race Matters: The Social Construction of Whiteness* (Minneapolis: University of Minnesota Press, 1993), 2.

19   C. Pajaczowska and L. Young, "Racism, Representation, Psychoanalysis," in *Race, Culture and Difference*, ed. J. Donald and A. Rattansi (London: Sage Publications in association with The Open University, 1992), 202.

20 M.L. de Zwart, "Past Roots: Annie B. Juniper," *Canadian Home Economics Journal* 48, no. 3 (1998): 101.

21 David Wilson, "Free Text-Book Branch Report," 47th Annual Public Schools Report of the British Columbia Department of Education (Victoria: King's Printer, 1914), A74.

22 "Former Victoria Teacher Now English Principal," *Victoria Daily Colonist*, 26 August 1926, 1.

23 *Girls' Home Manual*, 2.

24 Uma Narayan, "Eating Cultures: Incorporation, Identity and Indian Food," *Social Identities* 1 (1995): 63–87.

25 *Canada Year Book* (Ottawa: King's Printer, 1922–23), 207.

26 J. Strang and J. Toomre, "Alexis Soyer and the Irish Famine," in *The Great Famine and the Irish Diaspora in America*, ed. A. Gribben (Amherst: University of Massachusetts Press, 1999), 66.

27 *Girls' Home Manual*, 120.

28 Ibid., 5.

29 Janice Rutherford, "A Foot in Each Sphere: Christine Frederick and Early Twentieth-Century Advertising," *Historian* 63, no. 1 (2000): 67–87.

30 W. Peter Ward, *White Canada Forever: Popular Attitudes and Public Policy Toward Orientals in British Columbia*, 2d ed. (Montreal: McGill-Queen's University Press, 1990), 53–76, 79–93.

31 Timothy Stanley, "White Supremacy and the Rhetoric of Educational Indoctrination: A Canadian Case Study," in *Making Imperial Mentalities: Socialization and British Imperialism*, ed. J. Mangan (Manchester: Manchester University Press, 1990), 144.

32 For more information on Alice Ravenhill, see M.G. Smith, "Alice Ravenhill: International Pioneer in Home Economics," *Illinois Teacher* 33, no. 1 (1989): 10–14, or Ravenhill's own autobiography, written when she was over ninety years old: A. Ravenhill, *Alice Ravenhill: The Memoirs of an Educational Pioneer* (Toronto: Dent, 1951); Alice Ravenhill, *Women's Institute Quarterly* 1 (1915): 1, quoted in Angus McLaren, *Our Own Master Race* (Toronto: McClelland and Stewart, 1990), 26.

33 Rosalinde Esson Young, "Rejuvenation of Domestic Science," *Western Woman's Weekly*, 26 July 1924.

34 J.H. Putman and George Weir, *Survey of the School System of British Columbia* (Victoria: King's Printer, 1925).

35 Putman and Weir, *Survey of the School System*, 339.

36 K. Arnup, *Education for Motherhood: Advice for Mothers in Twentieth Century Canada* (Toronto: University of Toronto Press, 1994).

37 Franca Iacovetta, "Recipes for Democracy? Gender, Family and Making Female Citizens in Cold War Canada," in *Rethinking Canada: The Promise of Women's History*, ed. V. Strong-Boag, M. Gleason and A. Perry, 4th ed. (Don Mills: Oxford University Press, 2002), 299–312. For further reference, see Franca Iacovetta and Valerie J. Korinek, "Jell-O Salads, One-Stop Shopping, and Maria the Homemaker: The Gender Politics of Food," in *Sisters or Strangers? Immigrant, Ethnic, and Racialized Women in Canadian History*, ed. Marlene Epp, Franca Iacovetta, and Franca Swyripa (Toronto: University of Toronto Press, 2004), 190–230.

38   M.L. de Zwart, "Jessie McLenaghen," in *The Homeroom: British Columbia's History of Education Web Site*, ed. Patrick A. Dunae, [online] Nanaimo, BC: Malaspina Univesity College, 2001: <http://www.mala.bc.ca/homeroom/Content/Topics/People/Jessie.htm> (30 May, 2002).

39   Jessie McLenaghen, "Foreword," *Foods, Nutrition and Home Management Manual, Circular One* (Victoria: King's Printer, 1931), 3.

40   Mary Drake McFeely, *Can she bake a cherry pie? American women and the kitchen in the twentieth century* (Amherst: University of Massachusetts Press, 2000), 53.

41   *Foods, Nutrition and Home Management Manual*, 39.

42   Ibid.

43   *Purity Cook Book*. 2d ed. (Toronto: Purity Flour Mills, [1932] 1945), 4.

44   McFeely, *Can she bake a cherry pie?*, 50.

45   M. Kerman, "Chinese Chews": <http://www.jewishfood-list.com/recipes/cookies/bars_brownies/barschinesechews01.html> (10 June 2002), A Treasury of Jewish Holiday Baking.

46   "Red envelopes and oranges": <http://allrecipes.com/cb/w2m/seaspec/holiday/Chinesenewyear/default.asp> (10 June 2002), Allrecipes.com website.

47   "No Bake Chinese Chews," *Hamilton Spectator*, 27 February 2002: <http://www.hamiltonspectator.com/bidwell/539040.html> (10 June 2002).

48   Edward Said, *Orientalism: Western Conceptions of the Orient* (London: Penguin, 1978).

49   Narayan, "Eating Cultures," n.p.

50   Jean Duruz "Haunted kitchens: Cooking and remembering": <www.ipsonet.org/congress/5/papers-pdf/jd.pdf> (17 January 2003), the V Congress of the Americas.

part three

FAMILY, REGION, NATION

nine

"Complicated and Clouded": The Federal

Administration of Marriage and Divorce among the

First Nations of Western Canada, 1887–1906

SARAH CARTER

Influenced by Benedict Anderson's work on regions, nations, and empires as "imagined communities," feminist and postcolonial scholars have since argued that regions and nations were imagined in racialized and gendered terms. Images of domestic life were incorporated into late-nineteenth-century ideologies of imperial domination and nation-building. The Canadian west was marketed to potential immigrants as a place of "fruitful land and happy homes." As Burnett, Erickson, and de Zwart's contributions to this volume illustrate, "happy homes" were envisaged as patriarchal, Christian, and White. As was the case in other settler societies and colonial "frontiers," the legal and cultural management of sexual arrangements – within Indigenous communities, and between colonized and colonizer – became a critical component in the erection of colonial boundaries. Although the law served as the "cutting edge" of colonialism, Sarah Carter argues that the regulatory power of Canadian marriage law, as applied to First Nations communities, was never certain; it was subject to resistance, manipulation, evasion, and the persistence of Aboriginal law on the part of Aboriginal communities, and legal and moral uncertainty on the part of missionaries, Indian agents, and administrators. By intricately tracing the evolution of federal marriage law in the early years of its application on the Prairies and in British Columbia, Carter highlights how reshaping the gender order lay at the heart of colonial agents' efforts to refashion Aboriginal societies in their own image.

Marriage, historian Nancy Cott writes, is of fundamental concern to a nation as it "facilitates a government's grasp on the populace"; it "is the vehicle through which the apparatus of the state can shape the gender order."[1] In late-nineteenth-century western Canada, deliberate measures were taken to facilitate the government's grasp on the populace, and to shape the gender order through the monogamous, Christian model of life-long marriage. The West was an ancient and, in other cases, new home to people with diverse approaches to marriage and divorce; the life-long monogamous ideal of marriage was not shared by all. This chapter focuses on the efforts of the Canadian federal Department of Indian Affairs (DIA), to impose the monogamous model on the Aboriginal peoples of prairie Canada and, to a lesser degree, British Columbia. A snapshot of these years reveals these measures as invasive and disruptive, but far from entirely successful. The authority of the DIA on matters related to marriage and divorce rested on an unstable foundation; the hold was tenuous and fragile. The DIA's efforts illustrate, as Antoinette Burton argues in her introduction to *Gender, Sexuality and Colonial Modernities*, the "limited capacity of the state and other instruments of social, political and cultural power to fully contain or successfully control the domain of sexuality"; that modern colonial regimes are "always in process, subject to disruption and contest and [are] never fully or finally accomplished, to such an extent that they must be conceived of as 'unfinished business.'"[2] "Unfinished business" reflects the perspective of the colonizing power; but from the perspective of Aboriginal people, unfinished business points to an important degree of persistence of Aboriginal law. As legal historian Sidney L. Harring has written, it is essential that we study, not only the history of the extension of Euro-North American law over Aboriginal people, but that we also trace the "right of Native Americans to live under their own law as an attribute of their sovereignty."[3]

The marriage laws of the Aboriginal people of the Plains differed from their English common-law counterparts in their flexibility and adaptability: They drew on traditions, but evolved according to changing conditions. In Aboriginal communities, the kinship system provided expectations about proper behaviour and shared responsibilities of wives, husbands, daughters, sons, daughters-in-law, sons-in-law, and others, which were conveyed through oral traditions and rituals.[4] Any brief description of marriage law greatly simplifies complex arrangements that involved far more than simply the spouses. Among the Blackfoot for example, marriages were extended-family affairs – both sets of relatives had to give their consent as the families were from then on joined together in an intricate web of kinship that had an influence on how all family members interacted in other social, political, economic, and religious roles.[5] Marriages were arranged generally among Elders, relatives, or close friends of the people to be married, and the relationship involved reciprocal obligations among the sets of relatives. The marriage was validated, and the reciprocal obligations of both parties established, through an exchange of gifts that could be initiated by either set of relatives.

There were various models of conjugal union, not just one, as was the case in the Christian and European tradition. Same-sex marriages were accepted in many Plains societies. One or more of the spouses might be a "two-spirit," who took on the activities, occupations, and dress of the opposite sex.[6] In his narrative of his many years among the Plains Ojibway of southern Manitoba, John Tanner wrote about the son of a celebrated chief who was "one of those who make themselves women, and are called women by the Indians."[7] She (Tanner's pronoun) had several husbands in the past and now wanted to marry Tanner. When he refused, another man, with two wives, married her. As this example also illustrates, most western Canadian Aboriginal nations practiced polygamy, and it was particularly prominent in Plains societies.[8] These marriages were not seen as a departure from a norm, but rather as a desirable family unit. Often sisters were married to the same man, but the term "sister" did not always conform to the European use of the term.

Marriages were dissolved for reasons of incompatibility, lack of support, or abuse. Ethnographer David Mandelbaum described divorce among the Plains Cree: "If a couple proved to be incompatible, either the man or the woman returned to the tipi of his or her parents. The one who remained cared for the children and kept the household effects. After a time, both were free to marry again."[9] But divorce was not the norm. According to Cree Elder Glecia Bear, divorce was much less common in earlier times, before the introduction of marrying "in church": "And this business of getting married in church ... in the old days there was none of that marrying business; when you found someone, a man for yourself to marry, you straight away married him, you never separated from him.... As you had married him, so you remained by virtue of that fact ... there was no church marriage and thus they lived together until one of them would depart this world."[10]

Marriage among Plains people, therefore, did not always conform to the monogamous model; it was not always one man and one woman, and it was not always for life. Some scholars have wondered about applying the word "marriage" at all to the variety of conjugal relations to be found in Aboriginal societies, suggesting that "marriage" is not a universally applicable concept, that it denotes a particularly Western concept, and only some relationships in any Aboriginal society might approximate this.[11] Are concepts such as "marriage" and "wife" categories of colonial control not commensurable with the practices of Aboriginal peoples? Have they been imposed by administrators, the courts, anthropologists, and historians to create order and clarity, and eliminate flexibility and diversity?[12]

Certainly many Euro-Canadian observers did not see these as "true" marriages because they did not all conform to the most widely accepted definition of marriage as the voluntary union of one man and one woman for life to the exclusion of all others. They simplified and dismissed Plains Aboriginal marriages as a form of purchase, an exchange of property in which men struck bargains according to the market value of women. As Kristin Burnett revealed in chapter 6, there was an insistence that Aboriginal marriage enslaved women. There was no love, courtship, or ceremony; a commodity simply changed hands. (Yet oddly, the rate of conjugal dissolution was seen by outside observers, not in a sympathetic light, as a means of the supposedly enslaved women to achieve freedom, but rather, as a sign of moral deficiency and dangerous autonomy.) But, as we know so well today, definitions of marriage change over time. Marriage in Plains Aboriginal societies was not the same as Christian and English common-law marriage, but the term, no matter how imperfect, can be used if it is understood that there were diverse definitions of marriage. Like the term "family," there is no fixed or homogenous definition. As presented in any undergraduate class today on the sociology of the family, marriages and family are "social constructs whose meanings have changed over time and from place to place."[13]

The DIA pursued a remarkably consistent policy on the question of First Nations marriage and divorce in western Canada from 1887 until 1951. This chapter examines how this policy emerged and was solidified by 1906 – despite doubts, consternations, confusions, prevarications, numerous suggestions for change, volumes of correspondence, and denials of any such regulations. The main features of the policy were that marriages according to Aboriginal law were recognized as valid, but they could not be dissolved according to Aboriginal law. This might, on the face of it, appear somewhat non-interventionist and even respectful of diverse legal regimes; however, this was not the case. Administrators were compelled to recognize the validity of Aboriginal marriage law for a variety of reasons, but largely because First Nations people were unable or unwilling to marry otherwise. As Nancy Cott argues in regard to the United States government's tolerance of consent or self-marriages, tolerance did not represent a retreat of state authority; it drew the couple into the obligations set by the law for married people.[14] In the case of those defined as "Indians" in Canada, recognition of the validity of their marriages drew them into the obligations set by the 1876 Indian Act. DIA officials recognized the validity of Aboriginal marriage rites, no matter how informal (despite doubts and confusions about whether these actually constituted marriage ceremonies), but the marriage thereafter was expected to be exclusive and permanent, which reflected an intolerance for many dimensions of Aboriginal marriage and divorce. As historian Joan Sangster has argued, Aboriginal marriages were "applauded if they looked exactly like Christian ones, if they were lifelong and monogamous, if husbands undertook their roles as providers, wives their roles as domestic caregivers."[15]

The involvement of government administrators, especially Indian agents, in the marital affairs of First Nations began with the establishment of reserves in the 1870s. For the purposes of annuity payments,

Indian agents determined which couples were to be recognized as married, which arrangements constituted a valid family unit, and which children were to be regarded as legitimate. Wives were paid annuities under the names of their husbands; that is a woman (White or Indian) was entitled to annuity payments if she was the legal wife of a treaty Indian. A woman's entitlement to an annuity had to be established separately if she was not a legal wife. Indian agents were guided by the ever-expanding Indian Act, which governed minute aspects of the lives of reserve residents by containing numerous clauses that referred to marriage and its obligations, expectations, and restrictions when applied to wives and husbands. Under the Indian Act, for example, "The term 'Indian' means: *First.* Any male person of Indian blood reputed to belong to a particular band; *Secondly.* Any child of such person; *Thirdly.* Any woman who is or was *lawfully married* to such person" (my emphasis).[16]

The reshaping of the gender order was at the heart of government efforts to reconstitute Aboriginal societies.[17] Creating men and women in accordance with European norms had to begin with the fundamentals. When paying annuities, Indian agents frequently had trouble, made mistakes, or were misled; notations in treaty pay lists indicate that agents struggled with the flexibility of gender roles: "wife shown as boy last year," "boy paid as girl last year," and "boy now a man formerly ran as a girl."[18] Clothing, hair, footwear, and personal decor did not differentiate men from women in the way that Euro-Canadians expected. An English visitor to western Canada, Edward Roper, wrote in his 1891 book, "most of us found it almost impossible to tell the young men and women apart; they were exactly alike in face, [the men had no 'beards or whiskers'], and being generally enveloped in blankets the difficulty increased."[19] All wore similar, beautifully decorated moccasins, bangles, and earrings. Dress, deportment, housing, work patterns had to be reconfigured to create and sustain proper categories of men and women. Fashioning husbands and wives through the introduction of the institutions of monogamous marriage and the bourgeois patriarchal family was the key to reshaping the gender order. Obedient and submissive wives, under the power and leadership of men, was the goal. To bring about this goal, Indian agents became embroiled in the most personal affairs of the people they administered: dispensing advice on marriage, arranging marriages, denying permission to marry, intervening to prevent couples from separating, bringing back "runaway" wives, and breaking up marriages they regarded as illegitimate.

Wedding of Winnie Crowchild and Alec Bull, Tsuu T'ina Nation, 2 October 1912. *L-R*: Mark Crowchild, Lucy Crowchild, Mrs. Crowchild, Mrs. Deans (girls' matron), Mrs. J. W. Tims, Winnie Crowchild, Alec Bull, Archdeacon J. W. Tims, and John Starlight. Glenbow Archives, NA-192-17.

Yet despite the assault on domestic life, DIA authorities were limited in their ability to impose non-Aboriginal marriage law and ideals. From the earliest years of settlement on reserves, government officials would have liked to have insisted on what they regarded as legal, or Christian marriage, but found this to be an impossibility. All of the marriages in existence at the time of the treaties of the 1870s, even those that were polygamous, were recognized as valid. Government administrators simply could not declare all of these marriages invalid, the children "illegitimate." Indian agents were obliged to recognize the post-treaty marriages of people according to their own law because people were unwilling, and in some cases unable, to marry otherwise. Even if people wished to get married in a Christian or civil ceremony, it was not always possible in the more "remote" regions, and this was the case well into the twentieth century. People did not have the means or opportunity to obtain licences, and the visiting missionary seldom remained long enough to enable him to publish the banns the requisite number of times to legalize a marriage. To insist that "legal" marriages were the only valid marriages would have made it impossible to enforce many clauses of the Indian Act. In an 1889 decision, discussed further below, a judge held that the Indian Act amounted to a statutory recognition of marriages according to Aboriginal law. The federal DIA was also hampered in its ability to impose laws of marriage because, in Canada, marriage is a provincial rather than a federal matter. The Department would not and could not consider enacting federal legislation relating to First Nations marriages. Instead, they had an "official stand" on marriage and divorce that was first articulated in 1887, and reinforced in a memorandum of 1906 that was distributed and maintained until 1951, although never codified by any statute of the Dominion.

Indian agents, inspectors of agencies, and other "men-on-the-spot" were unhappy with the ease with which divorce could be acquired, and they were alarmed at the numbers of second or more marriages with resulting children. They were convinced that only the "authorized wedding ceremony" would instil an appreciation for the permanence of the marriage bond. Manitoba superintendent inspector Ebenezer McColl's description was typical. He complained of how, "on some flimsy pretext one of the contracting parties to these unholy alliances abandons, with impunity, the other for a more congenial, or desirable companion, and the law is impotent to inflict punishment upon these transgressors for their unfaithfulness."[20] In the hope of preventing divorce and subsequent remarriages, Indian agents requested, with regularity, that legislation be adopted that would prohibit and abolish Aboriginal marriage law; however, no such steps were ever taken.

The government of Canada's official stand on Aboriginal marriage in western Canada was first articulated in an extraordinary October 1887 report of a committee of the Privy Council, which was approved by Governor General the Marquis of Lansdowne and related to "the alleged sale of Indian girls to white men in the Canadian North West."[21] It was drawn up in response to demands made by the Aborigines Protection Society of England that White men in relationships with Aboriginal women should be held responsible for their children.[22] Several missionaries had claimed that, in western Canada, Aboriginal women were being sold to White men, that these women were "rejected" after a few years or months, and that these men were not assuming responsibility for their children.[23] Were the children to be reclaimed and redeemed by the colonial community or allowed to be raised with their mothers as government wards? Questions concerning the validity of Aboriginal marriage were central to these debates. As H.T. Bourne, Church of England missionary to the Peigan of the Blackfoot Confederacy, wrote in a 2 July 1886 letter to *The Toronto Mail*, the men who "purchased" girls claimed that "The Indian custom of marriage is quite good enough." Bourne continued, "The Indian custom is nothing more than a right of possession by purchasing – as a man would buy a horse or a slave. Is ours a land where such a thing can be done with impunity? Let the Government of Canada and the North-West answer by legislating on this serious question, and setting it at rest forever."

The Aborigines Protection Society contacted Canada's High Commissioner in London concerning Bourne's allegations and the matter was then referred to Canada's Privy Council. The response was drafted by Sir John Thompson, minister of justice (and later prime minister from 1892–94), with the assistance of Department of Justice clerk George Burbridge; it was presented as the opinion of Sir John A. Macdonald, then prime minister, and the superintendent general of Indian Affairs (SGIA). The document reflected dominant representations of Christian marriage as an institution that honoured and elevated women, and of Aboriginal marriage as enslaving and demeaning women. It is also clear from the document that a view of Aboriginal women, as prostitutes and potential prostitutes, as women who were purchased and accustomed to numerous partners, prevailed among officials at the highest level of Canada's government. Thus, the White men allegedly deserting their Aboriginal partners and children were not to blame; the problem was the women themselves.

As set out in the 1887 report of the committee of the Privy Council, John A. Macdonald's opinion was that the "evil complained of results from the habits and customs of the Indians themselves, with whom 'marriage' requires only the consent of the parties and of the father of the female without any rite and without the idea of continuing obligation."[24] The validity of these marriages was established in the *Connolly* case, it was noted, but "the validity of such a divorce has never been affirmed." Here was the core of the policy to be pursued for the next sixty years and more. Aboriginal marriages were to be regarded as valid, but their divorces were invalid. The document established that no legal steps would be taken to prohibit or abolish Aboriginal marriage law, but the hope was that their "gradual civilization" would bring about change. It was deplored that the Indians did not have "a higher conception of the dignity of marriage," but it was doubted whether a better condition of affairs could be brought about through legal means. Prohibiting their own marriage customs would, it was claimed, "convert women, now regarded as reputable, by themselves and the society in which they live, into prostitutes, and thus, by causing them to lose their own self-respect greatly to aggravate the evil which it is desired to cure."[25] The final words of SGIA Macdonald, to be quoted often in future years by DIA officials to explain or in answer to critics of their policy, was as follows:

... that the true remedy of this lax state of things must come from the gradual civilization of the Indians, and more especially by the inculcation into their minds of the views which prevail in civilized communities as regards women's true position in the family, and of the Christian doctrine respecting the sanctity and indissolubility of the marriage tie. When they come to grasp this higher morality, it will no doubt be easy to bring about the desired change in their social relations.

Critical to this document, and to the subsequent official position of the DIA, was the case *Connolly v. Woolrich* (1867). Justice S.C. Monk, of the Superior Court of Lower Canada, held that the 1803 marriage of a Cree woman and a White man, which took place at Rivière-aux-Rats (in what is now northern Alberta) in accordance with the customs and usages of the Cree nation, was valid.[26] William Connolly, a chief factor of the Hudson's Bay Company, and Suzanne had lived together for twenty-eight years and had six children together. The Connolly family moved to Montreal in 1831, but the next year Connolly married again, this time in a Roman Catholic ceremony, to Julia Woolrich, the daughter of a prosperous merchant. After William's death, his eldest son by Suzanne Connolly contested the will that left the sizeable estate to Julia and her two children. The court held that English law was not in force at Rat River in 1803, and that a marriage "between a Cree Squaw, without any religious or civil ceremony, but according to the custom of the Cree Indians, and followed by constant co-habitation and repute and bringing up of a numerous family, during a series of years is valid ... if the right of divorce or repudiation be not exercised whilst the parties reside in the territory in question."[27] Suzanne was found to be the lawful widow, and Connolly's subsequent marriage was declared bigamous. Justice Monk's decision was not an unqualified vindication of marriage according to Cree law; he found that the marriage was valid because it conformed to the monogamous model, exhibiting voluntariness, exclusivity, and permanence.

Cree marriage, then, was upheld, as it was concluded that Cree law was in force in the area of northern Alberta in 1803. *Connolly v. Woolrich* is interpreted today as the leading case respecting Canada's recognition of Aboriginal marriage law and its nation-to-nation relationship with Aboriginal peoples. In addition to being interpreted as an early recognition of Aboriginal self-government, the case also stands as evidence that Canadian law is pluralistic, deriving from diverse written and unwritten sources in Aboriginal law and the English common law tradition.[28] But as legal scholar Douglas Sanders commented in a 1981 article, the case is meaningless as a precedent, and "could not govern the legality of later custom marriages."[29] The Connolly marriage preceded the first Imperial or Canadian legislation for the area and the introduction of English law to the Northwest. But the federal government insisted, well into the twentieth century, that the validity of marriages according to Aboriginal law was established by this case. They overlooked or ignored subsequent cases that challenged this position, such as the 1886 decision *Jones v. Fraser*.[30] The federal government also ignored another finding of the judge in the Connolly case – that Cree divorce by repudiation would have been possible in that jurisdiction, while it could not be exercised in Lower Canada.[31]

An 1888 opinion of the Department of Justice attempted to clarify the 1887 report of the Privy Council by advising the DIA on the policy to pursue with regard to marriage, divorce, and the legitimacy of children:

...marriages of Pagan Indians which have been contracted in accordance with tribal customs should be treated by your Department as *Prima facie* valid and the issue of such marriage as legitimate. If, however, an Indian so married deserts the woman who is recognized or is entitled to recognition as his wife, and during her life time lives with and has children by another woman, the Minister does not think that such cohabitation should in any case be recognized as marriage, unless there has been an actual divorce from the first wife. The resulting issue should therefore be treated as illegitimate and as having no right to share in the annuities of the band.[32]

Further strengthening this DIA position was an 1889 decision in the case of *Regina v. Nan-e-quis-a-ka*, which involved a Cree man charged and tried for assault.[33] The question arose during the trial as to whether his two wives were wives in law, and therefore competent to testify against their husband. Under English common law, husbands and wives were prohibited from testifying if their spouses were tried for an indictable offence. The first wife, Maggie, was dismissed as a witness when the judge determined that there was sufficient evidence to prove that she had entered into a legally binding marriage with the accused. Nan-e-quis-a-ka had promised to keep Maggie for all her life, and she had promised to stay with him. Justice Wetmore concluded that it would be monstrous to hold that the laws of England relating to forms and ceremonies of marriage were applicable in the North-West Territories "*quoad* the Indian population, and probably in any case." Wetmore also interpreted the Indian Act, with its numerous references to marriage, wives, husbands and widows, as recognizing Aboriginal marriage.[34] Mr. Justice Wetmore wrote, "I cannot conceive that these references were intended only to Indians married according to Christian rites. No doubt there are many such Indians, especially in the East, but I think these expressions were intended to apply to all Indians, Pagan and Christians alike. If so they amount to a statutory recognition of these marriages according to Indian custom in the Territories." The accused's second wife, however, was admitted as a witness, as she was not regarded by the court as a legally valid wife.

There were many compelling reasons for the maintenance of the policy outlined by the 1887 report of the Privy Council and opinions of the Department of Justice, despite criticisms, doubts, and vacillations that emerged continually over the next sixty years. Officials of the DIA at the highest level found themselves defenders of the validity of Aboriginal marriage law, even though, as one Ottawa bureaucrat wrote in 1911, "the ceremony may have been of ever so simple or crude a character."[35] As mentioned previously, Aboriginal people were determined to retain their own marriage law. Officials had no ability to compel people to marry otherwise, and they were reluctant in any circumstance to give orders that could not be enforced. The DIA hesitated to take any steps that might allow married people to claim that their marriage was not binding. DIA officials even advised missionaries and school officials to take care in asserting the superiority of Christian marriages, as it was feared that this could raise doubts as to the validity, especially the binding nature, of Aboriginal marriage law.[36] Officials also argued that efforts to impose Christian and English common law marriage might encourage people to disregard all marriage law in favour of co-habitation; it was feared they would see this as a "loophole" that would free them from all potential legal penalties and constraints.[37] It was also the case that marriages according to Aboriginal law had to be recognized as valid in order to successfully prosecute for bigamy or polygamy, or more to the point, to be able to threaten to do so. Even when couples were married by clergy, there was no guarantee that these would be viewed as absolutely indissoluble, and people continued to apply their own divorce law.

There were also compelling reasons to deny the validity of Aboriginal divorce. In nineteenth-century Canada, divorce was almost unknown. It was expensive and troublesome. Between 1870 and 1900, there were only 213 divorces in all of Canada, an average of just over nine per year.[38] The vast majority of marriages were dissolved only by the natural death of one of the parties. As historian Cynthia Comacchio has written, "The inflexible divorce law was another available means to enforce particular standards of morality, domestic life, and sexual conduct, strengthening 'norms' and actively establishing the hegemony of the middle-class family model."[39] The marriage of divorced persons, as rare as it might be, was also condemned in non-Aboriginal Canada. At a 1902 meeting of the General Synod of the Anglican Church in Montreal, the question of the marriage of divorced persons filled four long sessions. These marriages, it was reported in the missionary magazine *The Far West*, "are so repugnant to the feelings of the church that very few clergymen could be found to remarry, under any circumstances, even the 'innocent party.'"[40] DIA bureaucrats shared these attitudes toward divorce, subsequent marriages, and the need to enforce their standards of morality. As the concerns of Reverend H.T. Bourne indicate, and as is clearly articulated in the 1887 Privy Council report, Aboriginal women were classified as an immoral and corrupting influence on the emerging settler society of western Canada. They were viewed as prostitutes who threatened morality and health.[41] The monogamous life-long model of marriage and associated gender roles would have the effect of controlling and constraining Aboriginal women. DIA officials could not make it compulsory for Aboriginal people to be "legally" married, but they could do whatever was in their power to promote the monogamous model by discouraging, preventing, or refusing to recognize divorce.

There were also compelling financial reasons for the government's refusal to recognize the validity of Aboriginal divorce law and insistence that first marriages alone were valid. As a man on the Broken Head Reserve was advised in 1905, he could not collect payment for the wife of his "second so called marriage," as the marriage was "illegal."[42] New families formed following such divorces would mean adding more children to the pay lists. As the Department of Justice clerk advised in 1888, "the resulting issue should therefore be treated as illegitimate and as having no right to share in the annuities of the band." Officials remained insistent that only "legal" divorces would be regarded as valid, while recognizing that this was virtually impossible for Aboriginal people.

The DIA's insistence on monogamy, that marriage was indissoluble except through the death of a spouse or a "legal" divorce, presented a host of puzzling issues. People were not permitted their former range of options for new family formation in the event of desertion, separation, divorce, or such problems as cruelty. The position consistently taken by officials of the DIA is illustrated in an example from 1905. The Indian agent at Moose Mountain wrote to Ottawa asking whether a woman, married according to Aboriginal law but deserted by her husband for many years, could marry again. The agent carefully detailed that the woman's behaviour was not the primary cause of the marriage breakdown. "In a case of this sort," the agent wrote, "would it be legal for the woman to marry again, and if not how long would it be before she could do so provided her husband persists in deserting her and refuses to support her and her family."[43] The very swift reply to this inquiry, from Frank Pedley, deputy superintendent general of Indian Affairs (DSGIA), was typical of the responses to all such inquiries. Pedley wrote that because Indian divorce was not recognized as valid, she could not legally marry another man until the death of her husband, unless she obtained a legal divorce. If she thought her husband was dead for six years preceding a second marriage, then she could not be prosecuted for bigamy; but if her husband was alive, and she knew him to be alive, then the second marriage would not be regarded as legal and she could be so prosecuted. There were numerous such requests for advice from across the West, well into the twentieth century, always with the same reply.

Indian agents supported husbands and wives whom they perceived as justifiably aggrieved in some cases, but were quick to judge others, particularly women, as "immoral" if they had left unhappy marriages and formed new families. Agents and farm instructors took steps to separate couples that they believed did not have permission to be together, and gave permission in other cases. They barged into homes and forced people apart. In 1906, the farm instructor for the Moose Mountain agency wrote for instructions from Indian Commissioner David Laird in the case of a woman who had formed a new marriage and had a child with the man. "They were together last winter," he wrote, "but were separated by the Agent and they went together again last night but I parted them this morning and took the woman home." He promised to "keep them apart until I hear your decision."[44]

Concerted action was taken by Indian agents, the North-West Mounted Police, missionaries, and school principals to break up what they saw as illegal marriages. In 1898, a widowed woman, formerly a pupil of the Qu'Appelle Industrial School, declared her intention to marry a man who had been married previously. Father J. Hugonnard, principal of the school, together with Indian agent W.M. Graham, went to his reserve intending to take her from the man and return her to her community. When they could not be located, the police were called in to find her and remove her to her own reserve. Within a few days of this event, Father Hugonnard arranged for the woman to be married to a widower of another reserve.[45]

Agents had a number of means at their disposal to attempt to enforce monogamy. Under the Indian Act, DIA officials could withhold and redirect the annuities of people who had deserted their spouses. If a man parented an "illegitimate" child, his annuities could be re-directed to the support of the child. Also, as a means of enforcing monogamy, a widow could not inherit the property of her deceased spouse unless she was "a woman of good moral character," which meant that the relationship had been monogamous. Agents sought to "punish" mothers that they thought were living immorally by having their children taken away to residential school, or to live with relatives of the father, or by threatening to do so.[46] People were continually warned and threatened with potential prosecution for bigamy; they were told that it was a serious crime that could mean seven years in a penitentiary.[47] In the event of a person involved in a second marriage attempting to re-locate to the reserve of the new spouse, agents were instructed to treat them as they would any other trespasser and to deny them permission to reside on the reserve, as stipulated in the Indian Act.[48] Agents on reservations across the border in the United States were called upon to co-operate with projects of reconciliation by sending errant spouses back across the border.[49]

Agents also simply denied permission for people to marry if they did not approve. In 1900, the Indian agent at the Muscowpetung Reserve in Saskatchewan did not approve of the women two young men had chosen to marry. The men were graduates of the Regina Industrial School and the agent wanted them to marry girls from that school. Instead, they wished to marry women he regarded as "very undesirable companions." With the approval of the Indian Commissioner, the agent refused to recognize their marriages and informed the men at the time of annuity payments that the women would not be recognized as their wives, nor would any children born to them be regarded as legitimate.[50]

As is clear from the actions of this agent and Father Hugonnard of the Qu'Appelle Industrial School, government and school authorities worked together to arrange suitable marriages and prevent the unsuitable. But Father Hugonnard was not, as yet, acting in accordance with DIA instructions in 1890 when he was chastised by Indian Commissioner Hayter Reed for allowing marriages between female pupils of the Qu'Appelle school and males not-so-educated without the "sanction of the Department having been first obtained."[51] The marriages had been arranged by the parents and the contracting parties. Reed expressed a "feeling of great regret" that Hugonnard had permitted these marriages, and he vehemently disagreed with Hugonnard's view about the role of the parents in arranging the marriages. Hugonnard wrote to Reed that "the arrangements were made by the parents alone. I did not consider that I had any right to make them myself, nor could I take upon myself the responsibility of preventing them from carrying out the arrangements that they had already made. Their future happiness or unhappiness may depend upon it and if I had interfered, they would undoubtedly have blamed me for it afterwards and not without reason."[52] Hugonnard stated that he could simply not have waited for Reed's permission; "it was not in my power to stop them, even by refusing discharges to the four girls. The refusal would not have stopped them." Reed sputtered in reply, "The contention that the parents have sole right to decide such matters cannot for one moment be admitted." Parents interfered in many directions to prevent actions that were for their own good, Reed contended. The great expense of educating the pupils meant that the Department had acquired "further right" in regard to them, according to Reed, and that these amounts would be "thrown away" if they were to "return to sink back to their old condition on the Reserve." Reed's approach prevailed. In 1900, a DIA circular was issued that called for the promotion of marriages among graduands.[53] School principals and Indian agents were to work together to recommend courses of action. A system of incentives was devised to encourage such matches, with approved wives given domestic articles such as sewing machines, and approved husbands assistance with farm equipment.

There were occasions and situations when departmental rules and policies were to some extent set aside. In 1906, a Manitoba woman who had three children with a previously married man was ordered to end the relationship and return to her own reserve. Although the DIA inspector of Indian agencies, S.R. Marlatt, acknowledged that it would be a "great hardship" to send the woman back to her reserve with three small children, "allowing them to remain together would be encouraging vice."[54] The father of the three children wrote to Marlatt asking "how are the children which I have with her now, to live. Have I to support them? If so in which way. I would be very glad to support them only I couldn't take and keep them now as they are too young yet to be taken from their mother ... I hope you will do your best for me in this matter as if I get into trouble and am sent to jail who is to support my children."[55] The chief of the reserve also wrote to the inspector to plead that the woman not be sent back to her own reserve: "If they had no children I would send her right back to where she belongs, but as it is I don't know what to do."[56] Laird's decision in this case was that, while "we do not approve of his living with this woman, and cannot recognize her as his lawful wife, or his children as legitimate," action to separate the couple and break up the family would not be taken.[57] In this case, it likely helped that the man's first wife was cast in the correspondence as "immoral and unfaithful to him."

In many cases, efforts of the DIA and missionaries to enforce the monogamy policy were far from successful. The power of Indian agents was limited and contested, their authority tenuous. They preferred not to give orders, as one agent wrote, "that may not be enforced."[58] Agents often reported that they did not always succeed in breaking up "matches" that they did not approve of, or reconciling estranged couples.[59] Agents were also reluctant to do anything more than threaten to prosecute for bigamy.[60] The DIA did not wish to risk prosecuting and failing to obtain a conviction, as it would mean a great diminishment of their authority.[61] The dilemma that agents found themselves in with regard to prosecution for bigamy was summed up by an Indian agent in 1906: "If I should send a case for prosecution and it fell through it would be a direct slap in the face at my authority and influence, and if I do not prosecute, it would show that I agree with their practices."[62]

A 1906 case of bigamy in British Columbia that was unsuccessfully prosecuted proved to be the perfect illustration of why the legal route was fraught with peril. To commit bigamy, as explained by a Department of Justice clerk in 1914, "one has to go through a form of marriage recognized as a valid form by the law of the place where it is gone through." The law clerk feared that "marriage according to Indian fashion would not be sufficient to constitute the offence."[63] His opinion did not mention the case, but this is precisely what had happened in 1906. The case of *R. v. Kekanus* was heard before Justice Hunter in the Supreme Court of British Columbia in May 1906.[64] The accused, from Alert Bay, had recently acquired a second wife through Aboriginal law. The testimony from the trial reveals the profound difficulties involved in conveying the intricacies of Aboriginal law through an interpreter to an unsympathetic court. There was lengthy questioning of a witness (Thomas Newell, an Aboriginal man from Fort Rupert) about marriage, all through an interpreter who was himself frequently in the witness box and questioned by the Court. Many of the exchanges reflected the deep gulf of understanding because of the Court's insistence that marriage was monogamous and for life: "Q: But as a rule when an Indian man marries an Indian woman doesn't he live with that woman for life? A: There is no such understanding – no such words pass as they shall live together as long as they live. Q: Yes, I know there are no words to that effect, but isn't that what usually happens? A: Yes – some of them."[65] The notion that some children would be regarded as "illegitimate" was likewise foreign to the Aboriginal witness. When asked if the children of a woman by a second husband following an Aboriginal divorce would be "looked on as legitimate," the answer was: "There is no ill-name given to the children; the children will be quite legitimate." The flexible attitude toward custody of children also perplexed the court, and the following exchange convinced the judge not to proceed with the case:

Q: When the wife has young children and the husband leaves her, who supports these young children, the first husband, or the new husband?
A: The next husband.

Q: He takes the children over with the wife?

A: Yes.

Q: And the first husband has nothing more to do with them, is that it?

A: Well he looks after the children as well.

Q: Well who do they live with – him or her?

A: In most cases they generally go with the mother.

Q: On the principle that a foal follows the mare, I suppose. Then there is no ceremony among the Indians by which a man and a woman agree to remain together for life?

A: No, there is no such understanding made.

Q: And the man and woman can't bind themselves to live together for life by any ceremony?

A: No.

Q: So that it is only a ceremony – the meaning of the ceremony is that both parties shall live together as long as they like?

A: Yes

Q: And not longer – and that either can quit?

A: Yes, either party can marry again though they may have lived 30 or 40 years together.

Q: And it doesn't make any difference about whether the property is paid back or not?

A: Yes

Court: Well what is the use of going further Mr. Maclean, in this case.

It was Crown Prosecutor H.A. Maclean, deputy attorney general for the province of British Columbia, who had to convince the judge and jury that Aboriginal marriage was valid in order to convict for bigamy, and that "English law with regard to marriage, has no application at all."[66] The Criminal Code could apply only if Aboriginal marriage was recognized as valid. Maclean argued that "the matter is not as plain as it might be," and tried to draw attention to the case law. But Justice Hunter did not wish to hear the case law and replied, "No I don't know anything about any English case, but it is common sense – it is no marriage ceremony within the meaning of [marriage], the essence of the marriage ceremony is that the parties shall be intending to take each other for life." When Maclean replied, "That is the English law, my Lord," Justice Hunter said, "This is a mere agreement to cohabit." The judge called back the witness Thomas Newell after Maclean submitted that "these Indians from time immemorial, have been living under their own customs with regard to marriage, but it is a species of marriage – it is different from our ideas, no doubt about that."

The exchange that concluded this case began with Justice Hunter's question:

Court: (with interpreter) What is the Indian word for "marry"?

A: No such word, only wife – taking a wife.

Q: Well what word do they use?

A: Well they use a certain word which I don't know its equivalent in English – I don't think – well there may be, but I don't know it, we have the word (carthaca?) which has nothing to do with marrying.

Q: Well what does that word mean?

A: It simply means as far as I understand the word, it is the parties going into the house – I take it this way, that is the husband go in to the father of the woman's house, we have no such word as marriage in our language.

Following this exchange, which weakened his case and confirmed Justice Hunter's opinion, Maclean concluded by stating that English law had no application, and that "the circumstances of those Indians are so peculiar that they are governed by their own local customs with regard to marriage up to a certain point, and not by the English law." Justice Hunter, however, found that this was not marriage at all, it was mere cohabitation. He disagreed sharply with the Crown prosecutor saying: "I don't see how you can call the ceremony a marriage when it is admitted on the face of the proceedings that it wasn't the intention of the parties to live together for life, and never is the intention – I don't see how you can call that a marriage, it is a mere agreement to cohabit."[67] Justice Hunter further stated that if he were to convict for bigamy, (and thereby invalidate the second marriage), the effect would be "that more than one-half the children in this man's tribe are illegitimate. I am not going to hold that, for the purpose of putting this man behind the bars for a so-called bigamy prosecution." He concluded, "the evidence clearly shows that there is no intention on the part of the Indians when they go through this ceremony to take each other for life, and that, in my opinion, is the essence of a marriage, or such marriage as is contemplated by a prosecution for bigamy." The case did not go to the jury; the prisoner was found "not guilty" and discharged.

The case caused a surge of anxiety among DIA administrators. The decision undermined their policy of recognizing the validity of Aboriginal marriage law and meant that people could not be expected, required, or cajoled to regard their marriages as valid. Administrators greatly feared the consequences if word got out that all their threats about prosecution and possible incarceration were hollow. As the prosecutor in the case wrote to one Indian agent who wondered about the implications of the decision, "Under the circumstances it would be idle to send for trial any more of such cases."[68] However, DIA officials decided to boldly ignore the decision, to hope that word of the decision would not widely circulate, and to proceed as usual. Very hastily, the first version of a circular letter outlining the official position of the DIA on marriage, to be used for many decades, was distributed to all Indian superintendents, agents, and farmer instructors in the Dominion in June 1906 (see appendix).[69] Threats of potential prosecution for bigamy continued, but there was a clear awareness that many aspects of the policy outlined in that circular could not be sustained if challenged.[70] As one Indian agent wrote in 1914, if section 4 of the circular that pertained to bigamy were to be enforced "then I am sorry to say that there would be very few Indians in this agency who would not be in the penitentiary."[71]

The DIA stayed the course despite a surge of criticism and pressure from women's, religious, and moral reform organizations to address the issue of Indian marriage. Henrietta Muir Edwards, as discussed by Patricia Roome in chapter 3, added her voice to the protest. Replies were consistent with the policy as established back in 1887 and reinforced in the circular of 1906. DIA official Frank Pedley informed the National Council of Women in 1909, for example, that "Existing marriage customs are recognized by law with a view to maintaining as far as possible due regard to the sanctity of the nuptial contract, and ... they are probably much more binding on their consciences than any more civilized methods whether christian or civil."[72] Well into the twentieth century, DIA bureaucrats continued to distribute the 1906 memorandum and to quote from the 1887 order-in-council, including that the "true remedy of this lax state of things must come from the gradual civilization of the Indians."[73] In the years prior to 1951, numerous alternative approaches and strategies were floated by DIA officials, sometimes applied tentatively, but ultimately rejected, including a clause in the Indian Act giving agents the power to deal with and punish bigamy cases, a clause in the Act legalizing marriages according to Aboriginal law, a system of compulsory registration of all marriages according to Aboriginal law, an effort to have the Aboriginal marriage ceremony defined so that all could know what was essential to making a union valid and distinct from "mere concubinage," and a proposal to allow a special form of divorce.[74]

"The whole question of Indian marriages is complicated and clouded," were the words that began a 1949 internal DIA memorandum that attempted to trace and analyze the policy of the past sixty years and more in western Canada.[75] Two years later, a new "official position" was adopted. There was a major revision of the Indian Act in 1951, and at that time it was determined that Aboriginal marriage law would be recognized in the reformulation of band membership lists, but that after that date, no "custom" marriages were to be recognized for membership purposes.[76]

In First Nations communities, the twentieth century was characterized by a diverse, complex marital terrain. Many who were born in the early years of the century were raised in households with more than one mother. There was a high degree of persistence of Aboriginal marriage law. "My mother was against a church wedding," said Kainai Elder Mary Blackwater.[77] Others married in church only under pressure. As George Faithful of Frog Lake wrote, "The white people seemed to think that Philomena and I weren't married and that our children were illegitimate, but we were married in the way of Indian custom. The woman keeps the name of her father or mother. To please our church and the Government of Canada we were married two years ago by a United Church minister who came to visit us from Saskatoon."[78] Some parents continued to arrange marriages, but not all.[79] Some marriages were "arranged" by missionaries or school principals.[80] Some people remained married for life, while others divorced and remarried according to Aboriginal law. This diverse marital terrain indicates that, despite a concerted, at times formidable campaign of intervention in domestic affairs to facilitate a grasp on the population, and to reshape the gender order through the monogamous model of marriage, there was much unfinished business. An apparently dominant regime was unstable, porous, and contestable.

Appendix

Department of Indian Affairs

CIRCULAR.

OTTAWA, 2nd January, 1914.

TO INDIAN AGENTS.

SIR,

Since there seems to be more or less confusion or uncertainty in the minds of officials and Agents of the Department with regard to the law as to the recognition of Indian marriages and Indian divorces, it is deemed advisable to inform you as follows:

(1) A marriage between Indians or between Indians and others solemnized or contracted in accordance with provincial or territorial law is valid.

(2) The validity of marriages between Indians contracted in accordance with the customs of their tribes has been established by the Courts, notably in the case of "Connolly vs. Woolwich and others," in 1867; nor does the fact that one or both of the contracting parties may profess adherence to Christianity affect the matter.

(3) It is particularly deserving of notice that the validity of Indian divorces has never been affirmed in Canada, and Indian marriages, if valid, cannot be dissolved according to Indian customs, but only in such manner as other marriages may be dissolved.

(4) If an Indian is validly married to one woman and has gone through a form of marriage with another which would make her his wife but for the fact that he was already married, he is guilty of bigamy and liable to the penalties for that crime, (Section 308, Criminal Code, R. S. C. 1906), and the Department of Justice has expressed the opinion that, even if there has been no valid marriage but the Indian intended by complying with the customs of the band relating to marriage to make more than the first married his wife or wives, or if, even without such intention, he has complied in the case of two or more women with the requirements of the tribal customs, he may be successfully prosecuted under Section 310 of the Criminal Code.

(5) With reference to a more or less prevalent idea that a man or woman can legally contract a fresh alliance if he or she in good faith and on reasonable grounds believes his wife or her husband to be dead or if his wife or her husband has been continually absent for seven years then last past and he or she is not proved to have known that his wife or her husband was alive at any time during those seven years, it has to be pointed out that, while such conditions would furnish a good defence against a charge of bigamy, they would not serve to legalize the second alliance in case of its being shown that both parties to the first marriage contract were alive at the time of the second purported marriage.

While the foregoing are legal principles for general guidance, their application to individual cases would of course depend upon the merits of such cases, and this declaration of these principles is not intended to authorize prosecutions without prior reference to the Department.

Your obedient servant,

DUNCAN C. SCOTT
Deputy Superintendent General of Indian Affairs

ENDNOTES

1   Nancy F. Cott, *Public Vows: A History of Marriage and the Nation* (Cambridge, MA: Harvard University Press, 2000), 1, 3.
2   Antoinette Burton, ed., *Gender, Sexuality and Colonial Modernities* (London and New York: Routledge, 1999), 1.
3   Sidney L. Harring, "Indian Law, Sovereignty and State Law," in *A Companion to American Indian History*, ed. Philip J. Deloria and Neal Salisbury (Malden and Oxford: Blackwell, 2002), 444. Following Harring I will not use the term "customary" when describing Aboriginal marriage law. He writes that "to call Indian law 'customary' law sets up a false dichotomy between Indian and English or European law – which is itself rooted in custom." Brad Morse is critical of the Canadian judiciary for failing to define the family law, and specifically marriage law, of the Aboriginal people of Canada as "law." "At best, the courts have referred to 'Indian marriages' or 'custom marriages,' .... This approach, which is reflected by the wording chosen, is to regard native marriages as being conducted pursuant to customs, traditions, or practices, rather than according to law. This then presents customary marriages as being somehow less important and less durable than Christian marriages that meet modern legal requirements developed in England." See Bradford W. Morse, "Indian and Inuit Family Law and the Canadian Legal System," *American Indian Law Review* 8 (1980): 219.

4   James [Sákéj] Henderson, "First Nations' Legal Inheritances in Canada: The Mikmaq Model," *Manitoba Law Journal* 23 (1996): 1. See also Raymond J. DeMallie, "Kinship: The Foundation for Native American Society," in *Studying Native America: Problems and Prospects*, ed. Russell Thorton (Madison: University of Wisconsin Press, 1998).

5   Sarah Carter, *Capturing Women: The Manipulation of Cultural Imagery in Canada's Prairie West* (Montreal and Kingston: McGill-Queen's University Press, 1997), 163–65.

6   Sabine Lang, *Men as Women, Women as Men: Changing Gender in Native American Cultures* (Austin: University of Texas Press, 1998), xiv–xv.

7   John Tanner, *A Narrative of the Captivity and Adventures of John Tanner During Thirty Years Residence Among the Indians in the Interior of North America*, prepared for the press by Edwin James (1830 rpt.: Minneapolis: Ross and Haines, 1956), 89.

8   The term "polygamy" embraces both "polygyny" (one husband taking multiple wives) and "polyandry" (one wife taking multiple husbands). Plains Aboriginal societies practice polygyny, but non-Aboriginal people of the nineteenth century and since have referred to this as polygamy. In Plains Aboriginal languages there are no terms for polygamy, polygyny, or polyandry. See Sarah Carter, "Creating 'Semi-Widows' and 'Supernumerary Wives': Prohibiting Polygamy in Prairie Canada's Aboriginal Communities to 1900," in *Contact Zones: Aboriginal and Settler Women in Colonial Canada*, ed. Myra Rutherdale and Katie Pickles (Vancouver: UBC Press, forthcoming).

9   David Mandelbaum, *The Plains Cree: An Ethnographic, Historical and Comparative Study* (Regina: Canadian Plains Research Centre, 1979), 150.

10 Freda Ahenakew and H.C. Wolfart, eds. and trans., *Kohkominawak Otacimowiniwawa: Our Grandmothers' Lives as Told in Their Own Words* (Saskatoon: Fifth House, 1992), 79.

11 Ann Marie Plane, *Colonial Intimacies. Indian Marriage in Early New England* (Ithaca and London: Cornell University Press, 2000), 6.

12 Sean Hawkins, "'The Woman in Question': Marriage and Identity in the Colonial Courts of Northern Ghana, 1907–1954," in Jean Allman et al., *Women in African Colonial Histories* (Bloomington and Indianapolis: Indiana University Press, 2002), 116–43.

13 Mary Ann Schwartz and B. M. Scott, eds., *Marriage and Families: Diversity and Change*, 3rd ed. (Toronto: Prentice-Hall Canada Ltd., 2000), xviii.

14 Cott, *Public Vows*, 40.

15 Joan Sangster, *Regulating Girls and Women: Sexuality, Family and the Law in Ontario, 1920–1960* (Don Mills: Oxford University Press, 2001), 179.

16 Sharon Helen Venne, *Indian Acts and Amendments, 1868–1975: An Indexed Collection* (Saskatoon: University of Saskatchewan Native Law Centre, 1981), 24.

17 Julia V. Emberley, "The Bourgeois Family, Aboriginal Women, and Colonial Governance in Canada: A Study in Feminist Historical and Cultural Materialism," *Signs: Journal of Women in Culture and Society* 27, no. 1 (2001): 59–85.

18 Glenbow Archives (GA), Sarcee Indian Agency, Treaty pay lists for Sarcee and Stoney, 1887–1903: October 1891 (Sarcee Reserve), September 1891 (Stoney Reserve), September 1893 (Stoney Reserve). Blood Agency fonds, Treaty pay list for September 1887. Thanks to research assistant Kristin Burnett, contributor to this volume.

19 Edward Roper, *By Track and Trail: A Journey through Canada* (London: W.H. Allen and Co., 1891), 120.

20 Canada. *Sessional Papers*, no. 14, vol. 27, no. 10, for the year ended 30 June 1893.

21 National Archives of Canada (NA), Record Group 10 (RG 10), Department of Indian Affairs, vol. 3762, file 3245-1, Certified Copy of a Report of the Committee of the Honourable the Privy Council approved by His Excellency the Governor General in Council on the 31 October 1887.

22 Ibid, George Burbridge to L. Vankoughnet, 5 October 1886.

23 Carter, *Capturing Women*, 166–69.

24 NA, RG 10, vol. 3762, file 3245-1, Report of the Committee of the Privy Council, 31 October, 1887: 1.

25 Ibid., 14.

26 See Henry H. Foster, "Indian and Common Law Marriages," *American Indian Law Review* 3 (1975): 83–102; Morse, "Inuit and Indian Family Law," 199–257; Norman Zlotkin, "Judicial Recognition of Aboriginal Customary Law in Canada; Selected Marriage and Adoption Cases," *Canadian Native Law Reporter* 4 (1984): 1–17.

27 Extracts from the case of *Connolly v. Woolrich*: <http://www.interlinx.qc.cq/wjones/marriage.htm>.

28 "Customary Marriages," Indian and Northern Affairs Canada: <http://www.ainc-inac.gc.ca/pr/pub/matr/cm_e.html>.

29 Douglas Sanders, "Indian Women: A Brief History of Their Roles and Rights," *McGill Law Journal* 21, no. 4 (1975): 661.

30 Sylvia Van Kirk, *"Many Tender Ties": Women in Fur Trade Society, 1670–1870* (Winnipeg: Watson and Dwyer, 1980): 241; Constance Backhouse, *Petticoats and Prejudice: Women and Law in Nineteenth-Century Canada* (Toronto: Women's Press, 1991), chap. 1.

31 Sanders, "Indian Women," 660.

32 NA, RG 13, Records of the Department of Justice, int. 163, vol. 2406, file 1299-1914, Deputy Minister of Justice to Assistant Deputy and Secretary of the Department of Indian Affairs, 20 May 1914.

33 *Nan-E-Quis-A-Ka* (1889), 1 *Territories Law Reports* 211 (North-West Territories Supreme Court).

34 Zlotkin, "Judicial Recognition of Aboriginal Customary Law," 3.

35 NA, RG 10, vol. 3832, file 64,535, J. McLean to R.D. Hovell, 13 July 1911.

36 NA, RG 10, vol. 3990, file 180,636, J. McLean to the principal, Alberni School, 1900.

37 NA, RG 10, vol. 3762, file 32345, pt. 1, Secretary of the Department of Indian Affairs to M.R. Bogart, 2 December 1909.

38 Cynthia R. Comacchio, *The Infinite Bonds of Family: Domesticity in Canada, 1850–1940* (Toronto: University of Toronto Press, 1999), 61.

39 Ibid.

40 "General Synod Notes," *The Far West: Church of England Monthly Magazine*, 1902: 155.

41 Carter, *Capturing Women*, 186–87.

42 NA, RG 10, vol. 3559, file 74 pt. 28, Indian Commissioner David Laird to Indian Agent, Selkirk, Manitoba, 15 March 1905.

43 NA, RG 10, vol. 3559, file 74, pt. 3, Indian Agent, Moose Mountain to Frank Pedley, 20 February 1905.

44 Ibid., Thomas Cory to Laird, 7 August 1906.

45 NA, RG 10, vol. 3559, file 74, pt. 6, J.P. Wright to Indian Commissioner, 10 August 1898.

46 NA, RG 10, vol. 3881, file 94, 189, 26, letter of the Indian Agent, Crooked Lake Agency, 26 February 1897; vol. 3559, file 74, pt. 3, letter of Laird, 21 April 1906.

47 NA, RG 10, vol. 3559, file 74, pt. 16, Laird to Indian agent Sibbald, 16 December 1903.

48 NA, RG 10, vol. 3559, file 74, pt. 4, J. McKenna to Indian agent W. Mann, 5 October 1907.

49 GA, Blood Agency letterbook, vol. 1722, 23 November 1904.

50 NA, RG 10, vol. 3559, file 74, pt. 7, [illegible] to Indian Commissioner Laird, 9 July 1900.

51 NA, RG 10, vol. 6816, file 486-2-5, pt. 1, Indian Commisioner Hayter Reed to J. Hugonnard, 13 June 1890.

52 Ibid., Hugonnard to Reed, 31 May 1890.

53 J.R. Miller, *Shingwauk's Vision: A History of Native Residential Schools* (Toronto: University of Toronto Press, 1996), 22.

54 NA, RG 10, vol. 3559, file 74, pt. 30, S.R. Marlatt to Laird, 28 September 1906.

55 Ibid., Arthur Hall to Marlatt, 20 August 1906.

56 Ibid., Samuel Marsden to Marlatt, 20 August 1906.

57 Ibid., Laird to Marlatt, 29 September 1906.

58 NA, RG 10, vol. 3881, file 94,189, 7 September, 1898, from Indian agent, Birtle, Manitoba.

59 NA, RG 10, vol. 3559, file 74, pt. 12, W. Sibbald to Indian Commissioner, 22 December 1900.

60 In 1899, the Department of Indian Affairs did arrange to have a Kainai man, Bear's Shin Bone, charged with polygamy under Section 278 of the Criminal Code, after much prevarication and indecision. See Carter, "Creating 'Semi-Widows.'"

61 NA, RG 10, vol. 3559, file 75, pt. 18.

62 NA, RG 10, vol. 3881, file 94, 189, Halliday to A.W. Vowell, 7 August 1906.

63 NA, RG 13, int 163, vol. 2406, file 1299-1914, Memorandum for the Deputy Minister of Justice, by "J.C.," 15 May 1914: 4.

64 NA, RG 10, vol. 3881, file 94, 189, transcript of *R. v. Kekanus.*

65 Ibid., 12.

66 Ibid., 15.

67 Ibid., 17.

68 Ibid., H.A. Maclean to A.W. Neill, 7 July 1906.

69 NA, RG 10, vol. 3881, file 94,189, Department of Indian Affairs circular letter, 18 May 1906.

70 NA, RG 10, vol. 3559, file 74, pt. 4, Indian Commissioner to Indian agent Millar, 23 July 1907.

71 NA, RG 10, vol. 6816, file 486-2-8, W. Halliday to D.C. Scott, 23 February 1914.

72 NA, RG 10, vol. 3762, file 32345, Frank Pedley to the National Council of Women, 28 February 1910.

73 NA, RG 10, vol. 6816, file 486-2-8 pt. 1, Alec Cory to M. MacInnes, 13 August 1941.

74 NA, RG 10, vol. 3881, file 94, 189, Indian agent to A.W. Vowell, 9 July, 1906; Halliday to Vowell, 5 September 1906; McLean to Vowell, 19 September 1906;

McKenna to DIA Secretary, 5 October 1907; vol. 3990, file 180,636, Memorandum 24 February 1908.

75 Quoted in Sanders, "Indian Women," 665.

76 Ibid., 665–66.

77 *Sikotan* Flora Zaharia and *Makai'sto* Leo Fox, *Kitomahkitapiiminnooniksi: Stories From Our Elders*, vol. 1 (Edmonton: Donahue House, 1995), 2.

78 Frog Lake Community Club, *Land of Red and White: 1875-1975*.

79 Emma Minde, *Kwayask e-ki-pe-kiskinowapahtihick = Their Example Showed Me the Way: A Cree Woman's Life Shaped by Two Cultures*, told by Emma Minde; ed., trans. with glossary by Freda Ahenakew and H.C. Wolfart (Edmonton: University of Alberta Press, 1997).

80 See the three volumes of Kainai Elder interviews in *Kitomahkitapiiminnooniksi*.

ten

Advice Ideals and Rural Prairie Realities: National

and Prairie Scientific Motherhood Advice, 1920–29

NADINE I. KOZAK

Ever since Joan W. Scott published her influential Gender and the Politics of History *(1988), women's history has increasingly become part of gender history: the study of how masculinity and femininity are defined, and redefined, over time. Nadine Kozak explores the interplay of gender and region in rural women's responses to motherhood advice, as published in Canada's national "Blue Books" and the* Grain Growers' Guide *in the 1920s. Just as Sarah Carter's article highlights the cultural assumptions that underpinned the Department of Indian Affairs' policies on marriage and family, Kozak's contribution explores the biases that permeated "scientific" motherhood advice literature that was intended to acculturate Aboriginal, working-class, and immigrant women to urban, middle-class, and British-Canadian conceptions of family and motherhood.*

Unlike nineteenth-century Catholic clergymen and nuns, who looked to Mary as the ideal mother, advocates of scientific motherhood elevated physicians as the true "experts" on pregnancy and infant care in the hope that their advice would circumvent potential "race suicide" and ensure the future health of the nation. However, the "experts" overlooked the degree to which regional realities precluded many women from adhering to their advice. Advice literature defined women exclusively as "wives and mothers" and men as "breadwinners"; yet, rural prairie women continued to labour in their gardens and fields during pregnancy, they gave birth without medical assistance, and they raised their children without recourse to basic amenities common to middle-class urban households. Kozak's article begs the question: Did discrepancies between representation and reality give birth to a distinct regional women's culture on the Prairies?

Scientific motherhood literature, widely available in Canada during the 1920s and originating from both national and regional sources, provided women with medically sanctioned advice for pregnancy and infant care. Advice authors assumed that Canadian mothers' circumstances did (or ought to) mirror their own and that mothers would strive to implement their directives. The various realities of life in Canadian homes, however, rendered adherence to the authors' prescriptions difficult, if not impossible, for some mothers. This chapter contrasts the scientific motherhood literature with conditions in rural areas of the Prairie provinces in the 1920s and concludes that existing material challenges made observance of the instructions impossible. Ultimately, both national and prairie advice authors failed to adequately address the conditions of rural prairie women.

Given that the three Prairie provinces – Alberta, Saskatchewan, and Manitoba – were primarily rural and agricultural in the 1920s, the women of the region had significantly different life experiences than urban women in central Canada.[1] There were specific constraints and difficulties of being a mother on the rural Prairies that the advice literature did not take into account. First, prairie residents were more ethnically and racially diverse than those of the rest of Canada. Second, as was the case elsewhere, medical care was inadequate on the rural Prairies; as Florence Melchior's chapter on nursing education at Medicine Hat General Hospital illustrates (see chapter 15), it was also geared toward serving the interests of the privileged. Third, there were material hardships and physical burdens associated with life on the rural Prairies. Fourth, prairie mothers were subject to a climate of extremes, often with little moisture, wood for fuel, and shelter. Finally, distance from family and friends excluded rural prairie women from the traditional support networks of mothers, sisters, female friends, and neighbours. Such supportive relationships and the information that experienced women could provide were often only available to rural prairie women via letters.[2] These factors contributed to women's unique experiences on the Prairies.

Historians have well documented the hardships associated with life on the rural Prairies in the first half of the twentieth century, including the labour required of women for production and reproduction on the family farm. Despite unique rural prairie conditions, historians have not explored regional sources of scientific motherhood literature. Instead, they focus on the national literature and its reception. Historians Cynthia Comacchio and Katherine Arnup have studied the national advice literature available in central Canada, but the motherhood advice distributed on the rural Prairies has not received the same attention.[3] This study supports Comacchio, Arnup, and Dianne Dodd's argument that the material conditions in which women lived most heavily influenced the choices they made for childbirth and child-rearing. Like Dodd, it argues that scientific motherhood advice established unreal expectations for Canadian mothers, especially those who lived and worked in conditions of economic and material hardship and in isolated regions.[4] This study builds on these findings and explores the interplay of gender and region in rural prairie women's responses to the scientific motherhood literature available in the 1920s.[5] It also argues that scholars must consider regional advice sources and their adequacy for the local population.

Immediately following the First World War, the production of child-rearing literature exploded in Canada, prompted by the grave social and health concerns that reformers identified during the war. Canada suffered great losses during and after the conflict. The enormous wartime death toll and the ensuing Spanish Influenza epidemic led advice authors to idealize mothers as those who held the "Nation's hopes" in their hands.[6] Additionally, recruitment efforts found many Canadian men unfit for military service. This perception of an unfit population, combined with declining birth rates among "native-born" Canadians and high birth rates among immigrant groups, led doctors and others to fear that the future of the "white Imperial Nation" was at stake.[7] Dr. Helen MacMurchy, a eugenicist and medical doctor, illustrated these fears when she wrote:

The lines are fallen unto us in pleasant places, but our goodly heritage will go to the sons of the stranger, unless we put our hands and our minds earnest to the work of rearing an Imperial race.... The future of our Province, the future of our country, the future of our Empire, the future of our race, is signified by the same sign, and that sign is a child.... The keys that unlock the problem of Infant Mortality, are the keys of National and Imperial hope and power.[8]

Much like creators of domestic science textbooks discussed by Mary Leah de Zwart in chapter 8, parents and doctors were to answer MacMurchy's call to protect the Anglo-Canadian "race." One way to do this was to follow healthy child-bearing and rearing practices as defined by professionals. As a result, Canadian women in the 1920s were the objects of national and regional motherhood advice campaigns. An abundance of scientific motherhood literature made its way into many Canadian homes in the interwar period.[9]

Scientific motherhood, according to medical historian Rima D. Apple, "defined women in terms of their maternal role centered in the domestic sphere. At the same time, however, it increasingly emphasized the importance of scientific and medical expertise to the development of proper childbearing techniques."[10] Scientific motherhood literature introduced science and its principles into the home, the traditional sphere of women in the early twentieth century. Authors claimed that doctors held specialized knowledge that mothers did not possess, creating a gap between the scientifically trained physician and the expectant mother.[11] Literature advocating and describing the "proper" prenatal and postpartum care techniques for mother and child were available from many "experts," including doctors, nurses, middle-class reformers, and government agencies.[12] These "experts" published advice in a number of sources, as noted by Dr. Laura S. M. Hamilton, author of the *Grain Growers' Guide* series "Baby Stories," in 1920:

[F]rom the provincial governments down to the daily papers inquirers can get directions as to the best literature on the subject, and in many cases that literature

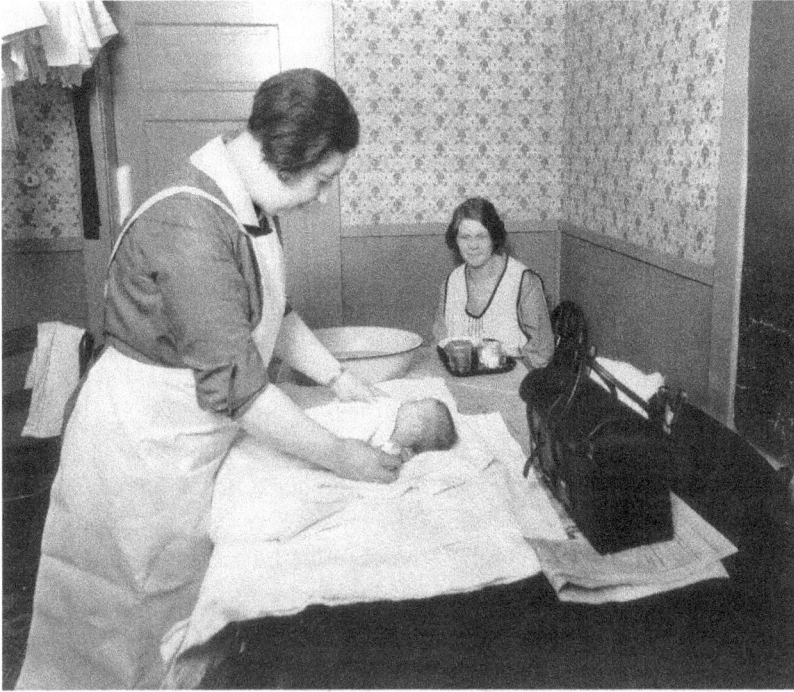

Expert Advice: Doctors, nurses, and government officials believed that their prenatal and infant care methods were the correct ones; they expected mothers to follow their prescriptions. In this photograph, Elizabeth Wedick, a member of the Victorian Order of Nurses, bathes a baby during a home visit as the child's mother observes, Calgary, Alberta, circa 1929. Glenbow Archives NA-3445-17.

will be supplied free. Most magazines have child welfare departments. Baby clinics are held in many of the large cities. In rural districts, Women's Institutes have taken up the work. All physicians are only too glad to give advice.[13]

The *Grain Growers' Guide* provided advice to the Prairie region during the 1920s. Hamilton's "Baby Stories" were the only sustained attempt during the decade to foster a regional advice program in the *Guide*, although articles on a variety of childcare topics appeared periodically.

The 1920s' early experiments in building a welfare state addressed proper mothering techniques through the publications of the Department of Health in Ottawa, authored by MacMurchy, Chief of the Division of

Child Welfare.[14] Canadians popularly labelled these books the "Little Blue Books," due to the colour of their covers. Literature from national government and prairie sources during the 1920s preached similar messages of the importance of medical care and the adherence to expert advice in favour of hygiene and routine in maternal and infant care. Prairie authors ignored regional problems of inadequate medical care, the burden of daily work, the lack of household technology, and rural conditions.[15] Doctors and authors offered idealistic advice – advice that presumed available and affordable medical care, access to labour-saving devices, and ample time – hoping that women would strive to improve their conditions for mothering.

The published advice sources, the official texts produced and distributed by the state and medical "experts," excluded the voices of rural prairie women. Using these is problematic but does facilitate comparison of the national advice, regional literature, and rural conditions. This methodological choice prohibits the examination of the experiences of specific women and instead leads to a focus on women as a group, undifferentiated by class, ethnicity, race, age, religion, and region.[16] It allows for an exploration of the asymmetry between representations of ideal motherhood, espoused by those who held social and economic power, and the experiences of mothers.[17]

MacMurchy and Hamilton's scientific motherhood literature discussed all the daily activities of mothers and infants: preparing for the baby's birth; maternal and infant care; and infants' feeding, sleeping, and habit formation. In addressing a woman's "psychic" preparedness for pregnancy and motherhood, Hamilton advised, "Be happy and simple, not introspective or gloomy." MacMurchy wrote that the expectant mother should be glad, brave, cheerful, and well because she was receiving her "dearest wish" – to be a mother.[18] The authors also emphasized physical health, advocating loose maternity clothes, simple diet, exercise, fresh air, plenty of sleep, and routinization of the "elimination" functions of the body.[19] Hamilton and MacMurchy stressed that expectant mothers consult a reputable doctor throughout their pregnancy. They dedicated the majority of their advice to discussing the necessities required for birth and the baby. Hamilton and MacMurchy listed the supplies to have available, including clean linen, towels, pitchers, basins, soap, Vaseline, and boric acid. They also discussed the preparation of the mother's bed.[20] After the preparations for birth, MacMurchy and Hamilton's advice fell silent. Neither discussed labour or birth. Hamilton advised women to be ready for when the "rush and excitement" came. Her advice then picked up again postpartum, instructing untrained attendants to care for mother and infant.[21] In a section entitled "The Baby Comes," MacMurchy reassured women, "Don't be afraid. Send for the nurse when you need her and your husband or the nurse will get the doctor in good time.... Everybody will take care of you." The following paragraph advised parents to register their baby's birth.[22] Both advice sources then turned to descriptions of caring for the newborn infant, including proper bathing, care, and feeding techniques. MacMurchy provided strict rules for nursing, "The baby must be put to the breast with perfect regularity. Never break the time-table."[23] Advice literature operated on many levels: it provided women with the most up-to-date methods on caring for mother and infant, it contained a wealth of information for first-time mothers, and it reinforced the importance of the medical doctor to childbirth by proceeding directly from pregnancy to caring for the baby, leaving out discussion of labour and birth.

In ideological terms, MacMurchy and Hamilton's advice popularized behaviouralist ideas, stressing routine in the daily lives of pregnant women, infants, and children. The American behavioural psychologist, John Broadeus Watson, argued that parents could control their children's behaviour by "educating them in correct habits."[24] The ideas were a reaction against affectionate and overprotective parents who were thought to damage their children's futures. Behaviouralist physicians and psychologists argued for a more detached method of child-rearing, one based on "unemotional" and "objective" science, which would better prepare children for the impersonal world they would inhabit as adults. In addition, the routinization of children's days would assist in the development of independence and self-control, traits required for successful adult lives.[25] As a result, the advice provided by the doctors was impersonal; they advocated what mothers should do, but their directions did not account for individual preferences or circumstances. Instead, the advice was a generic prescription for infant care. The "experts" expected everyone to raise their babies in the prescribed manner, which they believed was the most efficient and healthful way to ensure the survival of future generations.

The language used in MacMurchy's books, including the phrase "how to," implied that there was only one way to mother correctly and that the right way was the one advocated in the "Blue Books." Scientific motherhood "experts" considered their directions crucial to the development of the infant and the care of the mother.[26] They considered those who did not follow the prescriptions bad mothers who jeopardized their children's chances for good futures. MacMurchy wrote in *The Canadian Mother's Book* that the "Canadian Mother" knows that nursing her infant is "the greatest safeguard for the baby's life."[27] Indeed, nursing infants was best for Canada because MacMurchy associated breastfed children with health and strength, while "the poor babies that die are nearly all 'bottle-fed.'"[28] The doctors argued that, due to the wide availability of "expert" advice, ignorance was inexcusable. Hamilton wrote, "there is no excuse for ignorance nor for the shocking infant mortality, nor injured health."[29] If children were impoverished, malnourished, or diseased, the "experts" scorned their mothers for their ignorance or neglect.[30] In 1924, *Grain Growers' Guide* columnist Margaret M. Speechly noted that a "well-known" doctor maintained, "very often a baby's worst enemy is his mother" because she used improper care practices.[31] When these writers assigned women the task of "mothering," they separated the father from both mother and family.[32] The children reflected mainly on women's ability to "mother," without consideration for factors such as poverty or environmental problems.

As the caretakers of infants and children, mothers were responsible for all aspects of childcare: infant feeding, the inculcation of values and morals, and religious training, to name but a few. Just as Grey Nuns at Red River taught their mixed-blood students to aspire to motherhood as their truest vocation (as described by Lesley Erickson in chapter 2), "experts" in the 1920s considered mothering to be a woman's highest profession. In her first article for the *Grain Growers' Guide*, Hamilton stated, "motherhood ... is attainment, is perfection" and "motherhood is holy."[33] For the Social Gospel minister Salem Bland, "motherhood and homemaking ... [were] the highest and richest of all vocations."[34] Such an idealization of motherhood created impossible standards for Canadian families. Mona Gleason argues that, following the Second World War, the "normal family that was constructed through psychological discourse was idealized and therefore largely unattainable; moreover, it entrenched and reproduced the dominance of Anglo-Celtic (as opposed to 'ethnic'), middle-class, heterosexual, and patriarchal values." The psychologists' "normalized ideal" became the only family type truly acceptable, despite the diversity existent in the country at the time.[35] Experts employed these same characteristics to describe the ideal mother of the 1920s: White, Anglo-Canadian, and middle-class. Comacchio argues, "Because notions about maternal ignorance respected no barriers

"Canadianization": Indian agents distributed the "Blue Books" to Native mothers. Disagreements between the Department of Indian Affairs and the Department of Health prevented the publication of editions specifically tailored to Native mothers' needs. This photograph shows Louise, a Blackfoot woman, and her baby, circa 1930s. Glenbow Archives NA-2966-14.

of class or race, the experts had a potentially unlimited audience of women who needed their instruction simply because they were women. Their true targets, however, were the working-class, immigrant, and 'racially inferior' mothers who were regarded as the most ignorant of all."[36] The "Blue Books" and scientific motherhood advice columns introduced mothers of all races, classes, and ethnicities to prenatal and postpartum methods supported by those who held social power – White, middle-class doctors.

MacMurchy's "Blue Books" and the *Grain Growers' Guide* received wide distribution.[37] In 1921, subscriptions to the *Grain Growers' Guide* fluctuated between a low of 76,000 copies weekly in January 1921, to 82,000 weekly in March 1921, out of a rural prairie population of 1,253,000 in the same year.[38] The government, the women's sections of the Grain Growers' Association, the Red Cross, the Victorian Order of Nurses, and the Imperial Order of the Daughters of the Empire distributed the "Blue Books" to Canadians at no charge. In Québec and French-speaking areas, Catholic priests distributed the books to their parishioners, and Indian agents from the Department of Indian Affairs dispensed them on reserves.[39] In 1926, 72,346 mothers received MacMurchy's major publication, *The Canadian Mother's Book*; 60 per cent were English editions and 40 per cent French versions. That year, the Department of Health recorded approximately 250,000 births. Nearly a third of all women giving birth in 1921, therefore, received *The Canadian Mother's Book*. Even though these statistics do not measure the acceptance of the advice, many women did receive the literature and some of these women lived on the Prairies.[40]

From the available archival record, it is impossible to discern who received the advice literature, what their responses were, and how many women, given their circumstances, were able to follow the strict directions. As Florence Melchior's article in this volume demonstrates, some middle-class women in Medicine Hat demonstrated a marked interest in learning the most "up-to-date" nursing and childcare techniques. Similarly, Cristine Bye's account of Kate Graves's attitudes towards marriage and motherhood in the 1930s (see chapter 11) suggests that some farm women internalized the ideals that underpinned advice literature. Others, however, did not believe or accept all of the infant care instructions. Farm woman and novelist Kathleen Strange wrote of the motherhood literature in circulation in 1921, "I had always felt that a good deal of sentimental nonsense, some of it altogether false had been written about motherhood."[41] Although some women may have rejected the motherhood advice due to ideological objections, this study highlights the material challenges that women faced in carrying out the advice.[42] Examination of the scientific motherhood advice campaign illustrates that the "expert" authors of advice literature did not understand the contemporary conditions in many Canadian homes, specifically rural prairie homes.

Cultural diversity was an important feature of prairie society. Between 1891 and 1921, nearly four million immigrants came to Canada. By the 1920s, several ethnic groups were present on the rural Prairies, including Icelanders, French Canadians, Hungarians, Scandinavians, Jews, British, Germans, Ukrainians, Mennonites, Doukhobors, and

Hutterites.[43] In addition, Aboriginal peoples lived on and off of reserves in each of the provinces. Despite the ethnic, racial, and class diversity of the Prairies, the regional advice literature dismissed and rendered the habits of "others" unacceptable. According to Hamilton "the traditions of many nations' 'old wives' fables' … are all in favor of wrong habit." She reproached women from the "old lands" who let babies run around "naked" in the winter.[44] By limiting her comments on ethnic diversity to a condemnation of ethnic mothers' practices, Hamilton reinforced dominant cultural practices.

Dr. Hamilton also preferred middle-class ways and smugly shared her perceptions about the mothering abilities of different classes with her readers. In "Forming Baby's Habits," Hamilton declared that the "public opinion of the better class … [is] in favor of right habit."[45] She criticized the ignorance of both the lower and upper classes, "I have seen the babies of the poorer class of English here, sitting naked on the floor in midwinter"; "in some of the most fashionable districts," she had seen "really tiny boys and girls with short dresses and short woolen stockings and a long piece of bare leg and knee exposed to frosty air."[46] While Hamilton impressed upon readers proper winter dress for children, her deeper message celebrated middle-class practices as appropriate and correct. She singled out the poor, rich, and ethnic, criticizing their mothering practices.[47]

MacMurchy's "Blue Books" likewise did not reflect the ethnic and cultural diversity of Canada, rather they introduced immigrants to the "Canadian way," to the country's conditions and customs.[48] When the Canadian government translated the "Blue Books" into French, officials did not even change their advice to reflect French-Canadian culture.[49] Similarly MacMurchy's books were never translated into other languages for the immigrant population.[50] She was aware, however, that different groups of Canadian mothers might require different ad-vice. When MacMurchy attempted to alter the "Blue Books" to address Aboriginal issues, Deputy-Superintendent of the Department of Indian Affairs Duncan Campbell Scott interfered. Although Indian agents distributed MacMurchy's books on reserves, the Department of Indian Affairs refused permission to the Department of Health for participation in Aboriginal health issues. In 1923, MacMurchy offered to publish a special issue of *The Canadian Mother's Book* for Aboriginal mothers, which "'might be more suitable for them.'" Scott refused, stating that the "'complicated and confusing nature of the Indians'" would make the publication of such an edition impossible, rather he argued "'we would have to have several editions to cover the field adequately.'"[51] Inter-departmental rivalry and stereotyping circumvented the publication of literature tailored to the specific concerns of Aboriginal mothers that perhaps could have helped decrease the high infant mortality rate on reserves.[52] It is unclear, however, whether the special publications would have simply stressed the ideal or whether they would have truly addressed the conditions of Aboriginal mothers. Comacchio notes that the Department of Indian Affairs was committed to the "education" and "Canadianization" of Aboriginal women, commitments that she argues hindered progress in preventing the deaths of Aboriginal Canadians.[53] While translating the books into more languages or adapting them to different cultures could have increased readership across the Prairies, the regional and national literature largely ignored Canada's ethnic diversity.

Given the size and diversity of Canada, region is a central factor in the study of scientific motherhood advice. In the 1920s, the advice authors of central Canada and those of the Canadian prairies exhibited similar ideals of "modern" infant care, but the realities differed dramatically between Toronto and rural Alberta, Saskatchewan, and Manitoba. Mothers across the country did not have similar access to the resources required to carry out the tenets of scientific motherhood. One of the greatest problems on the Prairies was the lack of medical care. In the 1920s, physicians were still scarce and often too expensive in rural areas. When a farm was too far for a doctor to be present at the birth, women were dependent on public health, the Red Cross, and Victorian Order nurses for prenatal care and delivery.[54] In some areas, the outpost nursing stations of the Red Cross and small hospitals of the Red Cross and Victorian Order of Nurses were the only medical care available.[55] *Grain Growers' Guide* columnist Marion Hughes wrote in 1927, "The provision of adequate and efficient medical services is a problem that confronts many of the newer and more thinly settled rural communities."[56] In these cases, untrained attendants, commonly neighbour women, functioned as midwives. Many rural Canadian women also faced the birth of their children alone with no assistance from doctors or nurses. In contrast, most mothers in central Canada in the 1920s worried about the affordability of medical care, rather than its inadequacy.[57]

In response to the scarcity of doctors on the Prairies, Hamilton wrote an article entitled "Care of Mother and Babe" for the *Grain Growers' Guide* with a subtitle that read, "This Article is Specially Written for

Mothers Living Far From Doctors and Hospitals." The article, however, was not a substitute for doctors and nurses attending the birth. Instead, Hamilton wrote it for those cases where "the doctor, after the confinement, is of necessity only able to make one or possibly more visits."[58] It advised the "untrained nurse" how to clean up from the birth and care for the postpartum mother and infant. Hamilton did not address the reality of many prairie births where no doctor would attend at all, although her comment "where confinement takes place in the home, and possibly on some remote farm, the physician may not arrive till the last moment, or may not be in time at all" indicates that she was aware that unattended births did occur.[59]

In this instance, the national literature was more sensitive to the problems of western Canadian rural mothers far from doctors' care because it addressed the concern of births without attending physicians and provided advice for the situation. In general, the "Blue Books" contained as little medical information as possible to ensure mothers would have a doctor attend the birth. As a letter to Dr. MacMurchy from a western Canadian woman explained, women needed this education: "I know of two neighbours about to be confined. Both have already large families, neither one expects to have a doctor as they feel the expense will be hard to bear.... I can't refuse to help yet I do not feel equal to the task. ... This is the normal state of affairs all through western Canada except close in towns or cities."[60] MacMurchy included an excerpt from this letter in her 1928 report *Maternal Mortality in Canada*. In addition to this individual plea, the Home Branch of the Soldier Settlement Board wrote MacMurchy requesting help for mothers in rural areas "'who fear that medical and nursing aid may not be available at the time of birth.'"[61]

In response, MacMurchy published a 1923 supplement to *The Canadian Mother's Book*, a manual of midwifery directed at the "neighbour woman," who was to be present at the birth. To meet these women's needs, the supplement explained the stages of labour and what the attendant should do and could expect during the baby's birth.[62] While MacMurchy intended the supplement to make the untrained helper "feel equal to the task," the advice was only for cases the "experts" deemed "exceptional." On the front cover, government officials stamped the words "FOR DISTRIBUTION BY DOCTORS AND NURSES ONLY." Since the government requested that the distribution of the book be kept to a minimum, the Department of Health issued only one thousand copies in 1923. Neither the *Grain Growers' Guide* article "Care of Mother and Babe" nor the supplement was an adequate response to the inaccessibility of medical care.[63]

The inadequacy of Drs. MacMurchy and Hamilton's advice for births without an attending physician or nurse suggests that the "exceptional" case for middle-class families in central Canada and the prairie cities, the delivery of babies without medical attention, was much more common on the rural Prairies.[64] The requirement that doctors or nurses distribute the supplement illustrates MacMurchy's and the Department of Health's ignorance of rural prairie conditions. Women who lived too far from a doctor to have one attend the confinement probably could not obtain *The Canadian Mother's Book* supplement.

The long distance from medical care was problematic for most rural prairie families. In many cases, women delivered their babies – or in others, tragedy had struck – before the doctors could arrive.[65] In 1922, the United Farm Women of Manitoba conducted a "Rural Home Survey" to assess the living and working conditions of farm women in Manitoba, a survey that was illustrative of prairie farm conditions.[66] The "Rural Home Survey" revealed that 16.2% of the respondents lived 0 to 4.9 miles from a doctor, 49.5% lived 5 to 9.9 miles away, 20.6% had to travel 10 to 14.9 miles for medical care, 6.3% lived 15 to 19.9 miles from a physician, and 2.7% lived 50 to 74.9 miles from a doctor. The United Farm Women of Manitoba discovered that the telephone in part provided a solution to the geographic isolation of the Prairies. The survey revealed that 70 per cent of the respondents had a telephone. While telephones decreased the isolation for some prairie women, the survey found that the women living farthest from the doctor and other services were also less likely to have a telephone. These statistics and the discoveries about telephones illustrate that distance was still a problem for women in the 1920s and that, in many instances, the doctor or nurse did not arrive on time to deliver an infant.[67]

In areas where doctors and nurses were available, many women could not afford to pay their fees for natal care. In 1928, MacMurchy cautiously admitted that medical fees were too high, "From the point of view of the patient there is some reason to think that this may sometimes be the case."[68] At the time, it cost between sixty and seventy dollars to spend confinement at the Red Cross outpost hospitals; trained nurses commonly charged twenty to twenty-five dollars per week for home care; and it cost twenty-five dollars to have a physician attend the birth. Some Canadian women wrote the Department of Health angry letters because they could not afford the fee doctors charged for delivering a baby.[69] Showing surprising insensitivity, Hamilton chastised women who thought medical care was too expensive with "let me suggest that the doctor's fee is seldom as large as that of the undertaker."[70]

In *Giving Birth in Canada, 1900–1950*, Wendy Mitchinson suggests that occasionally women's lack of medical attention during birth may have saved their lives since maternal mortality was higher for women who had a doctor or nurse attending the birth. In the 1920s and 1930s, home births attended by a doctor had lower mortality rates than hospital births attended by a physician. Mitchinson notes: "The fact that during the first half of the century, mortality rates were lower when doctors or nurses were not even present was especially embarrassing for physicians." Finally, rural rates were lower than urban ones during the 1920s and early 1930s, even though fewer rural women had access to hospitals and prenatal care.[71] Ironically, rural families, probably unaware of the mortality statistics, accepted the official propaganda and the physicians' calls for the medicalization of childbirth.

Families' inability to afford physicians' fees rendered many other aspects of the motherhood advice futile. MacMurchy's "Blue Books" urged mothers to "call the Doctor" for every imaginable problem and stressed the importance of a "reputable" physician, one to whom the pregnant woman reported all headaches, pain, swelling, dizziness, and a host of other problems. The appeals for mothers to consult the "experts" strengthened doctors' authority over maternal and child health.[72] This advice, however, was not relevant for women far from doctors and for those who could not afford a doctor at the child's birth; it was an ideal many farm women could not attain.

The national advice literature, in addition, advocated that pregnant women limit their physical activities. MacMurchy wrote, "Most of us Canadians do our own housework, and you will be able to keep on with this."[73] Despite this statement, she maintained that women stop and rest when tired, limit work to six hours a day, sit down to work when possible, to take work easily, "not lift any heavy weight," and "not try to do the washing alone, except for 'a few little things.'"[74] Farm women's indoor and outdoor work in the 1920s depended on several variables, such as family size, type of housing, and the availability of tools, facilities, and labour-saving devices. Women cared for children, cooked, cleaned, sewed, washed laundry, carried wood and water, and often tended gardens and poultry. The "Rural Home Survey" found that only 14 per cent of women had domestic help.[75] As Sara Brooks Sundberg argues, the "female frontier" persisted into the 1920s although the frontier period had passed for men on prairie farms. Both "physical burden" and a lack of modern conveniences characterized farm women's work. Sheila McManus argues that the work done by Alberta farm women from 1905 to 1929 conflicted with urban understandings of the proper work for women. Indeed, "For many of these women, the experiences and challenges of indoor and outdoor farm work, reproductive and market-oriented, were a significant deviation from the gender constructions adhered to by 'respectable' White, English-speaking women in more urban settings."[76] Women on prairie farms in the 1920s worked hard, doing "unladylike" tasks to ensure the survival of family and farm. The labour of women on farms, labour required daily and weekly to foster production and reproduction, did not allow women to follow MacMurchy's advice. Nanci Langford reports that most pregnant farm and ranch women on the Prairies continued their chores as usual.[77] Hamilton, in contrast to MacMurchy, remained silent on the issue of work, perhaps aware of the futility of advocating reduced workloads for the expectant women given the realities of farm women's daily work. In some cases, the advice to reduce physical activity when pregnant conflicted with traditional practices. Mitchinson argues that for Aboriginal women living according to traditional custom, the reduction of work during pregnancy was simply not possible. Aboriginal women did not need reduced workloads because they believed birth was natural and that active women would have easier births; inactive women, according to custom, would have painful deliveries and give birth to lazy children.[78]

The discrepancies between the advice literature's ideals and rural women's realities continued beyond the birth of their children to infant and childcare. Many mothers on the Prairies were subject to "hostile" and "crude" environments that compared unfavourably to the standard assumed in the advice literature: middle-class homes with "modern" household technology.[79] One prairie woman remarked, "[Farm] Houses had no electric lighting, running water or central heating."[80] The "Rural Home Survey," according to Sundberg, found that "modern household technology remained a luxury in 1922."[81]

"Modern" household technology in urban areas reduced the difficulty of infant and childcare tasks, such as the pasteurization of milk. Although MacMurchy and Hamilton strongly advised that women able to breastfeed should do so, the advice authors provided instructions for

Farm Women's Work: Carrying water from the well was a particularly burdensome task on prairie farms. This photograph depicts Blanche Pope Johnston carrying a pail of water, Hanna area, Alberta, circa 1913–1930s. Glenbow Archives NA-3597-64

the care of milk for the infants of women unable to breastfeed and for children.[82] The "experts'" concern was that infected milk could spread diseases. In most cities, the officer of health monitored the supply to ensure that milk was healthy. In rural areas, however, there was no health inspector to guarantee purity. Hamilton noted that the people who were most likely to suffer were those without adequate inspection, therefore, MacMurchy and Hamilton stated that it was only safe to use pasteurized milk and they gave directions for milk's proper care.[83] To pasteurize, it was to be heated between 145 to 160 degrees Fahrenheit, or almost to a boil for those without a thermometer, for thirty minutes. After this, the milk was to be set in cold water and then kept cold, about forty degrees Fahrenheit, for up to twenty-four hours.[84]

Although "experts" encouraged women in rural homes to pasteurize milk, it was not easy for many to do so in the 1920s. Dodd notes that most rural homes had coal- or wood-burning stoves, with which it was hard to control the heat. Obtaining the correct temperature for pasteurization, therefore, was difficult and keeping pasteurized milk cold for twenty-four hours was even more problematic. Only a small percentage of farm homes had mechanical refrigerators and only a few more had iceboxes, hence keeping the milk cool was impossible in summer months. The advice about pasteurization was extremely difficult to implement for prairie women lacking "modern" household machines. The women, nonetheless, knew that non-pasteurized milk could spread diseases and "this knowledge served only to put unrealistic pressures on rural readers" of the advice literature.[85] Many rural women did not have the resources to carry out the advice, although the advice authors made them all too aware of the potentially dangerous or fatal consequences of their inaction.

Inadequate stoves complicated pasteurization, and they also made the heating of homes problematic. Wood- or coal-burning stoves heated 60 per cent of the Manitoba rural homes surveyed in 1922 and furnaces heated only 25 per cent. With stoves, it was more troublesome to achieve an even temperature.[86] It was difficult for those women heating the house by stove to obtain a temperature of seventy degrees Fahrenheit in the day and sixty-five degrees at night in the baby's room, as Hamilton advised.[87]

Not only did rural women find heating the baby's room difficult, attaining the advice authors' standards of cleanliness without running water was also a challenge. Running water was a rarity on the rural Prairies. Two-thirds of the women in the "Rural Home Survey" had no running water in their kitchens. As late as 1931, less than 2 per cent of Manitoba farm homes had running water in the kitchen or the bathroom.[88] Not having this convenience increased the difficulty of sterilizing the baby's bottles and bottle nipples and boiling its laundry as the advice literature suggested, because women had to carry large amounts of water from the well. According to the "Rural Home Survey," family wells were an average of sixty yards away from farm homes. The distances women traveled for water, however, could be much greater: one woman reported that the well was one mile from her house.[89] This example illustrates the glaring distinction between the advice authors' ideals and the realities of rural prairie life. Due to their lack of "modern" household technology, many rural prairie women were unable to follow the strict instructions given to them by advice authors. The advice literature contained unrealistic standards of childcare for many rural mothers. Farm women with no running water, electric heating, or refrigeration had a very difficult time achieving the ideal standards.[90]

In the 1920s, rural prairie mothers had access to several sources of scientific motherhood literature, including the "Baby Stories" of the *Grain Grower's Guide* and the "Blue Books" of the Division of Child Welfare in Ottawa. Although rural prairie women had significantly different life experiences than women in central Canada, including the scarcity and expense of medical care, days filled with hard labour inside and outside the farm home, and the lack of "modern" household technology, prairie women received similar advice literature from regional and national sources. Dr. Hamilton, writing in the *Grain Growers' Guide*, chose not to alter her instructions to reflect the special circumstances and conditions of the Prairies, whereas Dr. MacMurchy was barely more sensitive to the conditions of those living in hardship or isolation. Both authors upheld middle-class practices of mothering for all Canadians, regardless of region, ethnicity, race, class, or other factors. An examination of the availability and affordability of physicians' care, burdens of household and farm work, and the lack of "modern" household technology in rural homes illustrates that prairie farm women faced great barriers to implementing scientific motherhood principles. For many rural prairie women in the 1920s, the scientific motherhood ideals advocated by the medical "experts" stood in sharp contrast to the material realities of farm life.

ENDNOTES

1   In 1921, 64 per cent, or 1,253,000 of the 1,956,000 prairie dwellers were rural; 36 per cent, or 703,000, were urban: Gerald Friesen, *The Canadian Prairies: A History* (Toronto: University of Toronto Press, 1987), 511, 514; Veronica Strong-Boag, *The New Day Recalled: Lives of Girls and Women in English Canada, 1919–1939* (Markham: Penguin, 1988), 113; R. Douglas Francis, Richard Jones, and Donald B. Smith, *Destinies: Canadian History Since Confederation* (Toronto: Harcourt Brace, 1992), 133–38; Suzann Buckley, "Efforts to Reduce Infant and Maternal Mortality in Canada Between the Two World Wars," *Atlantis* 2, no. 2 (Spring 1977): 78; Ina J. Bramadat and Marion I. Saydak, "Nursing on the Canadian Prairies, 1900–1930: Effects of Immigration," *Nursing History Review* 1, no. 1 (1993): 108; Cynthia Abeele, "'The Infant Soldier': The Great War and

the Campaign for Child Welfare," *Canadian Bulletin of Medical History* 5, no. 2 (1988): 110–12.

2 Nanci Langford, "Childbirth on the Canadian Prairies, 1880–1930," in *Telling Tales: Essays in Western Women's History*, ed. Catherine A. Cavanaugh and Randi R. Warne (Vancouver: UBC Press, 2000), 149–50.

3 Cynthia R. Comacchio's book, *"Nations are Built of Babies": Saving Ontario's Mothers and Children, 1900–1940* (Montreal and Kingston: McGill-Queen's University Press, 1993), studies scientific motherhood advice in Ontario. Katherine Arnup's *Education for Motherhood: Advice for Mothers in Twentieth Century Canada* (Toronto: University of Toronto Press, 1994) focuses on Ontario, especially the city of Toronto, and to a lesser extent Alberta, British Columbia, Manitoba, New Brunswick, Nova Scotia, and Québec. Norah L. Lewis' article, "Creating the Little Machine: Child Rearing in British Columbia, 1919–1939," *BC Studies* 56 (Winter 1982–1983): 44–60, is a study of scientific motherhood in that province. Andrée Lévesque's *Making and Breaking the Rules: Women in Québec, 1919–1939*, trans. Yvonne M. Klein (Toronto: McClelland and Stewart, 1994), studies scientific motherhood literature in Québec. Historians write about the Prairies only fleetingly in their studies of scientific motherhood advice literature; however, as this study will show, the Prairies were also subject to the advice literature.

4 Comacchio, *"Nations are Built of Babies,"* 12; Arnup, *Education for Motherhood*, 156; Dianne Dodd, "Advice to Parents: The Blue Books, Helen MacMurchy, M.D., and the Federal Department of Health, 1920–1934," *Canadian Bulletin of Medical History* 8, no. 2 (1991): 212, 222–23.

5 For this study, I use anthropologist Nancy Bonvillain's definition of gender. She states "Gender is a social construct. It emerges from sex differences between females and males but, rather than reflecting biology, gender reflects and defines the social identities of women and men." Nancy Bonvillain, "Gender Relations in Native North America," *American Indian Culture and Research Journal* 13, no. 2 (1989): 2.

6 Arnup, *Education for Motherhood*, 19.

7 Abeele, "'The Infant Soldier,'" 107; Comacchio, *"Nations are Built of Babies,"* 56; Mariana Valverde, "'When the Mother of the Race Is Free': Race, Reproduction, and Sexuality in First-Wave Feminism," in *Gender Conflicts: New Essays in Women's History*, ed. Franca Iacovetta and Mariana Valverde (Toronto: University of Toronto Press, 1992), 5, 8; Arnup, *Education for Motherhood*, 21–22.

8 Helen MacMurchy's 1910 report *Infant Mortality*, 36, quoted in Arnup, *Education for Motherhood*, 22.

9 Dodd, "Advice to Parents," 223.

10 Rima D. Apple, *Mothers and Medicine: A Social History of Infant Feeding, 1890–1950* (Madison: University of Wisconsin Press, 1987), 97.

11 Julia Grant, *Raising Baby by the Book: The Education of American Mothers* (New Haven, CT: Yale University Press, 1998), 115; Apple, *Mothers and Medicine*, 17, 97.

12 This study focuses on motherhood advice provided by medical doctors. "Experts" thus refers to physicians who possessed credibility because they attained a medical degree. At the same time, placing the term in quotation marks calls into question whether a medical degree was sufficient preparation for giving advice

on mothering. It problematizes the term and suggests that perhaps there were other experts on childrearing; women who had given birth and raised children in similar regions and circumstances, including mothers, grandmothers, sisters, and neighbours: Apple, *Mothers and Medicine*, 97; Cynthia R. Comacchio, *The Infinite Bonds of Family: Domesticity in Canada, 1850–1940* (Toronto: University of Toronto Press, 1999), 98.

13   Laura S. M. Hamilton, "The Bottle Fed Baby," *Grain Growers' Guide* 13, no. 14 (7 April 1920): 53.

14   Hamilton's "Baby Stories" series was very similar to MacMurchy's "Blue Books," although Hamilton published her work in 1920, which was one year earlier than MacMurchy. The Dominion Government of Canada printed the first edition of *The Canadian Mother's Book* in March of 1921. That Hamilton published her articles first shows that she was not simply adopting MacMurchy's ideas on child-care; these were the dominant beliefs of the "experts." The seven articles published in the "Baby Stories" series were: Laura S. M. Hamilton, "Working With the Creator," *Grain Growers' Guide*, 13, no. 4 (28 January 1920): 42–43; Laura S. M. Hamilton, "The Hygiene of Pregnancy," *Grain Growers' Guide*, 13, no. 9 (3 March 1920): 44–45; Hamilton, "The Bottle Fed Baby"; Laura S. M. Hamilton, "Care of Mother and Babe," *Grain Growers' Guide*, 13, no. 19 (12 May 1920): 46–47; Laura S. M. Hamilton, "The Breast-Fed Baby," *Grain Growers' Guide*, 13, no. 23 (9 June 1920): 30–31; Laura S. M. Hamilton, "Forming Baby's Habits," *Grain Growers' Guide*, 13, no. 29 (21 July 1920): 28–29; Laura S. M. Hamilton, "Fall Babies," *Grain Growers' Guide*, 13, no. 41 (13 October 1920): 29–30. Helen Mac-Murchy, *The Canadian Mother's Book* (Ottawa: Dominion of Canada Department of Health, 1925), title page; "The Countrywoman," *Grain Growers' Guide*, 13, no. 17 (28 April 1920): 39; "Another Baby Book," *Grain Growers' Guide* 14, no. 12 (23 March 1921): 30; Kathryn McPherson, Cecilia Morgan, and Nancy M. Forestell, eds., "Introduction: Conceptualizing Canada's Gendered Pasts," in *Gendered Pasts: Historical Essays in Femininity and Masculinity in Canada* (Don Mills: Oxford University Press Canada, 1999), 9; see Arnup, *Education for Motherhood*, 52, for information about the first publication of *The Canadian Mother's Book*.

15   By using the *Grain Growers' Guide* and the "Blue Books" as the sources for the dissemination of advice, this study excludes women unable to read and women unable to read English. Thus, I am studying only literate Anglo-Canadian women and immigrant women literate in English. Another limiting factor is subscription. It is impossible to determine who subscribed to the *Grain Growers' Guide* and who shared their copies with non-subscribing friends and family. The two prerequisites for receiving motherhood advice through the *Grain Growers' Guide* were that women must be able to read English and they must have access to the journal. The limitation for the "Blue Books" was only that women must be able to read English or French, as the government distributed the books free. Indeed, these factors may limit the study to a small group of the larger prairie population.

16   Lévesque, *Making and Breaking the Rules*, 24, 34; McPherson, Morgan, and Forestell, "Introduction," 2; Mary Kinnear, *A Female Economy: Women's Work in a Prairie Province, 1870–1970* (Montreal and Kingston: McGill-Queen's University Press, 1998), 5; Comacchio, *The Infinite Bonds of Family*, 5.

17 McPherson, Morgan, and Forestell, "Introduction," 3–4; Joy Parr, "Gender History and Historical Practice," *The Canadian Historical Review* 76, 3 (September 1995): 365; Sarah Carter, *Capturing Women: The Manipulation of Cultural Imagery in Canada's Prairie West* (Montreal and Kingston: McGill-Queen's University Press, 1997), 9–10.

18 Hamilton, "The Hygiene of Pregnancy," 44; MacMurchy, *The Canadian Mother's Book*, 8–9.

19 Hamilton, "The Hygiene of Pregnancy," 44–45; MacMurchy, *The Canadian Mother's Book*, 15–26.

20 Hamilton, "The Hygiene of Pregnancy," 44–45; MacMurchy, *The Canadian Mother's Book*, 34-41.

21 Hamilton, "Care of Mother and Babe," 46.

22 MacMurchy, *The Canadian Mother's Book*, 59–60.

23 Ibid., 60–132; Hamilton, "Care of Mother and Babe," 46–47; Hamilton, "The Bottle Fed Baby," 53–54; Hamilton, "The Breast-Fed Baby," 30–31; Hamilton, "Forming Baby's Habits," 28–29; Hamilton, "Fall Babies," 30.

24 John Broadeus Watson quoted in Grant, *Raising Baby by the Book*, 140, see also 42.

25 Comacchio, *The Infinite Bonds of Family*, 97; Grant, *Raising Baby by the Book*, 41–42.

26 Dodd, "Advice to Parents," 204.

27 MacMurchy, *The Canadian Mother's Book*, 72.

28 Ibid., 30–31.

29 Hamilton, "The Breast-Fed Baby," 31.

30 Hamilton, "Fall Babies," 30; Arnup, *Education for Motherhood*, 36, 38; Lévesque, *Making and Breaking the Rules*, 33.

31 An unidentified doctor quoted in Margaret M. Speechly, "When Mother Acts as Nurse," *Grain Growers' Guide* XVII, no. 11 (12 March 1924): 11.

32 This study will only discuss scientific childcare literature in relation to mothers. The advice authors largely viewed fathers solely as breadwinners. MacMurchy, in *The Canadian Mother's Book*, gave fathers a role as "Mother's Helper." This role had little to do with the infant directly. It was the father's job to build baby furniture, take care of the mother, read *The Canadian Mother's Book* so that he knew how his wife should be taking care of the baby, hang curtains and pictures so that his pregnant wife need not stand on chairs to reach, register the baby's birth, encourage his wife to nurse the baby, be a good role model for the children, ensure that mother and child received proper medical care, and care for the mother during pregnancy. There is no mention in the literature that fathers were to hold the baby or help with it in any direct way. Instead, the father's role was secondary; he was the provider for the family. Most of the scholarly literature largely ignores the role of the father, a fact prompting Comacchio to publish an article entitled "'A Postscript for Father': Defining a New Fatherhood in Interwar Canada" in 1997. Comacchio's 1993 book, *"Nations are Built of Babies,"* does not mention fathers in its 340 pages. Grant, *Raising Baby by the Book*, 3; MacMurchy, *The Canadian Mother's Book*, 21, 60, 67–92, 127, 132; Helen MacMurchy, *Maternal Care* (Ottawa: Department of Pensions and National Health, Canada, 1931), 3, 5–6; Helen MacMurchy, *Mother: A Little Book For Men* (Ottawa: Dominion of Canada Department of Health, 1928), 5, 10, 23; Cynthia R. Comacchio, "'A

Postscript for Father': Defining a New Fatherhood in Interwar Canada," *The Canadian Historical Review* 78, no. 3 (September 1997): 385; Comacchio, *"Nations are Built of Babies"*; Arnup, *Education for Motherhood*, 33.

33 Hamilton, "Working With the Creator," 42.

34 Salem G. Bland, "The Woman and the Child," *Grain Growers' Guide* 15, no. 50 (13 December 1922): 5; Francis, Jones, and Smith, *Destinies*, 241.

35 Mona Gleason, *Normalizing the Ideal: Psychology, Schooling, and the Family in Postwar Canada* (Toronto: University of Toronto Press, 1999), 4.

36 Comacchio, *The Infinite Bonds of Family*, 93.

37 Dodd, "Advice to Parents," 204.

38 After March 1921, the *Grain Growers' Guide* did not record subscription numbers on the cover, possibly indicating a decrease in subscriptions due to the worsening prairie agricultural crisis of the 1920s: *Grain Growers' Guide*, (5 January 1922): cover; *Grain Growers' Guide* (16 March 1922): cover; Friesen, *The Canadian Prairies*, 329, 514.

39 The back covers of the "Blue Books" listed the available titles and encouraged mothers to send for those they wished. The government mailed the books to them free of charge. Dodd, "Advice to Parents," 204, 210; Comacchio, *The Infinite Bonds of Family*, 96; Pamela Margaret White, "Restructuring the Domestic Sphere – Prairie Indian Women On Reserves: Image, Ideology and State Policy, 1880–1930" (Ph.D. diss., McGill University, 1987): 240–41.

40 Dodd, "Advice to Parents," 211.

41 Kathleen Strange, "'I Hadn't Believed That There Was So Much Pain in the World,'" in *No Easy Road: Women in Canada, 1920s to 1960s*, ed. Beth Light and Ruth Roach Pierson (Toronto: New Hogtown Press, 1990), 181; See also, Light and Pierson, *No Easy Road*, 173.

42 At least one woman, the unnamed mother of George James Macdonald, born 26 September 1928, followed MacMurchy's advice. She neatly penned the baby's name and birth weight in the proud hand of a new mother at the top of the "Weight Chart" in the back of her copy of *The Canadian Mother's Book*. From 26 September 1928 until 21 August 1929, Macdonald's mother followed MacMurchy's advice and recorded her son's weight, his height, and other comments as well. Studies that illustrate the various levels of acceptance and implementation of the scientific motherhood advice are Grant's *Raising Baby by the Book*, 137–60, which considers the United States; Arnup's *Education for Motherhood*, 120–26, which studies central Canada; and Comacchio's *"Nations are Built of Babies,"* 181–212, which provides evidence for the province of Ontario. None of these volumes discuss rural prairie Canada, where conditions were harsher than in central Canada. Arnup bases her exploration of mothers' acceptance of parenting advice largely on studies done in the 1980s. She assumes that parents' responses to the literature were similar earlier in the century.

43 To American immigration historian Roger Daniels, an ethnic group is "a number of people who conceive of themselves as being alike by virtue of their common ancestry, real or fictitious, and who are so regarded by others." "Ethnicity," to American religious historian Harold J. Abramson, "develops from the history and migration of culturally differentiated races, nations, and tribes, not to mention the unique social experiences of religious creeds." Roger Daniels, "Eastern European Jews," History 389 – Origins of North American Immigration, 1600 to

Present – Lecture, 23 October 1996; Harold J. Abramson, "Religion," in *Harvard Encyclopedia of American Ethnic Groups*, ed. Stephan Thernstrom (Cambridge, MA: The Belknap Press of the Harvard University Press, 1981), 869; Friesen, *The Canadian Prairies*, 242, 249, 257, 262, 265, 267, 269, 273.

44 Hamilton, "Forming Baby's Habits," 28; Hamilton, "Fall Babies," 29.

45 Hamilton, "Forming Baby's Habits," 28.

46 "Class," according to historian Edward Thompson, "happens when some men [or women], as a result of common experience (inherited or shared), feel and articulate the identity of their interests as between themselves, and as against other men [or women] whose interests are different from (and usually opposed to) theirs." E. P. Thompson, *The Making of the English Working Class* (London: Penguin Books, 1968), 8–9; Hamilton, "Fall Babies," 29.

47 Comacchio, *"Nations are Built of Babies,"* 12–13.

48 MacMurchy specifically designed her books *Beginning Our Home in Canada*, *How to Make Our Canadian Home*, and *How We Cook in Canada*, to introduce new immigrants to the "Canadian way." The simple language used in all of the "Blue Books" was likely a mechanism intended to assist people who were new to reading English. "Helpful Booklets," *Grain Growers' Guide* 14, no. 49 (7 December 1921): 18; MacMurchy, *The Canadian Mother's Book*, 70; Dodd, "Advice to Parents," 206.

49 Dodd, "Advice to Parents," 211.

50 The "Little Blue Books" from 1921, 1923, 1925, 1926, and 1928 all ask mothers requesting the literature to "[p]lease mention whether the English or the French Edition is desired." Dominion of Canada, Department of Health, *How to Take Care of the Family* (Ottawa, Dominion of Canada Department of Health, 1921); Helen MacMurchy, *How to Take Care of the Baby* (Ottawa: Dominion of Canada Department of Health, 1923); Helen MacMurchy, *How to Take Care of the Children* (Ottawa: Dominion of Canada Department of Health, 1923); Helen MacMurchy, *How to Take Care of the Mother* (Ottawa: Dominion of Canada Department of Health, 1923); Helen MacMurchy, *Canadians Need Milk* (Ottawa: Dominion of Canada Department of Health, 1926); Helen MacMurchy, *Mother: A Little Book for Men* (Ottawa: Dominion of Canada Department of Health, 1928); MacMurchy, *The Canadian Mother's Book*.

51 White, "Restructuring the Domestic Sphere," 240–41.

52 In 1925, the Native infant mortality rate was 170 per 1,000 live births and the non-Native rate was in the mid-40s. Almost one in four Native children died. Strong-Boag, *The New Day Recalled*, 153; White, "Restructuring the Domestic Sphere," 244; Arnup, *Education for Motherhood*, 83.

53 Comacchio, *The Infinite Bonds of Family*, 94.

54 "Home Nursing Courses," *Grain Growers' Guide* 17, no. 31 (30 July 1924): 18; Marion Hughes, "Health Services in the Country," *Grain Growers' Guide* 20, no. 11 (1 June 1927): 26; Bramadat and Saydak, "Nursing on the Canadian Prairies," 107; Comacchio, *The Infinite Bonds of Family*, 95.

55 Buckley, "Efforts to Reduce Infant and Maternal Mortality," 78; Bramadat and Saydak, "Nursing on the Canadian Prairies," 109–10.

56 Hughes, "Health Services in the Country," 26.

57 Comacchio notes that many families dwelling in urban areas "could not pay the high costs of private physician care." Dodd, "Advice to Parents," 218; Strange,

"'I Hadn't Believed,'" 181; Abeele, "'The Infant Soldier,'" 110–12; Bramadat and Saydak, "Nursing on the Canadian Prairies," 108; Buckley, "Efforts to Reduce Infant and Maternal Mortality," 78; Comacchio, *The Infinite Bonds of Family*, 95; Wendy Mitchinson, *Giving Birth in Canada, 1900–1950* (Toronto: University of Toronto Press, 2002), 167–69.

58   Hamilton, "Care of Mother and Babe," 46.

59   Hamilton, "The Hygiene of Pregnancy," 44.

60   An unidentified prairie woman quoted in Buckley, "Efforts to Reduce Infant and Maternal Mortality," 78.

61   Soldier Settlement Board request quoted in Dodd, "Advice to Parents," 218.

62   Dodd, "Advice to Parents," 218–19.

63   Ibid., 219.

64   Ibid., 218; Langford, "Childbirth on the Canadian Prairies," 151–52.

65   Mitchinson, *Giving Birth in Canada*, 167.

66   The United Farm Women of Manitoba sent the "Rural Home Survey" to 364 women. Of these women, 330 returned their fully completed questionnaires. The survey of 1922 favoured women who were more likely to benefit from modernization. The women who responded had to be literate in English because the survey was published in English. They were also from slightly wealthier families based on where they owned land and how much they owned. These biases serve to underscore the relevance of the findings in terms of the lack of modern conveniences in farm homes. The underrepresented women, those less wealthy and non-English speaking, experienced home conditions as primitive, and maybe even more so, than those represented in the survey did: Mary Kinnear, "'Do you want your daughter to marry a farmer?': Women's Work on the Farm, 1922," in *Canadian Papers in Rural History VI*, ed. Donald H. Akenson (Garonoque: Langdale Press, 1988), 144–45; Sara Brooks Sundberg, "A Female Frontier: Manitoba Farm Women in 1922," *Prairie Forum* 16, 2 (Fall 1991): 185, 187, 189, 190.

67   Langford, "Childbirth on the Canadian Prairies," 152, 169; Kinnear, "'Do you want your daughter?'" 144–45; Sundberg, "A Female Frontier," 193.

68   Helen MacMurchy's 1928 report *Maternal Mortality in Canada* quoted in Buckley, "Efforts to Reduce Infant and Maternal Mortality," 79.

69   "Outpost Hospitals," *Grain Growers' Guide* 13, no. 7 (18 February 1920): 47; Bramadat and Saydak, "Nursing on the Canadian Prairies," 108; Dodd, "Advice to Parents," 219.

70   Hamilton, "The Bottle Fed Baby," 53.

71   There are a variety of statistical problems to consider, such as under-representation and the fact that problem cases might have specifically sought out hospitalization or a doctor's care and such cases may contribute to some of the deaths recorded. Despite these problems, it is significant to note that maternal mortality rates were lower for births not supervised by medical personnel, while advice authors deemed a doctor or nurse's presence necessary at birth: Mitchinson, *Giving Birth in Canada*, 264–65.

72   The advice to "call the Doctor" also presumed telephone ownership. Not all prairie farms had telephone service in the 1920s; in 1921, one-third of prairie farm homes had a telephone and, by 1931, the ownership rate had fallen to 25 per cent: Nadine I. Kozak, "'Among the Necessities': A Social History of Communication Technology on the Canadian Prairies, 1900 to 1950" (master's thesis, Carleton

University, 2000): 91–92; Dodd, "Advice to Parents," 213, 218; MacMurchy, *The Canadian Mother's Book*, 11; Hamilton, "The Hygiene of Pregnancy," 42.

73　MacMurchy, *The Canadian Mother's Book*, 20.

74　Ibid., 20–21.

75　Kinnear, *A Female Economy*, 69, 94; Sheila McManus, "Gender(ed) Tensions in the Work and Politics of Alberta Farm Women, 1905–29," in *Telling Tales: Essays in Western Women's History*, ed. Catherine A. Cavanaugh and Randi R. Warne (Vancouver: UBC Press, 2000), 130.

76　McManus, "Gender(ed) Tensions," 123.

77　Langford, "Childbirth on the Canadian Prairies," 166.

78　Mitchinson, *Giving Birth in Canada*, 106–7.

79　Strong-Boag, *The New Day Recalled*, 113; Sundberg, "A Female Frontier," 185.

80　An unidentified prairie woman quoted in Bramadat and Saydak, "Nursing on the Canadian Prairies," 112.

81　Sundberg, "A Female Frontier," 190.

82　Hamilton, "The Bottle Fed Baby," 53; Hamilton, "The Breast-Fed Baby," 30; MacMurchy, *The Canadian Mother's Book*, 30–33.

83　MacMurchy, *Canadians Need Milk*, 7; Hamilton, "The Bottle Fed Baby," 53.

84　The metric conversions for these temperatures are 45 to 53.4 degrees Celsius for pasteurization and 4.4 degrees Celsius as the holding temperature: MacMurchy, *Canadians Need Milk*, 9; Hamilton, "The Bottle Fed Baby," 54; MacMurchy, *The Canadian Mother's Book*, 108–9.

85　Dodd, "Advice to Parents," 223.

86　Kinnear, "'Do you want your daughter?'" 145.

87　Mothers were to keep the baby's room at 21.1 degrees Celsius in the day and 18.3 degrees Celsius at night: Hamilton, "Fall Babies," 30.

88　Kinnear, "'Do you want your daughter?'" 145; Sundberg, "A Female Frontier," 190–91.

89　The wells were an average of fifty-five metres from the farm homes. MacMurchy, *The Canadian Mother's Book*, 84; Hamilton, "The Bottle Fed Baby," 53; Sundberg, "A Female Frontier," 190.

90　Dodd, "Advice to Parents," 221.

eleven

"I Think So Much of Edward": Family, Favouritism,

and Gender on a Prairie Farm in the 1930s

CRISTINE GEORGINA BYE

As Nadine Kozak suggests, feminist historians seeking to rewrite the West often struggle with a dearth of sources that shed light on how motherhood advice literature, which privileged men as "breadwinners," constrained the beliefs and activities of rural women in their daily lives. By using a personal collection of letters, written by Saskatchewan farm woman Kate Graves to her daughter during the Depression, Cristine Bye explores power relations within the patriarchal farm family that have often eluded the grasp of historians. Graves's letters suggest the extent to which she favoured her son; they recount the manipulations, power struggles, arguments, and unhappiness that emerged as her adherence to prevailing notions of the "ideal" wife and mother brought her into conflict with her daughter-in-law. By placing her study of family power dynamics within the context of a burgeoning international literature on rural women, Bye argues that women who lived in strong patriarchal cultures internalized dominant notions of masculinity and femininity. By privileging their sons over their daughters, and by holding their daughters-in-law to the strictest standards of femininity, rural women like Kate Graves participated in their own oppression. By doing so, they ensured the survival of the family farm, but impeded the formation of a strong women's culture. In the late nineteenth century, imperialists and nationalists in both Britain and Canada planted their hopes for a reinvigorated masculinity and reinstituted patriarchy on the colonial "frontiers"; by subjecting the Graves family correspondence to critical gender analysis, Bye details one of the more subtle ways that these hopes came to bear fruit in a regional context.

Saskatchewan farm woman Kate Graves was thrilled on 5 December 1932, when her twenty-five-year-old son Edward asked her to help him choose the fabric for a new, tailor-made suit. "Has to be specially nice suit this time, for he is going to be married," she wrote her daughter Georgina. "Just think of it! The last of eight to jump the broomstick."[1]

Thus began an eight-and-a-half-year saga of joy, sorrow, anger, and betrayal that would demonstrate the profound sense of love and responsibility Kate felt towards Edward, the lengths she would go in order to support him and his family, and the patriarchal notions that undergirded Graves family relations during the Great Depression. Kate's bond with Edward was a dominant theme in her life throughout this period. Although she supported her other children and relatives in many ways, she consistently invested more money, energy, and emotion in her only natural-born son. This strategy not only helped Edward and his young family endure, but reinforced assumptions about male and female roles within the Graves family. Ultimately, it fed Kate's identity as a good wife and mother, and sustained a family system that favoured males.

This chapter is based mainly on a collection of letters Kate Graves wrote to her fourth eldest daughter, Georgina Edith (Graves) Griffiths, between 1930 and 1941.[2] The letters reveal a woman who was devoted to her family and was largely responsible for getting them through the

Depression. They also shed light on the Graves family's internal dynamics, especially Kate's relationships with Edward, her daughters, and Edward's wife Dorothy. Historians and other scholars have explored the patriarchal underpinnings of western Canadian society and the institution of the family farm.[3] Many prairie farm women wrote the agrarian press in the early decades of the twentieth century to complain about male domination in society and the home and to express solidarity with their overworked, undervalued peers.[4] But others – perhaps the silent majority – acquiesced to the gender status quo. Noted women's historian Gerda Lerner argues that women have historically "participated in the process of their own subordination because they have been psychologically shaped so as to internalize the idea of their own inferiority."[5] Several scholars have detected a similar pattern among rural women in various periods and settings.[6] Kate's letters allow us to observe this process in one particular farm family. Kate Graves occasionally expressed subtle resentment of, but did not publicly challenge, male authority. Rather than risk her reputation as a respectable farm woman, she subordinated her own interests and those of other female family members to those of men. The extent to which she internalized notions about male superiority – favouring her son, discounting her daughters, and scapegoating her daughter-in-law – is striking.

Before our story begins, it is important to mention that this is mainly Kate's tale. Her letters tell us far more about her than other family members. We do not know Edward and Dorothy's side of the story. Nor do we know how Kate's husband Tom saw events, beyond what Kate tells us. Kate and Tom appear to have enjoyed a solid marriage, but Tom played a peripheral role in her letters, and thus in the account that follows. That said, the growing literature on farm women and families can add to our understanding of the story's various players.

The woman at the centre of this paper was born into an English-speaking Presbyterian family on 11 March 1866 at Franklin Centre, Quebec (then Canada East). Kate Edwards married small-scale foundry owner and blacksmith Tom Graves in 1885 and, over the next sixteen years, bore seven daughters and welcomed a five-year-old foster son from England into her home. The birth of Kate and Tom's only natural-born son in 1907, after a string of daughters, was a particular source of pride and pleasure in the Graves family. Kate and Tom must have felt their family was finally complete.[7] They named the baby Thomas Edward, after his father, but called him Edward. Congratulations poured in from relatives and neighbours, and Edward's sisters vied with each other to shower him with attention. Fourteen-year-old Georgina liked to hold "our baby," and mentioned him daily in her diary. "I was the first to kiss Edward on his first Christmas day," she wrote.[8] Kate later told Georgina that she loved her daughters and would have liked a dozen. But Edward was destined to have a paramount place in her heart.[9]

In 1914 Kate, Tom, and most of their children moved to a homestead in southwestern Saskatchewan near the future town of McCord, about two hundred kilometres southwest of Regina. The Graves were what western Canadian historian Gerald Friesen would call a "respectable" farm family.[10] They operated an average-sized, 375-acre grain farm, enjoyed a moderate income that allowed them to employ seasonal workers, belonged to Saskatchewan's British-Canadian, Protestant majority, and held respected positions in the community's church, school, and agricultural organizations. Georgina left for Alberta in the early 1920s and another daughter moved to British Columbia, but Kate's remaining five daughters and foster son settled within a thirty-five-kilometre radius of Kate and Tom's farm. The 1930s found the couple, then in their sixties and early seventies, sharing their home with Edward, his growing family, and various grandchildren.

No part of Canada or the world suffered more during the Great Depression than the province of Saskatchewan. Drought, plunging wheat prices, and the prolonged contraction of the Canadian economy conflated to almost destroy Saskatchewan society. Between 1928–29 and 1933, the province's per-capita income fell by 72 per cent, compared with 42 per cent for Canada as a whole. Provincial net farm income fell to minus $34-million in 1931; individual farm operators' average net income was minus $255. Saskatchewan farmers, who were largely dependant on wheat, saw per bushel prices plummet to a four-hundred-year, worldwide low. Hot winds, dust storms, and insect hordes destroyed many farm families' crops and gardens for six, seven, or more years in a row. Saskatchewan's environmental and economic problems had enormous social consequences. Many residents were hungry, poorly clothed, illhoused, and in poor health. By 1937, two-thirds of the rural population was on government relief. For residents over seventy, relief often came in the guise of the dominion-provincial old age pension program; the number of Saskatchewan pension applicants more than tripled over the course of the decade. Thousands of families abandoned their farms for new homes in northern Saskatchewan or other parts of Canada. At

Kate Graves with husband Tom and grandchildren Billy and Gordon Graves, 27 June 1937. Courtesy: Cristine G. Bye.

least one-fifth of the population left the province over the course of the decade. Southern Saskatchewan's fortunes did not begin to brighten until the drought lifted in 1938. Crop yields improved, but grain prices and farm incomes remained low. It was not until farmers reaped a bumper crop in 1942 and wheat prices rose in 1943 that the province could genuinely say the Great Depression was over.[11]

The Graves' experiences with crop failure, poverty, illness, and family dislocation mirrored those of many Saskatchewan families. Drought and other environmental hazards hit Kate's region particularly hard. Crop District No. 3, which encompassed much of southwestern Saskatchewan, recorded the lowest crop yields in the province for six of the ten years between 1929 and 1938. Wheat yields in Kate's municipality dropped from twenty-five bushels an acre in 1928, to five bushels in 1929, and stayed low for most of the decade. Farmers harvested no wheat at all in 1931 and 1937.[12] "Don't seem like it can rain here," Kate wrote Georgina on 11 June 1937. "Not one bit of anything. No wheat on the field."[13]

Some years, virtually every farm family in the area required government help. Kate's letters and Rural Municipality of Mankota relief ledgers show that she and Tom received relief each year between 1930 and 1938. Relief records also list the names of Kate's neighbours and the families of five of her children.[14] Kate and Tom applied for the old age pension in 1937, when they were seventy-one and seventy-three, respectively. Kate wrote in June of that year that a pension administrator was considering her application. "I hope he hurries a little. Times are hard."[15] Several family members developed nutritional-deficiency diseases and other ailments, often postponing necessary medical treatment for lack of money. The most tragic case was Kate's eldest daughter Mary, who died of tuberculosis in 1933. Kate's region lost more than 22 per cent of its farm population. The number of farms in the Rural Municipality of Mankota fell from 478 in 1931 to 383 in 1941 – the second highest decrease out of eight municipalities in the area.[16] Kate's foster son and natural son both joined the exodus. Charley moved briefly to northern Saskatchewan in 1934, and Edward left for Quebec in 1937. Kate and Tom did not live to see the end of the Depression; both died in 1941. But thanks largely to Kate's efforts, the family farm – and Edward – endured.[17]

Like thousands of other poverty-stricken Canadian families, Kate and her kin pulled together to help each other through the Depression.[18] They regularly offered each other direct financial support in the form of loans and gifts of food, clothing, household items, and cash. Kate sent Georgina and her family used clothing, rag rugs, handmade mittens, and coins. She gave one daughter her sewing machine, bought castor oil and clothes for some grandchildren, and lent money to male relatives who needed train fare. Kate's relatives, in turn, gave her wild berries, garden seeds, chickens, meat, vegetables and – for Christmas and birthdays – everything from tea towels to stationery.

The Graves also employed gendered work strategies on behalf of their immediate and extended circles. Men owned the land and were responsible for fieldwork and large livestock. They were the family's representatives in the community. Often they worked, attended agricultural and political meetings, and conducted business together. Kate, like the authors of motherhood advice manuals (described by Nadine Kozak in chapter 10), saw her menfolk as breadwinners and heads of households. In her view, they must work hard, assume overall responsibility for the farm and family, and provide dependents with adequate shelter and physical comforts. She praised male relatives for being "good workers" and showing "ambition." A son-in-law who bought a large supply of groceries for his family was "a good provider."[19]

The task of nurturing Graves family members physically, socially, and emotionally fell mainly to women – as it did in a vast number of Canadian homes in the 1930s.[20] Kate and her female relatives physically supported their families through their work in the house and yard – cooking meals, gardening, caring for children and sick adults, and earning vital income from poultry and dairy products. The women's egg money and economizing efforts helped offset the family's loss in wheat income, making them – like countless other North American farm women – the farm's true economic mainstay in the 1930s.[21] Socially, the women sustained their kin by providing food for community events, organizing family gatherings, and exchanging letters with far-flung relatives. The women also played a vital emotional role in the family. They were its "tension managers," offering sympathy, affection, and advice to stressed kin.[22] They supported men who felt "blue and discouraged" about failed crops, consoled each other when Mary died, and generally served as each other's best friends and confidants.[23]

As was the case in Henrietta Muir Edwards's relationship with Aboriginal women at the Blood Reserve in southern Alberta (discussed by Patricia Roome in chapter 3), Kate's close relationships with her daughters and other female kin suggest the presence of a "women's culture" that supported women in ways men did not.[24] The women often performed domestic work, worked at community events, and attended women's meetings together. Kate regarded the extended visits she paid her daughters and a niece as holidays that helped keep her cheerful and healthy. Her contact with female kin, more than anything else, may have been the strategy that sustained her during the Depression. As we will see, however, the Graves women did not nurture all female family members equally. Kate and her daughters criticized Dorothy's conduct as a homemaker, wife, and daughter-in-law. And they failed to nurture women to the degree that they nurtured men. Often, they supported Edward at women's expense.

If Kate expected men to be the family's chief decision-makers and providers, she expected women to be its capable-but-submissive caregivers. The ideal farm woman excelled at homemaking and mothering. She was hard-working, efficient, selfless, and stoical. "Katey is so clever," she said of her fifth eldest daughter. "How she manages and keeps things running so smoothly these days – and no complaints."[25] The ideal woman also knew her place in the family hierarchy. Kate was a strong-willed, competent woman who knew the value of her contribution to the family and farm. But she often deferred to male family members, even on matters that were important to her. And she publicly portrayed mild-mannered Tom as a dominant figure and herself as his compliant wife. Accurate or not, it was important to Kate to project an image that was compatible with patriarchal notions that prevailed in rural Saskatchewan and the rest of Canada in the 1930s.[26]

Most Saskatchewan farm families would have agreed with the standards Kate used to measure male and female behaviour. The ideal of the male farmer/provider and the female homemaker/dependent was firmly entrenched in rural society.[27] John W. Bennett and Seena B. Kohl, who studied families in the Maple Creek area of southwestern Saskatchewan in the 1960s, found that men were judged mainly on their skills as ranch or farm operators and their performance as family providers, and women were judged mainly on their "goodness" as mothers and homemakers.[28] Of course, the Depression prevented many families from fully conforming to gender ideals. An increased number of prairie farm women performed fieldwork and other male-designated tasks because their families could not afford male workers. And women supported the family farm economy by intensifying their subsistence and income-generating activities in the household, garden, hen house, and barn. Women's dairy and poultry-related work allowed families in parts of Saskatchewan to meet almost half their own food needs, and made a substantial contribution to the province's overall agricultural economy. The percentage of agricultural revenue from dairy and poultry products rose from 4 per cent in 1928, to 23 per cent in 1937. Meanwhile, the percentage of revenue from wheat – which Saskatchewan society and the Graves family associated with men – fell from 80 per cent to 33 per cent. In short, women often became their families' true providers and kept them on the land. However, women's vital labour was not publicly acknowledged or rewarded in the 1930s. Economically, legally, and socially, prairie society continued to privilege men.[29] If anything, the notion of the male breadwinner strengthened. Concern for male morale prompted many Canadian families to cling to the fiction of the male as the economic head of his family and the female as his dependent mate. "There remained at least a facade of the traditional family to present to the outside world and to organize relations within," writes family historian Cynthia Comacchio.[30]

This brings us back to the Graves' family story. Edward married a local woman, Dorothy Hamilton, on 19 January 1933, when he was twenty-five and she was eighteen. From the very beginning, Kate and Tom took a keen interest in the young couple's finances. They considered moving a small house onto the farm for Edward and Dorothy – Tom made an offer on the house by mail – but in the end the two couples decided to live together until they could afford to build an addition onto Kate and Tom's house. It was not uncommon for young married couples and elderly parents to share accommodation as a survival strategy during the Depression. Depending on the province, four to nine per cent of households were multiple-family in 1931, and historian Denyse Baillargeon found that most of the couples in her sample of working-class Montrealers lived with family members, usually the husband's parents, for the first few months to two years of their marriage.[31] It is interesting to note the patrilocal nature of these arrangements. The Graves and many other Canadian families assumed the bride would throw her lot in with the male side of the family. Farm families, especially, assumed that a son and his wife would live with or near his parents because the son was expected to work with his father and to eventually assume ownership of the farm.[32]

At first, Kate was pleased with her daughter-in-law and enjoyed her company. She reported that they shared an interest in house plants and planned to work in the garden together. Dorothy showed considerable promise as a homemaker and wife. She was "very industrious" and mended clothes "nicely." "I tell you Edward's clothes are kept in order." Dorothy was also "kind" to Kate, giving her a cake with "Mother of Mine" written on it for Mother's Day.[33]

Two years later, Kate's opinion of Dorothy had plummeted. Edward was "a comfort," but Dorothy was difficult. "She has sulky spells and don't speak to me for hours."[34] The women's working relationship was often strained. Kate resented the fact that Dorothy disappeared upstairs on butter churning day. "It is a lot of work for me and she won't turn her hand over if I churned all hours."[35] By this time, Dorothy and Edward's son Gordon had joined the household, and Kate and Tom's avid interest in their grandchild had become a source of tension. Kate was stung when Dorothy accused her and Tom of spoiling him. "She plainly said she wished we would let her bring him up and so I am more than willing.... She has lots to learn. One thing she was never taught [was] respect for her elders."[36] The popular press in the 1930s regularly raised the spectre of the "mother-in-law bogey": the difficult female elder who interfered in younger family member's lives.[37] But Kate saw herself and other elderly women in her family as victims of heartless daughters-in-law. She blamed Dorothy for their fractious relationship. "Never think for a moment I am hard with D. I have been so lenient that she got thinking everything was hers here and was very independent and openly wishing we would get out."[38] Kate saw Dorothy as immature, grasping, and prone to "loud, uncontrolled" rants. She saw herself, on the other hand, as controlled, civilized, and superior. "I try to be pleasant," she insisted.[39]

Kate was relieved when she and Tom finally moved into the newly completed addition to their house in June 1935, two and a half years after Dorothy and Edward's wedding. Although the two families continued to have considerable contact – they were separated by a single door, and Kate and Tom continued to use a bedroom in Dorothy and Edward's section – relations between the women apparently improved. "They all seem to be getting on fine together now that they have their own part of the house," Kate's daughter Katey (Graves) Hatlelid wrote Georgina in March 1936.[40] Kate could not resist subtly criticizing Dorothy in her letters to Georgina, however. She reproached her for not helping local women cook for a community meal, and derided her mothering and homemaking skills. She hinted that Gordon had a cold because his mother did not always keep him in stockings. And she noted on a windy spring day in 1937 that "Dorothy picked this horrid day to wash all her quilts great and small," and when the clothes line broke, several quilts "wallowed in the dust."[41] Kate apparently shared her opinions with Katey, who said: "Dorothy ... is a poor manager, but mother helps her by tending the babies whenever asked."[42]

Dorothy's life with Kate cannot have been easy. The two women had vastly different personalities and interests. Dorothy was a jovial young woman with a hearty laugh and a penchant for romance novels.[43] Kate was an elderly, proper woman who preferred newspapers and serious conversation. Kate seemed to think she had considerable experience to share with Dorothy, but that Dorothy was not open to her wisdom. The two families were likely aware that their living situation was not ideal. Historian Veronica Strong-Boag says many Canadians in this period "believed that living together in a two or three generation group was fraught with danger."[44] Most of the Montreal women Baillargeon interviewed said they tried to get along with their mothers-in-law and willingly conformed to their expectations; some credited their mothers-in-law for teaching them how to cook.[45] Scholars of twentieth-century rural women and families say women who marry into farm families (which is the way most enter farming) often face special pressures. They may be constantly scrutinized, expected to share their mother-in-law's social interests and work patterns, and marginalized within their husband's family and the male-owned farm business.[46] Perhaps Dorothy – who was as strong-willed as Kate in her own way – resisted the subordinate role she was expected to play in the Graves family hierarchy.

Problems aside, Kate, Tom, Edward and Dorothy all benefited from their living arrangement. It saved Edward and Dorothy the cost of purchasing or renting a separate household, and allowed both parties to share livestock, household and farm equipment, and relief allotments for fuel and food. The arrangement also had emotional advantages. It fed Kate and Tom's bond with their son and his children, and it made the older pair feel good to know they were aiding Edward financially. Historian James Snell says many elderly Canadians in the first half of the twentieth century "enjoyed the status and power that came from their interaction with their sons and daughters or other relatives – aiding them in 'getting a start,' sharing a home or farm ... or providing less tangible assistance."[47]

Just how financially and emotionally intertwined the two families were became clear in 1937. Anxiety in the Graves household escalated in the spring as the family realized that they were facing their worst year yet. "Edward is discouraged out and out," Kate wrote on May 11. "We have had a terrific dust storm all day and our crop is blowing out same as other people's and he says all the hard work and early rising going for naught. He would like to move right off." Kate expressed her distress through that of Edward and Dorothy. "I do not think people should stay on here. This is about enough.... [Dorothy] says she is going to walk out if she has no other way."[48]

A month later, the family's mood had switched to excited anticipation. "Well, I can hardly tell you the latest news at our place," Kate wrote. "Edward had me write to Colin B. Edwards and ask how chances were back there. We all felt we would like to go back if we could get a house to live in, and Edward wanted work." The years Kate had spent writing to, and sustaining connections with, Quebec kin paid off. Word came that Franklin Centre farmers expected to reap abundant hay and apple crops, and that there were several farms available for rent or purchase. "And Edward decided to go east," said Kate. "Go in our car."[49]

At the end of June, thirty-nine neighbours and friends gathered at Kate and Tom's house for a farewell party for Edward and Dorothy. The young couple stood in the doorway between the two parts of the house as their friends presented them with an envelope containing $4.95. Kate thought her son acquitted himself well in his role as the Graves family standard-bearer. "Edward spoke so well, thanking them and in a good clear voice.… He should have been an orator."[50] Far from seeing Edward's leave-taking as an admission of defeat, Kate and her family saw it as evidence of a desire to provide for his family. He was proving his worth as a man. "He has been a good, hard working man and he is tired of not being able to earn his living ... and he did not like living on relief," said Kate. Dorothy earned rare praise for supporting her mate; Kate called her "brave" and "willing."[51]

The departure of Edward and his young family in Kate and Tom's 1926 Chevrolet left an aching void in the older couple's life. "We miss the folks so much," Kate wrote the day after they left.[52] Kate and Tom deliberated over following Edward east, torn between remaining on the farm in which they had invested so much energy and capital, and giving their son the financial and emotional support he seemed to need and expect. A small part of them realized that Edward was overly dependent on them. "Father says we can live much better without Edward than he can live without us," Kate wrote on 26 July 1937. But they found it very difficult to deny him. "Edward now wants the horses to plow and work his rented farm and the cows also," Kate wrote. "We have decided if we stay here to keep the cows and horses, and of course it bothers me to know that Edward needs them to start farming."[53]

Kate's letters from the summer of 1937 are among the most emotionally intense of the collection. This was one of the lowest points of the Depression for her, not because she experienced unparalleled environmental and economic disaster, but because she was separated from her precious son. She was uncharacteristically rattled and indecisive – much more distraught than when foster son Charley left for northern Saskatchewan three years earlier. Well aware of Kate's feelings, her daughters visited her often and did their best to advise and comfort her. They seemed to believe Kate and Tom were more emotionally reliant on Edward than the reverse. "Both Mother and Dad are so bound up in them," said Katey.[54]

Kate had just made up her mind to join Edward when a female relative wrote to say that Dorothy opposed her coming. Kate felt betrayed,

Kate Graves's daughter-in-law Dorothy and son Edward with children Billy and Gordon on 27 June 1937 – the day before they left Saskatchewan for Quebec. Courtesy: Cristine G. Bye.

but acted out her feelings by saying she hated to disappoint her son. "I think so much of Edward and know he would like to have us there."[55] Bolstered by her daughters, Kate decided to remain in Saskatchewan. Prior to this, she had expressed little regret at leaving her female kin in the West in order to be with her son. Only after that option became unfeasible did she elect to see herself as the fortunate mother of "good loving daughters and granddaughters who would not want me to go and be under that Dorothy again." Edward urged Kate to re-think her decision. Perhaps wishing to prove he was the head of his household, he insisted that Dorothy had agreed to "do whatever he said" on the matter. But Kate would have none of it. "We know her. A very selfish woman she is."[56]

Although they did not go to live with Edward, Kate and Tom decided to send him most of their possessions. In mid-September, Tom left for Quebec in a railway car containing Kate's good cook stove, the kitchen table and all of their farm livestock – including "*my* two cows." Edward's side of the house was stripped bare. "I miss everything," Kate wrote the day after Tom left. "Even Lady, our dear old faithful dog went to Edward, and some three dozen fowls."[57] Shipping the goods took most of Kate and Tom's meagre resources, including Kate's first old age pension cheques. Left with little money, no livestock, and few furnishings, the couple were willing to jeopardize their own ability to farm in order to give their son every opportunity to succeed.

Kate had mixed feelings about supporting Edward's venture. She was proud of the generosity she showed the young couple, but begrudged the help she gave Dorothy. "She never appreciates a thing we did. Like the leech's daughter, cried more, more." Not only was Dorothy an ungrateful daughter-in-law, but she was a poor wife – a "spender" who squandered her husband's (and his parents') resources.[58] Part of Kate's animosity towards Dorothy sprang from deep-seated doubt about Edward's business sense. Edward had rented an expensive farm for two years, with hopes of buying it. "He has no capital at his back," said Kate. "Just brawn and muscle and a good man. He is a good worker and does want to get ahead ... but I cannot believe he will ever own the place."[59] Kate said Edward would have to pay $325 a year in rent, and at least $200 in living expenses, because "his wife knows nothing of being economical."[60] Somehow, it was Dorothy's fault that Edward was getting in over his head financially. Rather than admit that Edward was financially dependent on them, and that his ability to make business decisions and support his family was flawed, Kate scapegoated Dorothy. She could not allow herself to see Edward as anything but "a good man."

After Tom returned from Quebec in late 1937, he and Kate went to stay with their daughter Katey and her family for several months. "Katey is a fine daughter," Kate wrote on 24 January 1938. "Always in good humour and so thoughtful of our comfort."[61] Kate often referred to Katey and her other daughters as "kind" and "good company." She knew she could count on them to take care of her emotionally and physically. She and most of her kin conformed to the widespread belief that it was up to daughters – and daughters-in-law – to care for elderly family members. To the Graves women, Dorothy's worst crime was that she was unkind to her mother-in-law.[62]

Not only did Kate expect her daughters to be solicitous of her, she expected them to understand when she and Tom favoured Edward with their affections, money, and physical presence. Georgina was informed that Kate was writing her less often because she was penning two letters a week to Edward. "He seems anxious to get them, poor boy." And, she heard how delighted Kate was to receive a birthday phone call from "our son" urging her and Tom to visit. It seems Kate had written Edward to say Tom might go east a second time.[63] In the meantime, Georgina, who had not seen her mother for thirteen years, was told repeatedly that her parents had neither the money nor the will to visit her. Kate said Tom missed Edward too intensely to leave home. But she may have been speaking of her own bond with Edward. "Everybody around here knows Edward and I were very much attached in every way. So many things we thought the same about."[64] Whatever the excuse, the fact is that Kate found the resources to finance Edward and Tom's trips to Quebec, and seriously considered sending Tom again. Clearly, "our son" was more important than Georgina.

Ultimately, Kate's doubts about Edward's ability to make a go of it proved correct. In the fall of 1939, Edward announced that he was relinquishing his farm, trading his parents' car in on a newer model, and returning to Saskatchewan. As soon as Tom heard the news, he began building a new bedroom for Kate and himself in the "west part" of the house; he hoped to prevent friction between the two families by giving Edward's family the entire east section. "Your Pa decided we must give them all this part," Kate wrote Georgina. "I hated to give up my bedroom for 25 years, but one must give in at times." Kate gave the impression that she bowed graciously to her husband's will and wanted what was best for her son. "I want to have peace for Edward's sake. He is dear to me."[65] Kate dreaded Dorothy's return, however. "She is large and aggressive as it were. *Enough said.*"[66] When Edward's family arrived in early December, Kate was so excited that she was almost rude when she told Georgina for the umpteenth time that she could not travel to see her. She did not judge Edward harshly for his failed sojourn – though she was sorry he had sold the cattle to pay down his debts. So much for her two cows.

Besides the fact that Edward had depleted his resources and missed his parents, it made sense for him to return to Saskatchewan when he did. The drought had broken, Kate and Tom's farm was again producing grain and, thanks to their old age pension cheques, the elderly couple were in a better position to help him than two years earlier.[67] In addition, the family may have thought it wise to locate Edward on the farm he was expected to inherit. "This farm is to be his, of course," said Kate.[68] Georgina and her sisters were given to understand that, not only did Edward take first place in his mother's heart, he had first claim on his parents' land. Kate and Tom adhered to the belief – common among farm families to the present day – that land should be passed down to sons rather than daughters.[69] It was assumed that Edward would get the farm, and Kate's daughters would get her dishes. The daughters did not contest Edward's right to the farm. Letters they wrote later suggest that they thought the farm should be in Edward's name. Ensuring that the farm retained the family name has traditionally been very important to farm families.[70] Foster son Charley may not have qualified for a share of the farm because he was not a "true" Graves. Kate seemed fond of Charley, but sometimes failed to think of him as a son. For instance, when she spoke of Edward as the eighth child to "jump the broomstick," she forgot that, counting Charley, she had nine children.[71]

Soon after Edward and Dorothy returned, family relations on the Graves farm resumed their former pattern. Kate and Tom continued to subsidize the young couple economically, giving them a stove and buying them a barrel of coal oil. "We help them all we can," said Kate.[72] And conflict between Kate and Dorothy resurfaced. The two women were clearly engaged in a tug of war for Edward's affections. "Dorothy and Edward are not generous with helping us," Kate wrote. "She seems to demand all his time in a way. If he comes and sits down, generally calls or sends for him.... We feel he is bossed too much."[73] Rather than blame Edward for neglecting his parents, Kate accused Dorothy of failing to defer to her husband and in-laws. Hostilities continued off and on until Kate died of a heart attack on 3 May 1941, at age seventy-five. One of Kate's daughters noted, with some disdain, that Dorothy "broke down and cried" at the funeral.[74] When Tom died less than three months later, Edward – with his sisters' approval – took over the family farm.

To explain the favouritism Kate and her family showed Edward in the 1930s, we must look to the patriarchal nature of the family farm and prairie society. Definitions of patriarchy vary, but Lerner defines it broadly as "the manifestation and institutionalization of male dominance over women and children in the family and the extension of male dominance over women in society in general. It implies that men hold power in all the important institutions of society and that women are deprived of access to such power."[75] Catherine Cavanaugh and other historians argue that patriarchal notions formed the very basis of prairie society in the late nineteenth and early twentieth centuries. Many Anglo-Canadians saw the West as a male preserve – a place that grew wheat and men. Settlement mythology depicted men as brawny, enterprising farmers and women as "gentle tamers" and "helpmates." Male government officials and legislators viewed women as dependents rather than direct contributors to the agricultural economy. Drawing on middle-class gender ideals, they developed laws and policies that reinforced patriarchal family structures.[76] Anthropologist Max Hedley, who has studied family farming in twentieth-century western Canada, argues that the term "family farm" was something of a misnomer. All able-bodied family members were expected to contribute their labour to the enterprise, but it was usually owned by an individual male. Without direct access to land, women and children were dependent on the male "head of household." Relationships within families varied, but the power to direct labour, collect profits, and dispense rewards ultimately rested with the senior male.[77] With male dominance came the notion that men were superior to women.[78] Rollings-Magnusson notes that settler families valued sons more than daughters – for their physical labour, their ability to enlarge family holdings by acquiring homesteads, and the likelihood that they would continue the farm.[79] Families favoured men mainly because they owned and controlled the land that was the source of family wealth and status. "Land – the most valuable resource in farming – leads families to associate more frequently with, or to favor in other ways, relatives who are its source," writes cultural anthropologist Sonya Salamon.[80] Of course, customs and laws favouring men ensured that they were more likely than women to gain access to land in the first place.

As mentioned, a range of state policies and laws reinforced women's subordinate position in western Canada. For instance, "the Dominion Lands Act of 1872 was specifically designed to prevent most women from acquiring free homestead property."[81] Women could homestead only if they were widowed, divorced or separated and had dependents. Other laws severely restricted married women's claims to family property. The federal government abolished dower in the Canadian West in 1886, which meant that a widow could not claim an interest in her husband's estate. And English common law did not entitle wives to a share of farm profits or a say in the disposition of the family farm – no matter how hard they worked on its behalf. Reformers agitated for homesteads for women from early in the twentieth century to 1930, without success. However, between 1915 and 1920, the Prairie provinces introduced legislation which guaranteed a widow a share of her husband's estate and prevented a husband from selling or mortgaging the homestead without his wife's consent. The changes gave women some protection "but no real security."[82] They did not prevent husbands from selling or willing to others the farm equipment, livestock, and household goods that made farms viable. Nor did they entitle wives to an equal share of the marital property while their husbands were living. Elizabeth Ann Kalmakoff argues that the dower campaign failed "to elicit an acknowledgement in law of the value of women's economic contributions to the development of a farm and to agricultural settlement as a whole."[83] Although the new legislation put some limits on husbands' absolute economic power, many legislators, judges, and even dower supporters continued to assume that men owned the land and were entitled to conduct their families' financial affairs.[84] Few women gained legal ownership or control of farm assets, either during the course of their marriages or upon divorce; as late as 1988, most Saskatchewan farm women did not own part of the "family farm."[85] Despite reformers' best efforts, women saw "patriarchy preserved on the prairies."[86]

Sociologist Sally Shortall argues that farming culture in Western countries has traditionally afforded women less power than men because they rarely have independent access to land and because farm families typically transfer land from father to son. The custom of patrilineal farm transfer is so powerful that "women's disinherited position is relatively unquestioned."[87] In Saskatchewan, girls learned that farmers were male and that women could not expect to own or control farm land. The only way they could enter farming was "through the back door" as a farmer's wife. Historically, most young Saskatchewan women cleared the way for their brothers to assume the family farm by leaving to pursue work, education, or marriage, which was seen as a woman's chief objective.[88] A 1931 survey of the Swift Current-Gull Lake district found that "few girls remained on the home farm after their seventeenth year." Many farm boys, however, stayed to assist with farm work "preparatory to farming for themselves."[89] Sons were taught to see themselves as farmers and to make succession to the family farm their main life goal. Rather than push sons from the household, farm families expected them to apprentice themselves to their fathers for a considerable period. For the likely heir, the farm succession process could be difficult. He was in a position of "bound-dependency" – bound to the family enterprise and obliged to defer to his father's authority.[90] Often, there was friction between fathers anxious to retain control of farm assets and decision-making authority, and sons anxious for more autonomy and responsibility. Mothers tended to serve as buffers between fathers and sons, smoothing the farm transfer process.[91] Several rural women's scholars argue that farm women were more intent on maintaining family unity and the farm enterprise than serving their own interests. "They asked only for success of the farm family in reproducing itself, of passing the farm on to the next generation," writes historian Joan Jensen.[92]

It is important to note that, as Lerner argues, "patriarchy does not imply that women are either totally powerless or totally deprived of rights, influence, and resources."[93] Publicly and privately, many Canadian farm women resisted male domination in the early decades of the twentieth century. Ontario women complained in the agricultural press about inheritance practices that disadvantaged daughters, especially hardworking spinsters who cared for elderly parents.[94] Prominent western Canadian feminist Nellie McClung told of a wealthy farmer who left a farm to each of his three sons and, "to his daughter Martha, a woman of forty years, the eldest of the family – he left a cow and one hundred dollars."[95] *Grain Growers' Guide* women's page editor Isobel Graham chastised farm families for devoting more resources to sons than wives and daughters. "We are told that a son 'earns or helps to earn the land,' therefore, the land is sacredly reserved for him." Graham said families tended to place sons on pedestals "with our own work-hardened hands, then stand back and admiringly exclaim, 'behold how splendidly they have climbed to their eminence!' And we have heartlessly robbed our daughters and wives and mothers to place the sons there."[96]

In the 1930s, many women wrote the Saskatoon-based *Western Producer* and other publications seeking recognition for the vital work they performed on prairie farms and "a more equitable distribution of responsibilities, resources and rewards within the family."[97] But even the most disenchanted contributors tended to see women primarily as homemakers and nurturers. The vast majority of western Canadian women continued to assume that farming was a male pursuit and that men were entitled to own, control, and inherit the family farm. Four Saskatchewan women who became "farm wives" during this period "seem to have accepted without much anger or resentment the legal and other disadvantages that they experienced," reports researcher Julie Dorsch.[98] As late as 1963–64, Maple Creek families frowned on local women who operated farms or ranches. It was "just not done."[99]

We have seen that the Graves were not alone in favouring their successor male.[100] With Kate's encouragement, the daughters left home as young women and accepted the fact that they would never own the family farm.[101] No doubt, the family reasoned that Edward deserved the farm because he helped his parents work it. They discounted the fact that the daughters laboured in the house and yard when their parents were establishing the farm, and that they continued to support their parents physically and emotionally as they aged. Just before she mentioned that Edward would get the farm, Kate detailed the excellent care four of her daughters had given her when she was seriously ill with influenza. Kate valued her daughters' role as the family's nurturers, but did not consider rewarding them with a share of the family property.

To be fair to Edward, he may have found his position difficult. His parents expected him to farm, whatever his true desires and abilities. Kohl and Bennett argue that rural sons actually had fewer options than daughters.[102] Kate and Tom, like many rural Saskatchewan parents, encouraged their successor son's dependency. In the economically depressed 1930s, Edward may have seen no alternative but to accept their help.

The Depression failed to shake Kate's ideas about men's and women's proper family roles. The Graves men were no longer the family's true providers, but Kate and the other women in her family behaved as though they were. We know that Kate continued to see Edward as a model of proper manhood. She expressed some resentment of male dominance. It bothered her when her son appropriated "*my* two cows." As a woman, she had been largely responsible for the family's dairy operations. She had likely bought those cows with her own egg and butter money. But as a male "head of household," Edward outranked her. Kate acquiesced to his wishes rather than jeopardize her status as a respectable, compliant farm woman. Gretchen Poiner, who has studied gender relations in rural Australia, argues that when internal or external forces threaten men's power, women actively uphold male authority. "In those aberrant circumstances in which women come to the fore, the understanding that men ought to possess greater power is translated into the belief that they do."[103]

Scholars who have studied farm women in a number of contemporary settings argue that they often accept male dominance as natural, consenting to their own subordination and stigmatizing women who do not adhere to prescribed gender roles.[104] Shortall found that Irish farm women's "powerless position is so deeply internalized that it results in a negative reaction against any farm wife who breaks out of this mould." Shortall also noticed that mothers-in-law reinforced inferior positions for daughters-in-law.[105] We know that Kate did not see Dorothy as a model female family member, that she did not find her helpful, efficient, and submissive. Focusing on Dorothy's supposed flaws allowed Kate to believe that she, herself, was an ideal woman. *She* knew how women should behave. Margaret Alston suggests that farm women may collude in their own subordination in exchange for power in the domestic sphere.[106] Rather than challenge patriarchal ideas about men's and women's proper roles, Kate embraced and drew strength from them. They helped her to construct and reaffirm her identity as a "good" farm woman.

Ultimately, the story of Kate and her family illustrates the extent to which gendered ideas coloured Graves family relationships in the 1930s. Kate felt compelled to devote an inordinate amount of emotion, energy, and money to Edward because he was a man. The strategies she used to get him through the Depression – from sharing her home with him, to financing his migration east, to promising him the farm – were rooted in patriarchal ideas about the relative value of men and women. Kate loved her daughters and appreciated their emotional and physical support. She enjoyed spending time with them and giving them small gifts. She praised them for fulfilling their roles as good wives, mothers, and daughters. But she did not value them as much as she valued her son. "The girls" were only doing what was expected of women; good daughters did not compare with a good son. Nor did Kate support the other principal woman in her son's life: his wife Dorothy. She was willing to devalue her daughters and assail her daughter-in-law in order to elevate her son – and herself. Attacking Dorothy allowed her to bolster her image of Edward as the ideal breadwinner male, and her image of herself as the ideal mother, wife, and homemaker.

Prairie farm women in the 1930s lived with a patriarchal system that favoured men; the constraints they faced were enormous. Some women, like Kate Graves, coped by aligning themselves with the males in their families. No doubt, on some level, they believed this strategy would help them and their families survive. The example of the Graves family tempts us to conclude that the policy of privileging men worked. The family and its chosen male endured. But the narrative of Kate, Edward, Dorothy, and the others suggests that, for female family members especially, the policy had its costs.

ENDNOTES

1   I would like to thank David B. Marshall, Elizabeth Jameson, R. Douglas Francis, Tamara P. Seiler and the *Unsettled Pasts* editors for their helpful insights into my work on Kate Graves. I also thank Kate Logan, Tania Therien, Danielle Kinsey and Jeri Lynne Lorentzon for their editing advice and encouragement. Kate Graves's letter to Georgina Edith (Graves) Griffiths, 6 December 1932, Kate Graves Family Papers, author's possession. All letters by Kate and other Graves family members originate from McCord, Saskatchewan, unless otherwise noted. For a detailed study of Kate Graves, see Cristine Georgina Bye, "'Times are Hard': A Saskatchewan Farm Woman's Experience of the Great Depression" (master's thesis, University of Calgary, 2001).

2   Kate Graves was my great-grandmother. Her daughter Georgina Edith (Graves) Griffiths farmed with her husband and children near Fleet, in east-central Alberta. Georgina preserved more than 150 of the letters Kate wrote her during the Great Depression. When Georgina died in 1973, she left the letters to her daughters – my mother Muriel (Griffiths) Bye and aunts Jean (Griffiths) Checkel and Anna (Griffiths) Rodvang. I am grateful to them for entrusting the letters to me. The letters form the bulk of the Kate Graves Family Papers, a collection of Graves family documents dating from the mid-nineteenth to the mid-twentieth century.

3   On the patriarchal foundations of prairie society, see Catherine Cavanaugh, "'No Place for a Woman': Engendering Western Canadian Settlement," *Western Historical Quarterly* 28 (Winter 1997): 493–518; Catherine Cavanaugh, "The Limitations of the Pioneering Partnership: The Alberta Campaign for Homestead Dower, 1909–25," *Canadian Historical Review* 74 (June 1993): 198–225; Sandra Rollings-Magnusson, "Canada's Most Wanted: Pioneer Women on the Western Prairies," *Canadian Review of Sociology and Anthropology* 27 (May 2000): 223–38; Sandra Rollings-Magnusson, "Hidden Homesteaders: Women, the State and Patriarchy in the Saskatchewan Wheat Economy," *Prairie Forum* 24 (Fall 1999): 171–83; Margaret E. McCallum, "Prairie Women and the Struggle for a Dower Law, 1905–1920," *Prairie Forum* 18 (Spring 1993): 19–33. On the patriarchal structure of the family farm in western Canada and elsewhere, see Max J. Hedley, "'Normal Expectations': Rural Women Without Property," *Resources for Feminist Research* 11 (March 1982): 15–17; Max Hedley, "Relations of Production of the 'Family Farm': Canadian Prairies," *Journal of Peasant Studies* 9 (October 1981): 71–85; Jean Burnet, *Next-Year Country: A Study of Rural Social Organization in*

Alberta (Toronto: University of Toronto Press, 1951), 31; Carolyn E. Sachs, *The Invisible Farmers: Women in Agricultural Production* (Totowa, NJ: Rowman and Allanheld, 1983), 65, 72–74, 81–82; Marjorie Griffin Cohen, *Women's Work, Markets, and Economic Development in Nineteenth-Century Ontario* (Toronto: University of Toronto Press, 1988), 42–45, 57–58.

4   Veronica Strong-Boag, "Pulling in Double Harness or Hauling a Double Load," in *The Prairie West: Historical Readings*, ed. R. Douglas Francis and Howard Palmer, 2nd ed. (Edmonton: Pica Pica Press, 1992), 401–23; Christa Scowby, "'I Am A Worker, Not A Drone': Farm Women, Reproductive Work and the *Western Producer*, 1930–1939," *Saskatchewan History* 48 (Fall 1996): 3–15; Christa L. Scowby "'Divine Discontent': Women, Identity, and the *Western Producer*" (master's thesis, University of Saskatchewan, 1996); Barbara E. Kelcey and Angela E. Davis, eds., *A Great Movement Underway: Women and The Grain Growers' Guide, 1908–1928* (Winnipeg: Manitoba Record Society, 1997); Norah L. Lewis, ed., *Dear Editor and Friends: Letters from Rural Women of the North-West, 1900–1920* (Waterloo, Ontario: Wilfrid Laurier University Press, 1998).

5   Gerda Lerner, *The Creation of Patriarchy* (New York: Oxford University Press, 1986), 218.

6   Sally Shortall, "Power Analysis and Farm Wives: An Empirical Study of the Power Relationships Affecting Women on Irish Farms," *Sociologia Ruralis* 32 (1992): 431–51; Sally Shortall, *Women and Farming: Property and Power* (London: Macmillan Press; New York: St. Martin's Press, 1999); Michael Gertler, JoAnn Jaffe and Lenore Swystun, "The Old Same Place? Gender Relations on Cooperative and Conventional Farms in Saskatchewan," *Prairie Forum* 29 (Fall 2004): 253–77; Wendee Kubik, "Women's Contradictory Roles in the Contemporary Farm Economy," *Prairie Forum* 29 (Fall 2004): 245–52; Margaret Alston, *Women on the Land: The Hidden Heart of Rural Australia* (Kensington: UNSW Press, 1995); Gretchen Poiner, *The Good Old Rule: Gender and Other Power Relationships in a Rural Community* (Sydney: Sydney University Press, 1990); Carolyn E. Sachs, *Gendered Fields: Rural Women, Agriculture and Environment* (Boulder: Westview Press, 1996), 27; Sachs, *The Invisible Farmers*, 108–9; Sarah Whatmore, *Farming Women: Gender, Work and Family Enterprise* (London: Macmillan, 1991); Kristi Anne Stølen, "The Gentle Exercise of Male Power in Rural Argentina," *Identities: Global Studies in Culture and Power* 2 (April 1996): 385–406; Deniz Kandiyoti, "Bargaining with Patriarchy," *Gender and Society* 2 (September 1988): 274–90; E.A. (Nora) Cebotarev, "From Domesticity to the Public Sphere: Farm Women, 1945–86," in *A Diversity of Women: Ontario, 1945–1980*, ed. Joy Parr (Toronto: University of Toronto Press, 1995), 222–23.

7   This is how prominent Saskatchewan Co-operative Commonwealth Federation supporter Gertrude S. Telford and her husband felt when their son arrived in 1927, after the birth of two daughters. See Ann Leger-Anderson, "Marriage, Family, and the Co-operative Ideal in Saskatchewan: The Telfords," in *Telling Tales: Essays in Western Women's History*, ed. Catherine A. Cavanaugh and Randi R. Warne (Vancouver: UBC Press, 2000), 305.

8   Georgina Edith Graves diary, 1907, Kate Graves Family Papers. For an example of a letter congratulating the Graves on Edward's birth, see Maude (Graves) Peacock letter to Kate Graves, Downsville, Wisconsin, 2 July 1907, Kate Graves Family Papers.

9 Kate Graves letter to Georgina Edith (Graves) Griffiths, September 1932. Also see Enid (Wallace) Kolskog interview, 13–14 August 1998.

10 Gerald Friesen, *The Canadian Prairies: A History* (Toronto and London: University of Toronto Press, 1987), 316–17.

11 G.E. Britnell, *The Wheat Economy* (Toronto: University of Toronto Press, 1939); H. Blair Neatby, *The Politics of Chaos: Canada in the Thirties* (Toronto: Macmillan of Canada, 1972), 31, 136; John Herd Thompson with Allen Seager, *Canada 1922–1939: Decades of Discord* (Toronto: McClelland and Stewart, 1985), 119, 351; S.M. Lipset, *Agrarian Socialism: The Cooperative Commonwealth Federation in Saskatchewan* (1950; reprint, Berkeley: University of California Press, 1971), 118–33; Vernon C. Fowke, *The National Policy and the Wheat Economy* (Toronto: University of Toronto Press, 1957), 259; *Rural Roads and Local Government: A Summary*, Saskatchewan Royal Commission on Agriculture and Rural Life (Regina: Queen's Printer, 1956), 6; F.H. Leacy, *Historical Statistics of Canada*, 2nd ed. (Ottawa: Statistics Canada, 1983), M119-128; James H. Gray, *Men against the Desert* (Saskatoon: Western Producer Prairie Books, 1980), 1–65; Blair Neatby, "The Saskatchewan Relief Commission, 1931–1934," *Saskatchewan History* 3 (Spring 1950): 41–56; E.W. Stapleford, *Report on Rural Relief Due to Drought Conditions and Crop Failures in Western Canada, 1930–1937* (Ottawa: King's Printer, 1939); Bye, "Times are Hard," 49–70.

12 E.S. Hopkins, A.E. Palmer, and W.S. Chepil, *Soil Drifting Control in the Prairie Provinces*, Canada, Department of Agriculture, Bulletin 32 (Ottawa: King's Printer, 1946), 53–55; Bruce Baden Peel, "R.M. 45: The Social History of a Rural Municipality" (master's thesis, University of Saskatchewan, 1946), 220–390. Also see Bye, "Times are Hard," 49–70.

13 Kate Graves letter to Georgina Edith (Graves) Griffiths, Lafleche, Saskatchewan, 11 June 1937.

14 Rural Municipality of Mankota, No. 45, Mankota, Saskatchewan, Relief Ledgers, 1930–40. Also see Bye, "Times are Hard," 49–70.

15 Kate Graves letter to Georgina Edith (Graves) Griffiths, 29 June 1937.

16 D.M. Loveridge and Barry Potyondi, *From Wood Mountain to the Whitemud: A Historical Survey of the Grasslands National Park Area* (Ottawa: Parks Canada, 1983), 320; Britnell, *The Wheat Economy*, 202–3.

17 Kate and Tom Graves' farm remains in the family more than sixty years after Kate's death. It is currently owned and operated by Kate's grandson Murray McCrea, son of Kate's sixth eldest daughter, Ethel (Graves) McCrea.

18 Cynthia R. Comacchio, *The Infinite Bonds of Family: Domesticity in Canada, 1850–1940* (Toronto: University of Toronto Press, 1999), 126–30.

19 Kate Graves letter to Georgina Edith (Graves) Griffiths, 10 January 1935. For a detailed discussion of gendered work strategies and power relationships in the Graves family, see Bye, "Times are Hard," 71–113.

20 Veronica Strong-Boag, *The New Day Recalled: Lives of Girls and Women in English Canada, 1919–1939* (Markham, Ontario: Penguin Books, 1988), 113.

21 Carolina Van de Vorst, "A History of Farm Women's Work in Manitoba" (master's thesis, University of Manitoba, 1988); Strong-Boag, "Pulling in Double Harness," 401–23; Scowby, "I Am A Worker, Not A Drone," 3–15; Scowby, "Divine Discontent"; Dorothy Schwieder and Deborah Fink, "Plains Women: Rural Life in the

1930s," *Great Plains Quarterly* 8 (Spring 1988): 79–88; Deborah Fink and Dorothy Schwieder, "Iowa Farm Women in the 1930s: A Reassessment," *Annals of Iowa* 49 (1989): 570–90; Dorothy Schwieder, "South Dakota Farm Women and the Great Depression," *Journal of the West* 24 (October 1985): 6–18; Joan Jensen, "'I've Worked, I'm Not Afraid of Work': Farm Women in New Mexico, 1920–1940," in *History of Women in the United States: Historical Articles on Women's Lives and Activities*, ed. Nancy F. Cott, vol. 6, *Working on the Land* (Munich: K.G. Saur, 1993), 423; Pamela Riney-Kehrberg, ed. *Waiting on the Bounty: The Dust Bowl Diary of Mary Knackstedt Dyck* (Iowa City: University of Iowa Press, 1999), 21–22; Pamela Riney-Kehrberg, *Rooted in Dust: Surviving Drought and Depression in Southwestern Kansas* (Lawrence: University Press of Kansas, 1994), 97–98, 147–48; Katherine Jellison, *Entitled to Power: Farm Women and Technology, 1913–1963* (Chapel Hill and London: University of North Carolina Press, 1993), 103–4, 114–15, 117; Laurie Mercier, "Women's Role in Montana Agriculture," *Montana: The Magazine of Western History* 38 (Autumn 1988): 50–61; and the following works by Deborah Fink: *Agrarian Women: Wives and Mothers in Rural Nebraska, 1880–1940* (Chapel Hill and London: University of North Carolina Press, 1992), 106–7, 123–24; "Sidelines and Moral Capital: Women on Nebraska Farms in the 1930s," in *Women and Farming: Changing Roles, Changing Structures*, ed. Wava G. Haney and Jane B. Knowles (Boulder and London: Westview Press, 1988), 55–70; *Open Country, Iowa: Rural Women, Tradition and Change* (Albany: State University of New York Press, 1986), 45–75.

22 Pat Armstrong and Hugh Armstrong, *The Double Ghetto: Canadian Women and Their Segregated Work* (Toronto: McClelland and Stewart, 1984), 67–68, 100–101.

23 Ethel (Graves) McCrea letter to Georgina Edith (Graves) Griffiths, 4 November 1934, Kate Graves Family Papers.

24 See Carroll Smith-Rosenberg's influential article, "The Female World of Love and Ritual," *Signs* 1 (1975): 1–29, which argues that nineteenth-century middle-class American women created an emotionally sustaining world for themselves apart from men. Also see Monda Halpern, *And On That Farm He Had a Wife: Ontario Farm Women and Feminism, 1900–1970* (Montreal and Kingston: McGill-Queen's University Press, 2001), 61–65; Margaret Conrad, "'Sundays Always Make Me Think of Home': Time and Place in Canadian Women's History," in *Rethinking Canada: The Promise of Women's History*, ed. Veronica Strong-Boag and Anita Clair Fellman, 2nd ed. (Toronto: Copp Clark Pitman, 1991), 97–112; Eliane Leslau Silverman, "Writing Canadian Women's History, 1970–82: An Historiographical Analysis," *Canadian Historical Review* 63 (December 1982): 521. Scholars who critique the concept of women's culture include Linda K. Kerber, "Separate Spheres, Female Worlds, Woman's Place: The Rhetoric of Women's History," *Journal of American History* 75 (June 1988): 9–39; Bari Watkins, "Woman's World in Nineteenth-Century America," *American Quarterly* 31 (Spring 1979): 116–27; Nancy Grey Osterud, *Bonds of Community: The Lives of Farm Women in Nineteenth-Century New York* (Ithaca and London: Cornell University Press, 1991), 5–9, 89–92, 118, 123, 136, 257; Aileen C. Moffatt, "Experiencing Identity: British-Canadian Women in Rural Saskatchewan, 1880–1950," (Ph.D. diss., University of Manitoba, 1996), 19–21, 35–38, 266–67.

25   Kate Graves letter to Georgina Edith (Graves) Griffiths, 18 December 1934.

26   Bye, "Times are Hard," 32, 106–9. Also see interviews with Kate Graves' grand-daughter, Enid (Wallace) Kolskog, 13–14 August 1998, 27 January 2000, 16 September 2001, 31 August 2002, 17 November 2002, 23 November 2002. On the impact of patriarchy on English-Canadian girls and women in the interwar years, see Strong-Boag, *The New Day Recalled.* In *Northern Plainsmen: Adaptive Strategy and Agrarian Life* (Chicago: Aldine Publishing, 1969), 188, John W. Bennett says rural Saskatchewan women sometimes downplayed and concealed their involvement in ranch enterprises, acting as "a quiet but important force." Parvin Ghorayshi, "The Indispensable Nature of Wives' Work for the Farm Family Enterprise," *Canadian Review of Sociology and Anthropology*, 26 (1989): 584, wonders if farm women, "under pressure of gender ideology," consciously present themselves as quiet partners so as not to jeopardize "the social status of their husbands as farmers and the 'heads of the enterprises' within a male-domi-nated community."

27   On the promotion of domestic ideology in the West by women's organizations, agricultural educators, and farm publications, see Jeffery Taylor, *Fashioning Farmers: Ideology, Agricultural Knowledge and the Manitoba Farm Movement, 1890–1925* (Regina: Canadian Plains Research Center, 1994), 68–89; Moffatt, "Experiencing Identity," 129; Kerrie A. Strathy, "Saskatchewan Women's Insti-tutes: The Rural Women's University, 1911–1986" (master's thesis, University of Saskatchewan, 1987); Saskatchewan Women's Institute, *Legacy: A History of Saskatchewan Homemakers' Clubs and Women's Institutes, 1911–1988* (Saskatoon: Saskatchewan Women's Institute, 1988), 1–10, 17, 21; Catherine C. Cole and Judy Larmour, *Many and Remarkable: The Story of the Alberta Women's Institutes* (Edmonton: Alberta Women's Institutes, 1997), 8; Linda Rasmussen et al., *A Harvest Yet to Reap: A History of Prairie Women* (Toronto: The Women's Press, 1976), 88–89.

28   John W. Bennett, with Seena B. Kohl and Geraldine Binion, *Of Time and the Enterprise: North American Farm Management in a Context of Resource Marginal-ity* (Minneapolis: University of Minnesota Press, 1982), 164–71; Seena B. Kohl, *Working Together: Women and Family in Southwestern Saskatchewan* (Toronto: Holt, Rinehart and Winston of Canada, 1976), 19–21, 67–71. Bennett and Kohl note that women derived part of their status from, and helped to bolster, their husbands' status in the community. They also achieved independent reputa-tions based mainly on "behaviors acted out in the domestic sphere." Although women had performed a range of enterprise-related roles since the settlement era and did not distinguish the household from the enterprise, they received little "social credit" for non-domestic work. The community valued industriousness, efficiency, frugality, sociability, and self-reliance on the part of both sexes.

29   Bye, "Times are Hard," 71–113; Van de Vorst, "A History of Farm Women's Work," 79–86, 100, 135–39, 126–45, 169; "Prairie Wife," *Chatelaine*, May 1935, 29; Scowby, "Divine Discontent," 56–87, 128–46; Strong-Boag, "Pulling in Double Harness," 401–23; Strong-Boag, *The New Day Recalled*, 126; Mary Kinnear, *A Female Economy: Women's Work in a Prairie Province, 1870–1970* (Montreal and Kingston: McGill-Queen's University Press, 1998), 85–99; C.A. Dawson and Eva R. Younge, *Pioneering in the Prairie Provinces: The Social Side of the Settlement*

Process, Canadian Frontiers of Settlement, 8th vol. (Toronto: Macmillan Company of Canada, 1940), 142–43; R.W. Murchie, *Agricultural Progress on the Prairie Frontier*, Canadian Frontiers of Settlement, 5th vol. (Toronto: Macmillan Company of Canada, 1936), 223–24, 248–49, 263–64; Britnell, *The Wheat Economy*, 71–72; *A Submission by the Government of Saskatchewan to the Royal Commission on Dominion-Provincial Relations (Canada, 1937)* (Regina: King's Printer, 1937), 173.

30   Comacchio, *The Intimate Bonds*, 125. Also see Nancy Christie, *Engendering the State: Family, Work and Welfare in Canada* (Toronto: University of Toronto Press, 2000), 246–47; Cynthia Comacchio, "Bringing Up Father: Defining a Modern Canadian Fatherhood, 1900–1940," in *Family Matters: Papers in Post-Confederation Canadian Family History*, ed. Lori Chambers and Edgar-Andre Montigny (Toronto: Canadian Scholars' Press, 1998), 294; Strong-Boag, *The New Day Recalled*, 47–48; Strong-Boag, "Pulling in Double Harness," 409.

31   Comacchio, *The Infinite Bonds*, 128; James Snell, "The Family and the Working-Class Elderly in the First Half of the Twentieth Century," in *Family Matters: Papers in Post-Confederation Canadian Family History*, ed. Lori Chambers and Edgar-Andre Montigny (Toronto: Canadian Scholars' Press, 1998), 499–510; Strong-Boag, *The New Day Recalled*, 122; Fink, *Agrarian Women*, 98, 102, 105–6; Denyse Baillargeon, *Making Do: Women, Family and Home in Montreal during the Great Depression*, trans. Yvonne Klein (Waterloo: Wilfrid Laurier University Press, 1999), 63–65, 159.

32   Kohl, *Working Together*, 60; Seena Kohl and John W. Bennett, "Succession to Family Enterprises and the Migration of Young People in a Canadian Agricultural Community," in *The Canadian Family*, ed. K. Ishwaran, 2nd ed. (Toronto: Holt, Rinehart and Winston of Canada, 1976): 255–56; Sonya Salamon, *Prairie Patrimony: Family, Farming, and Community in the Midwest* (Chapel Hill and London: University of North Carolina Press, 1992), 41; Ramona Marotz-Baden and Claudia Mattheis, "Daughters-in-law and Stress in Two-Generation Farm Families," *Family Relations* 43 (April 1994): 132–37.

33   Kate Graves letters to Georgina Edith (Graves) Griffiths, 3 April 1933, 2 May 1933, 15 May 1933.

34   Ibid., 18 March 1935.

35   Ibid., 27 May 1935.

36   Ibid.

37   Strong-Boag, *The New Day Recalled*, 186.

38   Kate Graves letter to Georgina Edith (Graves) Griffiths, 1 July 1935.

39   Ibid., 21 April 1941; 18 March 1935.

40   Katey (Graves) Hatlelid letter to Georgina Edith (Graves) Griffiths, Lafleche, 20 March 1936, Kate Graves Family Papers.

41   Kate Graves letters to Georgina Edith (Graves) Griffiths, 17 June 1935, 17 April 1937.

42   Katey (Graves) Hatlelid letter to Georgina Edith (Graves) Griffiths, Lafleche, 20 March 1936.

43   Enid (Wallace) Kolskog interview, 13–14 August 1998; Kate Graves letter to Georgina Edith (Graves) Griffiths, 15 April 1940.

44   Strong-Boag, *The New Day Recalled*, 186.

45 Baillargeon, *Making Do*, 64.

46 Kohl, *Working Together*, 61, 68; Salamon, *Prairie Patrimony*, 126; Sachs, *Gendered Fields*, 136; Alston, *Women on the Land*, 63, 142; Margaret Alston, "Women and Their Work on Australian Farms," *Rural Sociology* 60 (Fall 1995): 525–26; Research, Action and Education Centre, "Keeping Women Down on the Farm," *Resources for Feminist Research* 11 (March 1982): 13; Candyce S. Russell et al., "Coping Strategies Associated with Intergenerational Transfer of the Family Farm," *Rural Sociology* 50 (Fall 1985): 372–73; Marotz-Baden and Mattheis, "Daughters-in-Law and Stress," 132–37; Ramona Marotz-Baden and Deane Cowan, "Mothers-in-Law and Daughters-in-Law: The Effects of Proximity on Conflict and Stress," *Family Relations* 36 (October 1987): 385–90; Barbara Heather et al., "Women's Identities and the Restructuring of Rural Alberta," unpublished paper (2002), 8. (My thanks to Prof. Heather, of Grant MacEwan College, Edmonton, Alberta, for making this unpublished paper available to me.)

47 Snell, "The Family and the Working-Class Elderly," 500.

48 Kate Graves letter to Georgina Edith (Graves) Griffiths, 11 May 1937. In a decade's worth of letters, this was one of the very few times Kate spoke with frustration about the Depression. And then, she did it through Edward and Dorothy. Normally she did not permit herself to express emotions in her letters that she considered to be unfeminine, such as anger, irritation, or disappointment.

49 Ibid., Lafleche, 11 June 1937.

50 Kate Graves letter to Georgina Edith (Graves) Griffiths, 29 June 1937.

51 Ibid., 19 June 1937, 29 June 1937. Also see Katey (Graves) Hatlelid letter to Georgina Edith (Graves) Griffiths, Lafleche, 18 June 1937.

52 Kate Graves letter to Georgina Edith (Graves) Griffiths, 29 June 1937.

53 Ibid., 26 July 1937.

54 Katey (Graves) Hatlelid to Georgina Edith (Graves) Griffiths, Lafleche, 18 June 1937. On rural parents' and successor sons' mutual dependency, see Salamon, *Prairie Patrimony*, 123.

55 Kate Graves letter to Georgina Edith (Graves) Griffiths, Wood Mountain, Saskatchewan, 8 October 1937. Dorothy appears to have confided to Tom's niece, the female relative in Quebec with whom Dorothy and Edward were living temporarily, that she did not want to be saddled with nursing Kate in her old age.

56 Kate Graves letters to Georgina Edith (Graves) Griffiths, 23 September 1937, 3 September 1937.

57 Ibid., 3 September 1937, 14 September 1937.

58 Ibid., 3 September 1937, 23 September 1937.

59 Ibid., 14 September 1937; also see 26 July 1937 and 3 September 1937.

60 Ibid., 14 September 1937.

61 Ibid., Lafleche, 24 January 1938.

62 Beth Light and Ruth Roach Pierson, eds., *No Easy Road: Women in Canada 1920s to 1960s* (Toronto: New Hogtown Press, 1990), 316; Snell, "The Family and the Working-Class Elderly," 502; Katey (Graves) Hatlelid letter to Georgina Edith (Graves) Griffiths, Lafleche, 27 August 1937.

63 Kate Graves letters to Georgina Edith (Graves) Griffiths, 3 September 1937, 24 March 1939.

64 Ibid., 23 May 1938. Kate had not seen Georgina since she visited her at Fleet, Alberta, in 1924. Aside from a preference for Edward and his family, there is

no clear explanation as to why Kate failed to make the two-day train trip to see Georgina between 1924 and her death in 1941. Lack of money was not necessarily an impediment; on at least two occasions, Georgina's husband, Bert Griffiths, offered her the fare. Kate may have believed she could not leave her domestic and farm responsibilities, but nearby female relatives could have assumed her chores. Georgina was probably unable to travel to see her mother herself due to bouts of serious illness and her own heavy workload. She was the mother of six young children and had no nearby female kin to help her. Kate Graves's letter to Georgina Edith (Graves) Griffiths, Kerrobert, Saskatchewan, 25 November 1924; Muriel (Griffiths) Bye interview, 31 May 2002.

65 Kate Graves letter to Georgina Edith (Graves) Griffiths, 10 October 1939.

66 Ibid., 25 September 1939.

67 On ways in which the dominion-provincial old age pension program empowered elderly Canadians to help their families in the 1930s and 1940s, see Snell, "The Family and the Working-Class Elderly," 506. Kate and Tom's combined monthly pension income was $30.

68 Kate Graves letter to Georgina Edith (Graves) Griffiths, 29 May 1939.

69 Kohl and Bennett, "Succession to Family Enterprises," 246–65; Bennett, with Kohl and Binion, *Of Time and the Enterprise*, 149–60, 373–74; Kohl, *Working Together*, 56, 78–84, 107; Faye Davis, *Legal, Economic and Social Concerns of Saskatchewan Farm Women* (Saskatoon: Saskatoon Branch, Women's Legal Education Action Fund, 1989), 12; Michelle Boivin, "Farm Women: Obtaining Legal and Economic Recognition of Their Work," in *Growing Strong: Women in Agriculture*, ed. Diane Morissette (Ottawa: Canadian Advisory Council on the Status of Women, 1987), 67; Norah C. Keating, "Legacy, Aging, and Succession in Farm Families," *Generations: Journal of the American Society on Aging* 20 (Fall 1996): 62–63; Cohen, *Women's Work*, 54–57; Béatrice Craig, "Families, Inheritance and Property Transmission in Rural Central Canada in the Nineteenth and Early Twentieth Centuries," in *Family Matters: Papers in Post-Confederation Canadian Family History*, ed. Lori Chambers and Edgar-Andre Montigny (Toronto: Canadian Scholars' Press, 1998), 159–75; Shortall, *Women and Farming*, 1–45, 68–69; Shortall, "Power Analysis and Farm Wives," 444; Salamon, *Prairie Patrimony*, 41; Fink, *Open Country*, 202–6; Joan Jensen, *Promise to the Land* (Albuquerque: University of New Mexico Press, 1991), 1–2; Kenneth Michael Sylvester, *The Limits of Rural Capitalism: Family, Culture, and Markets in Montcalm, Manitoba, 1870–1940* (Toronto: University of Toronto Press, 2001), 135–67; Malcolm Voyce, "Testamentary Freedom, Patriarchy and Inheritance of the Family Farm in Australia," *Sociologia Ruralis* 34 (1994): 71–83; David G. Symes, "Bridging the Generations: Succession and Inheritance in a Changing World," *Sociologia Ruralis* 30 (1990): 287–89; Osterud, *Bonds of Community*, 62–67; Alston, *Women on the Land*, 30; Poiner, *The Good Old Rule*, 123; Cebotarev, "From Domesticity to the Public Sphere," 209. Some scholars argue that farm families in particular regions and ethnic communities tried to treat all offspring fairly in the inheritance process. Still, daughters were more likely to be treated unfairly than sons, and were less likely to receive land. See Stephen John Gross, "Handing Down the Farm: Values, Strategies, and Outcomes in Inheritance Practices Among Rural German Americans," *Journal of Family History* 21 (April 1996): 192–217; Royden Loewen, *Hidden Worlds: Revisiting the*

Mennonite Migrants of the 1870s (Winnipeg: University of Manitoba Press, 2001), 33–49; Mark Friedberger, "The Farm Family and the Inheritance Process: Evidence from the Corn Belt, 1870–1950," *Agricultural History* 57 (October 1983): 1–13; Jane Marie Pederson, *Between Memory and Reality: Family and Community in Rural Wisconsin, 1870–1970* (Madison: University of Wisconsin Press, 1992), 165.

70 Katey (Graves) Hatlelid letter to Georgina Edith (Graves) Griffiths, Lafleche, 25 August 1945; Georgina Edith (Graves) Griffiths letter to Ethel (Graves) McCrea, Fleet, Alberta, 21 October 1945, Kate Graves Family Papers. Kohl, *Working Together*, 58, 81, 84; Salamon, *Prairie Patrimony*, 142, 150, 163, 222; Shortall, *Women and Farming*, 39; Poiner, *The Good Old Rule*, 122; Symes, "Bridging the Generations," 288–89.

71 Kate and Tom Graves had planned to adopt Charley when he joined their household in 1900, at the age of five, but for some reason the adoption did not proceed. Charley's full name was Charles William Fothergill Graves. He was twelve years older than Edward. Like his sisters, he does not appear to have contested Edward's right to the family farm. Genealogical documents, Kate Graves Family Papers; Enid (Wallace) Kolskog interview, 13–14 August 1998; Arthur Graves interview, 29 December 2002.

72 Kate Graves letter to Georgina Edith (Graves) Griffiths, 28 May 1940.

73 Ibid., 10 June 1940. On competition between mothers-in-law and daughters-in-law for the son/husband's affections, see Marotz-Baden and Cowan, "Mothers-in-Law and Daughters-in-Law," 386, 389.

74 Emma (Graves) Hatlelid letter to Georgina Edith (Graves) Griffiths, Wood Mountain, Saskatchewan, 6 May 1941, Kate Graves Family Papers.

75 Lerner, *The Creation of Patriarchy*, 239.

76 See footnote 3 above. Also see Friesen, *The Canadian Prairies*, 304; Sara Brooks Sundberg, "Farm Women on the Canadian Frontier: The Helpmate Image," in *Farm Women on the Prairie Frontier: A Sourcebook for Canada and the United States*, ed. Carol Fairbanks and Sara Brooks Sundberg (Metuchen, NJ: Scarecrow Press, 1983), 71–90; Kathryn McPherson, "Was the 'Frontier' Good for Women?: Historical Approaches to Women and Agricultural Settlement in the Prairie West, 1870–1925," *Atlantis* 25 (Fall/Winter 2000): 75–86.

77 Hedley, "Normal Expectations," 15–17; Hedley, "Relations of Production," 71–85. Also see Burnet, *Next-Year Country*, 31; Cornelia Butler Flora and Jan L. Flora, "Structure of Agriculture and Women's Culture in the Great Plains," *Great Plains Quarterly* 8 (Fall 1988): 195–205; Fink, *Open Country*, 202–13, 226; Fink, *Agrarian Women*. In *Preserving the Family Farm: Women, Community, and the Foundations of Agribusiness in the Midwest, 1900–1940* (Baltimore and London: Johns Hopkins University Press, 1995), 18, Mary Neth argues that "patriarchal structures made familial relations hierarchical, not mutual, and created the potential for an unequal distribution of labor and rewards within farm families." Hedley and Neth note that, in reality, power relationships within families could take a variety of forms, and that women and children had a degree of agency.

78 Allan G. Johnson, *The Gender Knot: Unraveling Our Patriarchial Legacy* (Philadelphia: Temple University Press, 1997), 5.

79 Rollings-Magnusson, "Canada's Most Wanted," 233.

80 Salamon, *Prairie Patrimony*, 41. Also see Shortall, *Women and Farming*, 1–70.

81 Rollings-Magnusson, "Hidden Homesteaders," 174.

82　Linda Silver Dranoff, *Women in Canadian Law* (Toronto: Fitzhenry and White-side, 1977), 50. Also see Cavanaugh, "No Place for a Woman," 507–8.

83　Elizabeth Ann Kalmakoff, "Woman Suffrage in Saskatchewan" (master's thesis, University of Regina, 1993), 52.

84　McCallum, "Prairie Women," 30–31.

85　Since 1 January 1980, Saskatchewan women have been entitled to a legal share in family property upon divorce. The legislation came in the wake of a case in the 1970s involving an Alberta woman, Irene Murdoch, who lost her bid for a share of the ranch she worked with her husband. However, Saskatchewan's Matrimonial Property Act did not alter the belief that farm land should be owned by men and passed down to men. Judges continued "to ensure that the family farm remained intact in the hands of the husband at the expense of the woman's fair share of the assets," says Davis, *Legal, Economic and Social Concerns of Saskatchewan Farm Women*, 20. Also see Jean E. Keet, "The Law Reform Process, Matrimonial Property, and Farm Women: A Case Study of Saskatchewan, 1980–1986," *Canadian Journal of Women and the Law* 4 (1990): 166–89; Jean E. Keet, "Matrimonial Property Legislation: Are Farm Women Equal Partners?" in *The Political Economy of Agriculture in Western Canada*, ed. G.S. Basran and D.A. Hay (Toronto: Garamond Press, 1988), 175–84; Dranoff, *Women in Canadian Law*, 51–54; Boivin, "Farm Women," 53, 61–63; Gertler, Jaffe and Swystun, "The Old Same Place?" 253–77. Forty-three per cent of Saskatchewan farm women who responded to a 1988 survey reported that they jointly owned the farm with their husbands; it is not known whether these were legal or informal arrangements. Only 2 per cent of respondents said they had a legal partnership with their husbands. See Davis, *Legal, Economic and Social Concerns of Saskatchewan Farm Women*, 3, 13.

86　Cavanaugh, "The Limitations of the Pioneering Partnership," 199.

87　Shortall, *Women and Farming*, 7.

88　Kohl, *Working Together*, 107; Bennett, with Kohl and Binion, *Of Time and the Enterprise*, 158; Kohl and Bennett, "Succession to Family Enterprises," 248–49; Jensen, *Promise to the Land*, 26. In *Legal, Economic and Social Concerns of Saskatchewan Farm Women*, 3, 12, 14, Davis notes that only 4 per cent of Saskatchewan farm women surveyed in 1988 had inherited their farms or taken up farming "by some means outside of marriage." Sixty-seven per cent entered farming by marrying a man who farmed.

89　*The Farm Business in Saskatchewan, Study Number Four: Survey of the Swift Current-Gull Lake District*, Agricultural Extension, Bulletin No. 52 (Saskatoon: University of Saskatchewan, College of Agriculture, July 1931), 28. Also see William Allen, *The Farm Business in Saskatchewan, Study Number One: Grain Farming on the Prairie – The Belbeck District, North of Moose Jaw*, Agricultural Extension, Bulletin No. 37 (Saskatoon: University of Saskatchewan, College of Agriculture, June 1927), 23.

90　Bennett, with Kohl and Binion, *Of Time and the Enterprise*, 149, 151; Kohl, *Working Together*, 58, 81.

91　Bennett, with Kohl and Binion, *Of Time and the Enterprise*, 118, 138–40; Kohl, *Working Together*, 81; Janet Edgar Taylor, Joan E. Norris, and Wayne H. Howard, "Succession Patterns of Farmer and Successor in Canadian Farm Families," *Rural Sociology* 63 (December 1998): 553–73; Burnet, *Next-Year Country*, 31; Russell et al., "Coping Strategies," 363–64; John Hutson, "Fathers and Sons: Family Farms,

Family Businesses and the Farming Industry," *Sociology* 21 (May 1987): 221–23; Salamon, *Prairie Patrimony*, 143, 146–47, 167; Wendee Kubik, "The Study of Farm Stress and Coping: A Critical Evaluation" (master's thesis, University of Regina, 1996), 59. As for farm successors' wives, they generally had little influence on the farm transfer process and often found it stressful; a daughter-in-law's chances of becoming a legal owner and equal partner with her husband in the extended family enterprise were slim. See Russell et al., "Coping Strategies," 372–73; Alston, "Women and Their Work on Australian Farms," 525–26.

92 Jensen, *Promise to the Land*, 238; Sarah Elbert, "Women and Farming: Changing Structures, Changing Roles," in *Women and Farming: Changing Roles, Changing Structures*, ed. Wava G. Haney and Jane B. Knowles (Boulder and London: Westview Press, 1988), 245–64; Pederson, *Between Memory and Reality*, 165. Also see Davis, *Legal, Economic and Social Concerns of Saskatchewan Farm Women*, 12, who says Canadian farm wives were taught that "the woman's reward for devoting her life to working on the farm came when she witnessed the transfer of ownership of the farm from her husband to her son. The woman should not expect to pass on the farm to her daughter because the daughter, by virtue of her sex, does not possess the interest, management skills or physical abilities needed to operate a farm."

93 Lerner, *The Creation of Patriarchy*, 139.

94 Halpern, *And on That Farm He Had a Wife*, 42–43.

95 Nellie McClung, *In Times Like These*, quoted in Rasmussen et al., *A Harvest Yet to Reap: A History of Prairie Women* (Toronto: The Women's Press, 1976), 154.

96 Isobel, "Around the Fireside," *Grain Growers' Guide*, quoted in Rasmussen et al., *A Harvest Yet to Reap*, 156. On Isobel Graham and the *Guide's* other feminist women's page editors, see Kelcey and Davis, eds., *A Great Movement Underway*, x–xxii.

97 Gail Cuthbert Brandt, "Postmodern Patchwork: Some Recent Trends in the Writing of Women's History in Canada," *Canadian Historical Review* 72 (December 1991): 461. Also see Strong-Boag, "Pulling in Double Harness," 401–23; Scowby, "Divine Discontent."

98 Julie Dorsch, "'You Just Did What Had to be Done': Life Histories of Four Saskatchewan 'Farmers' Wives,'" in *"Other Voices": Historical Essays on Saskatchewan Women*, ed. David De Brou and Aileen Moffatt (Regina: Canadian Plains Research Center, 1995), 128.

99 Kohl, *Working Together*, 56. Farm women's tendency to view farming as a male occupation and to define themselves as homemakers and "helpmates," rather than farmers, has proven remarkably resilient. On western Canadian farm women, see Wendee Kubik and Robert J. Moore, "Women's Diverse Roles in the Farm Economy and the Consequences for their Health, Well-being, and Quality of Life," *Prairie Forum* 27 (Spring 2002): 118–19; Lenore Swystun, "Women in Farming: A Social Economy of Multi-Family and Single Family Farms in Saskatchewan" (master's thesis, University of Saskatchewan, 1996); Heather et al., "Women's Identities and the Restructuring of Rural Alberta," 1–17; Milagros Ranoa, *Women and Decision-making in Agriculture: Barriers to Participation*, RDI Report Series 1993–2 (Brandon, Manitoba: Rural Development Institute, Brandon University, 1993); Jennifer J. Young, "Farm Women of Alberta: Their Perceptions of Their Health and Work" (master's thesis, University of Alberta, 1997). On farm women

in the United States, see Jean Kinsey, *Women in Agriculture: The U.S. Experience,* United States, Department of Agricultural and Applied Economics, Staff Papers Series, P87-2 (St. Paul: University of Minnesota, 1987); Rachel Ann Rosenfeld, *Farm Women: Work, Farm, and Family in the United States* (Chapel Hill and London: University of North Carolina Press, 1985); Sachs, *Invisible Farmers,* 108–9.

100 Many Canadians in general in the early decades of the twentieth century believed that men were superior to women, and sons were superior to daughters. Some families made no secret of the fact that they favoured boys. Edward and Dorothy hoped their own first child would be a boy, and Georgina, who had three daughters and three sons, filled her private papers with poems and articles extolling boys. See Strong-Boag, *The New Day Recalled,* 8; Light and Pierson, *No Easy Road,* 178–80; Kate Graves letter to Georgina Edith (Graves) Griffiths, 8 March 1934; "Mother's Boys," "One Way to Rear a Boy," "Boys Make Men," "The Boy of Yesteryear," "My Baby No Longer," Georgina Edith (Graves) Griffiths scrapbook, ca.1910–1973, Kate Graves Family Papers. Not all families preferred boys. Suzanne Morton, "'To Take an Orphan': Gender and Family Roles Following the 1917 Halifax Explosion," in *Gendered Pasts: Historical Essays in Femininity and Masculinity in Canada,* ed. Kathryn McPherson, Cecilia Morgan, and Nancy M. Forestell (Don Mills, Ontario: Oxford University Press, 1999), 110, suggests that many North Americans cherished daughters for their domestic labour and "for what were believed to be their distinct emotional attributes and qualities. The value placed on girls was especially true in the case of adoptions, where there was a consistent preference for girls over boys." Often, adoption applicants sought girls to provide companionship for women or to care for elderly family members.

101 Five of Kate's seven daughters taught school for a time when they were young women. All eventually married; at least six chose farmers.

102 Bennett, with Kohl and Binion, *Of Time and the Enterprise,* 151, 160, 373–74; Kohl, *Working Together,* 76, 107.

103 Poiner, *The Good Old Rule,* 136, 143.

104 See footnote 6, above.

105 Shortall, "Power Analysis and Farm Wives," 447, 450 n15; Sarah Ann Shortall, "Farmwives and Power: An Empirical Study of the Power Relationships Affecting Women on Irish Farms," (Ph.D. diss., National University of Ireland, 1990), 322–26, 365.

106 Alston, *Women on the Land,* 16, 63–65. Also see Cebotarev, "From Domesticity to the Public Sphere," 222–23; Kandiyoti, "Bargaining with Patriarchy," 274–90.

part four

FROM THE INSIDE LOOKING OUT

Femininity *and the* "Frontier"

twelve

My Mother's Trunk

OLIVE STICKNEY

*When eighty-eight-year-old Olive Fimrite Stickney took
the podium at the "Unsettled Pasts" conference, she was
expected to comment on her experiences as the first woman
in Alberta elected to a rural municipal council; instead,
she provided her audience with this beautifully crafted
and lively tribute to her mother, Inga Alexander Fimrite.
Born in 1914, Olive Stickney learned the hardships of rural
farm life at an early age. She was only two years old when
her single mother, with three children, joined a group of
Scandinavian settlers who followed the Reverend Halvar
N. Ronning over the Edson Trail to establish a Norwegian*

Olive Fimrite outside
The Rite Shoppe, her
restaurant in Valhalla
Centre, Alberta, 1937.
Courtesy: Frances
Stickney Newman.

Lutheran settlement in the Peace River Country in northern Alberta. In 1939, Olive married Lewis Stickney and moved to the town of Hythe, where the couple farmed and raised five children. She was elected to the County of Grande Prairie Council in 1966, and dedicated herself to the development of rural Alberta by promoting better health and social services, higher education, and housing for senior citizens.

Prior to her death, Stickney's daughters wrote a tribute to their mother wherein they stated: "How often we read about women who have managed to break into the male-dominated worlds of medicine, law, engineering, business, and politics.... But how seldom we advert to women who have devoted their lives to family, church, and community, without ever having drawn a salary, without ever having had the opportunity to contribute to a pension." Like Kate

Graves, whose life is explored by Cristine Bye in the previous chapter, Olive Stickney belonged to this latter group. So, too, did her mother. In "My Mother's Trunk," Stickney relates the hardships, and fulfillments, that Inga Fimrite encountered as a single woman homesteader. Like many contributions to this volume, Stickney's piece reminds us that historical models – such as "separate spheres" for men and women, and the "patriarchal family farm" – fail to capture the experiences of many rural women and children. With the aid of her children and bachelor homesteaders (who traded their labour for laundry and food services), Inga Fimrite managed to "prove up" and raise a family within a society that privileged the male landowner and breadwinner. "My Mother's Trunk" discloses how oral tradition, collective memory, material possessions, and religious belief worked within the Fimrite family to preserve ethnic identity and foster hope in the face of adversity.

Many an evening we gathered around the trunk. It stood in the hall at the top of the stairs. Seated on stools or on the floor, we waited while Mother lifted one corner, took the key from its hiding place and turned the lock to other lands.

Inside the trunk, there were three layers, each unfolding a past of wonder and romance. In the top compartment were letters and documents; old records and newspaper clippings. The most important article here, however, was the tin box. It too had a lock and key and in it was the first money we ever saw. As children, we were fascinated with the silver and thought it was much more valuable than paper bills. Nearby was a large black leather-covered book upon which Mother put a value above that of the precious money. She called it the "Family Bible." As we gathered around her, she would read to us from the Book, and then at our insistence would turn to the middle page and point out our names – "Adolph Olof Matthew," "Oliva Margereta," and just "Martin."

Once she explained to us that Martin was born after our father became *ill* and he, looking down at the child, simply said, "Call him 'Martin'."

As we would watch, off would come the second divider. This was even more exciting. Our attention would be drawn to a gold jewelry box. Mother would reach into its velvet fold and lift out a beautiful gold locket-watch and matching bracelet – gifts to her from our father before they were married. Our curious eyes would move on to quaint carved boxes, odd shaped brooches, and rich ostrich plumes that at one time must have been in high style. Folded neatly in one corner were pieces of her finest Hardanger embroidery from far-away Norway.

Then would come family photographs. I remember one phrase that stood out, linking us with the past, "Yes, Olive, you look just like her – your aunt Marie. She was your father's sister. You have the same lovely smile."

All this time, my older brother would sit quietly by holding a picture of our dad in his hands. No one needed to speak – same high forehead, large expressive eyes and handsome features. At six years of age, Adolph was the image of our dad.

Little Martin would stand on the other side of the trunk, gripping the edge with one hand for support and holding in his other hand a luxurious muff – his treasure, his "kitty." His eyes took in everything. Martin resembled no one. He was just "Martin."

On those evenings, gathered together for comfort and support, we heard more of the story. Our mother told us of her home in Norway, of her nine brothers, of the untimely death of her parents. At eighteen, she ventured alone across the ocean to the "States." Here she met our dad and his lovely sister, Aunt Marie. Mother sketched in a bit about dad's brothers. She was not one to dwell on the sad parts and there wasn't too much that wasn't sad.

The story would progress as we would work toward the bottom of the trunk, from which all the happy tales seemed to come. That gorgeous wedding dress made by a seamstress friend in the "States"! It had a twenty-two inch waistline and fell in creamy folds to the floor. The veil was lavishly fashioned out of yards and yards of tulle with an artificial orange-blossom headpiece. Through the years, the dream grew with me, that should I stand before the altar some day, it would be in *that* dress.

As the treasures were put back into the trunk – three layers – bits more of the story would be pieced together. I must have been very young the first time I remember her relating this part of the story. A coal-oil wall-bracket lamp shone on the trunk and its contents. Its rays illuminated her strong features as she reached down and picked up Martin. She lovingly cradled him in her arms as she described her wedding, then went on to tell of our father's decision to leave the "States" for a new country – Canada. They bought land at Kingman, Alberta, near Edmonton. One day our father left by team to take a load of grain to market. A bitter winter storm came up. His ears were badly frozen resulting in brain infection. During his illness, the mortgage came due and they lost their land.

I often think now how thoughtless children can be, for as she closed the trunk we argued over which treasure would belong to whom when "Mamma dies." Even as a child, my eye was on the gold locket-watch and bracelet.

Other details of the story came to light when friends visited mother. I always seemed to be out of sight, yet within hearing distance. She told them of such sad episodes that she would never have wanted to burden our young hearts with the same.

Mother told of the most unusual circumstances that led her to the Peace River Country in northern Alberta. A missionary from China praised this new unsettled homestead land – this district that he later named "Valhalla," meaning "The Home of the Gods."

To her queries, he answered that there was lots of land. The Peace River Country was a land of opportunity, a land of the future. Could she go with the settlers he planned to take? That was doubtful! How could she manage with three small children? There were no roads, no schools, and not even a house for her. She explained to him that she had nowhere to go. Her husband, who was not a Canadian citizen, had been sent back to Norway when he "took sick." At that time, she had connections in the "States." An invitation had been sent to her by a doctor for whom she had worked, suggesting she come back, but when she started back, she was denied a passport. While she was an American citizen, she had three Canadian-born children and was without money or means of support. Friends at Kingman, the Rorems, heard of her plight and invited her to bring the children to their home until she got her bearings. But after that what?

"Well!" said Missionary Ronning upon hearing the story, "I don't know how you can manage; but God is able and the church does have a responsibility to widows and to the fatherless. Yes, you may come with the next group of settlers." Thus we ventured by rail to Sexsmith and then started out by wagon. It was July 1916. Mother sat in the bottom of the wagon surrounded by three small children. Nearby was the trunk. We jogged for miles, through mud holes and deep ruts, over the pioneer trial, and all the way rain! Rain! RAIN! Pastor Ronning guided the horses and finally we reached Valhalla, the landsite.

Mother was deeply touched when she saw her quarter of land. The school was to be erected across the road. Kind, thoughtful settlers who had heard her story had refused to file on this central quarter. A creek ran through it, the bush was sparse; in fact, much of the land could be broken without brushing.

Inga Alexander
Fimrite, 1941.
Courtesy: Frances
Stickney Newman.

She was glad she had refused offers to adopt the children. Somehow, she would build a house; for the present, a tent would do. She would prove the land. She would blaze a trail and give her children a path to follow – a future. The trunk was the key to the past but in her strong hands lay the present. Nothing daunted her. She never went to bed until one in the morning – sometimes later. At daybreak, she was up and at work. A plan began to formulate. Some land had been taken up by families but many of the surrounding homesteads had been filed on by bachelors. These men had no one to bake their bread, to wash and iron their clothes. Perhaps she could exchange her labour for theirs. By fall, the lumber was out of the mill and the first frame house in the district was erected. Rough sheds were put up for our animals. All this was accomplished before winter set in.

During the first difficult years, the boys learned to help Mother through the days. In the evenings and into the night hours I was with her. She was never afraid if I were to sit by the ironing board or near the stove where she was at work. We didn't talk, but I was company and I never tired. Love was on guard.

As time slipped by, the days must have become lonely for Mother for soon we were all at school. We did not always come home light-hearted. But at the end of trying days, she seemed to sense our need. She gathered us around the trunk and transplanted some of the magic of the past into the tragedies of the present. There was that never-to-be-forgotten day in school when a mean boy told us our dad wasn't "sick" but "CRAZY!" A horrible word! As her explanation reached us over the trunk, it shed a new light on our sorrows and eased our pain.

Mother had her frightening experiences as well. There was that one dark night when the cow strayed. We had to have milk, and as I recall she put us on a blanket on the floor, hid the matches for fear of fire. Then out she went into the dusk to search. There were no fences – only trees and darkness. Soon she was lost in the night. For hours, she wandered in circles until finally she saw a light. She called, was recognized, and soon was drawn out of the darkness. It was two in the morning and only because there was sickness in the home did they have a light. She was so confused, they had to lead her home, to three small children asleep with tear-stained faces. This was the only time anyone saw her break down. She, who had endured so much fear, knew what we had gone through before sleep came. Kind neighbours brought the cow home the next day.

During those first difficult years, we never bought anything that wasn't absolutely essential. Somehow we managed by bargain and barter and finally some money came into the house. Needless to say, it went into the trunk. Soon we were old enough to help decide when to reach for the key to our resources – a team of horses, a set of harrows, a wagon, and always just enough money.

As a very young child, I don't remember what my mother looked like. I only observed the work she did. As I grew older, I began to notice *her*. She spoke with wit and laughed easily and often; yet she had a tongue that could lash and it came down, stroke upon stroke when we deserved it. She had a figure, too, that was the result, not of diet, but of duty.

Soon my mother's hands were calloused and large as a man's. Her fingertips and nails were cracked from summer's work and winter's cold. Alone she waged a winning battle against wind, snow, and drifts. Even at fifty degrees below zero, there were chores to do and, in summer, plowing and fencing to be done.

Ploughing could be an adventure on a homestead. One day she stopped her horses at the far end of the field and looked toward the "Big Trees." Lurking in the bushes a few rods from her was a cougar. She was terrified: all the more so when it inched toward her and the horses. She unhooked the traces and turned the horses toward home. Speaking reassuringly to the nervous animals, she dared not take her eyes off the beast as she backed up step by step. The cougar followed at a few yards distance and, not until the buildings came in sight, did he slink away. Turning, she raced the horses for home.

At this time, things improved somewhat. Adolph was old enough to drive the team when Mother held the plow. Meanwhile Martin and I washed the dishes and the loathed separator. All went well until his boyish instincts developed and Martin closed the door forever on what had been a congenial arrangement (for me). He moved outside to the place of all men and busied himself with wood and chores; calves and colts.

We learned many things the hard way. There was a law that no food was ever to be wasted. At supper, we often had either Norwegian mush or bread and milk. Martin hated bread crusts and many a night I had to slip down and swallow dry crusts to rescue a tearful boy.

Adolph was solemn and serious-minded. Martin and I were more alike. The responsibility of homesteading didn't rest too heavily on our shoulders. In the evenings we gaily set off, arms entwined, composing poetry as we looked for the cows. As we followed the path across the "Ditch," the "Stones," and the "Big Trees," Martin put our words to music. Such happy days!

We were growing up. Adolph was taking a man's place on the farm. I had finished public school and wanted high school but where was the money to come from? The trunk? There was surely not enough, for we were in the Depression of the 1930s. The trunk held very little – perhaps enough for books and I could work for my board, but what about clothes? Then Adolph came to the rescue by selling his prize heifer. My mother sewed. Thus, I left home for the first time clothed in love and style.

We who had battled the elements and surmounted every difficulty then found ourselves at war. Adolph did not pass the medical examination, but, in 1939, Martin joined the forces. About this time too, my dreams were fulfilled as I stood at the altar in *that* dress. Over my shoulder, I caught the expression in my mother's eyes of the lost hopes, loneliness, and struggle in her own life, but quickly it was replaced by that brave expression she had learned to wear so well.

Our ways were about to divide. The years had taken their toll and soon Mother would have to give up active farming and just sit down.

How quickly another twenty years go by! Not too long ago I drove out to the "farm." Sitting quietly beside me was my mother. I wondered what was on her mind as she looked serenely across the land to watch Martin ploughing the same furrows she had once turned over. We drove past her fence, still standing. My eyes followed hers across the "Ditch," past the "Stones" and to the "Big Trees." There wasn't too much change.

In the house, she picked up a scrapbook full of the activities of her eldest son; telling of his election and re-election to the Alberta Legislature where he today represents the district she pioneered.

Mother stayed to visit and I drove away alone; back to my own home and my own family. On entering our home, I felt strangely drawn to the trunk. It stands in the hall at the top of the stairs. Some of its secrets I will never know, but wrapped up in it were all our dreams and out of it emerged our destinies.

A note from Olive's daughter, Frances Stickney Newman, May 2005: "In recounting the story of 'My Mother's Trunk,' Olive Stickney set her narrative in about 1975, nearly a decade after Inga Fimrite passed away in her mid-eighties. Quite fittingly, Olive's final public appearance was at the "Unsettled Pasts" conference. Although she died in May 2003, she lived long enough to learn that her – and her mother's – story would not be forgotten."

thirteen

Washtub Westerns

ARITHA VAN HERK

Given that our approach to western Canadian, women's, and gender history is informed by an emphasis on inclusiveness, dialogue, and diversity, we welcomed contributions to the "Unsettled Pasts" conference that moved beyond the prerequisite scholarly articles and paper presentations. Walking and research tours explored prominent women's history sights in Calgary and provided guided introductions to the sources for studying women's and gender history at the Glenbow Museum and Archives and at the Calgary Public Library. Evening events included a documentary film night and the debut of a play by Nancy Millar called

"Singing Up the Hill," which centred on Alberta's "Famous Five" women who won women recognition as "persons" within the British North American Act (discussed by Patricia Roome in chapter 3). This chapter is a ficto-critical version of a performance piece that novelist and writer Aritha van Herk wrote for and performed at the conference. As van Herk explains in her introduction, it is a monologue that explores, re-enacts, and interprets femininity on the "frontier" using verse, historic photographs, and remnants from the past – a clothesline, a washtub, and a scrub board. She demonstrates how creative writing, in this case a commentary on laundry in the West, can reach a broader and more diverse audience than most academic histories, drawing attention to an overlooked and undervalued aspect of the West's unsettled past.

In Calgary at the turn of the century, Chinese laundries and houses of ill-repute had an equal number of barrels of water delivered to their establishments every week. These two (un)clean margins thus ironically embodied a larger weekly ritual connected to a socially peripheral concern with cleanliness. The metaphorical impact of filth and its eradication was an unspoken but upfront matter in the settlement period. That conjunction of clean and dirty speaks to an aspect of the West's unsettled past that has been largely overlooked and undervalued, the quotidian but tyrannical question of cleanliness, especially the maintenance of clean apparel. Somehow, in a world without running water, without easy access to soap or extra clothes or, in an unpredictable climate, line-drying time, women (and their feminized doubles, the Chinese laundries) did the literal laundry, a task inescapable as death and taxes but accorded far less importance.

Here follows a ficto-critical monologue on laundry in the West, what it meant and how it worked, how it inflected class and economics, how it reflected both culture and nature, how it speaks as a text of the unsettled side of settlement. The perspective is aware of how such work would be viewed or read now, and so crosses the hundred years between a woman's perspective at the turn of the twentieth century and what she might know now.

Glenbow Archives NA-4195-6

A Woman Standing at a Washtub, Scrubbing

Her voice is steady rather than strident, hoarse with exertion but not coarse. She is realistic rather than evangelistic. Her apparel is practical, enabling her to move freely, but dark so that the splashes and dirt won't show. She has wrapped up her hair, and her sleeves are rolled past her elbows.

Let me tell you, cleanliness is an over-rated virtue. I'd like to consign it to perdition, but that's always easier said than done. I swear, were I the swearing kind, that I've spent half my life leaning over murky water, and not in an effort to catch a glimpse of my reflection, either. Although what would I see? Just myself, looking pinched and dissatisfied, dishevelled as a woman always ends up looking when she is forced to make an occupation of cleaning the world around her.

At least in the summer I can work outside – that's why I've got this washtub balanced on two chairs out here in front of the house – well, it's hardly a house, more like a shack. I could use a workbench or something

Glenbow Archives NA-3731-8

practical, but there's never any time for the men to hammer together helpful furniture like that, so I try to manage with what I have.

I am most intimate with tubs and washboards, flatirons and buckets. I'd give my arm for a proper clothesline but the boys don't have the time to dig deep holes and settle two stout posts into the ground. And I need both my arms. Scrubbing is an arm job, and a modern woman would be bragging how many calories this work burns up and how much it helps her metabolism. Not to mention how it gets to those isolated muscle groups under the arms, and in the shoulders, teres minor and major, as well as the triceps. That's for an age that will not have to do laundry by hand.

And I'm working this washboard after I've dragged the water something like half a mile from the creek. The bucket brigade work comes first. Plumbing? Plumbing in this house consists of a bucket filled with fresh water, a dishpan for the dishes, of course, a basin for hand-washing, a slop pail for dirty water (which I throw on the garden) and a ceramic pot with a cracked lid under the bed.

Of course, we have an outhouse, that indispensable amenity. The standard outhouse joke is that it's too close in summer and too far away in the winter. The principle of an outhouse is this: dig a hole, put a little shed over it with a board across a pit, and move the whole venture when it gets too odoriferous. And it is a truism that you don't want to put the outhouse too close to the house.

So waste is simple enough, but every drop of water that I use I drag into the house; every drop of water that gets used for anything other than drinking I drag out of the house. Every drop of water that needs to be hot and not cold gets heated on my stove. Every fire in that stove gets fuelled by wood, wood that needs to be chopped, kindling and chunks and all the other variations that provoke different intensities of fire. But clean and dirty water, I carry and carry and carry. I carry every drop of water that I use for dishwashing, cooking, cleaning, child-bathing and laundry.

I've measured this out. The creek is a hundred yards away from the house. I drag water from the creek about ten times a day, sometimes on a slow day six, but on washday at least a dozen times. That's about one thousand yards a day, and in one year that works out to something around two hundred miles. Oh, you don't know what a mile is anymore? Almost twice as much as a kilometre. Does that help? Two hundred miles a year just carrying water. I've mentioned my arms but do you want to see my leg muscles? And I've been doing this for three years, which would add up to six hundred miles. And it's uphill too. If the boys would just dig a well with good water right next to the kitchen garden, I would be beyond happy. But I'm blessed enough to be close to a creek with good clear water. That in itself is a wonderful gift, out here in the scrub parkland of Alberta where potable water is not easy to find. And I treasure my rain barrels, because when they are full, I'm a rich woman.

But on this homestead, where the water that comes into the house is water that has to be carried out again, a woman becomes a natural conservationist. No doubt about that. I dream of a tap that you can open with a flick of the wrist, a stream of hot water that I can just plunge my head under. But then I dream that it all drains into slop pails, pails and pails that I have to carry outside and dump out, trying to channel them into the right areas of the garden. Come to think of it, I might just drown.

Glenbow Archives NA-5610-128

But here I am, trying to do the biggest job that faces me every week. I heard of that Sarah Roberts, you know, who wrote *Of Us and the Oxen*, she mentions doing a little washing every day, but I would rather get it all done at once. Not that it's ever done. At the end of the day, I feel as if I should be washing the dress I've done the washing in – it's stained and spattered so. I keep this one because I can roll up the sleeves and it doesn't show the dirt much. And when I take it off, the blouse underneath begins my pile of laundry for next week.

This is how women in the West get by, although none of us are about to earn any titles as queen of Alberta. We read the catalogue to comfort ourselves for what we don't have. In my case, I linger over those new-fangled wringer devices, but so far, I've got to rely on my hands, which are rough and chapped from so much hard wear, especially when the winter cold sets in. And why should I worry about clothes needing special care, when sheets and pillow cases, tea towels and underwear alike are pretty much made of flour sacks. The trick with flour sacks is to soak them, then bleach them, then boil them for about an hour – that gets rid of the red letters and beats the cotton softer. No one will ever know you're not wearing silk.

Some women feed their families cold Sunday leftovers on washdays, but I set bread to rise overnight, punch it down, let it rise again, roll it, punch it, and form it into loaves, then set the loaves to rise again. I've got the stove hot anyway, to boil water. And at the end of a tiring day, nothing could be better than a fresh cut crust spread with home-made butter and Rogers Golden Syrup.

But here's my washing routine. First, I chop enough wood to keep the stove burning all day. Sometimes the boys help, but they're usually working too far off, so I have to be ready to do it myself. Then, I carry pails and pails of water from the creek, and start to heat it on the stove. Some of it I just want warm, some I heat until it boils. Then I get out my soap, grate some into the boiling water, and start. Yes, of course I make my own soap. I save the grease and the ashes, mix them together with a little lye and then cut them into blocks. I laughed and laughed the day Royan brought home from Calgary a box of that granulated soap, with instructions on the side for Whiter Washing with Less Work. "Sprinkle granulated soap into the tub or washer. Add lukewarm or hot water and stir. A few seconds will give a clear, rich, soapy solution. Use enough soap to produce creamy, lasting suds even after the clothes are in. Let the suds be your guide." Let the suds be your guide. Homemade soap doesn't get up the suds much, but it gets clothes clean, or at least clean enough for us.

I do soak the whites overnight if I can get the boys to fetch a few pails on Sunday evening, but usually in cold water that I can start boiling early in the morning. And if something is soiled with grass or blood, I scrub it out with cold before I put it into the hot.

Did you know, one wash, one boiling, and one rinse uses something like fifty gallons of water? About four hundred pounds that is. You want to know what that is in litres? About one hundred and seventy-six litres. I only gave you the distance to the creek, not the weight I carry. Buckets

Glenbow Archives NA-2607-2

and buckets. Did I tell you about my trapezius muscles? And wet clothes weigh a ton. Even after you've squeezed the water out, they feel like lead.

I'm only grateful I don't have a lot of tablecloths, or fine linen napkins. And that the boys are all out of diapers. I've got sheets and pillowcases, lots of tea towels and hand towels, the coloured shirts and my dresses, and then the really grimy stuff, the boys' work clothes, overalls, socks. I must say, I'd rather do laundry than darn socks. At least my fingernails get clean.

I did learn how to do this properly, you know, in domestic science class back in Ontario. Note any spots or staining, roll garments and push well under water. Be sure that water covers the clothes. Rinse thoroughly, one hot water rinse, and one cold-water rinse. Colourfast clothes should soak not more than fifteen or twenty minutes. Hah. Here everything gets one rinse, with cold. I haven't got the energy to wring them out and then do it all over again. Although when I can get it, I do use a little bluing, just to make the whites seem whiter. It looks nice against the sky. I don't bother with starch anymore – although I tried for a while, on the white shirts and my collars. But I got shirt fronts that were stiff as a board or just too limp, so I gave up. Potato water doesn't work as well as proper starch. And I don't soak the work clothes overnight, just throw them in and pound them up really good. By that time, the water is so dirty that it doesn't matter much anyway.

Here I do the washing in this galvanized tub, punishing the clothes over this corrugated board, eyes stinging from the yellow carbolic, the only soap that will take out the heavy stains. At least this time of year, things get a chance to dry. In the winter, it's just a case of hanging the wet clothes outside until they're frozen before carrying them in like a stack of boards.

Funny, I don't mind washing as much as ironing, the flat iron heating on the wood stove like a ball and chain, and who out here notices whether anything is ironed or not. Although I do make some effort, making sure the creases are more or less repressed. I'd rather be milking the cow, or even churning (it all uses the same muscles) with the wooden dasher. And my favourite job is picking saskatoons, down in the hot coulee, thick with mosquitoes and thunder. Saskatoons, gooseberries, chokecherries, I even found a wild strawberry patch and the first time, I confess, I lay down on the ground next to those tiny plants and ate every one, all by myself, cramming them into my mouth so selfishly. Well, now I've started a few raspberry canes. And for all the water it takes to get the canning done, I don't mind that, boiling and bottling fruit. It's so pretty, jars of jewels, when I'm done.

Better than ironing, heating the iron and then having to test it on an old tea towel, make sure it isn't too hot or that the bottom isn't sooty, then pressing away. And I've only got the table to work on, it's hard to get creases and sleeves done properly on a flat surface. But ironing, the end of my laundry chores, just consolidates my aching back and my raw hands.

This is work. Work, you know, is the character that gets subsumed in the history books. Oh, they've changed their tune, they're interested in women's work now, they even dare to praise and admire how hard women worked, but they'd rather talk about women's political work, mouth work, hand work (the pretty stuff, knitting or crocheting), all the

Glenbow Archives NA-2674-3

maidenly stuff where no woman gets down on her knees except to pray. Although you could say that now most of our professions have been redeemed from dishonour.

Funny how in the future when the historians start hunting through those old pictures, they'll find so many photos of men doing their washing. Now I'm trying to figure out the reason for this healthy documentation of something that I can't get one of my boys even to help me with. Either those men have no woman to do the job for them, which is likely enough, or it was so amazing and unusual when they plunged their hands into a tub-full of water, someone just had to take a picture of them. How many photographers roamed the West looking for men doing their laundry? How many men posed doing their laundry? There's one famous picture that is going to get used over and over again. It's of a woman washing while she listens to the radio. But it's easy to tell that she isn't moving around too much, tethered to that machine. Seems like someone wants to persuade us that work is supposed to give us pleasure.

Glenbow Archives NA-1319-1

But if I lived in Calgary, I'd send my laundry to Hop Wo's or Sam Wing's and pretend to be a glorious society dame. I wonder how that works. I heard that the two places that use the most water in Calgary are Chinese laundries and whorehouses – both of them get at least six barrels of water delivered a week. Delivered. I'd love that. "Just deliver my water please." No, I'd never set a whorehouse on fire, it's just another form of work. And they must have understood soap and water, no matter what the magistrates call disorderly. A disorderly house. Ha. They should see this one. But after all, there are so many more men than women out here, lonely and isolated, and I can understand hard-handed men being hungry for a little touch. Some women marry their customers, I hear,

Glenbow Archives NA-2186-33

although why they would do that is beyond me. Marrying likely means giving up living in relative comfort (I am still marvelling that they get those six barrels of water delivered!) for squeezing into a dark and dirty shack like this one. I guess they wouldn't have to deal with countless men, but they'd be toiling at different tasks, just as unsavoury, if you ask me. I'd say the gain in propriety would be counterbalanced by sheer dismal discomfort. And work.

Out here there are three men for every woman and any woman who wants marriage doesn't last long. Did you see the advertisement last summer? Wanted, a "girl who is kind to dogs and a good cook." Don't know if they got any replies. Of course, what they really want is someone to look after chickens and pigs and to do the milking, and of course, to sleep with. And the *Lethbridge Herald* headline. "Alberta needs women more than men or money." Ha. I wish we got paid as much as men. They've put ads in the newspapers back home. "Urgent: thousands of nice girls are wanted in the Canadian West. Over 20,000 men are sighing for what they cannot get – WIVES! Shame! Don't hesitate – COME AT ONCE. If you cannot come, send your sisters. So great

Glenbow Archives NA-3931-19

is the demand that anything in skirts stands a chance. No reasonable offer refused. They are all shy but willing. All Prizes. No Blanks. Hustle up now Girls and don't miss this chance. Some of you will never get another." I laughed myself breathless over that one.

No blanks? I could tell them a thing or two. And what kind of woman would respond to that advertisement? Spinsters gambling that they'll find a cravat and a waistcoat rather than a bristle-faced burper who doesn't know the difference between a knife and a fork? And what happens if she lays eyes on the fellow and then won't have him? Does she have to refund her fare out west? They say it's better to come out here if you have family, at least you'll have a support system or a network. But nice girls think twice about marrying west. Cunning, desperate, imaginative, courageous and foolhardy girls come, and don't I wonder if they aren't the kind of women that this part of the country needs, the kind who are likely to do well under these circumstances, rubbing clothes on an old scrub board out under the raw June sky.

My old scrub board. This is the everyday one. When I got married, my mother gave me a dainty, personal scrub board. I know, an oxymoron, right. No, that was my travel deluxe, trousseau-happy DURI HANDI, ideal for silks, hosiery and lingerie or handkerchiefs. I think I still have a pile of lawn handkerchiefs but I don't use them out here. They're in the sulky trunk, where I try to keep things I might get a chance to use someday. I've got no silks at all, and as for hosiery, well, I hoard and harbour my hose, since I don't know when I'll be able to buy another pair. But there it is, my Duri Handi. I get it out every Monday, to remind me that I once dreamed of travelling, and thought I would need a travel scrub board, "Just the right size to fit in a bucket, pail or lavatory. Packs easily into suitcase or travelling bag."

I dream of travelling. If I were a travelling lady, I could stay at the Palliser and spend $1.55 a week on laundry. I dream of living in Calgary, and having Hop Wo come to the door to pick up my dirty laundry. I dream of his hands, cleaning my clothes, that man doing my work, my doing his work, the two of us in the same boat, only those with no power allotted the most important job of all, this intimate skill, this awful smelly back-aching task.

I boil soup, I render lard, I churn butter, I scatter grain for the chickens, I gather their eggs, I salt the pork that was Elmer the pig who ate table scraps and rooted in my garden, I hoe weeds and hill potatoes, I milk cows. I can make a fine cake out of a few raisins and a handful of flour, and I make soap for laundry. There is no measurement of how many times I've quietly turned over this washtub and gone behind the house and cried.

But then I get busy. I stuff mattresses with straw, I stitch away at a quilt from the patches of clothes that are too ragged to wear. Sometimes I pray for a chinook.

Eventually, I'll get one of my wishes. A post office, a party line, a neighbour with a sense of humour. Eventually, I'll get a two-storey house made of wood, complete with a mud room, three bedrooms upstairs, a front and a back parlour, a dining room, a pantry, a kitchen, and a

Glenbow Archives NA-2685-98

clothes line strung taut between the sky and hope, sheets hanging clean and white beside the back door.

And my grandmother will send a barrel of apples from Ontario. While in town, grubby cowboys will visit the steam baths at all hours and even baths on "Tuesdays and Fridays for Ladies." I might go and take one sometime, just to immerse myself in a tub of water that I haven't carried. Meanwhile, I'm dancing the washtub dance, me and my scrub board, inseparable we are, and what would I do without it? Where would I be?

So I'll finish this load, stretch all these wet clothes over the fence, tip the dirty water next to the garden, and set myself down with a cup

Glenbow Archives NA-4186-7

of tea in one of the mugs that hasn't cracked. I'll plan how to dress up the rhubarb for dessert tonight, without resorting to too much sugar. There's cream for on top. That always helps. And later, I'll allow myself a moment, bury my nose in those same threadbare sheets, just to catch the smell of cloth that has dried in a hot sunny breeze, incomparable perfume.

I know you want me to declare that the compensations are few, but mighty. I won't go that far. But if they ever do a Washboard Western, I'll be the first to read it.

fourteen

Delicious Moments: Uncovering the Hidden Lives

of Western Canada's Black Pioneer Women

CHERYL FOGGO

In Canada, documentary films like Great Grandmother *(1987) and* Women in the Shadows *(1991) reflected and enhanced popular and academic enthusiasm for western women's history. In recognition of the role played by documentary and film makers, the "Unsettled Past" conference offered an "evening of film," which included a discussion with writer-director Penny Wheelwright and a screening of her docudrama,* The Orkney Lad: The Story of Isabel Gunn. *In addition, Alberta writer and director Cheryl Foggo gave a presentation entitled "Black Faces in Unexpected Places: Pioneer Black Women in the Canadian*

Prairies," in which she screened segments from a forthcoming documentary entitled "Happy Endings," which was inspired by her lifelong passion for her ancestors' story. Her work builds upon a filmmaking tradition that includes documentaries like Sylvia D. Hamilton's Black Mother, Black Daughter *that have introduced popular and academic audiences to the diverse experiences of African-Canadians. Just as Olive Stickney 's mother inspired her political activism and writing, the women of Calgary's small but tight-knit Black community inspired Foggo to collect, preserve, and disseminate the stories of their collective past.*

In 1985, Foggo began researching and writing Pourin' Down Rain, *a book that chronicles her forbears' transnational, cross-border journey from Africa to the United States and from Oklahoma to Canada. Through* Pourin' Down Rain, *Foggo hoped to correct the mistaken assumption that western Canada had been settled exclusively by White homesteaders. This article, which appeared originally in* Legacy *magazine, has been revised to highlight the triumphs and the hardships – racism, hard work, dislocation, and poverty – of Black "pioneer" women in Alberta. Based upon stories and reminiscences that were passed on to Foggo as a child, and in oral interviews with the "grandmothers" of Calgary's Black community, Foggo's article – like many pioneer narratives across the cultural spectrum – draws attention to the importance of religion, family, community, and collective memory as bonds that sustained Black women and their communities in times of need.*

When I was growing up it seemed that I was who I was, living where I was because of divine intervention.

One of six children born to a woman who was the granddaughter of slaves, I lived in Bowness, a former small town that had been swallowed up by Calgary. The little brown faces of my brothers, sister, and I were usually the only little brown faces, wherever we went. Usually, but not always. There was the Standard Church in Inglewood, pastored by my uncle, Andrew Risby, where every Sunday my family gathered with the other remnants of northern Black communities. And, there was our neighbourhood. Down the street in one direction from the small green and white bungalow we inhabited lived the old Hayes, grandparents to our friends Randy, Ricky, and Debbie, who lived across the alley behind them. Across our alley and three houses down lived old Mrs. Carrothers. Up the street in the other direction from the Hayes, nearly directly across the street from each other, were the Saunders and the Lawsons. My mother swears this proximity was an accident.

To my mind, as I grew older, the stories about the Black settlements of northern Alberta and Saskatchewan deepened into legends, and I came to doubt her protestations. It had to have been part of The Plan. Hayes, Carrothers, Lawson, Saunders – these were all names that could be found on immigration logs at Emerson, Manitoba, in the early part of the last century, alongside the names of my own great-grandparents. They were coming from the same place, the southern United States, for the same reason – God had called them away from oppression and enslavement to the Promised Land. Just as our grandparents and great-grandparents had pulled up stakes, ridden the long train together, banded together to form the northernmost Black communities that had ever existed in the world, we had banded together on 70th Street in Bowness because it was our destiny.

During the first decade of the twentieth century, the place where my maternal great-grandparents had been enjoying relative freedom, and some human rights, became Oklahoma. Whites who had pressed hard for the establishment of Oklahoma, then, as a first priority, used politics and violence to attack the Blacks who had settled there. In his book, *Deemed Unsuitable*, Bruce Shepard quotes prominent Oklahoma citizen Roy Stafford who wrote in the *Oklahoman*: "The law is as powerless to curb the debased, ignorant and brutal negro as it is to restrain vicious animals that attack men. Does not this alone explain the hangings, burnings and horrible forms of mob violence visited upon those of the black race who shatter the law?"

Lynchings frequently followed such tirades, which dominated newspaper editorials and election platforms of the time. Numerous towns saw the burning and dynamiting of Black homes and beatings of Black citizens. A racist mob descended on the town of Wairuka and gave its Black citizens twenty-four hours to leave. Politicians won seats by promising to introduce segregation in all aspects of public life; their promises took place during elections where Blacks were denied participation through various, illegal means.

My forebears – the Glovers and the Smiths – believed absolutely that they were God's people and that God had a place for them. When the Canadian government began running ads in southern newspapers for farmers to come north and settle the wild regions of Alberta and

Saskatchewan, they were certain they had found that place. They had heard of Canada: it was the last stop on the Freedom Train, the Underground Railroad. It was the place their own forebears had sung about in code in their spirituals. Canada's secret names were Canaan, Heaven, the other side of Jordan. Along with between one and two thousand others like themselves, my great-grandparents were going to the Promised Land.

The communities formed by these pioneers were in and around Maidstone and North Battleford in Saskatchewan, and Keystone (now Bretton), Campsie, Junkins (now Wildwood), and – the largest and best known – Amber Valley, in Alberta. They lived in abandoned railroad boxcars or tiny log cabins with dirt floors and tarpaper roofs. Some of the pioneers described enduring temperatures of sixty degrees below zero, in shacks where the wind and snow blew through the cracks. They ate moose and pork when they could get it; rabbit and squirrel when they had to. In *The Window of our Memories*, a book of Black pioneer stories collected by Velma Carter and Wanda Leffler Akili, Sally Carrothers recalls, "Baby, I love rabbit until this day. You know why I love it? Because it saved my life. It kept us from starving to death.... Don't you worry honey, I'm not going to ever say I don't like rabbits." The pioneers wrestled rocks, trees, and bushes to clear their land. Old Mrs. Bush, a sweet, small woman who attended my uncle's church, described walking twelve miles through rain-clogged muskeg and bog to buy groceries in Edmonton.

Worst of all, their welcome was not what they'd hoped for. Petitions were circulated against their presence. Editorials were written in Alberta newspapers, denouncing them as a threat. Legislation to keep them out was introduced. This type of activity was discouragingly familiar. Some of the people stumbled and lost their way. There was infighting and backstabbing. A small number adopted crime and despair as a way of life; yet, the majority thrived. Most of the pioneers, including my ancestors, became fiercely loyal Canadians. What they had left behind in the South was so dehumanizing that hardship in Canada was simply incorporated into the legend. God never promised it would be easy – He only promised the Promised Land. They ignored the petitions because racist Canadians usually didn't deliver their petitions with violence; and the other kind of Canadians, the righteous ones, were some of the best friends they'd ever had.

The women of the community often formed the first bonds with their new neighbours, and in the usual ways – through quilting and cooking. When nearby settlements arrived for baseball games, the women played an important role in winning hearts – it would appear that friends were easily bought with double-basted southern fried chicken, button bone spare ribs, potato pie, and home made ice cream.

The workload and hardship of the women's lives was astonishing. They laboured alongside the men in the fields, and tended the gardens and animals. They raised huge families, overseeing chores for everyone. Clothing was hand-sewn, hand-mended, scrubbed on washboards, and hung out to dry. Some of them walked or drove wagons miles for supplies. The cultural stereotype of the good cook was very much alive in these Black settlements. When I hear my elderly aunts reminiscing about the wood stove, my mind boggles. These monstrosities required a chemist's knowledge and incredible patience – when do you add wood, when do you take it away, how do you know the precise moment when the bread must go in? For that matter, how do you prepare ingredients to feed fifteen people in a log and sod hut that would be smaller than most modern kitchens? Somehow, these women fed their families three times every day, and many of them fed everyone within miles after church on Sundays.

When you have had to run for your life, community takes on added importance. Many of these Black pioneer women worked hard outside their homes to build up the community: running the post office, delivering babies, applying sophisticated knowledge of local herbs and plants to the medical needs of their children and neighbours, lobbying for schools. None of these activities or hardships set the lives of these women apart from those of their White neighbours. What set them apart was the draining, painful task of raising children to love themselves when the teacher turned them away from the schoolhouse, and salving the bruised egos of men who were denied respect when they valued it so highly.

I took their sweet, sweet spirits for granted when I was a child. If I had known what they had been through, I would have marvelled more. They weren't bitter. They called me "honey" and "baby" and hugged me and fed me homemade rolls and glazed ham, and turkey with cornbread dressing after church on Sunday. By the time I was born, most of the surviving pioneers and their second generation had moved away from the farms. They were the backbones of our tiny Black communities in the cities. There were so many strong women like my grandmother, Arrenna Glover Smith, who passed down a legacy of grace, warmth, and deeply resonant survival skills.

The pioneers raised many successful men, such as Floyd Sneed, the drummer for seventies superstar rock band "Three Dog Night," civic engineer Oliver Bowen, who oversaw the construction of Calgary's Light Rail Transit (LRT), *Edmonton Journal* cartoonist Malcolm Mayes, and His Honour, Judge Lionel Jones, whose father Jesse was a world-class track athlete. Perhaps more remarkably, they also produced women who excelled in a time when both their skin and their gender were disadvantages. Violet King became the first Black female law graduate in Canada, and the second woman to be admitted to the bar in Calgary. Velma Carter, one of five sisters who all became teachers, also achieved widespread recognition as an author.

My own career as an author was launched with a 1980 article for *Calgary Magazine*. The magazine piece, titled "Aunt Gotchie," was about Calgary's Black community, which by that time had grown to include people from all over the world. Although I found it interesting to meet and interview people who had been born in Africa, the United States, and the Caribbean, I was most drawn to the stories of the first generation of children born to the Black pioneers – people like Joan Armstead and her husband Alge, who, as Calgary's first Black bus driver, was forced to make practice runs before he was hired, so his employers could determine whether White Calgarians would accept him. Willa Sneed, or "Aunt Gotchie," and her husband Nap (parents of "Three Dog Night" drummer Floyd) invited me for tea and didn't mind that I brought my tape recorder.

These were people who had been acquainted with Calgary in the first decades of the twentieth century, and who had known me virtually from the day I was born. I sat with Aunt Gotchie and Uncle Nap (they weren't my aunt and uncle, but my brothers and sister and I called them so because they were our cousins' aunt and uncle and we saw them every Sunday at church) in their kitchen, drinking tea and eating fresh, warm cinnamon buns and thought to myself, "I'm working! This precious, delicious moment is my work!" I was, in fact, employed as an orthodontic assistant at that time, and my freelance writing career was very much in the fledgling stage. The tea, the buns, and Aunt Gotchie and Uncle Nap's beaming faces marked the beginning of the end of my dental career. Rereading the piece recently, I experienced a chill looking

The author's mother, Pauline (Smith) Foggo, on her wedding day. On the bride's left, her twin sister, Pearl (Smith) Hayes. On the bride's right, her friend, future lawyer Vi King. The flower girls are the bride's nieces; to her left, Sharon Risby and between Pearl and Vi, Elaine Lewsey. Scarth Street, Regina, 1 August 1953. Courtesy: Cheryl Foggo.

over the prescient words I had written. Aunt Gotchie and Uncle Nap had been lamenting the loss of closeness the community had inevitably experienced when Black pioneers sold their farms, moved to the cities and, by prospering, began to spread out into the suburbs:

Aunt Gotchie sighed. "Everything was so different then, honey. I used to listen to the old people talk about forty years ago and wonder how they could remember that far back. Now here I am talking about forty years ago."

I look gloomily into my teacup, thinking that before I know it I'll be telling some whippersnapper how I used to be rocked to sleep on Aunt Gotchie's knee at Watchnight service.

How right I was. The work of my life has become the preservation of those memories and the dissemination of those stories. Many of the people I interviewed for that article have died; I loved them, and I wanted the world to know who they were. Since that time, my career as a writer of poetry, screenplays, journalism, stage plays, and books has been built on the depths of their experiences. My identity, values, commitment to community and my connection to humanity have grown out of my family's history. I am who I am because of who my mother was and who her mother was and who her mother was. I grew up hearing my existence framed as a combination of legend, myth, and ordained entitlement. I knew that our history – tragic and painful – had been turned to good. I was a writer because that is what was meant for me. There were important and interesting stories to be told.

I grew weary of mainstream Canadians' assumptions that only White pioneers had settled Canada's west. From time to time, I saw something sinister in those assumptions. I wrote *Pourin' Down Rain* to answer the question I have been asked by other Canadians countless times since I was a child: "Where are you from?"

The book is an account of my own family's journey from slavery to Calgary. Some years after writing it, I was chatting on the phone with my cousin Glenda in Vancouver. She told me she had just finished rereading it. "I wanted to ask you something, though," she went on to say. "I mean, I laughed and I cried. But what kind of response do you get from strangers who don't know us?"

Her question was a good one, one that I had wrestled with before writing the book. *Pourin' Down Rain* is a highly personal memoir. If my intention was to shed light on the long history of Black pioneers on the Prairies, shouldn't the book have been more encompassing, less specific to my own family? In the end, it was more important to me to touch readers personally, rather than adding significantly to their general understanding of a people's history. I was hoping that specificity would breed universality. *Pourin' Down Rain* says, "My family endured long, hot trips by car across the prairies too. My family got lost in snowstorms, just like yours. We walked lazily along the railroad tracks looking for fool's gold, just like you."

The book also says that my ancestors and the other pioneers were not defined by racism. They were not victims; they were survivors:

More than once Aunt Daisy recalled for me in detail how happy they were that it was autumn as they prepared for the winter ahead. She would hold her hands up in front of my face, so that I could imagine how black they became after two hours of pulling vegetables from her mother's garden. There were turnips, carrots, beets, potatoes and cabbage, which her mother transformed into a huge barrel of sauerkraut and stored in the cellar...

After school, the children were sent with buckets into the woods, to collect a variety of berries. Drucilla would can or make jam from the saskatoons, raspberries, strawberries, gooseberries, pin cherries and other berries that the children gathered.

"When everything else was ready," Aunt Daisy said when she spoke to me of this happiness, "Papa slaughtered two of the hogs. Us children felt like we were ready. Ol' Winter could just come on and he wasn't going to bother us none."

She rested her head back, paused, closed her eyes. She was recalling herself and her family as they had been in their contentment in 1916 – loved, sheltered and well fed.

I was happy to tell Glenda that people "get" *Pourin' Down Rain.*

Occasionally I run up against publishers or producers who pass my work over because they believe there are not enough Black people living in western Canada to justify its existence. Their attitude is misguided and sells Canadians short. Many people prefer an accurate and full accounting of their country's history to a false, incomplete history. Many from across the spectrum of Canada's multiracial, multicultural population embrace one another's stories.

I revel in the opportunity to represent the stories of Black girls and women like those of the pioneers and their descendants who have inspired me, and who have never before been represented on Canadian stages, screens, or pages. In my play *Heaven*, a fictional teacher named Charlotte Williams arrives from the east to teach in Amber Valley in 1927. Charlotte, a descendant of Underground Railroad fugitive slaves, is a third-generation Canadian and her perspective puts her in conflict with the more recently arrived Canadian residents of Amber Valley. The incident, where Charlotte gets into trouble for demanding books for her classroom, is based on a story from the school days in Amber Valley shared with me by Peggy (Bowen) Brown, who is a cousin to the Oliver Bowen who shepherded the Calgary LRT. Along with her husband Sidney, who is one of those pictured in the famous Amber Valley baseball team photo, Peggy opened her collection of artefacts from her parents' Amber Valley homestead to the actors who performed in *Heaven* for its Calgary run at Lunchbox Theatre.

During *Heaven*'s run at Lunchbox, I picked up my mother, Aunt Gotchie, and her sister Helen Lyons to take them to see the show. The traffic was heavy that day. As I manoeuvred through the downtown congestion and into a parking spot, I heard Helen say to Aunt Gotchie, "This little girl knows what she's doing." Aunt Gotchie replied happily, "She sure does."

They were not condescending. I may have been forty-four years old at the time, but they saw me as one of their own little girls who had given them a voice, had written a story from their lives, and found an audience for it; one who had, furthermore, the courage and skill to drive through traffic-clogged freeways to take them to see it.

I marvel at their lives, they marvel at mine. It's a good deal.

fifteen

Nursing Students at Medicine Hat

General Hospital, 1894–1920

FLORENCE MELCHIOR

Within the patriarchal constraints imposed on women at the turn of the twentieth century, nursing emerged as one of the few acceptable professions for women in the public sphere. Yet nursing education, like mission work, was governed by the same assumptions and intentions that underpinned the larger colonial and nation-building projects. By describing how medical, Christian, and British-Canadian gender ideals shaped perceptions of nurses and their daily practice at Alberta' first school of nursing, Florence Melchior highlights how the emergence of the profession accompanied and enhanced the consolidation of middle-class, British-

Canadian identity formation and power in prairie towns and cities. Contrary to popular stereotypes that represented nurses as exploited drudges, nursing students at Medicine Hat were privileged women from British-Canadian and Protestant families who were trained to be "moral icons," examples of the feminine ideal, in local communities. Melchior's research indicates, however, that although nursing students earned higher wages and more respect than working-class women labouring in Medicine Hat's factories, they were held to gender norms and ideals that enhanced the process by which nursing came to be regarded, and undervalued, as "women's work." As Siri Louie's article on female mountaineers will illustrate (see chapter 16), women's lives, experiences, and potentials were historically constrained, even in the absence of official barriers to achievement or advancement.

The time has also come when a training school for nurses should be started. We are constantly receiving applications from young ladies who are anxious to acquire a nurses' [*sic*] training. This could be done with very little additional outlay. There are few ways in which the hospital can benefit the public more than by being able to supply a nurses' [*sic*] training to those who are anxious and willing to acquire one, and who are willing to give their time and work gratuitously for the sake of the information they receive.[1] – Dr. J. G. Calder (1893)

With these words, the impetus for the first school of nursing in the first hospital west of Winnipeg, Manitoba, and east of Vancouver Island, British Columbia, was born. Who were these women that desired a nurse's training? From what strata of the community did they come? Who was considered a desirable nursing student? On what criteria was that desirability based? As historian Kathryn McPherson has noted, in the early twentieth century nursing students were a privileged group of women who benefited from a higher social standing and enhanced opportunities for higher education than the average working woman.[2] Was that privilege derived, or partly derived, from ethnicity? As others have suggested, my research indicates that, like valued masculine professional and political positions, professional nursing in English-speaking Canada's early years was occupied and reserved for women of the dominant British-Canadian group.[3] Moreover, the qualities deemed desirable for nurses were based on middle-class feminine ideals.[4] This chapter explores this argument further as it applies to the formation of the Medicine Hat General Hospital School of Nursing and the identity and work experience of its nursing students.[5]

While ethnicity is central to this analysis, the variables of gender, class, and age are also considered. Although ethnic groups other than the dominant British-Canadian, Protestant group developed cohesive ethnic identities in the prairie West, they did not belong to the elite that created political and institutional policies. As de Zwart, Kozak, and Louie's contributions to this volume illustrate (see chapters 8, 10, and 16), the British-Canadian middle class played an active and public role in the Prairies, often creating policies and directives that benefited their own members.[6] Nursing education was shaped by similar goals and assumptions. Studying who became nursing students highlights, not only ethnicity and (to a lesser extent) class as variables that complicate nursing history, but also the wider socio-economic and cultural forces that governed nursing education in a regional context.

Although medical staff would have had a vested interest in ensuring quality nursing care for their patients, it is not clear whether the idea for a Medicine Hat school of nursing originated with the medical or nursing staff. In late-nineteenth and early-twentieth-century Medicine Hat, the medical superintendent presented the lady superintendent's report to the board of directors, and probably had editorial licence over its content.[7] It is likely that plans for a school of nursing had been in the making since the hospital opened in 1890, with the first lady superintendent, Nurse Grace Reynolds, and her assistant, Nurse Mary Ellen Birtles, playing an instrumental role in its planning.[8] In 1891, however, Reynolds left to marry Dr. John Calder. Birtles also left, and three years later took up the position of lady superintendent at the Calgary General Hospital. Consequently, it was Nurse Agnes Miller, a Royal Infirmary of Edinburgh graduate, who replaced Reynolds and supervised curriculum development for student nurses.[9] As the wife of the medical superintendent, Reynolds likely had influence over the curriculum. As Tony Cashman notes in his history of nursing in Alberta: "It was apparently the joint work of Miss Miller and Miss Reynolds and represented the Nightingale method from two angles."[10] Yet, the cultural context of the community, which would have been defined by its settlers, may have equally affected the development of the hospital and training school.

The first European settlers in Medicine Hat were of British origin. Whether transplanted from Ontario, the United States, or the British Isles, the British were always, as Howard Palmer argued, "rated as the most desirable settlers by Alberta's newspapers and by immigration officers."[11] The Canadian government actively recruited them in North America and Britain.[12] In the view of government policymakers, they were model Canadians, embodying an ideal from the British Isles that illustrated Canada's pride in being part of the British Empire. Perhaps, more importantly for this study, their wages for labour were also higher than any other immigrant group.[13] The first British-Canadian settlers in the Medicine Hat area were either ranchers, employees of the Canadian Pacific Railway (CPR), entrepreneurs, church ministers, or professionals such as physicians and lawyers. These settlers later formed a Medicine Hat elite, which included the mayor, the members of town council, hospital, and school boards, and the owners of most businesses and industries.[14]

Other settlers were of Scandinavian and German origin, with Germans comprising the largest group. The earliest Germans arrived in 1889 and settled in Dunmore (east of Medicine Hat) and Josephburg (in the Cypress Hills).[15] Reports from German colonies in the Cypress Hills appeared in the *Medicine Hat Times* as early as 1890. The editor of the local paper referred to them as "worthy settlers."[16] Between 1908 and 1916, the areas north and east of Medicine Hat (around Schuler, Hilda, Burstall, Irvine, and Walsh) were likewise settled by these groups.[17] Palmer concluded that, except for some isolated religious minority groups, Germans and Scandinavians assimilated easily into Canadian society for several reasons. First, they were regarded as culturally similar to the dominant British. Second, they were industrious, embodying the ideal British work ethic. Third, diversity within the groups, including religion and place of European origin, precluded a strong national identification such as that experienced by Ukrainians. With the influx of massive non-British immigration after 1896, Alberta's population grew to include over 41,000 Germans and almost 30,000 Scandinavians by 1911.[18] Until the First World War, Germans enjoyed the distinction of being the second most "desirable" immigrants after people of British descent.[19]

The original inhabitants of the Medicine Hat area, the Blackfoot and Cree, like other First Nations, were subject to Canada's Indian policy. The goals of this policy were "civilization," assimilation, and gradual enfranchisement. Part of this process included placing "Indians" on reserves where they could take up farming and forego their traditional migratory economy. By 1883, when the CPR reached Medicine Hat, Treaties 4 and

7, which concerned land in southern Saskatchewan and Alberta, had been signed, relegating the Blackfoot and Cree to reserves. Although no reserves are located in the immediate Medicine Hat area, Medicine Hat is between the boundaries of Treaty 4 and 7.[20] Until at least 1916, peoples of both nations continued to camp at their accustomed meeting ground – the flood plain at Medicine Hat – sometimes causing consternation among newly arrived Europeans.[21]

Other ethnic groups that received less than favourable review in the local paper included Chinese and Italians. Headlines that proclaimed "Keeping out the Chinese" appeared often. The Chinese were considered less desirable than the Japanese, who were described as "undoubtedly superior."[22] However, the Japanese were not considered wholly desirable either. One journalist noted, "a large immigration of the lower class of Japs would be almost as great an evil as the influx of Chinamen [sic]."[23] In 1894, the headline "Italians Give Trouble: A Number of the Dagoes Wounded in the Fray"[24] likewise appeared; the article's content reflected prevailing perceptions about the desirability or undesirability of immigrants, and their place in the "ethnic pecking order."[25]

The tone of the *Medicine Hat Times* and the *Medicine Hat News*, as noted above, was consistent with the view of British-Canadian settlers in other parts of western Canada who believed that British society was the epitome of civilization – one to which all others should aspire.[26] The goal of transplanting and re-creating that ideal on the Prairies, and in Medicine Hat, can be inferred from club and leisure activities, traditions such as Orangeman Parades, and the articles that appear in the local paper.[27] It was this attitude that also set the tone for building the local hospital and school of nursing. At the official opening of the hospital, Reverend James Herald of the Presbyterian Church stated, in reference to the history of hospital construction in Great Britain, "the erection of hospitals was essentially the outcome of the spread of Christianity."[28] The ideal, which was assumed to be Great Britain, could be achieved in Medicine Hat and the construction of a Christian hospital was seen as a step in that direction.

The need for a hospital was recognized in 1888 as typhoid, injuries, and illnesses among farmers, ranchers, and railway workers motivated leading citizens to make it a top priority.[29] As implied earlier, the community leaders were also committed to and practised Christian charity, a prime motivator in raising the necessary funds for such an enterprise. Other reasons, more selfish in origin, probably derived from boosterism

Medicine Hat General Hospital, 1894. Medicine Hat Museum and Art Gallery, 0180-0015.

– the promotion of the community as attractive to settlers and entrepreneurs.[30] John M. Niblock, superintendent of the CPR in Medicine Hat, a "teetotaller, Orangeman, rigid Methodist, and rumoured member of the extremist Protestant Protective Association ... accused of discriminating against Catholics in hiring and against unfriendly railway customers in business," was instrumental in its founding.[31] He initiated fundraising for the hospital's construction and furnishing, and applied to the Legislative Assembly of the North-West Territories for its incorporation. For seven years, he also served as president of the hospital's board of directors.[32]

In January 1890, the first patients were admitted and the official opening ceremony was held in June. The building, an impressive sandstone construction, was decorative and in most ways functional. The hospital offered three general and five private wards for both male and female patients on the first and second floors. The nurses' quarters were located in one half of the mansard flat, an attic space that included a sitting room and three bedchambers. The other half of the flat contained the contagious diseases ward, which nurses entered through a separate stair-case located on the outside of the building. Furnishings for the hospital came primarily through local donations.[33]

Reynolds, Birtles, and an unnamed assistant, who appears to have trained under their tutelage, staffed the hospital. The three women provided patient care, assisted in surgery, ordered supplies, served meals, and generally managed the hospital.[34] The work was both arduous and demanding. For example, the *Medicine Hat Times* reported in 1890: "An operation known as ovarian resection (removal of ovarian tumours, in this case three in number) was successfully performed at the hospital here on May 12th, by Doctors Olver and Calder.... The operation is generally recognized as 'The most serious and difficult operation in the whole field of surgery' is the first in the Territories."[35] Besides the nursing work performed during surgery (Reynolds administered the anaesthetic while Birtles assisted the surgeons), the nurses had the patients' recovery to attend to after a long day spent in the operating room.[36]

Reports to the board of directors indicate that the hospital was well used. In its first year of operation, 124 patients were admitted with a 28.2-day average length of stay. One hundred and one operations were performed with an average surgical stay of 40.6 days. The total number of patient-days was 3,591, for an average of about ten patients a day; however, the hospital did have as many as twenty-two beds occupied at one time.[37] In Marcel Dirk's history of the hospital, he found that, in the first year of operation, only thirty-five of the patients admitted were from Medicine Hat. The rest were sent to the hospital from an outlying area that encompassed Winnipeg to the east, Edmonton to the north, and Field, British Columbia, to the west. Seventy-five per cent more men than women were admitted, reflecting the population mix of the time. The religion and ethnicity of the patients were also noted carefully, most being of British-Protestant extraction: "twenty seven English, eleven Scottish, nine Irish, twenty eight Ontarians ... four Germans, four Russians, two Swedes, and one Italian."[38] Interestingly, despite policies of protection and civilization, only one First Nations person was registered: she died of breast cancer.[39]

By the time the school of nursing opened in 1894, the hospital staff in the previous year had provided care to 193 patients for a total of 5,804 patient-days.[40] Therefore, the workload for three nurses was increasingly heavy and would have been, at times, unmanageable. Without an adequate supply of available trained nurses, a school of nursing must have seemed a perfect solution to the problem. Much-needed staff would be immediately available and, in the long term, a cadre of trained nurses could benefit the well-being of the growing community.

The Medicine Hat General Hospital School of Nursing officially opened in August 1894. Nursing students had been on staff, however, for some months. In anticipation of the opening, Reynolds and Birtles initiated the two-year program with at least three students in late 1893 or early 1894.[41] Although there was no notation in the local paper in 1894, at the 1895 "Annual Meeting of the Medicine Hat General Hospital" the president of the board reported:

Nurses' Training School. – The Training School which has been established in our hospital under the supervision of Dr. Peters must in a short time result in much good being done. Already nurses are in demand and it is the desire of your Board of Directors to keep two or three competent nurses available for all kinds of outside nursing, and thus giving trained service at the lowest possible cost.[42]

The following week, the medical superintendent's report again mentioned the school:

The commencement of a training school for nurses has filled a long felt want in connection with this Institution. Since August 1st lectures have been given weekly to the nurses. A number of ladies of Medicine Hat having expressed a desire to attend these lectures, it was decided to allow all interested ladies to attend. The lectures embrace medical, surgical, maternity and other subjects of interest to a practical nurse. They are of a practical nature and are supplemented by teaching at the bedside by the matron. Three of our nurses have already been engaged in nursing cases outside the hospital. That their services are appreciated is shown by increased desire for them, which is becoming so great that we will have to increase our staff in the near future.[43]

The first two graduates, Gertrude Hales and Jean Miller (the younger sister of Lady Superintendent Miller), wrote their examinations in January 1896.[44] As reported by the president: "The papers are now all in and show both nurses as having passed their examinations very creditably, having taken over 90 per cent of the total number of marks. Both the nurses and their teachers are to be congratulated on this splendid showing."[45]

In the following years, the number of nursing students accepted each year increased, reflecting the growth of the community, the extra staff needed after the opening of the Lady Aberdeen Maternity Hospital in 1895, the demand for private nursing care, and perhaps the increased acceptability of hospital care.[46] Where hospitals had once been feared as places where the sick and poor were treated and often died, the Medicine Hat General was lauded in the opening ceremonies as a necessary institution for the whole community.[47]

Women who entered the school were subject to the control of the board of directors and under the supervision of the medical and lady superintendent. First, however, the prospective student had to apply and be accepted for admission. Information about desirable qualities in a nursing student was gleaned partially from admission criteria. In 1895, the *Rules and Regulations of the Training School for Nurses in connection with Medicine Hat General Hospital* set the following questions for potential students:

1. Name in full and present address of candidate.
2. Religion.
3. Are you married, single or a widow[?]
4. Your present occupation or employment.
5. What has been your occupation[?]
6. Age last birthday and date and place of birth.
7. Height. Weight.
8. Where educated.
9. Are you strong and healthy and have you always been so[?]
10. Have you ever had any uterine disease?
11. Have you any physical defect?
12. Have you any tendency to pulmonary complaints?
13. If a widow have you any children? How many? Their ages. How are they provided for?
14. The names in full and the addresses of two persons to be referred to. State how long each has known you. If previously employed, one of these.[48]

The *Rules and Regulations* also stipulated that applicants "of superior education and cultivation, when equally qualified for nursing, will be preferred to those who do not possess these advantages."[49] Character was believed to be more important than knowledge and skill when women's work, including nursing, was evaluated.[50] Indeed, a speaker at the Women's Literary Club of Medicine Hat asserted in 1907, when considering "the highest type of girl ... character is higher than intellect."[51]

Using data from annual reports published in the local newspaper, Dirk was able to formulate a table demonstrating acceptance rates of prospective nursing students. The data indicates that many women desired a nurse's training, and positions were highly sought (see Appendix A for acceptance rates from 1907 to 1920). From 1894 to 1920, acceptance rates for applicants ranged from 15 to 30 per cent. In subsequent years, the lowest rate (6 per cent) occurred in 1934 when 248 women applied for 16 positions.[52] That so many women applied to the school of nursing probably reflects the lack of employment and educational opportunities for women in Medicine Hat. Courses in domestic science, piano, and languages alone were available, unless a woman left the city for further education.[53] In addition, employment for women, as advertised in the local paper, was restricted to domestic service with rare secretarial and teaching opportunities.

Nursing, a profession that was exclusively the domain of women, was respectable and highly valued.[54] For example, in an article in the *Medicine Hat Weekly News*, a journalist wrote: "There is always more or less romance in the mind of the young girl about the profession of nursing, which is rightfully considered one of the very highest professions open to women."[55] The journalist went on to recount the experiences of a Chicago nurse who debunked the myth of the ministering angel and exposed the physical and "un-dainty" reality of nursing work. However, working outside the home seemed to be incentive enough. Although the women's emancipation movement was not whole-heartedly supported in the local paper, many young women in the city and surrounding area were clearly eager to expand their horizons beyond domestic science.[56]

Acceptance as a probationer did not automatically translate into acceptance as a student; consequently, acceptance rates were even lower than the data suggests. In 1908, Lady Superintendent Sarah McKinlay's annual report to the board read: "75 applications were received, thirteen probationers taken into the school and nine were accepted," for an acceptance rate of 12 per cent.[57] Lady Superintendent Jean Sims reported that, in 1909, "six probationers were taken into the school, three being accepted and two are still on probation."[58] Acceptance as a student still did not guarantee graduation. Attrition in intermediate and senior years was not uncommon: sometimes students were expelled and sometimes they left of their own accord.[59] Obviously, many women believed they were qualified; however, given the low acceptance rates, few realized their aspirations. Unfortunately, the data cannot tell us whether women who failed the probationary period reapplied to the program.

All applicants also required a "letter from a clergyman or other responsible person, testifying to her good moral character."[60] Religion was the second question on the application. Why was the religion of the nursing students important? The ideals of the men on the hospital board, who belonged to the elite of the community, might be helpful in answering this question. For example, a journalist commenting on the 1890 opening ceremonies in the *Medicine Hat Times* noted: "A temporary platform was erected in this ward for the use of the presiding clergymen. These were, Rev. James Herald of the Presbyterian Church; Rev. Walter G. Lyon of the Episcopal Church [Anglican]; and Rev. C. Teeter of the Methodist Church."[61] The news item is noteworthy for several reasons. First, the members of the hospital board found it necessary to include a Christian presence at the ceremonies. This harkens back to the British ideal that community leaders were trying to create in Medicine Hat. Second, Christian service legitimized women's presence in the public sphere; the attendance of clergy ensured the respectability of the hospital, nurses, and nursing students. Third, although the Roman Catholic, Baptist, and Lutheran churches were active in the community, the hospital board and President Niblock did not solicit their participation in the event.[62]

The ideal qualities that were desired and inculcated in nursing students are inferable from the *Rules and Regulations of the Training School for Nurses*. Nursing students were expected to attend church each Sunday. They were to "spend at least fifteen minutes in the open air every day, either within or off the hospital grounds." The nursing students were also to bear in mind that, in addition to their knowledge and skills, they were to develop "a character of steadiness, thoughtfulness, modesty and tact, which will justify confidence in those who employ them or recommend them for employment, and reflect credit on themselves and on the school." The women were also cautioned to "avoid boisterous laughing or loud talking either in the wards or corridors or in their own parlor or bedrooms." Visitors were to be received in the sitting room, but gentlemen required special permission from the lady superintendent.[63]

The expected behaviour of the nursing students conformed to that of the ideal Victorian woman. Nursing, which was believed to stem from women's natural nurturing qualities, was lauded as a perfect vocation for women – outside of marriage and motherhood (discussed by Nadine Kozak in chapter 10). However, when examined more closely, the "perfect fit" becomes contradictory. First, the supposedly weak but nurturing woman in need of male guidance and protection was not congruent with the daily realities of the nursing profession, which required women to make decisions concerning the care of sick patients. Second, a woman's perceived mental and physical frailty (which was allegedly expressed through modesty and "shrinking" from the public sphere) was at odds with the demanding and physically intimate work of nursing.[64] The design of nurse's uniforms reflected these contradictions: it symbolized an outward expression of repressed sexuality and high moral values, which possibly disguised the work that nurses performed. Although religious or charity works were the only permissible reasons for a Victorian woman to be out of the private sphere, nursing, a profession supposedly based on the Christian ideal of nurturing, was an exception. However, considering the reality of her work, the nurse still had to tread carefully to ensure an outward appearance of the ideal through behaviour and dress.[65] The *Rules and Regulations*, as enforced, became a formal public indicator for the respectability of the nursing school and its students.

That nurses were held to the ideal became apparent in 1917, when it was rumoured that an applicant had been rejected because she had worked in a hotel. The furore in the community forced the hospital board to form a committee to investigate the matter. William Cousins and Dr. Smyth reported that the woman had received an application form, but had not submitted it.[66] They also disclosed that a "deputation from the Trades and Labour Council waited on the Board" for information regarding acceptable qualifications of applicants.[67] The deputation was told that the applicant must have a good character, testified to by a clergyman, and a fairly good education. Despite evidence to the contrary, Cousins and Smyth informed the deputation that the class of applicants was not considered.

The rejection of the applicant may have gone unnoticed in earlier years, but the First World War and the suffrage and labour movements may have affected community attitudes.[68] The dissenters, who were not mentioned specifically in the minutes of the board, could have been educated women who were familiar with feminist thought and literature

Medicine Hat School of Nursing graduates, 1901; Top to bottom: Josephine Yates, Agnes Ridpath, and Rose Krause. Medicine Hat Museum and Art Gallery, 0183.0004.

and buoyed by women's active participation in the war. Many British-Protestant women in Medicine Hat were active in the Imperial Order of the Daughters of the Empire where, in addition to planning good works, they discussed the issues of the day. Perhaps they believed there was nothing wrong with a woman's participation in the work force. These women may have been able to influence the formal political institution, in this case, the hospital board of directors, although they had no political capacity of their own.[69] On the other hand, it could have been the working class of Medicine Hat, as suggested by the involvement of the Trades and Labour Council, who discerned an inequality in the acceptance practices of the school of nursing. Regardless of the dissenters' identity, it was the first time issues of class in relation to the hospital and the school of nursing were addressed.

Although the board purported to accept students without reference to class, graduating lists reveal that the students were culturally homogenous (see appendix B for a list of graduates between 1895 and 1920). Assuming that ethnicity and religion can be gleaned from surnames,[70] students were, with few exceptions, British-Canadian, mostly of English or Scottish origin. Carol Bacchi noted in her work on Canadian suffragists that women of British origin likely belonged to Methodist, Presbyterian, and Anglican congregations.[71] The class or social status of the British-Canadian women accepted into the school of nursing is likewise inferable from surnames. In *All Hell for a Basement*, Ed Gould records the names of mayors, council members, presidents of the chamber of commerce, and board members from the schools, hospital, and library from 1899 to 1981.[72] With few exceptions, none of the students appeared to be the daughters of the elite or politically active families of Medicine Hat society. Instead, the hospital patient register (which lists most students at some time during their training) indicates that they were the daughters of farmers or, more rarely, church ministers from rural communities.[73]

One exception, Margaret Drinnan, who was the daughter of newspaper editor J. D. Drinnan and sister of hospital board president J. K. Drinnan, is noteworthy. She graduated in 1903 and then began work at the Macleod Hospital. In 1904, she visited her brother in Medicine Hat on her way to Wawota for her sister's wedding. The "Death of Miss Drinnan" in the *Medicine Hat Weekly News* reflected the ongoing dangers of nursing and the problems of a safe water supply. "While here she went to the hospital where a slight operation was performed for the removal of a small growth from her wrist. For a few days previous to this she had not felt well, and while in the hospital symptoms of typhoid fever developed. Within the past few days bad complications set in, followed by peritonitis. Death came at eight o'clock last evening."[74]

Two other nursing students, Evadina McCutcheon and Vivia Nicholas, likewise did not live to graduate as nurses. The Spanish influenza epidemic arrived in Medicine Hat in late 1918.[75] As was the case in other Canadian communities, the epidemic overwhelmed the resources of the city and its health care workers. On 10 March 1919, McCutcheon died of pneumonia after she had contracted influenza while allegedly nursing an influenza patient.[76] In the same year, on 9 December, Nicholas also died under the same circumstances.[77] A meeting of the hospital board was called on the days that the women died, indicating the severity of the concern.

Interestingly, McCutcheon was from one of Medicine Hat's prominent families. Bill and R. McCutcheon are mentioned in Reverend J. W. Morrow's *Early History of the Medicine Hat Country*. They were two of the first men who came to the area in 1883; they owned farms, livery stables, a delivery company, and served as auctioneers. Baby McCutcheon was listed as one of the first White babies born in Medicine Hat.[78] The McCutcheon family was also mentioned as being present at a "Presbyterian Picnic" in 1895, and a member of the McCutcheon family was on the Public School Board in 1898.[79] Significantly, after the death of Evadina McCutcheon, application numbers to the school dropped, suggesting the family had influence within the community from which most applicants were drawn.

Lady Superintendent Victoria Winslow, in her report to the board in September 1918, had lobbied for a shorter day and a shorter workweek for students. Winslow noted, "In view of the agitation and criticism by labour leaders and others of the public regarding to hours of duty for pupil nurses, it would be advisable to arrange that regulations should be changed to shorten the hours of duty."[80] After the death of McCutcheon, Winslow renewed her appeals to the board of directors.[81] An eight-hour day was implemented in 1921, but was not fully realized until the 1940s. In 1920, nursing students and graduates worked six days a week: They worked split shifts, with students working in the morning, attending class in the afternoon, and returning to duty in the evening. It was not until 1940 that the workweek was reduced to five days.[82]

Although there were sizeable populations of German and Scandinavian women in Medicine Hat and the surrounding area, only one individual attended the nursing classes of this period. They may have applied and suffered rejection when the number of applications was down. Evidence from the local factories and potteries suggests, however, that Medicine Hat's female (and male) labour force was structured hierarchically according to class and ethnicity. In her study of the Medalta Potteries strike in postwar Alberta, Cynthia Locke-Drake found that the "majority of workers were born in Canada and the predominant ethnic heritage was German."[83] Anne Hayward's work on *The Alberta Pottery Industry, 1912–1990*, indicates that the owners and managers were usually of Scottish or English origin, the artisans of English/Austrian/German origin,

Medicine Hat School of Nursing graduating class on the veranda of the nurses' residence, 1919. Medicine Hat Museum and Art Gallery, 0183-0009.

and the workers/labourers of German or Irish origin.[84] Tillie Schlenker, a woman of German origin, who began working for Gas City Pottery after completing high school stated: "It was a good job for women then. There was hospital work, but you had to work Sundays and evenings. The only other alternatives open to women were housework and jobs in stores."[85] Considering the ethnicity of nursing students, it is unlikely that Schlenker would have been accepted, had she applied to the school.

Schlenker's comment is more readily understandable if one compares wages and working conditions in the nursing school and potteries. From 1916 until 1922, Schlenker earned six dollars for a forty-eight-hour week (about twenty-five dollars a month) for "putting handles and spouts on teapots." This was about 65 per cent of what men earned in the same pottery factories.[86] By 1920, nursing students, depending on their status in the three-year program, earned twelve, fourteen, or sixteen dollars a month, which included room and board.[87] When it is considered that the cost of room and board ranged from five to nine dollars a week in 1905, to seventy-five cents a day in 1911 for a private duty nurse caring for a patient in the hospital, then the wage of the nursing student more than doubles.[88] In comparison to male workers, the nursing students also fared well. For example, in 1903 male conductors for the CPR received an increase in pay from twelve to eighteen dollars a month.[89] At this time, nursing students were earning ten to twelve dollars a month, which included room, board, and laundry services. Materials and patterns for uniforms were also provided, although students had to sew their own or find someone to do it for them.[90] Considering the cost of room and board, nursing students were more than on par with some male workers who had to provide their own lodging. Of course, the nursing students had to live by the strict rules and regulations of the hospital, something nursing students in later years would defy.

Nursing students' working conditions also compared favourably to those experienced by female factory workers. Although nursing was dangerous and demanding, pottery work also had its dangers – albeit over the long-term. Hayward reports that morbidity rates for silicosis, a disease of the lungs caused by inhaling silica dust (silicone dioxide, a major constituent of ceramics, prepared by grinding flint sand), was between 50 and 75 per cent higher for those who worked thirty years or more in pottery factories. When the air at Medicine Hat Potteries was tested in 1943, the levels were ten times the acknowledged levels of danger.[91] In contrast to the almost luxurious residence that nursing students lived in, the factory environment was less than wholesome. A former employee of the Medalta Potteries recalled the toilet facility: "It had two sides on it – no front, not even a curtain. I don't think from the day it was put in it was ever cleaned. To use it you had to sit there like a King of England with everybody looking."[92] Considering that nursing students were attaining an education that may have translated into financial and personal independence, something unknown to most women, and that working conditions were no worse (or better) than their compatriots in the pottery factory, it was a fair deal for the time.

Some nursing historians have suggested, however, that students were exploited by the "nurse hire" system.[93] The data from Medicine Hat challenges this argument. Nursing students were hired out by the hospital for $1.00 per day, which increased to $1.50 per day in 1902, with students receiving their regular pay while the hospital collected the difference.[94] The system lasted for only eleven years, by which time graduated nurses were offering private-duty services. For example, in 1906, the following advertisement appeared in the *Medicine Hat Weekly News*: "Nursing: Mrs. Dove is open for any engagements as a nurse to maternity cases."[95] It was at this time that the hospital's board of directors no longer reported income from nurse hire. The amount of money collected by the hospital for the outside work of nursing students was:

Year	Amount Reported
1894	$20.00
1895	$326.10
1896	$368.75
1897	$321.75
1898	$435.85
1899	$323.35
1900	$360.25
1901	$330.15
1902	$299.35
1903	No Data
1904	$70.75

Source: annual reports from the hospital board[96]

Considering the cost of replacing a nursing student with another worker, administration costs for the service, and that accommodation had to be provided for the nursing students (which included the building of residences), no great profit could be made from the venture.[97] More likely, it was a service to the community, created primarily for British-Protestant families who could afford it, which was part of the school's opening mandate. As Niblock reported about nurse hire in 1895: "Already nurses are in demand and it is the desire of the Board of Directors to keep two or three competent nurses available for all kinds of outside nursing, and thus give trained service at the lowest possible cost."[98]

Medical Superintendent Dr. Peters reported in the same year, "That their services are appreciated is shown by increased demand for them, which is becoming so great that we will have to increase our staff in the near future."[99] By 1896, the new medical superintendent, Dr. Smith stated: "The demand for trained nurses is steadily on the increase, taxing our resources to the utmost at times."[100] In light of the above, the nurse hire practice was probably more trouble than it was worth, in terms of monetary remuneration for the hospital.

The medical and lady superintendents, who formulated the rules and regulations, wrote: "The most desirable age for candidates to enter the school is from twenty-five to thirty-five, but every candidate should be over twenty years of age unless possessing some special qualification."[101] The age requirement stemmed back to the beliefs of nursing leaders, such as Florence Nightingale, who believed that women over the age of twenty-five had passed the stage of "being in love," and thus were more suitable for a career in nursing.[102] But, was the "most desirable age" criterion congruent with reality? Christopher Maggs, British nursing historian, found that the background (including age) of the average nursing student was distorted in order to attract the most desirable type of woman. He found that although the desirable age of prospective students was between twenty-five and thirty-five, most students were younger than twenty when they entered nursing schools.[103] Certainly, the background of Reynolds, who was educated in Leeds, England, at a hospital based on the Nightingale system, supports Maggs' findings about age.[104] She had been nursing for over ten years before settling in Medicine Hat, yet she married Dr. Calder who was then beginning his medical practice. Considering the mores of the time, it was unlikely that Dr. Calder would have married someone who was not his contemporary; therefore, she must have started nursing at an early age.

Reynolds probably transplanted English admission criteria to Medicine Hat.[105] As Nadine Kozak's work on scientific motherhood advice literature in this volume illustrates, however, official ideals pertaining to women often diverged from prairie realities. For instance, there may have been a shortage of young unmarried women in the community. In 1905, an article in the *Medicine Hat Weekly News* informed readers that women were scarce in Medicine Hat and that men were pining for wives.[106] The obituary of Nurse Mary Elizabeth Knisley in 1907 is also noteworthy. "Miss Knisley was 34 years of age. She took up the nursing profession many years ago and spent the last ten years in the West in faithful service in that noble profession."[107] Obviously, Knisley, too, began nursing at an earlier age than was desired. From the available information, most nursing students in Medicine Hat were less than twenty-five years of age upon entering the school.

The women attending nursing school in Medicine Hat were for the most part British-Protestant, middle-class women who were less than twenty-five years of age on admission to the program. The social standing of students fell somewhere between the political and social elite and the working class who worked as unskilled employees in the local pottery factories. Many nursing students were the daughters of farmers. Although there was a sizable population of German and Scandinavian women in the community, only one individual attended the nursing classes. Nursing work was arduous and sometimes dangerous, but the prestige, wages, working conditions, and opportunities for nursing students surpassed that of women working in pottery factories.[108] The experiences of Medicine Hat's nursing students support Kathryn McPherson's argument that nurses did indeed form a privileged group, which was not exploited outrageously, as some historians have suggested. This chapter points to the need for more studies that explore how nursing students and graduates were perceived in local communities and, in turn, how they perceived their own labour in comparison to other female workers.

Appendix A: Acceptance Rates of Students at Medicine Hat General Hospital

Year	Applied	Chosen	Acceptance Rate
1907	75	13	17%
1909	40	6	15%
1911	50	14	28%
1913	41	15	37%
1914	65	14	21%
1915	71	12	17%
1916	61	11	18%
1917	46	12	26%
1918	46	14	30%
1919	No figures available		
1920	14		

Source: Dirk, *Caps, Bibs and Aprons*, 10.

Appendix B: Graduating Nursing Students at Medicine Hat General Hospital, 1894–1820

1896	Gertrude Hales
	Jean Miller
1897	N. Knisley
	A. Andrew
1898	M. Manahan
1899	Margaret Black
1900	No data
1901	Josephine Yates
	Agnes Ridpath
	Rose Krause
1902	Margaret Grassick
1903	B. Evans
	Margaret Drinnan
	Three others unidentified
1904	No data
1905	No data
1906	Edna Auger
1907	New three-year program in place
1908	Edith Clark (last graduate of two-year program)
1909	L. McEachern
	C. A. Ashe
1910	Margaret Sherratt
	Mary Arnot
	Mary Borton
	Christine Dale
	Jean Brammall
	Jean Bell
1911	Annie Knox
	Ellen Rowe
1912	Ida McCorkle
	Lillian McDonald
	Lillian Ford
	Margaret Dunne
	Irene Trostem
1913	Edna Stewart
	Annie Frazer

	Edra Willett
	Annie Murray
	Alexandra Moore
	Nellie Scoville
	Elizabeth MacDougall
1914	No data
1915	Edith Hunter
	Elsie Charles
	Ethel McLuhan
	Emma Read
	Margaret Learned
	Mary Barter
	Augusta Kirkham
1916	Leslie Imes
	Jessie Gordon
	Matilda Green
	Mary Louise Hacker
	Emmeline Elliott
1917	Dorothy Alsop
	Annie E. Comber
	Florence MacClaren
	Florence Smith
	Annie Cheeseman
	Fanny Smith
	Annie Stothers
1918	No data
1919	Anna Belcher
	Gertrude Girling
	Hazel Moyer
	Mary Murray
	Alice Nash
	Edith Wales
	Ruth Peterson
	Joy Reid
1920	Margaret Mutrie
	Jean Johnson
	June Armstrong
	Sadie Smathers

Hannah Bell
Alma Coursey
May Lossee

Source: Dirk, *Caps, Bibs and Aprons*, 219–229, and excerpts from Annual
Report for 1896, MHM, M74.6.

ENDNOTES

1   "Third Annual Hospital Meeting," *Medicine Hat Times (MHT)*, 2 March 1893.
2   Kathryn McPherson, *Bedside Matters: The Transformation of Canadian Nursing,
    1900–1990* (Oxford: Oxford University Press, 1996), 16–18.
3   See, for example: Jan Noel, "Introduction," in *Race and Gender in the Northern
    Colonies* ed. Jan Noel (Toronto: Canadian Scholars' Press, 2000), 1–19; Howard
    Palmer, *Land of the Second Chance: A History of Ethnic Groups in Southern Alberta*
    (Lethbridge: Lethbridge Herald, 1972), 209–11; and Howard Palmer, *Patterns of
    Prejudice: A History of Nativism in Alberta* (Toronto: McClelland and Stewart,
    1982), 13–15, 87.
4   Among works reviewed: Patricia D'Antonio, "Revisiting and Rethinking the
    Rewriting of Nursing History," *Bulletin of the History of Medicine* 73 (1999): 268–
    90; Rondalyn Kirkwood, "Blending Vigorous Leadership and Womanly Virtues:
    Edith Kathleen Russel at the University of Toronto, 1920–1952," *Canadian Bulle-
    tin of Medical History* 11 (1994): 175–205; Florence Nightingale, *Notes on Nursing:
    What it is and What it is Not* (1859; reprint Philadelphia: Lippincott, 1946); and
    Veronica Strong-Boag, "Making a Difference: The History of Canada's Nurses,"
    Canadian Bulletin of Medical History 8 (1991): 231–48.
5   I am using a social-history approach, with ethnicity, class, age, and gender as
    categories of critical analysis. Included is an attention to the labour, or the work
    of nursing, and how it relates to the other categories. Kathryn McPherson and
    Meryn Stuart note that, while the influences of class and gender on nursing have
    received attention in Canadian historical scholarship, the influences of race and
    ethnicity require more research: "Writing Nursing History in Canada: Issues
    and Approaches," *Canadian Bulletin of Medical History* 11 (1994): 3–22. Ruth
    Roach Pierson's work: *"They're Still Women After All": The Second World War
    and Canadian Womanhood* (Toronto: McClelland and Stewart, 1986) is impor-
    tant for her focus on working women, their identity, and how they were received
    and perceived by a patriarchal society. See also Joan Sangster, *Regulating Girls
    and Women: Sexuality, Family and the Law in Ontario, 1920–1960* (Oxford and
    New York: Oxford University Press, 2001) and her discussion regarding a model
    for women's history. She contends that one model alone cannot fully explain
    women's subjugation or experience in a patriarchal hegemonic system. Her work

draws on Marxist, Foucauldian, Gramscian, and materialist-feminist frameworks. Primary sources for this study include minute books, financial ledgers, and school of nursing documents from the Medicine Hat General Hospital that are held at the Medicine Hat Museum and Art Gallery Archives. Another primary source includes issues of the *Medicine Hat Times, Medicine Hat News, Medicine Daily News,* and *Medicine Hat Weekly News* that are located at the Medicine Hat College Library.

6   R. Douglas Francis, "'Rural Ontario West': Ontarians in Alberta," in *Peoples of Alberta: Portraits of Cultural Diversity,* ed. Howard Palmer and Tamara Palmer (Saskatoon: Western Producer Prairie Books, 1985), 123–42.

7   According to the minutes of the Medicine Hat General Hospital Board of Directors (MHGH Minutes), a lady superintendent did not attend a board meeting until 1937, when Nurse Agnes Pederson read her own report: 10 December 1937, Medicine Hat Museum and Art Gallery Archives (MHM), M86.28.3. For a discussion of North American women and public speaking, see Kristina Minister, "A Feminist Frame for Interviews," in *Women's Words: The Feminist Practice of Oral History,* ed. Sherna Berger Gluck and Daphne Patai (New York and London: Routledge, 1991), 27–41. On nursing's loss of direct access to a board of directors, see Thetis M. Group and Joan I. Roberts, *Nursing, Physician Control, and the Medical Monopoly: Historical Perspectives on Gendered Inequality in Roles, Rights and Range of Practice* (Bloomington and Indianapolis: Indiana University Press, 2001), 39.

8   "The Hospital Opened," *MHT,* 30 January 1890. See also Marcel Dirk, *Caps, Bibs and Aprons: Memoirs of Medicine Hat General Hospital School of Nursing* (Medicine Hat: Modern Press, 1996), 5, and his exploration of the impetus for the formation of a school of nursing in Medicine Hat.

9   Dirk, *Caps, Bibs and Aprons,* 5, notes that specific details regarding the formation of the school cannot be found, except that it opened on 1 August 1894 under Lady Superintendent Agnes C. Miller and a new medical superintendent, Dr. J. B. Peters.

10   Tony Cashman, *Heritage of Service: The History of Nursing in Alberta* (Edmonton, Alberta Association of Registered Nurses, 1966), 25–27. Cashman makes special note of the connection that these nurses had with Florence Nightingale. Nurse Reynolds trained in Leeds, England, under Matron Gordon, a graduate of Nightingale's St. Thomas School. In Edinburgh, Nurse Miller took a course based on the Nightingale system that was laid out by Miss Pringle who was well known for her disagreement with "metallic" nurses.

11   Palmer, *Land of the Second Chance,* 210. Palmer reports that most of the people of British origin in Medicine Hat were from Ontario. Certainly, histories of the area indicate that newly arrived professionals, such as physicians, lawyers, and so on, were young men from Ontario. See, for example, Elliot Gould, *All Hell for a Basement: Medicine Hat, 1883–1983* (Medicine Hat, Alberta: Friesen Printers, 1981), 47–86.

12   Ninette Kelly and Michael Trebilcock, *The Making of the Mosaic: A History of Canadian Immigration Policy* (Toronto: University of Toronto Press, 1998), 61–65, 77–79, 119–21. By the early 1890s, Clifford Sifton realized that these two sources did not provide enough immigrants to settle the prairie West.

13   Palmer, *Land of the Second Chance*, 209–11. Local newspaper articles also indicate the preference for British immigrants. See, for example, "The Work of Immigration," *MHT*, 21 August 1890, and "Bonuses to Emigrants," *MHT*, 26 March 1891.

14   Sources reviewed include: Frank W. Anderson, *Frontier Guide to: Calgary to Medicine Hat* (Calgary: Frontier Publishing, 1970), 10–11; Gould, *All Hell for a Basement*, 47–58; David Jones, *Empire of Dust: Settling and Abandoning the Prairie Dry Belt* (Edmonton, University of Alberta Press, 1987), 9–16; and Palmer, *Land of the Second Chance*, 209–11. Also see *MHT*, 24 July 1890, 2; 30 July 1890, 4, for the importance of ranching to the region.

15   Sources include: Gould, *All Hell for a Basement*, 49; Palmer, *Land of the Second Chance*, 183, 185–86, 252; and Palmer, "Patterns of Immigration and Ethnic Settlement in Alberta," 1–27.

16   "The German Colonies," *MHT*, 24 July 1890, 2.

17   Palmer, *Land of the Second Chance*, 185.

18   Howard Palmer, "Strangers and Stereotypes: The Rise of Nativism," in *The Prairie West* , 2nd ed., ed. R. Douglas Francis and Howard Palmer (Edmonton: University of Alberta Press, 1992), 312–14. Also see Howard Palmer, *Patterns of Prejudice*, 22–27, who postulated a theory of preferred Whiteness in Canadian immigration and an "ethnic pecking order" that started with British, then Scandinavians, Germans, and central Europeans. See also David R. Roediger, *The Wages of Whiteness: Race and the Making of the American Working Class* (London and New York: Verso, 1991) for a detailed exploration of the formation of the "Whiteness" concept.

19   Kelly and Trebilcock, *Making of the Mosaic*, 168–70; Palmer, *Patterns of Prejudice*, 19, 47–50. See also, the changing attitude from acceptance/welcome to suspicion in the local paper after World War I started. For example, "German Spies Enlisted with Canadian Boys," *MWN* (*Medicine Hat Weekly News*), 19 November 1914, 8; "Winnipeg To Be Attacked (Perhaps?) 220,000 German Reservists," *MWN*, 14 January 1915; and "Germans in Canada," *MWN*, 24 February 1916, 4.

20   John L. Tobias, "Protection, Civilization, Assimilation: An Outline History of Canada's Indian Policy," in *The Prairie West*, 207–24. See also Sarah Carter, *Lost Harvests: Prairie Indian Reserve Farmers and Government Policy* (Montreal and Kingston: McGill-Queen's University Press, 1990), 17–25. Although the *MHT* refers to the Indians as Blackfoot, they may have been from the Blood Tribe – one of the tribes that make up the Blackfoot Nation, which includes the Blackfoot proper, Blood, and Peigan. According to Dempsey, *Indian Tribes of Alberta*, 22, the Blood tribe's first reserve after the 1877 Treaty 7 was a narrow strip of land extending from Blackfoot Crossing (near present-day Gleichen) along the Bow and South Saskatchewan Rivers to the Medicine Hat Area. Later in 1883, they settled at a reserve, which encompassed some of their traditional hunting grounds, between the Belly (Oldman) and St. Mary Rivers. Therefore, most of the Blackfoot Indians encamped around Medicine Hat, after the coming of the CPR in 1883, were probably from the Blood tribe. About the Plains Cree Nation who signed Treaty 4: Sarah Carter, *Aboriginal People and Colonizers of Western Canada to 1900* (Toronto: University of Toronto Press, 1999), 140–43, and Olive Patricia Dickason, *Canada's First Nations: A History of Founding Peoples from Earliest Times* (Toronto: Oxford University Press, 1997), 275–79. Note that one of the

clauses in the 1874 treaty, which encompassed southern Saskatchewan and part of southern Alberta, gave the Plains Cree the right to choose their reserve. But they were not allowed to settle in the Cypress Hills, the land they chose, and were removed to a more northerly reserve in 1882.

21   In the early 1880s and 1890s, mixed attitudes in the local paper towards Indians deteriorated to increasingly hostile ones. For example, "An Indignant Indian," *MHT*, 22 June 1893, reflected an acknowledgement of Indian rights as in this piece wherein a non-treaty Indian was trying to use the ferry at Medicine Hat to cross the river. "The Indian claims that being a non-treaty Indian, never having accepted a present from the Government and never having been accused of breaking the laws of the country that he is entitled to the same treatment as White settlers." But by 1912, the Indians were accused of "murderous intent," in "Damning Evidence Against the Indians," *Medicine Hat Daily News (MDN)*, 5 June 1912; "All Indians Must Go to the Reserve," *MDN*, 20 February 1916, 4, indicates that their presence was no longer tolerated: "Govt. Has Issued Order that they Must Discontinue Roving – Medicine Hat Indians Have Chosen Battleford or Piapot Reserves – Some 70 in this District Affected." The Indians referred to in this article must have belonged to the Plains Cree Nation.

22   "Chinese Immigration," *MHN (Medicine Hat News)*, 2 August 1900.

23   Ibid.

24   "Italians Give Trouble," *MHN*, 29 March 1894, 2.

25   Palmer, *Patterns of Prejudice*, 27.

26   Howard Palmer, "Patterns of Immigration and Ethnic Settlement in Alberta," in *Peoples of Alberta*, 3–4, 6–11.

27   A. W. Rasporich, "Utopian Ideals and Community Settlements in Western Canada, 1880–1914," in *The Prairie West*, 352–54, 358–62; Francis, "'Rural Ontario West:' Ontarians in Alberta," 123–42. See also articles in the local paper, for example, "The Glorious Twelfth: Medicine Hat Orangemen Celebrate it with a Picnic at Police Point," *MHT*, 17 July 1890; "The Temperance Lecture," *MHT*, 29 January 1891; "Masonic Church Parade," *MHT*, 22 June 1893.

28   "The Hospital Opened," *MHT*, 5 June 1890. The clergymen were all British Protestant despite the existence of Roman Catholic, Baptist, and Lutheran Churches within Medicine Hat. The clergymen in attendance were: Rev. James Herald of the Presbyterian Church; Rev. Walter G. Lyon of the Episcopal Church; and Rev. Ch. Teeter of the Methodist Church.

29   "The Hospital," *MHT*, 5 June 1890.

30   Marcel Dirk, *A Healthy Outlook: The Centennial History of the Medicine Hat Regional Hospital* (Medicine Hat: Holmes Printing, 1989), 7–10. Dirk explains that the typhoid epidemic in 1888 was one of the reasons for building the hospital. The ravages of this infection also struck Dr. Olver, the first medical superintendent, who succumbed to typhoid in September 1891. See his obituary: "Will Heal No More," *MHT*, 3 September 1891. Dr. Peters who succeeded Dr. Calder as medical superintendent in 1895 died the same year, also of typhoid. See "Death of Dr. Peters," *MHN*, 16 May 1895.

31   David Jones et al., *The Weather Factory: A Pictorial History of Medicine Hat* (Saskatoon, Saskatchewan: Western Producer Prairie Books, 1988), 4.

32   Sources regarding Niblock, his interest in the hospital, and some of his money-making schemes include: Dirk, *A Healthy Outlook*, 9–11 and Gould, *All Hell for a*

Basement, 233–44. See also, for example, "A Good Idea," *MHT*, 22 May 1890; and "The Hospital Concerts," *MHT*, 27 November 1890.

33 "The Hospital Opened," *MHT*, 5 June 1890. One barrier to optimal functioning was the surgery that was located directly off the main entrance in an obviously high traffic and less than antiseptic area was noted by Dirk, *A Healthy Outlook*, 13.

34 "The Hospital Opened," *MHT*, 5 June 1890. About the training of nurses, see, "Hospitals of the Northwest," *MHT*, 14 January 1892, in which the following appeared: "It is further interesting to note that Miss Reynolds trains nurses, with the aid of the medical staff, and so may be regarded as the Superintendent of the 'highest' nurse training school in the whole world – Medicine Hat being 2,150 feet above the level of the sea."

35 "Surgery at the Hospital," *MHT*, 22 May 1890.

36 For a more comprehensive list of the duties of a nurse in early Alberta, see, Sharon Richardson, "Frontier Nursing: Nursing Work and Training in Alberta, 1890–1905," *Canadian Journal of Nursing Research* 28, no. 3 (1997): 116–20.

37 "The Annual Report," *MHT*, 22 January 1891.

38 Dirk, *A Healthy Outlook*, 15–16.

39 MHGH Minutes, 17 January 1891, MHM, M71.268; MHGH Patient Register, MHM, M76.28.6.

40 "Annual Meeting," *MHT*, 8 February 1894.

41 *Rules and Regulations of the Training School for Nurses*, 1895, MHM, M74.6, unpaginated.

42 "The Annual Meeting," *MHN*, 24 January 1895.

43 "Report of the Medical Superintendent," *MHN*, 31 January 1895.

44 History of Nurses' Training School, MHM, M74.6, unpaginated.

45 "Hospital Meeting," *MHT*, 27 February 1896.

46 Lady Aberdeen, the wife of the governor general of Canada, laid the cornerstone of the Lady Aberdeen Maternity Hospital in October 1894. See, "The Aberdeen Visit," *MHN*, 18 October 1894. From 1893 to 1904, nursing students were hired out for private duty at a rate of $1.00 per day, which later increased to $1.50 per day in 1902. Nursing students received their normal wage; the hospital collected the fee and kept the balance. It is likely that the families who were able to afford private nursing were derived from the elite of Medicine Hat. See, "The Annual Meeting," *MHT*, 31 January 1895; "Hospital Items," *MWN*, 30 January 1902.

47 "The Hospital Opened," *MHT*, 5 June 1890. For a study on the history of hospital care, see Charles Rosenberg, *The Care of Strangers: The Rise of America's Hospital System* (New York: Basic Books, 1987). Rosenberg explores and explains the transition from home-based to institutional-based illness care in the nineteenth century. He argues that physicians and administrators had to overcome perceptions that hospitals were only for the impoverished who had no one to care for them.

48 Questions to be Answered by Candidate, MHM, M74.6, unpaginated.

49 Ibid.

50 Bella Crosby, "Registration," *Canadian Nurse* 7:1 (January 1911): 10–12.

51 Medicine Hat Women's Literary Club, MHM, M84.6.1, Program for 1907.

52 Dirk, *Caps, Bibs and Aprons*, 10.

53 Opportunities available might be surmised from articles and advertisements in the local paper. See, for example, "The Cooking School: Domestic Science

Classes this Week – Instruction Free of Charge," *MWN*, 23 August 1906; "Ladies College: Presbyterians Will Establish one in Lethbridge," *MWN*, 7 February 1907, 5; and "Miss Edith Harrison B.A.," *MHN*, 8 October 1903, 2. Miss Harrison offered teaching services in French, German, and music.

54 An exception to this was the use of male nurses/orderlies in mental nursing. See, for example, Geertje Boschma, "High Ideals Versus Harsh Reality: A Historical Analysis of Mental Health Nursing in Dutch Asylums, 1890–1920," *Nursing History Review* 7 (1999), 127–51.

55 "Profession of Nursing," *MWN*, 24 October 1907, 2.

56 See, for example, "Women Do Not Want Suffrage: Anti-Suffragists Take the Field In Opposition to Their Strident Sisters," *MWN*, 13 August 1908, 5; "The Modesty of Women," *MWN*, 13 August 1908, 5; and "Fight for the Vote Suffragists Advice Given Hat Mothers," 15 January 1913, 5.

57 "Annual Meeting of the Hospital," *MWN*, 13 February 1908.

58 "Medicine Hat General Hospital," *MWN*, 17 February 1910.

59 Dirk, *Caps, Bibs and Aprons*, 121–23. Numbers of students leaving the program after the junior year range from zero to three per year. As an example, in 1907, nine students entered as probationers and six graduated in 1910 for an attrition rate of 31 per cent after acceptance into the school. So, out of seventy-five applicants, only six became nurses.

60 First Division Rules, MHM, M74.6, unpaginated.

61 "The Hospital Opened," *MHT*, 30 January 1890.

62 From the time of the opening of the hospital, church times of other religious congregations are advertised in the paper. See, for example, "Church Directory," *MHT*, 17 July 1890; and "Roman Catholic Service," *MHT*, 11 December 1890, 3. Also see, "Religious Census," *MWN*, 14 October 1909, 4. An enumeration was undertaken by the Medicine Hat Sunday School Association showing that almost a third of Medicine Hat's population was Presbyterian. However, this census did not include farming settlements, many of which were made up of German and Scandinavian immigrants who did not belong to British Protestant congregations.

63 *Rules and Regulations of the Training School for Nurses*, MHM, M74.6, unpaginated.

64 For discussion on feminine ideals and Christianity, which became part of nursing see, for example, Patricia Hollis, *Women in Public, 1850–1900: Documents of the Victoria Women's Movement* (London and Boston: G. Allen and Unwin, 1979) 167–96; McPherson, *Bedside Matters*, 16, 35–37, 165–67; Wendy Mitchinson, *The Nature of Their Bodies: Women and Their Doctors in Victorian Canada* (Toronto: University of Toronto Press, 1991); Jan Noel, "Introduction," in *Race and Gender in the Northern Colonies*, ed. Jan Noel (Toronto: Canadian Scholars' Press, 2000), 1–19; Joan Perkin, *Victorian Women* (New York: New York University Press, 1993), 6–26, 51–72; Michelle Zimbalist Rosaldo, "Woman, Culture, and Society: A Theoretical Overview," in *Woman, Culture and Society*, ed. Michelle Z. Rosaldo and Louise Lamphere (Stanford, California: Stanford University Press, 1974), 17–42; and Strange, *Toronto's Girl Problem*, 23, 35, 53–88.

65 McPherson, *Bedside Matters*, 16–18.

66 MHGH Minutes, 14 May 1917, MHM, M86.28.2.

67 Ibid.

68 Carol Lee Bacchi, *Liberation Deferred? The Ideas of the English-Canadian Suffragists, 1877–1918* (Toronto: University of Toronto Press, 1983), 24–39; and Linda Kealy, *Enlisting Women for the Cause: Women, Labour, and the Left in Canada, 1890–1920* (Toronto: University of Toronto Press, 1998), 78–79.

69 Jill McCalla Vickers, "Feminist Approaches to Women in Politics," in *Beyond the Vote: Canadian Women and Politics*, ed. Linda Kealy and Joan Sangster (Toronto: University of Toronto Press, 1989), 20.

70 Bacchi, *Liberation Deferred?* 5, 152. Bacchi uses names to determine ethnicity, specifically Anglo-Saxon heritage. She writes that this is "a functional designation used to indicate British birth, Britain including Scotland and Ireland, or descendants of those of British birth." She cites A. H. Murray, ed., *New English Dictionary on Historical Principles* (Oxford, 1933) as the source for this method. She also uses religious affiliation to confirm heritage "because most (British) were either Methodists, Presbyterians, Anglicans, or members of smaller Protestant Churches." For this study, sources consulted included: *The Oxford Dictionary: Being a Corrected Re-Issue with an Introduction, Supplement, and Bibliography of a New English Dictionary on Historical Principles*, 13 vols., ed. James A. H. Murray, Henry Bradley, W.A. Craigie and C. T. Onions (1933; reprint Oxford: Clarendon Press, 1951) and Diane Snyder Ptak, *Surnames: Their Meanings and Origins* (Albany, New York: Author, 1993). Names that were not found in the dictionary were searched online: <http://search.swyrich.com> (1 May 2002) and <http://originsaffiliates.com> (1 May 2002) for their origins.

71 Bacchi, *Liberation Deferred?* 5–7.

72 Gould, *All Hell for a Basement*, 275–99. As a comment on the elite of Medicine Hat, significantly, the same names appear repeatedly in Gould's list of "A Who's Who." To name two as an example, during the period of this study W. T. Finlay was mayor of Medicine Hat as well as president of the hospital board. William Cousins served as president of the chamber of commerce, chairman of the public school board, as well as a member and president of the hospital board.

73 MHGH Patient Register, MHM, M86.28.6, M86.28.8.

74 "Death of Miss Drinnan," *MWN*, 27 October 1904.

75 MHGH Patient Register, MHM, M86.28.8. More than half the admissions for November 1918 were for influenza.

76 MHGH Minutes, 10 March 1919, MHM, M86.28.2.

77 MHGH Minutes, 9 December 1919, MHM, M86.28.2.

78 Morrow, *Early History*, 22–23, 44–45, 56, 65.

79 "Presbyterian Picnic," *MHN*, 15 August 1895; Gould, *All Hell for a Basement*, 283. A first name for the McCutcheon school board member was not recorded.

80 MHGH Minutes, 12 August 1918, MHM, M86.28.2. Winslow was first president of the Alberta Association of Registered Nurses. See, Cashman, *Heritage of Service*, 115–18.

81 MHGH Minutes, 14 April 1919, MHM, M86.28.2.

82 MHGH Minutes, 10 January 1921, MHM, M86.28.2; Dirk, *Caps, Bibs and Aprons*, 78.

83 Cynthia Loch-Drake, "Jailed Heroes and Kitchen Heroines: Class, Gender and the Medalta Potteries Strike in Postwar Alberta" (master's thesis, University of Calgary, 2001), 14.

84   Anne Hayward, *The Alberta Pottery Industry, 1912–1990: A Social and Economic History* (Hull, Quebec: Canadian Museum of Civilization, 2002), 32, 39, 54–55, 66–67.

85   Marylu Antonelli and Jack Forbes, *Pottery in Alberta: The Long Tradition* (Edmonton: University of Alberta Press, 1978), 44.

86   See Antonelli and Forbes, *Pottery in Alberta*, 44, 106; and Hayward, *The Alberta Pottery Industry*, 31, 62, 75, 76, 121.

87   Financial Ledger of the MHGH, MHM, M86.28.27. Although nursing students and nurses were required to live in the residence, the rooms allotted them in the Victoria Nurses' Home were luxurious compared to the lodgings of the working class in Medicine Hat. As Dirk, *Caps, Bibs and Aprons*, 21 asks: "Could it be all the hard wood floorings, rugs, and linoleum laid, all the antique buff chairs, chiffoniers, and chesterfield suites moved, and all the walnut writing tables, desk lamps, and other fixtures purchased were inducements to study? It appears so." In MHGH Minutes, 11 April 1927, MHM, M86.28.2, a board member states: "It is very desirable that the nurses be in their rooms a certain portion of the time for rest and study, but in order to encourage them to do so we feel the room should be more attractive and an evidence of this desire on the part of the Board we believe, add considerable to the morale and enthusiasm of those in training."

88   See "Room and Board," *MHN*, 15 June 1905, 2; "Board and Room Wanted," *MWN*, 18 May 1911, 11; and MHGH Minutes, 12 June 1911, MHM, M86.28.2.

89   "Increases in Pay," *MHN*, 20 August 1903.

90   First Division Rules, MHM, M74.6, unpaginated.

91   Hayward, *The Alberta Pottery Industry*, 109–10, 172.

92   Antonelli and Forbes, *Pottery in Alberta*, 45.

93   For example, see Janet Ross-Kerr, *Prepared to Care: Nurses and Nursing in Alberta* (Edmonton: University of Alberta Press, 1998), 49–50; Pauline Paul, "Nursing Education Becomes Synonymous With Nursing Service," in *Prepared to Care*, ed. Janet Ross-Kerr, 131–32, 134–35; and McPherson, *Bedside Matters*, 33, 43.

94   "Hospital Items," *MWN*, 30 January 1902; "The rates for nurse hire were changed from $1.00 a day to $1.50 a day or $10 a week."

95   "Nursing," *MWN*, 20 December 1906, 9. Whether Mrs. Dove was a graduated nurse cannot be ascertained from the advertisement.

96   See the annual reports from the hospital board: "The Annual Meeting," *MHN*, 24 January 1895; "Hospital Meeting," *MHN*, 27 February 1896; "Hospital Meeting," 4 February 1897; "Hospital Meeting," *MHN*, 24 February 1898; "General Hospital Annual Meeting," *MHN*, 23 February 1899; "Hospital Meeting," 8 February 1900, 1; "Annual Meeting Medicine Hat General Hospital," *MHN*, 14 February 1901; "General Hospital Annual Meeting," *MWN*, 13 February 1902, 7; "Hospital Meeting," *MHN*, 12 February 1903; "Annual Hospital Meeting," *MWN*, 11 February 1904, 5; and "Medicine Hat Hospital," *MWN*, 16 February 1905, 7. Nurse hire was reported as income for the last time in the 1904 budget.

97   Residences and additions were built in 1905 ($6,813.80), 1912 ($14,132), 1919 ($7,354.76), 1930 ($24,000), and 1957 ($671,000). In addition to construction, there were also costs including maintenance, utilities, furnishings, and the wages of a house-mother. See "The Nurses' Home Formally Opened," *MHN*, 15 June 1905; "Twenty Third Annual Report of General Hospital Shows Increase in Work," *MWN*, 14 August 1913, 3; "W. Cousins Elected President of the Hospital

Board," 13 January 1920; MHGH Minutes, 8 September 1930, MHM M86.28.2; and Dirk, *Caps, Bibs and Aprons*, 20–23.

98 "The Annual Meeting," *MHN*, 24 January 1895.

99 "The Annual Meeting: Report of the Medical Superintendent," *MHN*, 31 January 1895.

100 "Annual Hospital Meeting," *MHN*, 5 March 1896.

101 MHGH Minutes, 12 June 1911, MHM, M86.28.2.

102 Nightingale, *Notes on Nursing*, 75.

103 Christopher Maggs, "Nurse Recruitment to Four Provincial Hospitals, 1881–1921," in *Rewriting Nursing History*, ed. Celia Davies (London, England: Croom, 1980), 18–40.

104 "The Hospital Opened," *MHT*, 30 January 1890. Nurse Reynolds spent five years at her training hospital in Leeds, England, four years in Winnipeg, and two years at a hospital in Washington, DC before coming to Medicine Hat.

105 The same admission criteria were evident for the Winnipeg General Hospital School of Nursing, for example. Ethel Johns, *The Winnipeg General Hospital School of Nursing, 1887–1953* (Winnipeg: Alumnae Association of WGH School of Nursing, 1956), 19.

106 "Girls, Here's your Chance," *MWN*, 23 February 1905, 5.

107 "Nurse Knisley Dead," *MWN*, 28 February 1907. N. Knisley graduated from the Medicine Hat School in 1897 (see Appendix B). If she was twenty-four when she graduated, she must have been about twenty-two when she entered the program.

108 Loch-Drake, "Jailed Heroines," 29, 40. From 10 per cent in 1920, the proportion of female to male pottery workers reached 42 per cent by 1947.

part five

NEGOTIATING CONSTRAINTS

On Leaders *and* Leadership

sixteen

Peak Potentials and Performance Anxieties:

Gender, Mountaineering, and Leadership

in the Canadian West, 1906–40

SIRI LOUIE

In this article, Siri Louie addresses the issue of gender, power, and leadership in the West by examining the routine and exceptional activities of mountaineering men and women in the Alpine Club of Canada – a middle-class organization that distinguished itself from mainstream sports by encouraging women's involvement and advocating gender parity as official policy. While one might be tempted to conclude that the club constituted an example of the western "frontier" as "equalizer" – as a region that offered women freedom from Old World constraints – Louie avoids simplistic generalizations. The Club's inclusive policy derived from the nature of mountaineering technique (which opened the sport to novices and professionals, women and men) and the fierce activism of Elizabeth Parker, a journalist with the Manitoba Free Press *and the club's co-founder. Despite official policies of sexual equality, Louie concludes that the club's leisure and climbing activities were constructed upon hierarchies of race, class, and gender that promoted and enhanced middle-class, imperialistic notions of masculinity. Within the organization, men and women's physical capabilities were measured against each other; women's perceived biological limitations became the standard by which the best men were measured. Louie draws attention to the manner in which women's "peak potentials" were historically constrained in patriarchal contexts – even in the absence of formal laws, rules, and regulations. Eliane Silverman and Cora Voyageur's articles, which follow, explore how two women, Lena Hanen and Dorothy McDonald, navigated and negotiated these constraints in the world of twentieth-century politics and business.*

In 1906, the Alpine Club of Canada (ACC) was created to celebrate Canada's western mountains by teaching mountain climbing to Canadians – female and male.[1] Its officials promoted climbing as a crucible, through which the rigorous level of engagement with "wilderness" benefited all.[2] Unlike most North American mainstream sports institutions, the ACC (and other North American mountain clubs inaugurated around the turn of the century) welcomed women.[3] One year after its inception, over 30 per cent of ACC members were women. The percentage remained around 40 per cent until a decline in the 1950s. Singles formed, on average, two-thirds of the female membership.[4] They often joined with peers or relatives, and meeting future spouses through the ACC was common.[5] Female members' ages ranged from eighteen, the minimum allowed, to "venerable," and fitness levels were equally varied.[6] The exceptional degree of sexual parity that women found in the ACC was a distinction of which its members rightly remain proud.

Yet scholars have established that sport in early-twentieth-century North America perpetuated, as well as challenged, a social hierarchy where men's abilities were considered superior.[7] Was the ACC an anomaly? Gina La Force's study, which examines the interconnections between Canadian nationalism and Anglo-Saxon identity in ACC mountaineering, treats masculinity as normative.[8] PearlAnn Reichwein's doctoral dissertation notes that Club officials held conventional gender expectations regarding domestic or secretarial roles, but that the acceptance of women's leadership in regional administration and actual climbing indicate the ACC's openness to women's achievement.[9]

This chapter argues that the ACC's gender norms from 1906 to 1940 were exceptional in degree, but not in kind. Broader disparities in power that excluded or restricted the involvement of women, lower classes, and non-Whites in professional work and mainstream sports, marked the ACC in overt and subtle ways.[10] As was the case with students who attended the Medicine Hat School of Nursing (described by Florence Melchior in chapter 15), the membership at this time was overwhelmingly middle-class, White, urban, and Anglo-Canadian, with a strong American and British presence.[11] I am using "middle-class" in the sense of privileged socioeconomic position and access to cultural resources such as higher education, and "White" to indicate a racial identity perceived at the time as normative.[12] Alpine Club of Canada officials promoted a policy toward White middle-class women's physicality that was remarkably supportive compared to the restrictions of most mainstream institutions and sports. The policy was predicated, however, on an unofficial hierarchy structured around race, sex, and class – with exaggerated ideals of White masculinity on top.

To the few men and women of Jewish background who applied for membership in this period, even the bottom of the hierarchy was inaccessible, for ACC administrators and ordinary members rejected their applications.[13] Officials recruited middle-class members in an effort to legitimize mountaineering as a prestigious sport, and their pride in the membership's middle-class status and Anglo-Celtic heritage coexisted with their image of the Club as accessible to all: "[There is a] widely spread idea that the Club is very exclusive and for rich people only. We ... [are] open to every one of discreet behaviour and of clubable nature who has interest in the mountains."[14] While denying that members were "rich," officials had some awareness of the financial resources needed for leisure time, club trips, mountaineering equipment, and travel costs.[15] Women members shared this economic privilege with male members, but they were disadvantaged by perceptions of their sex's inferiority, which were held by the White, middle-class males who ran the Club.

This gender differentiation became more visible as new, ever-harder standards emerged in the ACC from 1906 to 1940, such as making the first ascent of a higher-altitude mountain, and climbing without a professional guide's assistance.[16] Officials responded by promoting unofficial codes of conduct that were splintered clearly along gender lines and, within the Club's White middle-class niche, the codes (despite their informality) perpetuated a traditional structure of unequal power relations.

Mountaineering at this time lacked a regulatory structure that enforced who could practise the sport, and how. The absence of codified rules to control the nature of men and women's participation contributed to the considerable degree of sexual equality that existed in the ACC; yet, it also fostered indirect, implicit expressions of a gender hierarchy. Mountaineering organizations were social clubs, not regulatory bodies. Standards of respected *style*, the manner in which a climb was done, provided the structure by which climbers measured ability.[17] In each generation of mountaineers, some individuals sought more difficult ways of climbing. These path-breakers introduced new stylistic ideals, while the ideals' difficulty made them prestigious. As others emulated the path-breakers, the new ideals gradually became universal and banal.[18] Women could not be directly prevented, therefore, from attempting to make climbs of great prestige alongside men. Women and men could be influenced only through social pressure – to climb at one standard or another.

Alpine Club of Canada women who engaged in routine climbs were motivated by enjoyment of the outdoors, companionship, and climbing's physical and mental rewards.[19] Many may not have felt that the prestige or personal satisfaction of climbing at a superior, difficult standard was worth the risk to life and limb, particularly since there was little social pressure to seek valour. Valour before perceived cowardice may have appealed more to men who felt social pressure to prove themselves, thus contributing to higher levels of achievement by men than women.[20] Renowned American climber Miriam E. O'Brien, one of the first women to climb prestigious routes without any man in her party, did so for "fun": "manless" climbing meant full autonomy, with all the pleasures and perils of being solely responsible for a climb's success or failure. Her analysis suggests that differential gender expectations may have fulfilled themselves, thus contributing to perceived differences in ability: "The [women] I know are more prudent than men of the same actual climbing ability.... Up to date women do not feel themselves so much driven by pride to persist on a climb when they ought to turn back. Being women, there is much less disgrace in their not making the peak."[21]

The ascents done by most ACC men and women, however, were too routine to provoke such musings. Annual summer camps in Canada's western mountain ranges were the ACC's primary way of introducing novices to mountain craft. Club administrators made the encouragement of women climbers an explicit, exceptional priority. The 1907 inaugural issue of the *Canadian Alpine Journal*, the ACC's official periodical, made this clear. Its opening articles were written, respectively, by William Whyte, second vice-president of the Canadian Pacific Railway, and Elizabeth Parker, co-founder of the ACC. Ten of twelve group photographs of ACC members featured women, and the "Report of the Chief Mountaineer," regarding the ACC's 1906 inaugural summer camp, emphasized that fifteen women were among the forty-two members who completed the requirements to become active members.[22] After the 1906 camp, where skirts proved incompatible with safe climbing, a dress code for climbs was instituted that minimized gender distinctions: "knickerbockers, with puttees or gaiters and sweater" were recommended to women, an outfit virtually identical to that suggested for men.[23]

Such parity contrasted sharply with the treatment of most urban White women of middle-class background in mainstream sports, where insistence on sex differences intruded more deeply than clothing concerns. Like Helen MacMurchy and Laura Hamilton, who wrote and disseminated motherhood advice literature based on the opinion of medical "experts" (described by Nadine Kozak in chapter 10), most doctors in North America at this time promoted the idea that, for these women, biology was destiny: reproduction dictated their life purpose. According to contemporary medical wisdom, a finite amount of energy was available to fuel women's physical and mental functions. Women who engaged in mental or physical strain that was considered excessive (such as higher education, or basketball played by men's rules) risked ruining their child-bearing capacity.[24] This pool of knowledge about White middle-class women's bodies was generated from the same system of gender-based power structures that underpinned relations of authority in law, medicine, higher education, and politics.[25] Its implication for mainstream sports was that men's bodies, unlike women's, were thought to be compatible with rigorous use. As a result, men were not only allowed, but also exhorted to push their bodies' limits in the quest for ever-better speed and strength records. The understanding that White middle-class women were unable to perform similarly, and that women who could were not truly female, resulted either in their exclusion from rugged sports such as sprinting, football, rugby, and soccer altogether, or the explicit division of men and women's competition.[26]

Recent publications by M. Ann Hall and Varda Burstyn on women, masculinity, and competitive sport in Canada offer comprehensive examinations of sport's historic and ongoing role in generating and sustaining male privilege. Both authors trace evolving forms of sexual differentiation in a wide variety of sports, they link those efforts to systems of hierarchical power relations in Canadian society, and suggest directions for dismantling sport's role in those systems to bring about equity. This study, in finding similar patterns in mountaineering – which was non-competitive and unregulated, and therefore (one might think) less susceptible to the perpetuation of hegemonic masculinity – confirms the pervasiveness of the structures that Burstyn and Hall identify.[27]

Given the contestation over gender in most other sports, why was there such a remarkable degree of support for women in the ACC? A factor may have been mountaineering technique. Propelling oneself across rock faces and glaciers in the wilderness involved such a variation of physical skills that it levelled physiological differences. Because a climb's length depended on many factors, speed was not precisely measurable and strength could not be privileged over other capacities. As a result, men had no biological advantage. In addition, in the routine, guided climbing typical at ACC camps, the extraordinary expertise of professional guides made the occurrence of pain and injury highly unlikely.[28] At his first camp in 1912, Paul A.W. Wallace, future professor of English and Aboriginal history, found that rope management was critical: "Dislodged stones did not slide, but bounced, and the hollow boom they left behind might have afforded food for reflection ... But ... we were, most of us, so new at the business, and so constantly engaged in disentangling ourselves from the rope, that we had not a moment for contemplating anything beyond our finger tips [*sic*]."[29] Tactile surety for rock was necessary, as K.B. Hallowes noted in a description of the 1913 Mount Robson camp:

I really liked the actual climbing ... except at those moments when I wondered if enough of me could ever be collected to make it worth while putting up a handsome tombstone with a touching inscription.... I should like to know why a foothold which had looked so all-sufficing ... as the guide went up, suddenly seems so ridiculously inadequate when it is a question of resting one's own weight on it. However, the moment passes [and] somehow one is at the top.[30]

Nimbleness and a good sense of balance were also vital as Ethel Johns, a pioneer of Canadian professional nursing, discovered on her graduating climb in 1909: "[On] the descent ... the steps on the snow slope were pretty well worn and the going was decidedly slippery. [The guide] Edouard's adjurations to 'the lady in the middle' became more and more peremptory. 'Stick your feet in,' said he, 'don't walk like a chicken' [sic]."[31] Without rope management, understanding of using holds in rock, and a sense of balance, physical strength was useless. Mountaineering craft demanded more physical versatility than most mainstream sports. Along with the low risk of physical jeopardy on routine climbs led by professional guides, which will be discussed further, mountaineering's physical requirements contributed to the ACC's support for middle-class White women climbers.

However, mountaineering technique alone is not a sufficient explanation for this phenomenon: the original Alpine Club in England, founded in 1875, was male-only until 1974.[32] That the ACC's co-founder was a woman accounts more readily for the enthusiasm. Arthur Oliver Wheeler was a surveyor whose desire to form a Canadian mountaineering organization nearly foundered on his countrymen's apathy. Wheeler was ready to form a Canadian section of the American Alpine Club when Elizabeth Parker took up the cause. Upon hearing of Wheeler's plans, Parker, a *Manitoba Free Press* journalist, protested in her column.[33] She implored Canadians to create an autonomous mountaineering organization, decrying those who cared little that Englishmen and Americans were racking up first ascents of Canada's mountains.[34] Parker's articles and editorials written by J.W. Dafoe, editor of the *Free Press*, stirred enough interest to make the Alpine Club of Canada a reality in March 1906.[35] Parker's fierce activism made the difference between a Canadian auxiliary to the American organization, and the autonomous Alpine Club of Canada.

Professional guides were another critical factor in the Club's welcoming atmosphere for women. In its early years, one mountaineering style was customary among amateur mountaineers of both sexes: guided climbing. Throughout this period, ACC climbs were led by both professional guides and civic-minded male members who were experienced mountaineers.[36] The professional guides were male White Central Europeans (Swiss or Austrian) with ambiguous class status in the ACC. Given the reverence with which club members referred to them, their status almost approached that of the superhuman skilled professional.[37] Climbing leadership in the ACC was, therefore, established (in the case of volunteers) as White, male, and middle-class, and in the case of the professional guides, as White, male, and ambiguously working class.

Professional guides' protective role applied to both experienced and novice members. Amateurs good enough to lead climbs themselves often preferred the safety margin of the professional's expertise. On the other hand, it was not uncommon for guides to coax, or physically drag up a mountain by the rope, a timid or weak client.[38] Whereas amateur leaders were known to make mistakes, professional guides' physicality and infallible grasp of mountain craft were legendary.[39] A. O. Wheeler, in his 1926 address to the membership at the Tonquin Valley Camp, commented on the extent to which a mountaineer's ascent and safe return could depend on the guide's heroic effort:

[Guides'] deeds of prowess lead their followers to almost believe them infallible in their profession. I once met [the Swiss guide] old Edouard Feuz ... returning from a climb of Mt. Sir Donald [3297 metres or 10,808 feet] with two very stout gentlemen, both in the last stages of exhaustion. "Edouard," I exclaimed, "How ever did you get them up" [*sic*]. He replied, "Dat is nothing. We could take up a dead man."[40]

ACC member John W. Hugill, an Alberta lawyer, explicitly identified the guides' superlative abilities as epitomizing masculinity.[41] Expressing regret at having missed several camps, Hugill remarked: "To think that I had irretrievably lost the association of these perfectly splendid specimens of physical, fearless, modest manhood for five years past!"[42] In the Club's early years, the mixed nature of groups customarily led by professional guides and volunteer members endorsed an extraordinary level of sexual equality. Leaders' authoritative role and the fact that they were exclusively male, however, masked underlying beliefs in middle-class White women's climbing inferiority. Those beliefs surfaced as a challenging standard emerged: "guideless climbing," or climbing without the security of a professional guide in order to test one's self.[43]

"Leading" climbs demanded a challenging level and variety of mental and physical skills.[44] Three things were required: first, the ability to plan a feasible route for the ascent and descent; second, the ability to execute the plan by physically leading every part of the route; third, the ability to abandon the old plan in an emergency, improvise a new plan, and lead it.[45] For example, a leader could minimize the risk of avalanche ("a fall of large masses of snow and ice down a mountain") with knowledge of how terrain and weather interacted.[46] Calculating avalanche risk involved many factors including, but not restricted to, the angle of the sun's rays on the snow, the angle of the snow slope, the amount and type of recent snowfall, and the velocity and type of wind.[47] The crux of leading competence was the ability to juggle variables. Every leader worthy of the role could analyze available options, judge the best course, and execute that decision.

Only in a life-threatening emergency, moreover, could a leader's competence be measured, and his or her authority over the other climbers verified. When caught by a thunderstorm on a ridge, for example, any previous plan had to be discarded at once, or climbers risked being struck by lightning. Snap decisions had to be made about the safest and quickest route down. "Safest" and "quickest" depended on the storm's severity, combined with the difficulty of surrounding rock, snow, and ice formations.[48] Climbs that seemingly proved the existence of sexual equality in mountaineering, therefore, on the basis of a woman's physical presence at the front of a mixed-sex party, actually proved nothing. In 1932, world-class American climber Miriam O'Brien commented:

A man may offer to let the woman lead [which she does] pleasantly enough for hours. Then an emergency comes up, like a thunderstorm on an exposed ridge, and it is imperative to get down at once. What happens? (Actual case.) The man wakes up, gives orders: "Traverse to the left by such-and-such a route" (not in fact the easiest or the quickest). It occurs to me that I am the logical leader ... considering that I am ahead and therefore have a much better view of the ground, while, aside from sex, I am competent to choose that particular type of route. But ... I have grown to recognize the fact that when a man lets a woman "lead" it is, for him, just a pleasant little fiction.[49]

The true leader was trusted by his or her fellow climbers to make crucial decisions instantly, with sound judgement, under life-threatening conditions. Under easy conditions, where a leader's mistake was unlikely to involve life-or-death consequences, underlying doubts about women's competence could lie dormant. Only a crisis could show whether men trusted a woman climber to perform at this rarefied level, the difficulty of which tested the abilities of the best of men. Unlike climbing with a professional guide, therefore, the guideless-climbing standard demanded intellectual and emotional, as well as physical, strengths that were no less than outstanding.

These fine distinctions did not apply to the routine, guided climbing done at annual summer camps by rank-and-file members of both sexes. Camps were usually of two weeks' duration with participants numbering, on average, between one and two hundred.[50] Ordinary climbing and instruction activities did not formally differentiate on the basis of sex. Climbing sheets were posted every evening for members to sign up for the next day's climbs. On each sheet was written the date of the climb, name of the mountain or pass to be attempted, maximum number of men and women to be accepted, and times of wake-up call, breakfast, and departure. A Climbing Committee, made up of the most experienced climbers, "reserved the right to limit the number in a party or strike off names of persons not thought qualified to make a particular ascent."[51] Afterwards, the leader or another competent member of the party would note on the sheet a description of the route, times spent, and comments about weather or the participants.[52] With rare exceptions, these authors discussed climbers solely in terms of mountaineering ability.[53]

The endorsement of women's aptitude for routine mountaineering was sustained in camp social activities, particularly the nightly campfire songs. Lyrics about mountaineering were set to existing melodies and, from 1906 to 1929, the songs were an indispensable part of the campfire.[54] The educational focus of the camps was brought out in songs meant for new members, celebrating newfound physical skills and the wilderness setting. Women's climbing ability in the guided style was particularly praised:

> Some girls spend their time in going out to tea,
>   But that sort of thing does not appeal to me.
> I had rather stand with my iceaxe in my hand,
>   And glissade down a thousand feet of snow.
> Mountaineering girls must all be true and tried
>   And must always try to imitate the guide;
> They must never stop until they reach the top,
>   And gaze upon the scene far below.[55]

This song and others cast women climbers in a very positive light. It must be noted, however, that the praise was lavished upon women for performing at a basic level.

Speeches and published writings of A.O. Wheeler, co-founder of the ACC, were similarly welcoming, yet patronizing when he promoted women as legitimate members of the fraternity who were comfortable with rough terrain and wild animals. In 1910, Wheeler's presidential address expressed admiration for women members:

The mountaineering ability of our girls is another feature of "that nice little Canadienne." ... I think our men members might accept the following as an axiom: "From Fairview to Lake Louise, by paths amidst the trees; on rock and ice and snow; wherever goats may go; if there's aught of worth to draw us, we find them there before us." Here's to our ladies, God bless 'em: formerly our superiors, now our equals.[56]

Wheeler also made a point of not using the term "men" to designate women by implication. Rather, he habitually added the phrase "and women."[57] His many efforts to publicly acknowledge women as visible, capable, and consequential to the membership were extraordinary, given the period and the physical risk and strain of mountaineering. Simultaneously, such pointed advocacy accentuated women's status as a special group. Men's ability to perform at basic levels was unquestioned, so they received no similar commentary. Despite condescension, however, women's climbing in the ACC was not generally resented or merely tolerated. Rather, repeated encouragement, by facilitating women's engagement with climbing's ruggedness, went against the custom of Canadian society and beyond the compromises of most mainstream sports.

Such encouragement could result in transforming a woman's understanding of the world and her place in it, claimed an article in the ACC's 1909 *Canadian Alpine Journal*:

As surely as there is a cliff to climb ... self-preservation [will make the woman novice] know herself as never before – physically, mentally, emotionally.... She ... gains confidence with every step, finds the dangers she has imagined far greater than those she encounters and arrives at last upon the summit to gaze out upon a new world. Surely not the same old earth she has seen all her life? Yes

– but looked at from *on top* – a point of view which now makes upon her mind its indelible impression.[58]

The author, Winnipeg obstetrician and social activist Mary Crawford, asserted that women who climbed gained self-confidence that transformed their lives; they learned that they could achieve previously unthinkable physical and mental challenges.[59]

Alongside Crawford's argument for women on top, however, is one that invokes customary gender norms of leadership based on the guided climbing style. Crawford emphasizes that only a basic level of physical ability, and no intellect at all, was necessary in routine guided climbing: "There are guides, men of experience, whom [a woman] has only to obey, and who will show her the right thing to do; ... She knows that every precaution against danger is provided."[60] That rank-and-file men were customarily dependent on guides alongside women, testifies to a substantial restructuring of traditional roles. At the same time, as unusual as such approbation was, the endorsement took place only within the context of White male leadership.

As new standards of excellence emerged, the encouragement that women received, relative to men, faltered. In 1913, ACC administrators organized attempts to make the first undisputed ascent of Mount Robson.[61] At 3,954 metres (12,972 feet), Robson was the highest mountain in the Canadian Rockies. The way in which ACC president A.O. Wheeler wrote of the climb suggests a link between an exaggerated ideal of masculinity, specific to mountaineering culture, and a universal standard of excellence embodied in the heroism of the first ascent of a higher-altitude mountain.

In this period, first ascents of higher-altitude mountains were coveted prizes because they could be virtually guaranteed to test the most expert mountaineer's capabilities. Two components to the challenge took the concept of engagement with "wilderness" to extremes: first, the size. Robson is not what climbers today consider high-altitude. Its upper reaches were, however, in the range of 2,700 to 5,500 metres (8,858 to 18,045 feet) – a height which physicians today consider capable of causing physiological problems from altitude.[62] Higher peaks also had much colder environments. The upper reaches were glaciated, or permanently covered with layers of snow and ice. Glaciation meant avalanche hazards and crevasses. Stronger winds found at higher altitudes exacerbated frigid temperatures, so frostbite and hypothermia were an ever-present danger. Finally, the sheer scale of such mountains meant greater distances to cover, which lengthened the time of exposure to the elements.[63] To not only survive, but also to achieve the summit necessitated physical and mental toughness.

Second, the attempted first ascent of such a peak augmented these factors because the terrain was unknown. If one route petered out in a maze of crevasses, climbers had to retreat and try a different route. If that one also ended in an insurmountable obstacle, the process had to be repeated. The factor of the unknown extended the length of time a climbing party was exposed to cold and snow. Spending a longer time on the mountain multiplied the chances of being caught in a storm. Subsequent ascents might encounter terrain and weather conditions more difficult than those on the first, but they generally conferred less prestige: the peak had already been measured against human capabilities and found to be, after all, conquerable.[64] Making the first ascent of a higher-altitude mountain, then, was a kind of trial-by-fire for mountaineers of the highest calibre to test themselves against unadulterated Nature.

In the summer of 1913, some of the Club's strongest climbers made three attempts from an ACC-organized camp to accomplish what they considered to be the first completed ascent of Mount Robson. The first party consisted of a professional guide, Conrad Kain, and two amateur mountaineers, Albert H. MacCarthy and W. W. Foster. This first group was the only one to reach the summit. All three parties, however, had their mettle tested. The successful party, despite ideal weather conditions, ran out of daylight on their descent. They had to bivouac, or camp out, overnight at 2,743 metres (9,000 feet) "without food or covering" before descending the next day. The other parties encountered severe storms that reduced visibility to almost zero and caused them to turn back, for safety's sake, before the summit.[65]

Some newspapers reported wrongly that a woman named Mary Vaux was in the successful party. Vaux, an active member of the ACC and the Society of Woman Geographers, was better known for mountain photography and botany than climbing. With her father and brothers, she contributed substantially to the advancement of glaciology in Canada.[66] Wheeler's refutation, however, was not based on Vaux's personal climbing ability. His objections were gender based:

The party who made the first complete ascent of Mt. Robson, 31 July 1913. Whyte Museum of the Canadian Rockies, M200 / AC 383 / 4, C.H. Mitchell

The accomplishment of the climb is, at the present time, quite beyond the physical ability of most women, and it is needless to say that no permission was given by camp management to any lady climber to make such an attempt, and none was made bu [sic] them. By and by, when a suitable shelter hut has been built high up on the mountain side, no doubt many ladies will succeed in reaching the summit, but at present such an attempt would be very unwise, and the Club was not taking any chances of loss of life in this direction.

When it is known that to reach the … summit, … Conrad Kain had to cut no less than sixteen hundred steps in snow and ice … necessitating hours of patient waiting [by the amateur mountaineers], *the difficultise* [sic] *will be partially understood*…. The frozen debris from the step cutting was blown for hours into the faces and eyes of the climbers, and *this fact alone exemplifies the great courage and determination necessary to attain success* [my emphases].[67]

Three points are important. One, the prestige of making the first ascent of Mount Robson was dependent on perceiving the unclimbed big mountain as a symbolic battleground upon which the climbers' abilities were tried and found equal to the adventure. Wheeler devotes half of his letter to the privations undergone by all three parties, because the first ascent of Mount Robson, he seemed to feel, was not simply a difficult climb: it was an absolute measure of the ability and skills of amateur mountaineers and (those epitomes of masculinity) the professional guides.

The second point concerns Wheeler's emphasis on a hut. He does not say that a hut several thousand feet up the mountain is important to successful ascents of weak climbers generally. Wheeler, who habitually made a point of addressing women as well as men, specifies here that a hut will help *women* attempting Robson. Rather than encouraging women to train hard to climb Robson without a shelter's aid, he advises that a hutless attempt would be "very unwise." This suggests that the challenge tested even the guides, whose competence embodied a White masculine ideal; implicitly, women attempting Robson without a hut would have contravened the unwritten hierarchy that underpinned power relations in the Club.

Third, Wheeler's language in his account of the difficulties surmounted includes phrases, emphasized in the quote, that indicate exasperation with non-mountaineers. The newspaper writers' ignorance, he seems to feel, made them incapable of understanding the achievement's magnitude. The placement of this paragraph immediately after his discussion of women suggests that, to Wheeler, the media's inclusion of a woman in the successful party emasculated the triumph of the party that did summit, and ridiculed the physical trials and disappointments of those that did not. He does not explicitly link masculinity with the trial that the Robson men survived; however, key phrases, and the letter's structure, suggest that his vehemence stemmed from a perception of gender as the splinter point of standards by which the best climbers in this White middle-class club were measured.

This was the impression of Phyllis Munday who, in 1924, made the first woman's ascent, guided by Conrad Kain and with the assistance of a High Camp at 1,067 metres (3,500 feet):

> That a woman would be allowed to attempt Mt. Robson was not credited at the camp of the Alpine Club of Canada at Robson Pass; much less was it thought possible that one could perform what was regarded as a prodigious test of physical endurance and mountaineering skill, so it was with amazed joy that I heard from Director A. O. Wheeler's lips that I was chosen to accompany my husband on the second 1924 party.[68]

Wheeler, therefore, upheld very public links between an ideal of overt masculinity, and the superior climbing standard of a higher-altitude first ascent: egalitarian expectations of women's climbing capabilities were readjusted in accordance with the ACC's exaggerated standards of White middle-class masculinity.

The other standard of excellence that emerged in the Club during this period was guideless climbing. Beginning in 1919, the *Canadian Alpine Journal* and administrators' speeches linked exemplary leading ability exclusively with the top male members. Women were not actively discouraged from excelling at leading climbs; administrators who believed in men's superiority simply neglected to honour, through the Silver Rope, women's achievements in this area.[69] ACC administrators indirectly encouraged and subtly confirmed the equation of masculinity with superior performance, by leaving the direction of ACC women's climbing to stagnate as the difficulty of mountaineering standards rose.

William J. Goode, in *The Celebration of Heroes: Prestige as a Social Control System*, discusses how those at the top of a socially stratified community maintain their prestige by recognizing, or overlooking, excellence. He argues that a hierarchical system of worth may be maintained, despite instances of excellence displayed by members of lower orders:

Climbers after a successful ascent of Mount Robson; Don and Phyllis Munday holding ice axes, lower left. British Columbia Archives I-61760.

By [praising] those below for their excellent performances at *lower* tasks, but not [interpreting] any excellence as proving the right to move upward. A system of ... control over upward movement need not deny merit where it appears. It is only necessary to be blind to *potential* merit. Since potential merit is often, perhaps even typically, ambiguous, that blindness can apparently be achieved quite easily.... In general ... members of the upper social strata *do not ... aim at improving the behaviour of the lower classes*, as judged by the standards of excellence ... that are widely held within that social system. There is no general commitment on the part of most social strata to move members of any lower strata very far toward higher achievements.[70]

Goode's discussion concerns class systems only, but since this study considers class, race, and gender to be aspects of the same hierarchical system of social organization, his insights are cogent.[71] When individuals from lower echelons display excellence according to the standards of the higher levels, they do not threaten the higher level's monopoly on excellence because they are so rare. Their ability may be regarded as deviant and their peers' cultivatable merit ignored, because potential for excellence is often inconspicuous. To protect the higher level's prestige, the number of members from below who excel to the higher level's standards should remain at the status quo. Actively constraining their achievement potential may be unnecessary; neglecting it may have the same result. Without ascribing malice or intent to ACC officials, therefore, their lopsided pattern of leadership nevertheless contributed to making the Club one where climbing at a level inspiring formal acclaim was the domain, almost exclusively, of middle-class White men.

Climbing guideless required amateur mountaineers to have a firm grasp of mountain-craft principles, both physical and mental. The 1920 *Canadian Alpine Journal* included the first written confirmation, by respected member Winthrop Ellsworth Stone, president of Purdue University from 1900 to 1921, of the attitude that men alone should, by coming to grips with wilderness dangers, learn how to lead:[72]

Too often ... climbers follow blindly, noting neither the route nor the surroundings. For the development of amateur mountaineering ... men of ability are not lacking. What is needed is a realization among our young men of the possibilities and the initiative to grasp them. One is not fully initiated as a mountaineer until he has ... [felt] a hold upon which [he] has thrown his weight, yielding; [suddenly found] his legs projecting through a snow bridge into a crevasse; [these] are dangers ... which threaten but also school the amateur in self-reliance.[73]

Because professional guides and the small body of put-upon volunteer men had become overworked, ACC executives had begun in 1919 to make similar appeals for more and more male members, not female, to learn how to lead.[74]

However, officials did not directly restrict the few women who had the initiative and drive to pursue leadership ability. From 1923 on, the occasional woman was listed on the climbing sheets as co-leader; from 1928 on, the occasional woman was listed as sole leader of a mixed climbing party.[75] The extent of their responsibility compared to male leaders, however, is unclear. Climbs ranged widely in difficulty, not only from mountain to mountain, but from year to year.[76] Moreover, the relevant climbing sheet comments do not indicate that the women

Phyllis Munday on Franklin Glacier carrying a 70-lb. pack. British Columbia Archives H-03440.

leaders encountered any emergencies. As noted earlier, the real test of sexual equality in climbing lay in whether the men in any party led by a woman trusted her abilities in a crisis.

Phyllis Munday was one female leader who handled mountain emergencies regularly. She and her husband Don were famous for making first ascents and exploring the Coast Mountains of British Columbia, an area previously disregarded by White climbers. Each trusted the other's ability to lead the way out of critical situations. Phyllis Munday was probably the ACC's best-known woman climber.[77] Yet her career in the

Club demonstrates how, for years, ACC administrators neglected women's potential for leading excellence by ignoring the issue altogether.

Officials withheld formal approval of women like Phyllis Munday, but gave approval to men of equal ability. In 1934, the executive board instituted a prestigious award called the Silver Rope. Theoretically, the Rope represented the Club's recognition of any mountaineer's superior leading ability; practically, it was an attempt to increase the number of male volunteer guides.[78] The Silver Rope could be granted two ways: one, the executive board could confer it on those members it considered worthy; two, any member could apply for it. The official terms of the award did not specify that only men were eligible.[79] Despite this, the issue of women's eligibility divided the three men, W. R. Tweedy, A. A. McCoubrey, and Cyril G. Wates, in charge of administering the award.[80] In January 1934, Tweedy wrote to McCoubrey, "It would seem from [Wates's] letter that he is only considering Males [who are presently] members. What about ... Mrs. [Phyllis] Munday?"[81] McCoubrey's reply was decidedly neutral:

I have no positive knowledge that Mr. Wates is compiling a list and I just received a denial from Mr. Wheeler this morning that he is working on a list. Mr. Wheeler's thought in this matter is that applications should come from members.... Regarding the question of ladies receiving the award . . . if there is no list, the onus should be on the applicant so that I do not think we should worry about that feature in the meantime.[82]

The issue, McCoubrey suggested, could remain dead until a woman actually applied.

The first three Rope recipients, however, did not have to submit applications. A. O. Wheeler received the first, by unanimous vote of the 1934 Annual General Meeting. The next two had their awards conferred upon them by resolution of the executive board.[83] It seems likely, therefore, that a male-only list of candidates existed. In the first year of its institution, thirty men were granted Silver Ropes, including Don Munday, whose major mountaineering accomplishments were the result of teamwork with his wife, Phyllis.[84] Women were officially eligible, but as long as none applied, influential officials were happy to sanction the leading abilities of middle-class White men alone.

In 1940, however, women's eligibility had to be dealt with. I have found no indication of how the issue came about, but in November 1940,

Wates, then president, wrote a memorandum "to certify that I have written to all members of the Executive Board asking for an ... opinion on ... whether the Silver Rope might be awarded to Lady Members of the Club on the same basis as to men."[85] Eleven out of thirteen board members approved. Four men, including Wates, then proposed the candidacy of Polly Prescott, who was granted the Rope within the year.[86] Prescott, an American, had been a rope leader at the ACC's summer camps since 1926 and completed several manless climbs.[87] Phyllis Munday was not granted the award until 1948, the year that her husband Don was the Club's western vice president.[88] The president, Sidney R. Vallance, wrote to Don: "We all know that no-one has more right to wear it than she; the only thing is that it should have been awarded long ago."[89]

The Silver Rope issue, then, demonstrates the subtle influence of an unofficial gender-based hierarchy of skills. The necessity of voting on women's eligibility betrays the prevalence of the idea, among ACC administrators, that only men deserved Club sanction for exemplary leading ability. As guideless climbing became a new standard of excellence, the guided climbing routinely done by rank-and-file members of both sexes became second rank. For officials who believed that men's abilities were superior, there was no need to suppress women such as Phyllis Munday who, in their rarity and lack of insistence for official recognition, presented little challenge to ideas of male superiority. Two policies sufficed to perpetuate the hierarchical gender-based relations of authority that prevailed in mainstream society: urging men to pursue the new standard, and neglecting women's potential to excel.

In conclusion, from the inception of the Alpine Club of Canada, administrators advocated an official policy of sexual equality in climbing. Women did find in the Club a remarkable freedom from restrictive ideas of femininity that prevailed in society generally. That freedom resulted, in part, from some officials' genuine desire to encourage women's physicality well beyond levels accepted in mainstream sports, if not at the level of the Club's male elite. It also resulted from the lack of formally enforceable rules in mountaineering at the time. Officials could never directly constrain women from climbing as strongly as the best men.

As it turned out, direct restrictions were not necessary to distinguish, by calibre, women and men's climbing. Women were encouraged to scale cliffs and jump crevasses alongside their male counterparts. Ultimate responsibility for the climbs, however, rested with almost exclusively male leaders, whether they be White Swiss or Austrian professional guides, or White middle-class amateur leaders whose expertise was publicly honoured, after 1934, through the Silver Rope. The superior calibre of men's abilities, in perception and practice, persisted throughout this period. ACC women's physical freedom was exceptional, but qualified. Unwritten and officially unacknowledged codes of gender-based skills perpetuated unequal power relations as effectively as explicit codes in mainstream sports.

As Canada's national mountaineering organization, the Alpine Club of Canada helped to shape early- to mid-twentieth-century perceptions and experiences of Canada's west as a "wilderness," where its female members could joyfully break away from stereotypes of delicate middle-class White femininity, and where leadership, denoted by proven superiority of physical and mental survival skills in a crisis, was publicly honoured as White middle-class male only. This study, therefore, may contribute to our understanding of the persistence of the White macho glamour of "the West" and wilderness, even in the face of deliberate attempts at change.

ENDNOTES

1   "Constitution," *Canadian Alpine Journal (CAJ)* 1 (1907); Whyte Museum of the Canadian Rockies (WMCR), PearlAnn Reichwein, "Beyond Visionary Mountains: The Alpine Club of Canada and the Canadian National Park Idea, 1906 to 1969" (Ph.D. diss., Carleton University, 1995), 140.

2   Many scholars have critiqued the concept of "wilderness" as forests, wild animals, and terrain unaffected by previous human habitation or imagination, since it involves selective amnesia about Indigenous peoples' relationship with the land. See for example Robert S. McPherson, *Sacred Land, Sacred View: Navajo Perceptions of the Four Corners Region*, Charles Redd Monographs in Western History, No. 19 (Salt Lake City, Utah: Signature Books, 1992); Mark David Spence, *Dispossessing the Wilderness: Indian Removal and the Making of the National Parks* (New York: Oxford University Press, 1999). The Stoney Nation currently makes claims to the mountain areas where most of the ACC's camps from 1906 to 1940 were held. See Chief John Snow, *These Mountains Are Our Sacred Places: The Story of the Stoney Indians* (Toronto: S. Stevens, 1977).

3   The original Alpine Club (London, England), inaugurated in 1857, was closed to women until 1974, resulting in the formation of all-women's climbing clubs. See Walt Unsworth, *Hold the Heights: The Foundations of Mountaineering* (Seattle: The Mountaineers, 1994), 68–69; "Our Founder," *Pinnacle Club Journal* 1 (1924):

1–3. North American mountaineering clubs open to women from the beginning were as follows: the Appalachian Mountain Club (1876), the Sierra Club (1892), the Mazamas (1894), the American Alpine Club (1902), and the British Columbia Mountaineering Club (1907). See Allen H. Bent, "The Mountaineering Clubs of America," *Appalachia* (December 1916): 9–11, 15; A. J. MacKintosh, "Mountaineering Clubs, 1857–1907," *Alpine Journal* (August 1907): 542–43; Rachel da Silva et al., "A Brief History of Women Climbing in the Coast and Cascade Ranges," in Da Silva, ed., *Leading Out: Women Climbers Reaching for the Top* (Seattle: Seal Press, 1992), 69. On gender differentiation in most mainstream sports, see note 7.

4   Reichwein, "Beyond Visionary Mountains," 89–99, 151–59.

5   For examples of women joining with peers or relatives, see *The Crag and Canyon*, 20 July 1907; *Lethbridge Herald*, 9 July 1908 and 16 July 1908; Glenbow Archives, V379/PD, Christina Bateman album; WMCR, M200/ AC 0M/ 32, A. A. McCoubrey Executive Papers, Records of Climbs and Articles Published sheets, Dr. Irene Barstow Hudson to A. A. McCoubrey; M200/ AC 0M/ 44, A. A. McCoubrey Executive Papers, Elizabeth Parker to William Whyte, July 20, 1906; and "Most of our membership is built up not through the newspaper editorial but through the local story and the personal contact in the Section," M200/ AC 0M/ 29, A. A. McCoubrey Executive Papers, A. A. McCoubrey to S. H. Mitchell; M200/ AC 0M/ 083, Laura Jamieson script, p. 1. On meeting future spouses through the ACC, see WMCR, M200/ AC 41/ 7, ACC Minute Books, Director's Address 1913, p. 311. On age range, *Calgary Daily Herald*, 6 August 1920, "Alpine Club Has Day of Rest in Mountain Camp"; WMCR, M200/ AC 090M/ 100, Annie M. Davies to S. H. Mitchell, 1913; M200/ AC 0M/ 102B, 1937 Upper Yoho Valley Camp, July 24, 1937, Mt. President. On fitness levels, WMCR, M200/ AC 041M/10, ACC Minute Books, Annual Meeting, communication from H. C. Boyd, 1924; M200/ AC 0M/ 083, Laura Jamieson script, p. 3.

6   Reichwein, "Beyond Visionary Mountains," 273; for examples of fitness levels, M200/ AC 00M/ 3, F. C. Bell Papers, S. H. Mitchell to T. B. Moffat, 6 September 1928.

7   Varda Burstyn, *The Rites of Men: Manhood, Politics, and the Culture of Sport* (Toronto: University of Toronto Press, 1999); Susan K. Cahn, *Coming On Strong: Gender and Sexuality in Twentieth-Century Women's Sport* (New York: Free Press, 1994); M. Ann Hall, *The Girl and the Game: A History of Women's Sport in Canada* (Peterborough, ON: Broadview Press, 2002); Colin Howell, *Blood, Sweat and Cheers: Sport and the Making of Modern Canada* (Toronto: University of Toronto Press, 2001); Bruce Kidd, *The Struggle for Canadian Sport* (Toronto: University of Toronto Press, 1996); Helen Lenskyj, *Out of Bounds: Women, Sport and Sexuality* (Toronto: Women's Press, 1986).

8   Gina La Force, "The Alpine Club of Canada, 1906 to 1929: Modernization, Canadian Nationalism, and Anglo-Saxon Mountaineering," *CAJ* 62 (1979): 39–47.

9   Reichwein, "Beyond Visionary Mountains," 99–104.

10   Alison Prentice et al. *Canadian Women: A History*, 2nd ed. (Toronto: Harcourt Brace, 1996); Veronica Strong-Boag et al., eds., *Rethinking Canada: The Promise of Women's History*, 2nd ed. (Toronto: University of Toronto Press, 2002).

11   WMCR, M200/ AC 0M/ 44, A.A. McCoubrey Executive Papers, Elizabeth Parker to William Whyte, July 20, 1906. M200/ AC 41/ 7, ACC Minute Books, 1914 AGM minutes, 343–45; M200/ AC 0/ 73, Mount Logan Expedition (1925) Papers – H.

F. Lambart Papers, S. H. Mitchell to H. F. Lambart, 7 December 1925; M200/
AC 041M/ 7, ACC Minute Books, clipping, n.d., n.p., Report of the First Annual
Report of the ACC, p. 24; Reichwein, 86–104.

12   Ann Hall et al., *Sport in Canadian Society*, 160–64; Edward Pessen, "Status and
Social Class in America," in *Making America: The Society & Culture of the United
States*, ed. Luther S. Luedtke (Chapel Hill, NC: University of North Carolina
Press, 1992), 362–75; David R. Roediger, *Towards the Abolition of Whiteness: Essays
on Race, Politics, and Working-Class History* (London: Verso, 1994).

13   In 1929, a Japanese applicant was only accepted because strong support from ACC
officials countered "strong feeling amongst many members against the Yellow
race." Quoted by Reichwein, "Beyond Visionary Mountains," 100–103; M200/
AC 00M/ 3, F. C. Bell Papers, S. H. Mitchell to F. C. Bell, March 27, 1928.

14   WMCR, M200/ AC 041M/9, ACC Annual Meeting 1918, Report of the Secretary
Treasurer; M200/ AC 041M/ 7, ACC Minute Books, Alpine Club Meeting, 2 June
1908.

15   WMCR, M200/AC 041M/ 7, ACC Minute Books, p. 245; M200/ AC 041M/ 9,
ACC Minute Books, Director's Address, 22 July 1915, 47; M200/ AC 041M/ 9,
Director's Address, 1917, 104; *The Gazette*, December 1921, 26. For the ACC's first
summer camp, in 1906, members paid (on top of annual dues of two to twenty-
five dollars depending on membership category) from one to two dollars per day
at camp. See *Constitution and List of Members*, 1906–08, and *CAJ* 1 (1907).

16   WMCR, M200/ AC 0/ 30-32, A. A. McCoubrey Executive Papers, Climbing
Records, *passim*; n.a., "Independent Mountaineering," *CAJ* 2 (1909): 137–38; W.
E. Stone, "Amateur Climbing," *CAJ* 11 (1920): 1–6.

17   Peter Donnelly, "On Verification: A Comparison of Climbers and Birders," in
Alan G. Ingham and Eric F. Broom, compilers, *Career Patterns and Career Con-
tingencies in Sport: Proceedings of the First Regional Symposium for the Sociology of
Sport, May-June 1981*, 487–88.

18   David Mazel, ed., *Mountaineering Women: Stories by Early Climbers* (College
Station, TX: Texas A&M University Press, 1994), 17–18; Trevor Williams and
Peter Donnelly, "Subcultural Production, Reproduction and Transformation in
Climbing," *International Review for the Sociology of Sport* 20 (1985): 3–4, 12–14.

19   WMCR, M200/ AC 090M/ 100, Annie M. Davies to S. H. Mitchell, 1913; Ethel
Johns, "A Graduating Climb," *CAJ* 2 (1910): 162–63; WMCR, M200/ AC 0M/ 083,
Laura Jamieson script, 3.

20   High-altitude first ascents and guideless climbing were challenges suited to those
most skilled in mountain craft. Fear of compromised masculinity, in which a
man's manhood was questioned or doubted, was often in other early-twentieth-
century contexts a powerful incentive to perform at the highest standard. Masculine worth had to be continually reiterated through sports, wars, and other media
that involved symbolic or actual conquest. See for example, Graham Dawson,
Soldier Heroes: British Adventure, Empire and the Imagining of Masculinities (London: Routledge, 1994); John M. Mackenzie, "The Imperial Pioneer and Hunter
and the British Masculine Stereotype in Late Victorian and Edwardian Times,"
in *Manliness and Morality: Middle-Class Masculinities in Britain and America,
1800–1940*, ed. J. A. Mangan and James Walvin (New York: St. Martin's Press,
1987), 176–98. When femininity and masculinity were defined as opposites, however, women could not prove their femininity by engaging in similar behaviour.

21 Miriam E. O'Brien, "Without Men: Some Considerations on the Theory and Practice of Manless Climbing," *Appalachia* 19 (December 1932): 194–97.

22 Elizabeth Parker, "The Alpine Club of Canada," 3–8, and M. P. Bridgland, "Report of the Chief Mountaineer," *CAJ* 1 (1907): 174.

23 WMCR, M200/ AC 0/ 129, ACC Camp Pamphlets, "ACC Third Annual Camp 1908 July 7th to July 15th." Skirts were still expected for women around the camp-fire, but this convention seems to have gone in and out of fashion. See British Columbia Archives (BCA), MS-0677, Frederick Victor Longstaff papers, Vol. 162, "ACC Camp O'Hara July 31."

24 See note 7.

25 Nancy F. Cott, *The Grounding of Modern Feminism* (New Haven: Yale University Press, 1987); Wendy Mitchinson, *The Nature of Their Bodies: Women and Their Doctors in Victorian Canada* (Toronto: University of Toronto Press, 1991); Margaret W. Rossiter, *Women Scientists in America: Struggles and Strategies to 1940* (Baltimore: Johns Hopkins University Press, 1982).

26 The effect of present-day gender equity in sport has resulted in the acceptance of masculinist standards of excellence privileging pain and injury, a phenom-enon that some scholars have begun to critique as pathological and indicative of the need for radical institutional reconstruction. See, for example, Cahn, 63, 218; Burstyn; Donald F. Sabo and Joe Panepinto, "Football Ritual and the Social Reproduction of Masculinity," in *Sport, Men and the Gender Order: Critical Feminist Perspectives*, ed. Messner and Sabo (Champaign, Illinois: Human Kinetics, 1990), 122–24; Kevin Young and Philip White, "Sport, Physical Danger, and Injury: The Experiences of Elite Women Athletes," *Journal of Sport and Social Issues* 19 (February 1995): 45–61; Kevin Young, Philip White, and William McTeer, "Body Talk: Male Athletes Reflect on Sport, Injury and Pain," *Sociology of Sport Journal* 11 (June 1994): 175–94.

27 Burstyn, *passim*; Hall, *passim*.

28 See note 26.

29 Glenbow Archives, Paul Wallace fonds inventory; D. B. Smith, "How Paul Wallace Came to Write *The White Roots of Peace*," unpublished manuscript, 9 August 1996; Paul A. W. Wallace, "Vermilion Impressions," *CAJ* 5 (1913): 115–16.

30 K. B. Hallowes, "Mount Robson Camp," *CAJ* 6 (1914–15): 215–16.

31 Margaret Street, *Watch-Fires on the Mountains: The Life and Writing of Ethel Johns* (Toronto: University of Toronto Press, 1973); Ethel Johns, "A Graduating Climb," *CAJ* 2 (1910): 162–63.

32 Unsworth, *Hold the Heights*, 68–69.

33 Cyndi Smith, *Off the Beaten Track: Women Adventurers and Mountaineers in Western Canada* (Jasper: Coyote Books, 1989), 71–73.

34 Elizabeth Parker, "A Holiday Tour in the West," *Manitoba Free Press*, 9 September 1905, 22; 16 September 1905, 21.

35 Esther Fraser, *Wheeler* (Banff: Summerthought, 1978); Raymond Huel, "The Creation of the Alpine Club of Canada: An Early Manifestation of Canadian Nationalism," *Prairie Forum* 15 (1990): 25–43.

36 Until 1944, each summer camp had two professional guides who were either loaned by the Canadian Pacific Railway or the Canadian National Railways, or hired by the ACC. See Alison Griffiths and Gerry Wingenbach, *Mountain Climbing Guides in Canada: The Early Years* (Parks Canada, 1977), 89; Andrew

J. Kauffman and William L. Putnam, *The Guiding Spirit* (Revelstoke: Footprint, 1986). On proportion of professional versus volunteer guides who led climbs at camps, see BCA, MS-2379, Don and Phyllis Munday Papers, Box 1, File 2, "ACC Formation." There were no female professional guides at this time. For comparison, present-day professional mountain guides' associations in Switzerland and Canada with internationally recognized standards of training have women members. One per cent of the Swiss Mountain Guides Association's 1350 members are women. See <http://www.4000plus.ch/e/cc2.cfm>. The Association of Canadian Mountain Guides' membership of 612 includes 129 female members, six of whom have earned full certification, the first, Diny Harrison, in 1992. Linda Heywood (ACMG staff) email to author, 28 January 2003.

37 WMCR, M200/ AC 27/ 14, Camp Notes by P. A. W. Wallace, Cathedral Mountain Camp, 25–27; M200/ AC 041M/ 10, ACC Minute Books, Director's Address, 1924; Peter H. Hansen in "Partners: Guides and Sherpas in the Alps and Himalayas, 1850s-1950s," in *Voyages and Visions: Towards a Cultural History of Travel*, ed. Jas Elsner and Joan-Pau Rubies (London: Reaktion Books, 1999) considers these guides imported to Canada as trivialized "commodities" paraded around to attract tourism for the Canadian Pacific Railway; but, the teacher-learner roles of guides and ACC camp participants surely resulted in higher status for the guides than Holger allows. Reichwein also points out that the guides "lent a European cachet to the camps in the Rockies and legitimated the Canadian alpine movement." Reichwein, "Beyond Visionary Mountains," 154.

38 Conrad Kain, *Where the Clouds Can Go*, ed. J. Monroe Thorington (Boston: Charles T. Branford, 1935), 219. From 1899 to 1949, the number of serious accidents that befell climbing parties led by professional guides rested at zero. Kauffman and Putnam, 113–14, 193.

39 "It is a marvel to me that the Alpine Club of Canada has had no fatal accidents for so many years. Amateurs who may have a little skill in pulling themselves over rocks are constantly entrusted with the lives of novices, not only on rocks but even on snow, of which they are almost entirely ignorant.... [yesterday] a party of twenty ... were together walking over the *length* of a concealed crevasse." WMCR, M200/ AC 27/ 14, Paul A. W. Wallace Papers, 5 August 1913, 106–8; Harold B. Dixon, "With the Canadian Alpine Club," *Alpine Journal* (February 1910): 28.

40 WMCR, M200/ AC 41/ 10, ACC Minute Books, 121.

41 Glenbow Archives, John W. Hugill fonds inventory.

42 John W. Hugill, "My Elopement with Martha," *CAJ* 9 (1918): 127.

43 1855 had marked the first guideless ascent by English climbers. See Peter Holger Hansen, "British Mountaineering, 1858–1914" (Ph.D. diss., Harvard University, 1991), 350, 381–82.
    From then on, this new standard of difficulty began to undergo the slow and difficult process of legitimization. The point of contention was whether climbing guideless was irresponsibly reckless. All agreed, however, that it was undeniably more difficult than climbing with guides. By the early 1930s in Britain, opinion was still divided regardless of generation as to the use of professional guides in the Alps. See J. L. Longland, "Some Guideless Climbs," *Alpine Journal* 245 (November 1932): 200–215; E.W. Young, review of "The Journal of the Fell and Rock Climbing Club," in *Pinnacle Club Journal* 4 (1929–31): 77.

Americans were practising guideless climbing, but articles published in *Appalachia* at the time made a point of discussing the style's merits, which suggests a similar lack of consensus. See Lincoln O'Brien, "Without Guides," *Appalachia* 18 (June 1930): 10–16; R. L. M. Underhill, "When Is A Climb 'Guideless'?" *Appalachia* 18 (December 1930): 181–83.

During the 1930s, however, guideless climbing seems to have become widely accepted as legitimate. Its prestige was widely acknowledged within the borders of Britain and the United States, where professional guides from the Alps were scarce. The occasional individual British or American climber hired a professional guide with whom to climb in North American ranges, but this seems to have occurred rarely. See Chris Jones, *Climbing in North America* (Berkeley: University of California Press, 1976), 38; R. W. Sandford, *The Canadian Alps: The History of Mountaineering in Canada*, vol. 1 (Banff: Altitude Publishing, 1990), 127–28.

In Britain beginning in the 1890s, the rock-climbing offered by North Wales, England's Lake District, and the Scottish Highlands aided the development of guideless rock-climbing as a sport separate from alpine mountaineering, in which snow and ice routes predominated over rock. Americans too were developing their own styles of rock, snow, and ice climbing in American and Canadian ranges. See Ronald W. Clarke, *Men, Myths and Mountains: The Life and Times of Mountaineering* (New York: Thomas Y. Crowell, 1976), 84–88; Unsworth, *Hold the Heights*, 155–69; Jones, *Climbing in North America*, 101–21.

44 WMCR, M200/ AC 50, *The Gazette*, January 1926, J. W. A. Hickson's President's Address, 7–8.

45 Underhill, "When Is A Climb 'Guideless'?" 181–83; Geoffrey Winthrop Young, ed., *Mountain Craft*, 2nd ed. (London: Methuen, 1921).

46 *Collins English Dictionary* (HarperCollins, 2000).

47 Geoffrey Winthrop Young, "Ice and Snow Craft," in Young, ed., *Mountain Craft*, 325–30.

48 Ibid., Geoffrey Winthrop Young, "Corrective Method," 276.

49 O'Brien, "Without Guides," 188.

50 Reichwein, "Beyond Visionary Mountains," 273; *CAJ* 1 (1907): 40.

51 WMCR, M200/ AC 00/ 10, H. E. Sampson Executive Papers, H. E. Sampson to W. R. Tweedy, 26 August 1930; BCA, Don and Phyllis Munday papers, MS-2379, Box 1, File 1, ACC Camps, "Alpine Club of Canada," ca. 1940s.

52 For example, WMCR, M200/ AC 0/ 101A, Climbing Sheets, 1930 Maligne Lake camp, "Charlton," 6 August 1930. WMCR, M200/ AC 0/ 101B, 1931 Prospector's Valley Camp, 22 July 1931, "Mount Neptuak," is instructive: Neptuak was considered to be one of the more difficult climbs of the camp so the wake-up call was to be at 3:30 in the morning, the climb was recommended to be "taken only by those in good condition," and the party was to be limited to five men and "nil" women. Climbing sheet records date back to the early years of the Club, but until the 1930s, unfortunately, offer only few and uninformative sentences.

53 From 1919 to 1940, the climbing sheets contain only two references to incidents where a woman in the party balked at doing something. See WMCR, M200/ AC 0M/ 102A, Climbing Sheets, 1934 Paradise Valley Chrome Lake Camp, 26 July 1934, "Bonnington Peak" by W. W. Dulley, and 28 July 1934, "Alcove" by W. W. Dulley.

54 *CAJ* 1 (1907): 40, *passim.*

55 WMCR, M200/ AC 179/ 3, Songbook, Cyril G. Wates, ed., *Songs of Canadian Climbers* n.p., n.d., #19.

56 WMCR, M200/ AC 41/ 7, ACC Minute Books, President's Address 1910, 201.

57 WMCR, M200/ AC 0/ 44, A. A. McCoubrey Executive Papers, Elizabeth Parker to William Whyte, 20 July 1906; M200/ AC 41/ 7-11, ACC Minute Books, President's Address 1910, 1915, *passim.*

58 Mary E. Crawford, "Mountain Climbing for Women," *CAJ* 2 (1909): 87–89.

59 See University Women's Club of Winnipeg Web site at <http://www.uwc-wpg.mb.ca/>.

60 Crawford, "Mountain Climbing for Women," 87–89.

61 Research by popular mountaineering historian Chic Scott has established that the claim of the Reverend George B. Kinney to have made the first ascent of Mount Robson in 1909, with outfitter Donald "Curly" Phillips, may be authentic despite having long been considered a hoax. However, as Wheeler, newspaper reports, and the 1913 climbers considered the 1913 climb to be the first ascent, that is how I will refer to it here. See Chic Scott, *Pushing the Limits: The Story of Canadian Mountaineering* (Calgary: Rocky Mountain Books, 2000), 70–82.

62 S. Sarkar et al., "High Altitude Hypoxia: An Intricate Interplay of Oxygen Responsive Macroevents and Micromolecules," *Molecular and Cellular Biochemistry* 253 (2003): 287–305; Michael P. Ward, James S. Milledge, and John B. West, *High Altitude Medicine and Physiology,* 3rd ed. (New York: Oxford University Press, 2000), 33; John B. West, *High Life: A History of High-Altitude Physiology and Medicine* (New York: Oxford University Press, 1998), 92–93, 128–31.

63 Kenneth A. Henderson, *The American Alpine Club's Handbook of American Mountaineering* (Boston: Houghton Mifflin, 1942), 86, 151, 163–64.

64 J. W. A. Hickson, "Psychological Aspects of Mountaineering," *American Alpine Journal* 1 (1931): 262; Charles E. Fay, "The Mountain As An Influence in Modern Life," *Appalachia* (June 1905): 27–40.

65 B. S. Darling, "First attempt on Robson by the West Arete (1913)," Conrad Kain, "The First Ascent of Mt. Robson, The Highest Peak of the Rockies," (translated by Paul A. W. Wallace), and Albert H. MacCarthy and Basil S. Darling, "An Ascent of Mt. Robson from the Southwest (1913)," *CAJ* 6 (1914–15): 29, 28 and 37, respectively.

66 Edward Cavell, *Legacy in Ice: The Vaux Family and the Canadian Alps* (Banff: Whyte Foundation, 1983).

67 WMCR, M200/ AC 27/ 21, Paul A. W. Wallace Personal Papers, letter from A. O. Wheeler to the editor of the *Winnipeg Free Press,* 20 August 1913.

68 BCA, MS-2379, Don and Phyllis Munday Papers, Box 10, File 12, "B.C. Woman First on Mt. Robson," 29 July 1924. This passage was toned down in the published version. See Phyllis Munday, "First Ascent of Mt. Robson By Lady Members," *CAJ* (1924): 68–75. The men in charge of determining who was fit to make the attempt cannot, however, have been unanimous in barring women from the first party. The relevant climbing sheet shows that two women were initially to be allowed, but that decision was apparently reversed, to judge from the fact that the "w," indicating the number of women to be allowed on the attempt, has been scribbled out. See WMCR, M200/ AC 0/ 100A, Climbing Sheets, 1924 Mount

Robson Camp, "July 23rd, 1924, Mt. Robson ... First Party for the High Camp," and "July 25th, 1924, Mt. Robson 2nd Party."

69   See notes 58 and 59.

70   William J. Goode, *The Celebration of Heroes: Prestige as a Social Control System* (Berkeley: University of California Press, 1978) 137, 145.

71   On race, class, and gender as aspects of the same hierarchical systems, see Gerda Lerner, *Why History Matters: Life and Thought* (New York: Oxford University Press, 1997), 131–98.

72   Jones Library (Amherst, MA) Web site at: <http://www.joneslibrary.org/special-collections/collections/stone/fa.htm>; WMCR, *Addresses Delivered at the Memorial Exercises held in Eliza Fowler Hall, Purdue University, October 12, 1921*, n.p., n.d., 70–72.

73   Ibid., Stone, 5.

74   "It is time ... that the younger men should take a hand in the game. The Club is in no position to work entirely upon a commercial basis.... You have all been here long enough to know what leading a rope means, but few take their mountaineering seriously enough to learn to do this, and the enjoyment of those who do is selfishly curtailed by the inertia of the many." WMCR, M200/ AC 41/ 9, ACC Minute Books, "Report of the Secretary-Treasurer [1919]," 147; "Quit yourselves like men, not sluggards. I should like to see ... more of the unselfish enthusiasm of the early Club days. Teaching beginners is not always an unmixed joy, but the rewards are great." M200/ AC 41/ 11, ACC Minute Books, "Letter from S. H. Mitchell [honorary secretary-treasurer 1933]," 60; BCA, MS-677, Frederick V. Longstaff Papers, Vol. 379, File 2, W. R. Tweedy to F. V. Longstaff, 29 May 1934.

75   For example, WMCR, M200/ AC 0/ 99B, Climbing Sheets, 1923 Larch Valley Camp, "Wenkchemna an Opabin Passes with Dr. Cora Best & Mrs. Shippam," 28 July 1923, and "Mt. Odarau [*sic*] from Lake O'Hara, Walter Feuz and Cora J. Best, guides," 4 August 1923; M200/ AC 0/ 102A, 1935 Magog Lake Camp, "July 18/35 (Mountaineering School) ... Guides ... Mr. Dickinson & Dr. [Evelyn] Gee," and "July 24/35 Aurora Creek Camp – climbers only. Party limited to 3 [Eric Bronglo, S.R. Vallance, Emmie A. Brooks], Guide (over and *above* the three) Eric Brooks." For women listed as leaders of mixed climbing parties, see: WMCR, M200/ AC 0/ 100B, Climbing Sheets, 1928 Lake of Hanging Glaciers Camp, "July 22/28 Traverse of Dorma Peak via Starbird Pass, Helen I. Buck, guide ... Party limited to 4 gentlemen and 1 lady [Helen I. Buck]"; M200/ AC 0/ 102B, Fryatt Valley Camp, "July 20/36, Outlier of Mt Fryatt ... Guide Miss L. Gest"; M200/ AC 0/ 103A, 1939 Goodsirs Camp, "July 21/39, Garnet Peak, Guide Mrs. Munday," "July 24/39, Mt. Vaux, [guide] Mrs. Munday," n.d. "Mt. Vaux and Mt. Ennis, [guide] Mrs. Munday."

76   WMCR, M200/ AC 00/ 122, E. O. Wheeler to A. W. Drinnan, 18 August 1933.

77   Kathryn Bridge, *Phyllis Munday, Mountaineer* (Montreal: XYZ Publishing, 2002); Susan Leslie, *In the Western Mountains: Early Mountaineering in British Columbia* (Victoria: Aural History Program of the Provincial Archives of British Columbia, 1980), 49–51; Smith, *Off the Beaten Track*, 189, 196–219; Don Munday, "Apex of the Coast Range," *CAJ* 16 (1926–27): 1–15; "Exploration in the Coast Range," *CAJ* 16 (1926–27): 121–40; and *The Unknown Mountain*, expanded edition (Lake Louise, AB: Coyote Books, 1993).

78 WMCR, M200/ AC 00/ 122, Miscellaneous Club Records; *Constitution and List of Members* 1939, 12–13.

79 WMCR, M200/ AC 00/ 122, Miscellaneous Club Records; *Constitution and List of Members* 1941.

80 Tweedy was secretary-treasurer and camp manager from 1929 to 1942, A. A. McCoubrey, president from 1932 to 1934 and editor of the *CAJ* from 1930 until his death in 1942, and Cyril G. Wates, vice-president from 1926 to 1928 and president from 1938 to 1940. See obituary by E. C. B, "Wharton Richard Tweedy 1889–1965," *CAJ* 48 (1965): 209; obituary by F.N., "Alexander Addison McCoubrey, 1885–1942," *CAJ* 28 (1941): 123; *Constitution and List of Members* 1941.

81 WMCR, M200/ AC 00/ 17, A. A. McCoubrey Executive Papers, A. A. McCoubrey to W. R. Tweedy, 24 January 1934.

82 WMCR, M200/ AC 00/ 18, A. A. McCoubrey Executive Papers, A. A. McCoubrey to W. R. Tweedy, 18 April 1934.

83 Arthur O. Wheeler, "Appreciation," *CAJ* 22 (1933): 230; WMCR, M200/ AC 00/ 19, A. S. Sibbald Executive Papers, A. S. Sibbald to W. R. Tweedy, 21 September 1934.

84 Don Munday documented his and Phyllis's climbs extensively. See, for example, "Apex," and "Exploration"; also "Expedition to Mt. Waddington," *CAJ* 17 (1928): 1–13, and "High Peaks of the Coast Range," *CAJ* 22 (1933): 1–23. See also Karen Routledge, "Shifting Seas of Ice: The Mundays and Mount Waddington, 1926–1934" (master's thesis, Simon Fraser University, 2002).

85 WMCR, M200/ AC 00/ 29, C. G. Wates Executive Papers, memorandum from Cyril G Wates, 6 November 1940.

86 WMCR, M200/ AC 00/ 125, Badge and Silver Rope Applications, "Badges and Ropes Awarded, 1934–43."

87 WMCR, M200/ AC 00/ 29, C. G. Wates Executive Papers, proposal of Polly Prescott's qualifications for the Silver Rope, enclosure with letter from Cyril G. Wates to W. R. Tweedy, 14 November 1940.

88 "The Silver Rope was awarded by unanimous Vote of the Meeting to the following: Mr. John Brett; Mrs. W. A. D. Munday; Mr. Alan Melville; and to Tom Merton." See BCA, MS-2379, Box 9, File 3, Don and Phyllis Munday Papers, ACC Executive Meeting Minutes, 23 July 1948.

89 WMCR, M200/ AC 90/ 22B, S. R. Vallance Executive Papers, S. R. Vallance to D. Munday, 22 October 1948.

seventeen

Lena Hanen and the Conflicts of

Leadership in the Twentieth Century

ELIANE LESLAU SILVERMAN

As Siri Louie's exploration of women's experiences in the Alpine Club of Canada illustrates, opportunities for female leadership in the sport of mountaineering were unofficially constrained by dominant middle-class and British-Canadian ideals of masculinity and femininity. In this article, Eliane Leslau Silverman examines how Lena Hanen, the daughter of Jewish immigrants to western Canada, became a successful businesswoman and leader in the twentieth century. Like many of the contributors to and women discussed in this volume – Sara Riel, Henrietta Muir Edwards, Clare Sheridan, Muriel Stanley

Lena with her parents and siblings. Front row (left to right): Esther (Lena's older sister) and her son Louis, Benjamin (Lena's youngest brother), Rabbi Smolensky (Lena's father); middle row: Noah Gordon (Esther's husband), Jennie Smolensky (Lena's mother), Lena Smolensky; top row: Jack (Lena's middle brother), Dave (Lena's eldest brother). Courtesy: Ayala Manolson.

Venne, Senator Chalifoux, and Dorothy McDonald – Hanen employed various strategies to negotiate a role for herself in the "public" space of business, politics, arts, and letters. Silverman uses oral interviews with friends, relatives, and business associates to construct a narrative of Hanen's life, one that traces how Hanen reconciled post-war ideals of femininity and domesticity with her increasingly active role on the public stage. Like many of the women discussed in this volume, Hanen's life cannot be broken down neatly into private and public spheres of activity: it was the private worlds of family and community that gave her the knowledge and strength to pursue her aspirations in business; paradoxically, they demanded that she sacrifice something of herself along the way. As Silverman argues, Hanen's story reveals tensions and conflicts experienced by women across the generations. She does so within a framework that acknowledges the problems and issues encountered by biographers who seek to "know" a woman's life.

Lena Hanen was a successful Calgary businesswoman whose life story exemplifies the conflicts experienced by women in positions of leadership. Although hers is a mid-twentieth-century story, her biography reveals tensions and conflicts experienced by women, past and present. Although she was autonomous in the world of work, which centered around her women's dress shops, in her private life she denied (or at least minimized) her strength and business acumen. She was born in 1906 and died in 1979; during that time, she moved from being a rabbi's daughter and a businessman's wife to being herself on a public stage. As the owner of a large western chain of women's clothing stores, the Betty Shops, Hanen became a leader to thousands of employees by exemplifying good management, intelligent commerce, and thoughtful employment practices. In her private life, however, she remained reticent: careful not to offend and not too forceful. The tensions and contradictions she experienced – between being a woman and being a businesswoman – provide insights into the difficulties of women's leadership.

Hanen never told her story in her own words; to the contrary, she remained quiet and modest, rarely speaking of herself. Her biography, therefore, can only be reconstructed through public records, like business directories, and through the recollections of the people who knew her.[1] This is only one of the possible narratives about her life; she would tell it differently. We can narrate a story about a woman, Lena Hanen, and a story about a place, Calgary, Alberta, but it is also a story about communities and connections. Lena Hanen's story is a story of a modern woman, rendered in silence and words; it is a story of a person divided, by time and place, between the private and the public realms, and how she created roles for herself in both, as best she could.

Hanen's background is important to the narrative. Her family of birth remained an influence, although one could never imply that she was simply a product of that family. To write that would be to minimize her capacity for self-direction, her determination, and her occasional unconventional behaviours. To some extent, Lena Hanen was a person of her own making, not simply an extension of her parents and her siblings, or

---

1   Interviews with family and friends comprise the major sources for this article. I am grateful to them all. *Henderson's Business Directories* at the Glenbow Archives as well as family papers and holdings of the Calgary Jewish Historical Society were the other resources that allowed me to create both a chronology and a context for Lena Hanen's story.

of the family she and her husband, Sam, made. To a degree, she became the agent of her own life, and a leader of others. However, her background was meaningful to her development: it helped to shape what she would become and provided her with the opportunity to shape herself. Her family communicated the beginnings of an identity and a way of understanding her future experiences.

Hanen learned how to be an observant Jew in the household of Rabbi Smolensky, her father. Lessons in family obligation came early to her, as did lessons in business. Hanen's parents taught her and her siblings at an early age to be out in the world, working in the stores of the extended family. To these experiences and lessons would be added the influence of place – Calgary, the urban frontier of the first quarter of the twentieth century; the influence of economy – the Depression decade of the 1930s, the booms that preceded and followed that decade, and the growing material desires of a thriving society; finally, the influence of ethnicity on members of minority populations. She found in prairie Canada the perfect niche for her women's clothing stores.

Personalities grow out of the interplay between individual experience, family histories, and the historical moment. The Smolenskys arrived in Calgary in 1917. Although they were Jews in a Christian world, they (like the Black pioneer women described by Cheryl Foggo in chapter 14) were able to thrive. There were only nine Jewish families in Calgary in 1905, and three hundred in 1919. By 1943, the Jewish community numbered 1,700; its members were bound together by profound loyalties to neighbour, church, and family. (Lena Hanen's later loyalty to family was legendary as she assiduously maintained family connections through phone calls, letters, and visits.) Calgary's Jews lived near each other and hired each other. Many had doors at the backs of adjoining stores so that family members and neighbours could go back and forth. Calgary likely offered the family community ties, economic prospects, and educational opportunities that were consonant with their expectations. Within the small Jewish community, there were few sharp disparities, and few huge disappointments. The Smolenskys were not overwhelmed by the shock of migration; they adapted to a "frontier" social environment that was constantly evolving.

Their success was influenced by their membership in a Jewish community that had institutions that kept its members together, supported them in their orthodoxy, and provided them with an ideology that did not denigrate worldly success. Culturally, the synagogue was joined by a *mikvah* (a ritual bath), a burial society, a school, a community centre, summer camps, and newspapers. Geographically, Jews maintained their connections by setting up their stores and buying their houses near each other. The bonds of community meant that the cataclysmic events of the twentieth century brought less dissonance to Lena Hanen's life than they did in many others. Immigration could have been disastrous, but was not. Lena Hanen came to adulthood during the good economic times of the 1920s; she was less affected than others were by the bad times of the 1930s. Economic security and predictability blanketed her during childhood. These came from a mother whose attention to domesticity was dictated and sanctioned by her religion, and from a father who was a community leader. Because good times coincided with Hanen's childhood and adolescence, she was liberated psychologically to take considered financial risks in ways that people born in the Depression decade could never do.

Although the rabbi had a strong presence during his daughter's childhood, relatives recall that Hanen's mother, Jennie Smolensky, did "all the doing" in the household – the laundry, the koshering of meat in the basement, certainly the cooking, and the cleaning. It is also possible that she influenced her daughter aesthetically. The extended family usually celebrated Jewish holidays at her house, where her china and glassware was an eclectic collection of bits and pieces that never matched. Despite the Smolensky's visibility in the community, the household apparently did not adopt the aesthetics of the 1920s, '30s, and '40s, which were being taught to Canadian girls and women by magazines and interior decorating manuals. We know that Jews were not exempt from their influences: other sources from the same period in Calgary describe murals and Tiffany lamps in Jewish households. Lena Hanen, by contrast, expressed discomfort at the least, contempt at the most, for extravagant display. As we will see, her own modesty was not dissonant with owning clothing stores for women: The Betty Shops found their perfect prairie niche among modest, not wealthy women whom Hanen had known all her life.

Lena Hanen was the middle of five children, coming after Esther, the "gorgeous" and "sociable" one. Relatives speculate that Hanen learned, from these descriptions of her sister, that she was "not the beautiful one." She seemed to think of herself as being less attractive than other women, even as she believed that attractiveness was superficial. Lena inherited her mother's physical build, which influenced adversely her perceptions of her body. She was not very tall, with large breasts that caused her to have her clothing made to order. In her working life and in her stores, Hanen wore dark suits and blouses, while her accessories were invariably costume jewellery. She was always modest in her personal display. When her husband, in later years, bought her a fur coat, she insisted that he return it because it was too ostentatious for her. Such accoutrements, she said, were only for "fancy ladies," women who dressed excessively well. She was not one of them, she did not respect them, and she thought of them as wasteful and self-centered.

Sadly, we know little about Hanen as a child, probably because, as an adult, she spoke little about herself. People concurred that she was self-effacing at the dinner table; she spoke very quietly and occasionally mumbled when expressing an opinion. "If you can't say something nice about a person, don't say anything at all," seems to have become her trademark. The phrase bespeaks a kindly person, certainly; but also one who avoided conflict and controversy. Perhaps Hanen's thoughts did not conform to the public persona that was later constructed for her, one that she helped to perpetuate. Perhaps her sense of privacy developed unselfconsciously as a necessary protection against the intrusions of a world with limited scripts for women. Perhaps she was critical of her own inner rebellion, remaining quiet, and protective of herself in the face of her own disapprobation. A habit of silence may have been fostered at an early age – we have no idea whether her parents listened to her. We are left to speculate since the boundaries between the self and the world, even the world of the family, were carefully drawn.

We do know that Hanen graduated from Grade 11 in 1923 with average marks and became a teacher one year later. She taught for one or two years (it is not clear) in a rural area that probably lacked basic supplies and teaching materials. Her personal possessions at the time of her death included hand-drawn maps for geography lessons and textbooks that she created herself. Despite these efforts, Hanen's teaching career did not last. Independence eluded her because her father, fearing for her safety, made her come home. She married Sam Hanen in 1926, at the age of twenty.

Friends and relatives recalled the respect this couple had for each other. Both were serious young people who were most likely idealistic about their future together. Sam was handsome, well dressed (he had manicures regularly and wore silk underwear and snappy hats with brims), and filled with a sense of possibilities; she was well-connected, steady, and capable. Seriousness and a respect for others characterized their relationships with business associates, employees, community members, and their children. In addition to recognizing each other's autonomy, they acknowledged each other's capacity to work toward their own, and their children's, futures. As partners in marriage and business, they brought optimism and creative energy to Calgary's growing economy and business community, and raised creative and energetic children. They were part of the process by which Calgary was transformed into a truly urban setting.

For twenty years, Lena and Sam Hanen ran profitable grocery and dry goods businesses together as they raised a family. As was the case in Jewish communities across North America, Lena and the children (male and female) worked in the family stores. Jewish children and women's unpaid labour in family businesses was integral to familial strategies of survival in the early decades of the twentieth century. Women also provided housekeeping services to boarders, worked as domestic servants, and laboured as factory workers in needle trade factories like Great Western Garment in Edmonton. They also produced through reproduction. Lena Hanen herself had three children. At home, she deferred to Sam, which befitted the daughter of a rabbi. Yet, Sam called upon Lena often to advise him on business decisions.

Lena's cooking was dispatched with the expediency necessary to a woman who was out of the house all day. She perfected the art of the pre-set oven timer and the pressure cooker. Although the Hanens had domestic help, Lena made efforts to keep house that were less than successful, according to interviews: puttering in the evenings, picking up a thing, perhaps cleaning it, perhaps leaving it to be finished by the household help. On Sunday mornings, she wandered the house with purpose, yet completed few tasks. She was like a whirlwind set in motion during the week that could not quite stop itself on the weekend. Each Sunday she cooked not one, not two, not three, but four frying pans full of blintzes, using all the burners on the stove like a production line. Although she loved the Calgary Stampede for the opportunity it provided to buy kitchen gadgets, she herself took no great delight in food or fine dinnerware. It was a matter of practicality and principled consistency. Unlike many Calgarian Jews who only kept kosher at home, she also did so when out. Although the Hanens rarely invited people in, the family occasionally held caravan-style, family picnic outings to Banff. In addition, relatives often stayed in the large Hanen house, which served as the site of many weddings and *bar mitzvah* parties. Lena did not cook for these events, however. One of her daughters said that her first priority was business, not a social life.

The couple's labours bore fruit materially when the Hanens moved into a prosperous Calgary neighbourhood in 1941. Contrary to dominant gender conventions, Sam was more interested in decorating than Lena, buying beautiful and expensive furniture. Although Lena bought kitchen gadgets, she maintained her disinterest in material things. For instance, she had her hair coloured and cut at the beauty school near her office, rather than at an expensive salon. Her one weakness was footwear; despite foot trouble, she insisted on wearing dainty shoes.

Six years after the Hanens relocated to a more prosperous area, Lena began to work as "manageress" (as *Henderson's Business Directory* lists her) of Malkin's, a women's clothing store in downtown Calgary. She thus began to write her own script, not in words, but in business endeavours. By 1950, she was listed as "manager" (the owner, actually) of the Betty Shop on 8th Avenue. By the age of forty-four, Hanen had made the transition – in fact, if not yet in name – from manager to sole owner of a dress store. For the remainder of her life, she would continue to open at least one, and sometimes two, stores a year. The act of buying the stores set Hanen apart from generations of Jewish women who worked in family businesses alongside their husbands without legally owning the fruits of their labour. Hanen served a long apprenticeship, but it served her well. Unlike the wives who knew exactly how many cases of soda to order, but whose husbands picked up the phone and did the ordering, she gained control of her own stores. In this control, she was able to express the person she was.

Hanen knew how to run the Betty Shops from the very beginning, having learned from experience. During the Depression and the Second World War, she learned to be creative. Flannelette, the material from which mothers made baby clothes and sheets, was hard to come by during these years. Consequently, Hanen kept track of the dates when women were expecting their babies and doled out flannelette to mothers when they needed it. By keeping their names in a notebook, she kept careful track of customers' needs and idiosyncrasies. Hanen, careful as always, grew the Betty Shops organically; by the time of her death, she had nearly one thousand employees who worked in nearly forty stores in Alberta, British Columbia, and southern Saskatchewan. There were some failures. In 1958, she opened a more expensive, stylish dress shop in downtown Calgary. Decorated by an interior designer, it was perhaps not her style; perhaps it catered to a clientele she considered too frivolous. It closed within the year. In the early 1970s, however, she opened and operated what may have been the first discount warehouse of ladies' wear in the West, drawing on her extensive contacts with eastern manufacturers.

Although managers had a certain control, the Betty Shops remained a one-woman operation. Hanen did the buying, either from salespeople who came west or from wholesalers in Montreal and Toronto. The merchandise was then shipped from the downtown Calgary location to the stores, which inhabited a unique niche in the women's retail clothing market in western Canada. They catered to a faithful clientele that knew it could find sizes in a certain style – not too flashy, not too expensive. Lena Hanen knew her customers well. The stores carried clothing for every occasion, from formal dress to outerwear. In contrast to large, impersonal department stores, customers to the Betty Shops encountered staff that came to know them well and treated them familiarly. The "foundation garments" departments, for instance, were extensive, with professionally trained sales personnel. The shops also carried a wide range of sizes, up to twenty-two, that met the needs of a clientele that ranged in age from eighteen to elderly, and in occupation from working women to the retired. For the most part, clients could expect that the women who waited on them were just like them: not wealthy, not extravagant, but rather solid frugal prairie women, who were themselves often immigrants.

Lena Hanen understood these women in some profound way. She could communicate with them by way of the stores she created, almost as if she were talking with them in a conversation unimpeded by the strictures placed on the rabbi's daughter, the wife, and the mother. In the store, she wrote her own story, one that spoke to unpretentious western women. The shops were a boon to farm women in small prairie towns who could not often get into cities, but were able to buy virtually everything they needed, even wedding dresses, in the Betty Shops. Her stores comprised the kind of self-expression she could value and indulge – unfrivolous, disciplined, and thrifty. They also gave her a setting in which to be both a good and fair employer and a devoted family person.

The Betty Shops were not simply an imitation of the businesses Hanen had come to know (the general and hardware stores), their growth and expansion was studied carefully. One of her relatives recalled that she read business and merchandising journals to improve her practices at a time when other Jewish businessmen were "flying by the seat of their pants." Consequently, she advertised the stores well and innovatively. "The Betty Shop Dance," which consisted of three hours of programming on CFAC TV, amounted to a long commercial. It appealed to a younger clientele, as did several daily five-minute radio spots with "Betty Bishop from the Betty Shops," a spokeswoman who discussed the latest styles. Hanen also joined downtown business organizations, including Toastmistresses, for their networking opportunities.

In the garment factories of the east, Hanen was praised as an astute businesswoman who went through the racks once, offered a price, and never bargained. She trusted store managers but, in the end, it was she who knew the stock, knew the market, knew the trends, knew the employees, the traveling salesmen, the books, and the seasons. To that knowledge and intelligence, she added almost limitless energy, which emerged out of one of her dictums: "Don't ask anybody to do anything you wouldn't do yourself." As a result, she knew every aspect of the stores: the cleaning, the selling, taking inventory, sending out stock, the buying, and the finances. One of her managers commented that it would be an understatement to say that Lena Hanen was on top of her business.

The Betty Shops, however, were also a setting where Hanen could express her devotion to family by employing nieces, granddaughters, and her own children. Virtually anybody in the family looking for work could help at the store (including a family member who worked poorly but received a paycheque for years). Retired family members could also pick up a few hours of pay working in the warehouse. One relative recalled that she worked and visited at the downtown store whenever she liked; she took along a sandwich and stayed as long as she wanted.

Although Hanen welcomed friends and family to her business, she was the boss. She could make her way through any part of the operation and notice staff who were lazy or dishonest; however, she also spoke proudly and approvingly of good staff. She shared her business acumen with anybody who needed to hear it: pay your bills right away; don't go to dinner with the traveling salesmen, because if he or she buys you an expensive meal you'll feel indebted; do your work before everything else; always keep a bank account in your own name because all women should have one; don't be afraid of innovations; "A woman should always have a car of her own so she can be independent." Acting on her own advice, Hanen bought each of her granddaughters a car on their sixteenth birthday.

Former employees and managers commented on her honesty with them, which was high praise in what they called a "dog-eat-dog business." They also recalled that she was thoughtful. For instance, Hanen arranged for the women who worked nights at the warehouse in stock control to have a taxi ride home so they would not have to walk through downtown to the bus stop. When she arrived at the opening of a new store, she introduced herself to the clerks and spoke quietly with them. Apparently, she never raised her voice or took over conversations; she allowed everyone to have his or her say. Finally, she mentored other women in the ways of business, quietly loaning them money and offering them advice. Not all managers, however, had completely positive memories of Hanen. One, who had a staff of five, felt that she ran the store on her own. There may have been a bit of resentment in her voice when she recalled that Hanen would come in without calling ahead. She did concede, however, that Hanen was "wonderful to work for."

Joan McCredie, who managed two large Betty Shops in the latter years (Southcentre and Chinook in Calgary), provides further insights into Hanen's business habits. Her story deserves telling, too, because it is a prairie narrative about another western woman who understood what other women needed. In 1943, McCredie's mother, using a tiny amount of start-up money, opened a dress store in Whitewood, Saskatchewan. At the time, silk stockings and lingerie were unavailable because of the war. In addition, traveling salespersons did not come through with samples. McCredie filled the vacuum by driving to the cities to buy materials from warehouses there. She then opened another store in Grenfell with her sister. Later, this sister opened a store of her own. These dress shops opened a new world for women in villages so small that the only shopping they could do was through the Sears catalogue. The dress shops offered women the chance to meet each other in women's stores, just like in the cities. Obviously energetic, McCredie's mother was also unconventional: she drove a car, wore slacks, and smoked cigarettes. As a child, Joan wondered why she could not have a mother like all the others; later, she became extremely proud of her.

Joan McCredie began working in retail stores at age thirteen. By 1950, she was married and working full time for $21 a week, nine to six every day, six days a week. By the time she became a manager for the Betty Shops, she had worked in and managed a variety of stores. When the controller of the Betty Shops called McCredie in 1973 to see if she would be interested in managing their new High River store, she had nine children; the youngest was ten. McCredie oversaw the construction and establishment of the High River Betty Shop, which was the twenty-third of the chain. Hanen told her that she trusted her to make decisions about things like display space and fitting room design. McCredie and the builder, however, often went to Calgary to consult with Hanen or to pick up supplies. McCredie recalled that they would meet Hanen at the warehouse, where she would ask questions like: Can you use this coffee can full of nails?; or, in reference to a broken mirror, "Do you think you can use that if you cut it down?"

Lena Hanen was always careful and thrifty. She did not have fire insurance, because the rates were too high. She kept stock in the basement, whether it would sell or not. And, for her precision, she became known as a "great" and a "shrewd" "businesswoman." Her capacity for mastering details was renowned, and the salespeople respected her for it. A few commented, "Wasn't she a gem!" or "Wasn't she a great gal!" Hanen likely would have relished McCredie's assessment of her as "the kindest woman I've had association with."

After Sam's death in 1972, Hanen's stoicism continued unabated. To her, the characteristic was a virtue: she had always impressed on others how important it was to avoid unnecessary emotional displays. Apparently, she never expressed anger. Most interviews commented on her restraint, her stoicism, and her tolerance. For instance, Hanen advised a niece – whose mother was in hospital, strapped to a chair – to avoid crying or showing emotion: "You have to get control." She followed this advice in her own life. Following Sam's death, his clothing stayed in the closet and Hanen changed nothing in the house. She talked about him often: "If Sam were here today...." Still, she carried on her family life and her shops almost as before, in the same dignified way. Hanen herself had many health problems later in life: she had shingles, *phlebitis*, bladder problems, high blood pressure, potassium deficiency, headaches, and, ultimately, a stroke. She dealt with these travails often by medicating herself with non-prescription drugs to treat the symptoms and falling back on her silent ways when she had a migraine.

Hanen's first stroke in 1977 caused partial paralysis in one arm. Although she became more dependent upon others for her physical needs, she remained very much the boss of the stores. When her staff held a birthday party for her at the Palliser Hotel in Calgary, she sat at the head table and talked with people, even though she was physically incapable of eating much. After another stroke, Hanen's legs became

Lena and Sam Hanen on the occasion of their 35th wedding anniversary, c. 1967. Courtesy Ayala Manolson.

paralyzed. She recovered slowly, showing almost childish delight in being able to wiggle her toes. She evinced pleasure in other physical realities: she loved the sun and lay appreciatively in patches of sunlight. In this, she manifested paradoxically more sensual pleasure than in her earlier years: she loved the rainbows cast by the bevelled glass of the windows, she was pleased by the soft blanket on the day bed, and she laughed at Jewish jokes.

But she was still disciplined. A niece who was working eighteen hours a day asked Lena, who was hospitalized, if she should come to see her right away. Lena answered, "Finish your work, and then come to the hospital."

And she was ambitious. It may be difficult in our day to associate that word with so mild-mannered a person, yet Lena Hanen pursued her aspirations single-mindedly. She did not neglect her family obligations (far from it), but she did not allow them to distract her from attending to her stores. Her stores were the vehicle that allowed her to form a self that belonged to herself. In them, she found an acceptable realm to express herself, one that built upon the time-honoured tradition of Jewish seamstresses, Jewish wives working in family stores, and Jewish daughters working in factories. She used her early exposure to business, combined it with her experience in retail sales, and added her own intelligence and creativity. The relational skills she had learned as a woman, combined with her respect for the integrity of other people, allowed her to run a respectful and successful organization. Her own self-respect, which was a realistic recognition of her unusual capacities, caused her to share her knowledge and experience with those who asked for it.

Clearly, Lena Hanen was determined to succeed. Her progression from one store to forty stores did not happen by chance. Her discipline and knowledge derived from observation, thoughtfulness, and listening to the needs of clients and suppliers. In no way did any of these contravene her commitment to "the good of the family." She was able to maintain a balance between an autonomous sense of herself – a voice of her own – and her connections to others because her voice was her stores. The business enterprise was consonant with other parts of her life. Her personal story was told in silence; it was a narrative constructed within the constraints of a society that did not allow women a public voice. Hanen kept her own counsel in order to avoid the conflicts of leadership that were particular to women, and to protect herself, by concealing her drive, her energy, and her ambition. The conflicts of leadership embodied the classic creative tensions between love and work. Lena Hanen found her own balance. Hers is the story, and the dilemma, of a modern woman and a modern leader.

eighteen

They Called Her Chief: A Tribute to Fort MacKay's

Indomitable Leader, Dorothy McDonald[1]

CORA J. VOYAGEUR

As the contributors to Part 1 illustrate, women's historic role as community builders and cultural mediators in western Canada was complicated and shaped by the race, class, and gender hierarchies that accompanied the construction of White settler colonies in the region. In this article, sociologist Cora Voyageur recounts how one Aboriginal woman navigated these constraints, and the region's colonial legacies, in order to assume a leadership role in the latter half of the twentieth century. Voyageur outlines the trials and

1 This article appeared previously in *Legacy: Alberta's Cultural Magazine* 7 (Winter 2002): 14–17.

tribulations of Dorothy McDonald, who, in 1980, became the first female chief of the Fort MacKay First Nation in northern Alberta. Like other women chiefs and elders across Canada, McDonald dedicated her tenure to preserving the "old ways" and the land, both of which were threatened by northern resource extraction and industrial development. McDonald's environmentalism brought her, however, into conflict with logging companies and the oil industry. While writers and researchers across the disciplines have, in recent years, drawn attention to the media and the law as sites that created and reproduced race and hierarchy in White settler societies, Voyageur highlights how McDonald skillfully used these two mediums to protest the hazardous activities of oil and logging companies that were threatening the safety and health of her First Nation. Like Sara Riel, Clare Sheridan, Henrietta Muir Edwards, and Lena Hanen, McDonald's faith and religion gave her the strength to navigate and negotiate the constraints that are placed upon Indigenous peoples and women (from diverse cultural communities) in colonial and postcolonial societies.

I admired her from afar. She was a dedicated, gutsy, straight-talking leader who took unpopular stands on controversial issues. She cared about the land when many others did not. She is a First Nations woman who would not be bullied – not by industry, not by government, and not by local politics. The object of my admiration is former chief of the Fort MacKay First Nation, Dorothy McDonald.

McDonald was the first woman to lead her First Nation. As chief, she followed in the footsteps of women like Martha Gladue of the Beaver Lake First Nation (near Lac La Biche in central Alberta) and Teresa Gadwa of the Kehewin First Nation (located by the Saskatchewan/Alberta border near Bonnyville), who first took up the mantle of Indian band leadership in the 1960s. At times during her tenure, McDonald was the lone female chief of Alberta's then forty-two First Nations.

I had the pleasure of interviewing the former chief of the Fort MacKay First Nation as part of my research into women leaders in Canada's First Nations community. My study examines the experiences of female Indian chiefs and other women in leadership positions as they negotiate their multiple roles as women, mothers, administrators, mediators, liaisons, community representatives, and decision-makers. My research findings show that life for women chiefs is not easy.

In Canada, First Nations people live under the Indian Act – an archaic piece of legislation developed shortly after Confederation that governs virtually every aspect of First Nations' lives. Among its paternalistic and patriarchal rules, this legislation deemed that only Indian men could be chief. However, 1951 Indian Act changes meant that Indian women were finally allowed to hold the office of chief. Elsie Knott, of Curve Lake, Ontario, made history by becoming Canada's first woman chief one year later. Since the 1990s, there has been a significant increase in the number of women chiefs across the country. According to the Assembly of First Nations, the national political organization representing 625 First Nations, currently 90, or about 15 per cent of the Indian Chiefs in Canada are women. Although the number of women chiefs increased over the years, the number is still slightly lower than females' 18 per cent representation in provincial politics, but on par with female representation in federal politics.

The community Dorothy McDonald led, the Fort MacKay First Nation, is located in the vast Treaty 8 territory. In the 1899 agreement, First Nations people surrendered a tract of land three-quarters the size of the province of Ontario to Queen Victoria's representatives. This resource-rich treaty area stretches across parts of the western provinces and the Northwest Territories and contains resources including tar sands, natural gas, oil, and diamonds. The presence of oil in the sand in this region was long known. Even early Canadian explorer Alexander Mackenzie's 1793 writings mention tar and oil oozing from the banks of Athabasca River. These tar sands would cause a whirlwind of change for the Indigenous peoples living on the banks of this same river some 170 years later.

McDonald was the fifth child of ten children born to Phillip and Victoria McDonald in the 1940s. Her childhood summers were spent at a fishing camp (located on the future Great Canadian Oil Sands site), where her family and other community members would fish, hunt, and pick berries. She remembers, "There was an abundance of ducks, fish, and moose. The [Athabasca River] water was clear and the air was fresh. When we rode a boat to McMurray, you could practically see the river bottom because the water was so clear." This was when McDonald developed her strong commitment to protecting the environment – a commitment she keeps to this day.

Her isolated community, Fort MacKay (named after an early Hudson's Bay Company employee), is located 65 kilometres north of Fort McMurray and did not have an all-weather road until the late 1960s. Prior to the road, the trek to Fort McMurray involved a four-hour boat ride down the river in the summer. In winter, community members travelled an ice-road after hailing taxis from Fort McMurray using the community's only telephone – a mobile telephone located in Fort MacKay's Hudson's Bay store.

McDonald spent her early years in Fort MacKay, where she attended the Fort MacKay Indian Day School until halfway through Grade 8. At fourteen, both she and her sister Elsie contracted tuberculosis and were placed in the Charles Camsell Indian Hospital in Edmonton. It was her first experience of a community larger than Fort McMurray, whose residents numbered approximately 1,200 at the time. Although they were away from their family, the sisters had each other and were able to make friends with the many Indian patients who had also contracted the disease. "There were only Indians in the Camsell. Most of us had TB. We were all there together," she recalls. During the girls' year-long stay, their father and brothers visited them. After release from the hospital, Dorothy boarded with a family in Edmonton and completed a high school diploma at St. Joseph's High School. She later attended Alberta Vocational College at Grouard. She was away from her community for a decade.

Life in Fort MacKay had changed drastically in her absence. Prior to major development in the region, Fort MacKay First Nation members lived a traditional life and earned their living primarily by trapping, hunting, and gathering, but some were also engaged in seasonal wage labour. The village was now connected to the outside world by an all-weather road. This road took community people to Fort McMurray and beyond with greater ease, but it also brought industry and people to Fort MacKay and to McDonald's doorstep.

McDonald comes from a lineage of leadership, like most of the sixty women chiefs who participated in my research project. Whereas her father, Phillip McDonald, was a hereditary chief who led his community for more than twenty-five years, she was elected for four terms. Dorothy loved and admired her father for his integrity and his concern for his community. She recalls, "He worked hard for our community, but government was not listening." During her tenure, she witnessed the fruition of environmental and community changes that had begun during her father's term.

First elected in 1980 after working as a band manager for the 450-member First Nation in northeastern Alberta, she recalls, "I used to help my dad with his correspondence and letters that he used to get from the government. It was hard for him, because he did not read English all that well. He used to read the dictionary to try to learn better English." Her move into leadership after her father's death seemed a natural thing for her to do. It was like continuing the family business.

Remembering when she began as chief, McDonald says, "There was so much to do. Our community had changed so much in such a short time. The people were not prepared to deal with the changes that come with industry – the increased traffic, the logging trucks, the noise, and the pollution." She felt it was her duty to look out for the best interests of her community to ensure that environmental concerns were addressed by industry. This sometimes made her a thorn in the side of industry.

McDonald used her position of chief to protect the land. She called for environmental assessments of new development projects and challenged the Energy Resources Conservation Board decisions on future resource development. For example, in June 1981 the Fort MacKay band fought a proposed road being built for drilling access north of the community. Road construction was halted. A year later, the band intervened in the planned expansion of Suncor operations and brought the First Nations' voice to the forefront with government and industry. Her leadership and her commitment to the environment caused her to be featured in a Health and Welfare Canada production *Many Branches* in the early 1990s.

While chief, McDonald tried to preserve culture by documenting the "old ways" through a series of interviews with community elders. They expressed sadness about the loss of the traditional livelihood and felt the environment should be preserved. "Change happened so quickly. The environment was being polluted and people were not able to hunt and fish as they used to. The fish were not fit to eat and the animals were all gone." A *Fort McMurray Today* article of the day supports this assertion by reporting that a warning against eating fish from the Athabasca River was in effect. McDonald's commitment to the environment was cemented when she witnessed polluted water that had a "red tinge to it, and river water turning black."

McDonald implemented a three-pronged initiative to help her community control its future. Her goals included: protection of traditional lifestyles for hunters and trappers, establishment of an economic base to move the community away from dependence on the Department of Indian Affairs, and opening better employment and training opportunities for community members. She achieved all of these goals during her tenure. Under her guidance, the community obtained much-needed infrastructure that had been unavailable to the band during her father's term. A band office, a nursing station, a fire hall, a fire truck, and a community hall were all part of McDonald's legacy. She was astute and able to capitalize on funding opportunities to move the community forward. She also established the Fort MacKay Group of Companies – six businesses that contract their services to the resource sector and now generate millions of dollars for the Fort MacKay First Nation. She negotiated employment opportunities for band members with companies working in the region and helped win one displaced trapper $50,000 compensation when his trapline was lost to a Syncrude lease. Although she felt satisfied with that particular case, she still laments that many other traplines were simply taken up by development while the owners were never compensated.

McDonald helped establish the Fort MacKay Interface Committee that brought ministers, deputy ministers, vice-presidents of the oil companies, and the Fort MacKay Band administrators together to discuss issues concerning government, industry, and the Fort MacKay people. Strategies to deal with employment, social programs, and environmental concerns resulted from those meetings.

McDonald was skillful at furthering her people's cause in the media. This was never more evident than when she and her band members set up a roadblock to protest logging trucks hauling through their community. Under her leadership, Fort MacKay members halted logging operations north of their community. The roadblock story occupied the front page of the *Fort McMurray Today* newspaper until the situation was resolved six days later. McDonald remembers, "it was a safety issue. Those trucks were driving right down the middle of our community. On the same road that kids walked to school on. I tried to talk to the owner of the logging company, but he just brushed me off. The roadblock got his attention." The blockade got everyone's attention including the media, the government, and some angry Fort McMurray citizens. Protesters received regular visits from the local RCMP. McDonald and others faced charges of obstructing a highway, with a maximum penalty of $500 and a six-month prison sentence. None of the protesters were charged. Truckers angry over lost wages wanted to sue her and the band – none did. A settlement was negotiated between the loggers, the government, and the Fort MacKay band, which included pilot cars escorting the logging trucks through the community and a reduced speed limit.

In 1982, McDonald personally brought five charges against the neighbouring Suncor oil sands plant while the Attorney General later added an additional fifteen charges under the Fisheries Act and the Clean Water Act. The company had been spilling oil, grease, and chemicals into the Athabasca River. They did not inform the government of the spill and did not inform the Fort MacKay band members who had been taking their water from the river. Newspaper accounts tell of the plant discharging fifty times the allowable limit of effluent into the river. The following year a provincial court judge found the company guilty of violating the Fisheries Act while charges under the Clean Water Act were dismissed. They received an $8,000 fine.

In 1999, McDonald was honoured by her community when the Fort MacKay First Nations' adult education centre was renamed the Dorothy McDonald Learning Centre. The learning centre, a satellite campus from Keyano College in Fort McMurray, provides adult upgrading and other educational programs. Her name continues to be recognized by many in this area for her contributions to First Nations people and for environmental stewardship.

Although her health has declined, McDonald still has a sharp mind, a magnificent memory, and an infectious laugh. Currently living in Fort McMurray with her husband, children, and grandchildren, she gladly shares her expertise and experiences with others.

When I asked McDonald about her legacy, she responded, "I tried my best when I was chief, but there are still so many things left undone. You cannot take things away from people's lives – like the land and the culture – without leaving a gap. Some of those people are really hurt, and the community must heal." However, she is optimistic about the community. "The community is in transition. There is always hope and a light at the end of the tunnel. I am confident that with the Creator's help the community can come through this rough time."

McDonald believes that people need to nurture mind, body, and spirit. She remarks, "First Nations people embody the spirit of the land.... Without our spirit we are nothing."

nineteen

Conclusion: Unsettled Futures:

Will Our Stories Be Forgotten?

ELIANE LESLAU SILVERMAN

When Eliane Leslau Silverman published The Last Best West: Women on the Alberta Frontier, 1880–1930 *in 1984, she influenced a generation of scholars who sought to reconceive the West by bringing to light women's individual and collective stories. Based on interviews and oral histories, the book celebrated the diversity of women's experiences in the region; it provided a perspective on the past from the back door or kitchen window. Since then, Silverman's interdisciplinary work has evolved to include adolescent girls, women and language, women and power, health issues, and material culture.*

Prior to her retirement in 2001, Eliane Silverman spent nearly twenty-five years at the University of Calgary where her scholarship and activism were supported by her lifelong commitment to feminism and her love for her daughters: she coordinated the Women's Studies program, advised the president on women's issues, and taught in the Faculty of General Studies. At the national level, Silverman served as director of research at Canadian Advisory Council on the Status of Women and as president of the Canadian Research Institute for the Advancement of Women. When she took the podium as the guest of honour at the "Unsettled Pasts" conference, however, Silverman chose to discuss her experiences as an activist in Calgary's local women's movement, where she was instrumental in founding status of women committees and abortion facilities. She disclosed the experiences of a generation of feminists, activists, and leaders whose stories and struggles rarely find their way into narratives of Canada's modern women's movement. Given the modern political climate, Silverman fears that these stories run the risk of being forgotten.

The banquet at which I spoke the following words was a beautiful event, notable for the presence of women of all ages, some the writers of our history and others the actors in it. It was notable for the level of laughter and enthusiasm, and for the palpable sense of relief that women's history of the western United States and Canada had achieved this outstanding moment. For me, one of the most touching moments of the evening came when I was given a corsage of roses by Pat Roome with a tentative explanation: we debated whether we should give you this, and some of the organizing committee thought yes, and others thought not, so I hope you don't mind! In my mind, I replayed countless feminist actions and activities at which we debated every point: should we or shouldn't we? The moment spoke to me of the attention to detail we have had to provide, sometimes to distraction; yet, we have been able to be attentive and still not lose sight of what we have been doing for over thirty years.

The evening was beautiful – friends and colleagues, wine, the play by Nancy Millar – and exciting for me because it provided the opportunity to say these few words on a subject that has long been on my mind. I began my talk with some words about how I came to collecting women's stories; how it was funded initially by a government ministry called Alberta Culture, which authentically believed that women's stories were worth telling and preserving, and the resistance I also experienced. But not from women who had stories to tell.

I had a secret weapon in my professional career. It was called Feminist Women of Calgary! More than my university colleagues, they became my support, my friends, my intellectual and activist companions. We found each other – different ages, religions, professions, ethnicities – we worked together, we made things happen. I believe we did this in much the same way as women in Alberta have always done: they find a problem, they seek ways to solve it, they sometimes succeed and sometimes fail, but they keep on working, agitating, acting. We too were powerfully propelled in our intellectual inquiry and our urgent need for changes for women.

And yet, the story of feminism in Calgary has barely been told. Will it be forgotten? The great and yet homely tradition of women's activism in Alberta from the early twentieth century was, until recently, virtually invisible, with the exception of those women who could be depicted as icons. Will the enormous and truly noble efforts of so many of our contemporaries in Calgary remain equally unknown?

I am worried. In recent books on women's equality-seeking movements in Canada, be they history, journalism, or political science, Calgary barely ever shows up. I wonder why this is so. It is surely not because Calgary's feminists have been quiet or laid low or daunted. They have followed in the path of early feminists, outspoken, bold, and accomplished, but many of you may not know that. They have seen the needs of women around them and have offered their best creativity and fervour to serve them. And yet, not unlike the story of the West in general, the experiences of Calgary's feminists do not appear on a national scholarly or journalistic agenda. You may not know about how much has happened here.

I want to tell you just a bit about our history here in Calgary. There have been successes, but also, of course, failures. Indeed, as is true in our individual biographies, our activist histories must be traced as much by false starts, errors, and meanderings, as by goals achieved. How many great ideas have we had that were never followed up? How many opportunities were lost, political errors made, feelings hurt? Those stories need telling too. But this was an evening of celebration of past and present, honouring the stories of great women who sought to make great changes. I hope that the books we write about the last thirty years of feminist history make room, a lot of it, for Calgary's feminisms.

Let me offer you a few of the stories. I begin in 1970 with the founding of the Calgary Abortion Information Centre. We were about ten

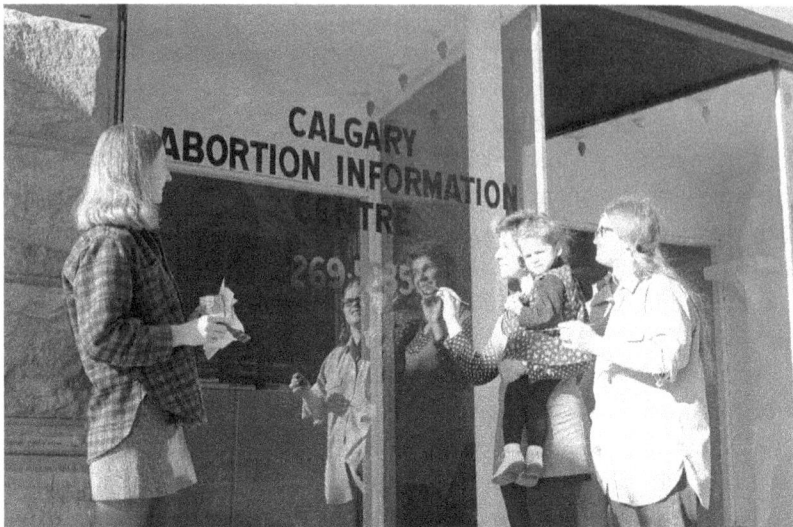

Finishing touches are applied to the window lettering of the Calgary Abortion Information Centre, November 1970. *L-R*: Heather Travers, Eliane Silverman with Monique Silverman (age 2), Linda Morill, with brushes. Glenbow Archives NA-2864-6833.

women, none of us at first known to each other, called together by an ad in the newspaper. We quickly became close friends, largely by telling each other our own stories. In response to the 1969 changes to the Criminal Code, our mission was to help women find the doctors (and the psychiatrists) who would, according to the law, approve and "allow" them to have the abortions that they had decided upon. We created a list of doctors, interviewing each of them in the city to determine which ones were amenable (some easily and others with specific criteria for the client) to performing abortions without humiliating their patients. To women who sought our services, we provided referrals and information about the procedure, as it was then. We listened to their stories. We also spoke in public settings – schools, clubs, medical associations, the medical school – to convey the narratives, making individual, legal, and cultural stories come together.

In our first two years, we became aware of the myths and lies about contraception; we then became a resource for women on the subject – methods, failure rates, pleasure, and aesthetics. We offered brochures

A police officer demonstrates a rape whistle at a Rape Crisis Centre meeting, Calgary, November 1977. Glenbow Archives NA-2864-17715.

and the best information we could, all the while cognizant of our mission – informed choice for women. Now called the Calgary Birth Control Association, members have discussed the use of the word "feminist" in the organization's publications, but ultimately retained it. The organization today has enlarged its vision from sexuality to include anti-racism and anti-homophobia education too. Nearly thirty-five years later, the organization is vibrant and responsive to new realities.

The Rape Crisis Centre followed in the early 1970s, at a time when the myths about sexual assault held that women enjoyed it, or were asking for it, or only got what they deserved. Similar jeering followed the establishment, a few years later, of the Women's Emergency Shelter. Women who were battered by their male partners must have been causing trouble. I need hardly elaborate that discussion, except to remind you that one of the earliest studies of wife battering had been a master's thesis in the Faculty of Social Work at the University of Calgary. The author, Kathy Sloman, reported on the bedroom community of Airdrie, and found that the rates of wife abuse were 18 per cent, about the same figure as people report today. The *Calgary Herald* editorial almost mocked her findings: that couldn't happen in our nice rural towns!

Another first: the first conference in the country on women and sport, in itself an important occasion made even better when the participants stormed the men's sauna at the University of Calgary gym wearing only towels. There was no women's sauna; they made their point dramatically! I believe that the first conference on pornography also took place in Calgary. One meeting room at the Palliser Hotel contained the first images of violent, woman-hating pornography that many of us had ever seen; it effectively addressed arguments that *Playboy Magazine* was all in good fun. We came to understand the range and the intensity of misogyny, its murderous rage.

We also organized one of the first Women's Studies symposia in the country. We were still groping for how to write women's stories from the inside out; and quickly we learned to do so, aided by our guest, the historian Jill Conway, who simply advised us, indeed berated us, to "Listen to women's stories. Stop listening to what men say about women." The Women's Centre on the University of Calgary campus was another setting that, hard fought for as it was, recognized that psychological and intellectual safety in dedicated women's spaces may be essential for women to talk openly. *Plus ça change, plus c'est la même chose*: the Centre's space was reduced from a decent office, to virtually a broom closet, then to a space too distant from the center of the campus; it now no longer exists. The struggle to re-open it continues.

Another early conference: "Women and the Law in the early '80s" was sponsored by the Faculty of Law at the University of Calgary. These conferences all offered radical new ways of thinking about issues, so that one could never again take anything for granted. And the Faculty of Law itself has been an example of academic feminism: its first dean, John McLaren, determined that fully half its staff would be women. They include outspoken feminist professors whose work influences students and shapes issues for the national legal community.

Calgary feminists have acknowledged women's activities as praiseworthy in a number of ways. An early organization, the Calgary Housewives Association, created by a handful of energetic young women, believed that raising children actually mattered, and they wanted to say so loudly. Similarly, the very first "Women Celebrate Women" event in the country took place in Calgary: It was sponsored by the YWCA and organized by active and visible feminists. In its first few years, the emphasis of the awards dinner was always on women who either dedicated their paid work and volunteer activism to the benefit of women, or who overcame the difficulties that face women every day. "Women Celebrate Women" lauded single mothers, welfare recipients, women working in feminist partnerships with other women, immigrant women, and educators who struggled in their various institutions for the lives of girls and women. In this tone, the event went on for ten years, until "achievement" and its benefits became more valued than "getting by," which is most women's lives. The first event was glorious. After the planning committee thought they might sell a hundred tickets, or perhaps two hundred, they made a huge leap of faith and booked the hotel for eight hundred! The temerity! Those tickets sold out quickly, and they had the hotel manager put an extra seat at each table: nine hundred women. "But that's more than the Premier's Dinner," he exclaimed. The entertainment included Margaret Atwood reading, Sylvia Tyson singing, and The Nellie McClung Players from Winnipeg. The evening went on until one o'clock in the morning; nobody wanted to leave.

People also came in huge numbers to Judy Chicago's exhibit, "The Dinner Party," at the Glenbow Museum. Dozens of women made that show happen, despite the reluctance of the museum. They raised funds, donated time, and made the arrangements for the massive exhibit. It drew the museum's largest attendance to that date. People came from all over the western states and provinces to see the beauty of the needlework and the power of the message about women hidden from history. Not any more! This conference, "Unsettled Pasts," was another proof of women's visibility to history, another affirmation of women's lives.

So many endeavours by women to celebrate, from the University Women's Club presentation in 1967, to the Royal Commission on the Status of Women. Irene Murdoch's dedication to the cause of divorcing women's rights, especially farm women. The establishment of the first provincial chapter, after its Toronto beginnings, of the Women's Legal Education and Action Fund, or LEAF, by Calgary women, in recognition of the legal work we would be doing for years to come. The presence of lesbian bars, from the 1950s on, in an unwelcoming city, which evinced lesbian women's knowledge that they needed places of their own. The organizations to help immigrant women in many ways – to establish their professional credentials, for instance, or to find housing or culturally sensitive medical care, or to provide them clothing for job interviews; such creativity in seeing issues and problems and seeking solutions. The Native Women's Shelter, which acknowledged the different needs of diverse populations. The Calgary chapter of the National Council of Jewish Women, which provided comfortable settings for women to learn how to become leaders. The new outdoor sculpture, which celebrated the girls and women who sold eggs to make a bit of extra money, acknowledged a different kind of frontier, one Betsy Jameson calls a "butter" frontier.

All these and countless more. But let me conclude with an allusion to the Famous Five Foundation, whose members literally put women downtown by commissioning and ultimately finding a space for commemoration of Alberta's Famous Five, the women who in 1929 went to the Privy Council in London to have women declared "persons." The sculpture is exuberant, larger than life. The Five are having tea, rejoicing in their victory as one of them holds aloft the *Edmonton Journal* front page. There is one empty chair, for us today to sit and join them in their celebration. It was a struggle – despite the money having been raised – to convince City Council to agree to a visible spot downtown, in Olympic Plaza, for the sculpture. However, there it is. Its unveiling was a fabulous event, celebrated by young people and adults alike, crowding the whole plaza, eager to hear the governor general, Adrienne Clarkson, and local women on a beautiful October day in 1999. Clarkson was in Calgary also to give out the Famous Five awards to five feminist activists. She strode into the ballroom of the Palliser Hotel, the very place where in the 1920s the first feminists gathered, seemingly innocuous, having tea, and began her speech with arms upraised and generous, addressing "Women!"

What a note to end on! I beg you, I beseech you, not to forget Calgary women of the last forty years – the feminists, the groups they started, the stories they tell, the connections they maintain among each other, their struggles and their victories in an especially hostile cultural climate. Can this be partly the reason for their solidarity? Perhaps. My mother, a feminist activist in California, often thought so. She used to marvel when she came to visit at how connected we all were with each other. As the culture becomes – we hope – more generous to women, we will tell other kinds of stories. No part of the narrative was or will be static; one event led to another, one part of a group might break away to form another, or another two. Meanwhile, tell the stories of western women, here in Calgary, to everyone you know. If their stories disappear, we face an unsettled future.

contributors

Kristin Burnett is a doctoral candidate in history at York University. Her dissertation research examines the health care work undertaken by Aboriginal and non-Aboriginal women in southern Alberta First Nations communities from 1880 to 1930.

Cristine Georgina Bye is a history Ph.D. candidate at the University of Calgary. She received the Governor General's Gold Medal for her master's thesis, "'Times are Hard': A Saskatchewan Farm Woman's Experience of the Great Depression." Her book on her great-grandmother, Kate Graves, is forthcoming.

Sarah Carter has taught Canadian history at the University of Calgary since 1992. Her books include *Capturing Women: The Manipulation of Cultural Imagery in Canada's Prairie West*; *Aboriginal People and Colonizers of Western Canada*; and the co-authored book, *The True Spirit and Original Intent of Treaty 7*, with Treaty 7 Elders and Tribal Council, Dorothy First Rider, and Walter Hildebrandt. In 2006 she will join the University of Alberta as H.M. Tory Chair in the Department of History and Classics, and School of Native Studies.

Mary Leah de Zwart holds a Ph.D. in Curriculum Studies. She has taught pre-service teachers at the University of British Columbia and at Okanagan University College in Kelowna and is presently teaching at Queen Elizabeth Secondary School in Surrey. Her research interests include women's history and the metaphoric application of theory to practice.

Lesley A. Erickson holds a Ph.D. in history from the University of Calgary. She is interested in the diversity of women's experiences in the North American west and is completing a manuscript entitled *Westward Bound: Gender, Criminal Courts, and the Creation of a White Settler Society, 1886–1940*. Her interest in gender, law, and moral regulation now extends to an examination of suicidal behaviour and its treatment during the colonization and settlement of the Prairie provinces and British Columbia.

Cheryl Foggo, a descendant of the Black Oklahomans who settled in Alberta and Saskatchewan in 1910, was born in Calgary. She studied journalism in Calgary. She is a prominent writer of fiction, non-fiction, poetry, plays, and screenplays for television and film.

Nadine I. Kozak is a Ph.D. candidate in Communication and Science Studies at the University of California, San Diego. Her research interests include the political economy of communication and the social history of communication and household technologies. A native Albertan, Nadine is also interested in the history of the Canadian prairies.

Siri Louie received her master's degree in 1996 from the University of Calgary and is currently a Ph.D. candidate in history at the University of Toronto. She lives in Boston.

Graham A. MacDonald has worked as a teacher, librarian, public historian, and heritage consultant. His writings concern the history of the fur trade and Native peoples. He is also interested in nineteenth- and twentieth-century British and European political philosophy. He currently lives in Victoria, British Columbia.

Florence Melchior holds a doctoral degree in nursing from the University of Calgary and is currently an instructor for the collaborative University of Calgary Nursing Program at Medicine Hat College. While her doctoral research examined the history of nursing education, student labour, and patient care in Alberta, her instructional focus is community and rural nursing.

Patricia Roome teaches Canadian history and women's studies at Mount Royal College in Calgary, Alberta. She served as a member of the organizing committee for the 2002 "Unsettled Pasts" Conference. An earlier version of her essay appeared in Valeria Gennaro Lerda and Roberto Maccarini, eds., *Oltre l'Atlantico. Ruoli di donne nelle societa del Canada e delle Americhe/Beyond the Atlantic: Women's Roles in Canadian and American Societies* (Milano: Selene Edizioni, 2004). She also recently published a biographical study of Alexander Cameron Rutherford in *Alberta Premiers of the Twentieth Century*, edited by Bradford J. Rennie.

Eliane Leslau Silverman is Professor Emeritus of Women's Studies at University of Calgary. Her children, her writing, her teaching, and her activism have informed her life and work, all meaningful as feminist. Today she lives at Salt Spring Island where she quilts, gardens organically, entertains friends, and swims daily in the ocean in a wet suit. Her latest book is called *Treasures: The Stories Women Tell About the Things They Keep.*

Charleen Smith completed a master's degree at the University of Calgary with a focus on women's legal history. Her research used a regionally based case-study approach to examine late-nineteenth to early-twentieth-century prostitution in British Columbia. She is currently co-owner of a historical research consulting firm focusing on women's and First Nations research and litigation management.

The late *Olive Fimrite Stickney* was the first woman in Alberta elected to a rural municipal council. She was elected to the County of Grande Prairie Council in 1966, and dedicated herself to the development of rural Alberta by promoting better health and social services, higher education, and housing for senior citizens.

Aritha Van Herk is the author of eight novels and works of creative non-fiction, most recently the novel *Restlessness* and the irreverent but relevant *Mavericks: An Incorrigible History of Alberta*, which won the Grant MacEwan Author's Award. She is University Professor and Professor of English at the University of Calgary. She is an avid reader and follower of contemporary culture and she is working on two books about melancholia and laundry.

Muriel Stanley Venne was the first Métis woman appointed to the Alberta Human Rights Commission in the 1970s and she has since championed human rights and the advancement of Aboriginal women. In 1998, she received the Alberta Human Rights Award and, in 2004, the National Aboriginal Achievement Award for Justice. She is president and founder of the Institute for the Advancement of Aboriginal Women, which honours and advocates on behalf of Aboriginal women.

Cora J. Voyageur is an associate professor in the Sociology Department at the University of Calgary. Her research focuses on the Aboriginal experience in Canada: women's issues, politics, employment, media, and economic development. She has conducted extensive community-initiated research with many First Nations and Aboriginal organizations and is currently completing a manuscript on female Indian chiefs in Canada.

bibliography

Abeele, Cynthia. "'The Infant Soldier': The Great War and the Campaign for Child Welfare." *Canadian Bulletin of Medical History* 5, no. 2 (1988): 99–119.

Ahenakew, Freda, and H.C. Wolfart, eds. and trans. *Kohkominawak Otacimowiniwawa: Our Grandmothers' Lives as Told in Their Own Words.* Saskatoon: Fifth House, 1992.

Alcock, F. J. *A Century in the History of the Geological Survey of Canada.* Ottawa: King's Printer, 1947.

Alston, Margaret. "Women and their Work on Australian Farms." *Rural Sociology* 60 (Fall 1995): 521–32.

———. *Women on the Land: The Hidden Heart of Rural Australia.* Kensington, NSW, Australia: UNSW Press, 1995.

Anderson, Benedict. *Imagined Communities: Reflections on the Origin and Spread of Nationalism.* London and New York: Verso, 1991.

Anderson, Frank, W. *Frontier Guide to Calgary to Medicine Hat.* Calgary: Frontier Publishing, 1970.

Anderson, Karen. *Chain Her by One Foot: The Subjugation of Women in Seventeenth-Century New France.* New York: Routledge, 1991.

Antonelli, Marylu, and Jack Forbes. *Pottery in Alberta: The Long Tradition.* Edmonton: University of Alberta Press, 1978.

Apple, Rima D. *Mothers and Medicine: A Social History of Infant Feeding, 1890–1950.* Madison: University of Wisconsin Press, 1987.

Armstrong, Pat, and Hugh Armstrong. *The Double Ghetto: Canadian Women and Their Segregated Work.* Toronto: McClelland and Stewart, 1984.

Arnup, K. *Education for Motherhood: Advice for Mothers in Twentieth-Century Canada.* Toronto: University of Toronto Press, 1994.

Bacchi, Carol Lee. *Liberation Deferred? The Ideas of the English-Canadian Suffragists, 1877–1918.* Toronto: University of Toronto Press, 1983.

Backhouse, Constance. *Colour-Coded: A Legal History of Racism in Canada, 1900–1950.* Toronto: University of Toronto Press, 1999.

———. *Petticoats and Prejudice: Women and Law in Nineteenth-Century Canada.* Toronto: Women's Press, 1991.

Baillargeon, Denyse. *Making Do: Women, Family and Home in Montreal during the Great Depression,* trans. Yvonne Klein. Waterloo: Wilfrid Laurier University Press, 1999.

Banks, Annie. "Jessie Donaldson Schutlz and Blackfeet Crafts." *Montana: The Magazine of Western History* 33 (1983): 18–25.

Barbour, Sarah. "Diverse Patterns of Relationalities: Expanding Theories of Women's Personal Narratives." *National Women's Studies Association Journal* 14, no. 2 (2002): 181–91.

Barclay, George. "Grey Nuns Voyage to Red River." *The Beaver* outfit 297 (Winter 1966): 15–18.

Barman, Jean. "Separate and Unequal: The Indian and White Girls at All Hallows School, 1884–1920." In *Rethinking Canada: The Promise of Women's History,* ed. Veronica Strong-Boag and Anita Clair Fellman, 11–27. Toronto: Copp Clark Pitman, 1991.

———. "Taming Aboriginal Sexuality: Gender, Power and Race in BC, 1895–1900." *BC Studies* 115–16 (Fall-Winter 1997–8): 237–66.

Beal, Bob, and Rod Macleod. *Prairie Fire: The 1885 North West Rebellion.* Edmonton: Hurtig, 1984.

Bell, Quentin. *Bloomsbury,* 2nd ed. London: Phoenix/Giant, 1986.

Bennett, John W. *Northern Plainsmen: Adaptive Strategy and Agrarian Life.* Chicago: Aldine Publishing, 1969.

Bennett, John W., with Seena B. Kohl and Geraldine Binion. *Of Time and the Enterprise: North American Farm Management in a Context of Resource Marginality.* Minneapolis: University of Minnesota Press, 1982.

Benoit, Barbara. "The Mission at Île-à-la-Crosse." *The Beaver* (Winter 1980): 40–50.

Bhabba, Homi. "Of Mimicry and Man: The Ambivalence of Colonial Discourse." In *Tensions of Empire: Colonial Discourse in a Bourgeois World,* ed. Frederick Cooper and Ann Laura Stoler, 152–60. Berkeley: University of California Press, 1997.

Birchall, Dianna. *Onoto Watanna: The Story of Winnifred Eaton.* Chicago: University of Illinois Press, 2001.

Boivin, Michelle. "Farm Women: Obtaining Legal and Economic Recognition of Their Work." In *Growing Strong: Women in Agriculture,* ed. Diane Morissette, 49–90. Ottawa: Canadian Advisory Council on the Status of Women, 1987.

Bonvillain, Nancy. "Gender Relations in Native North America." *American Indian Culture and Research Journal* 13, no. 2 (1989): 1–28.

Boschma, Geertje. "High Ideals versus Harsh Reality: A Historical Analysis of Mental Health Nursing in Dutch Asylums, 1890–1920." *Nursing History Review* 7 (1999): 127–51.

Boulton, Marjorie. *Zamenhof: Creator of Esperanto*. London: Routledge and Kegan Paul, 1960.

Bramadat, Ina J., and Marion I. Saydak. "Nursing on the Canadian Prairies, 1900–1930: Effects of Immigration." *Nursing History Review* 1, no. 1 (1993): 105–17.

Brandon, Piers. *Winston Churchill: A Brief Life*. Toronto: Stoddart, 1984.

Brandt, Gail Cuthbert. "Postmodern Patchwork: Some Recent Trends in the Writing of Women's History in Canada." *Canadian Historical Review* 72 (December 1991): 441–70.

Brewer, Aileen Mary. *Nuns and the Education of American Catholic Women, 1860–1920*. Chicago: Loyola University Press, 1987.

Bridge, Kathryn. *Phyllis Munday, Mountaineer*. Montreal: XYZ Publishing, 2002.

Bright, David. "'Go Home. Straighten Up. Live Decent Lives': Female Vagrancy and Social Respectability in Alberta." *Prairie Forum* 28 (Fall 2003): 161–72.

Britnell, G.E. *The Wheat Economy*. Toronto: University of Toronto Press, 1939.

Brooks, William Howard. "Methodism in the Canadian West in the Nineteenth Century." Ph.D. diss., University of Manitoba, 1972.

Brouwer, Ruth Compton. *New Women for God: Canadian Presbyterian Women and Indian Missions, 1876–1914*. Toronto: University of Toronto Press, 1990.

———. "Transcending the 'unacknowledged quarantine': Putting Religion into English-Canadian Women's History." *Journal of Canadian Studies* 27 (Autumn 1992): 47–61.

Brown, Jennifer S. H. "Métis, Halfbreeds, and Other Real People: Challenging Cultures and Categories." *The History Teacher* 27 (November 1993): 19–26.

Brownlie, Robin, and Mary-Ellen Kelm. "'Desperately Seeking Absolution': Native Agency as Colonialist Alibi?" *Canadian Historical Review* 75 (1994): 543–56.

Buckley, Suzann. "Efforts to Reduce Infant and Maternal Mortality in Canada between the Two World Wars." *Atlantis* 2 (Spring 1977): 76–84.

Burnet, Jean. *Next-Year Country: A Study of Rural Social Organization in Alberta*. Toronto: University of Toronto Press, 1951.

Burstyn, Varda. *The Rites of Men: Manhood, Politics, and the Culture of Sport*. Toronto: University of Toronto Press, 1999.

Burton, Antoinette. *Burdens of History: British Feminists, Indian Women, and Imperial Culture*. Chapel Hill: University of North Carolina Press, 1994.

———. "Thinking Beyond the Boundaries: Empire, Feminism, and the Domains of History." *Social History* 26 (January 2001): 60–71.

———. "The White Woman's Burden: British Feminists and the Indian Woman, 1865–1915." In *Western Women and Imperialism: Complicity and Resistance*, ed. Nupur Chaudhuri and Margaret Strobel, 137–57. Bloomington: Indiana University Press, 1992.

———. ed. *Gender, Sexuality and Colonial Modernities*. London and New York: Routledge, 1999.

Buss, Helen. *Mapping Our Selves: Canadian Women's Autobiography*. Montreal and Kingston: McGill-Queen's University Press, 1992.

Bye, Cristine Georgina. "'Times are Hard': A Saskatchewan Farm Woman's Experience of the Great Depression." Master's thesis, University of Calgary, 2001.

Cahn, Susan K. *Coming on Strong: Gender and Sexuality in Twentieth-Century Women's Sport*. New York: Free Press, 1994.

Cairns, Kathleen, and Eliane Leslau Silverman. *Treasures: The Stories Women Tell About the Things They Keep.* Calgary: University of Calgary Press, 2004.

Carter, Sarah. *Aboriginal Peoples and the Colonizers of Western Canada to 1900.* Toronto: University of Toronto Press, 1999.

———. "Categories and Terrains of Exclusion: Constructing the 'Indian Woman' in the Early Settlement Era in Western Canada." *Great Plains Quarterly* 13 (Summer 1993): 47–61.

———. *Capturing Women: The Manipulation of Cultural Imagery in Canada's Prairie West.* Montreal and Kingston: McGill-Queen's University Press, 1997.

———. "First Nations Women and Colonization on the Canadian Prairies, 1870–1920," In *Rethinking Canada: The Promise of Women's History,* 4th ed., ed. Veronica Strong-Boag, Mona Gleason, and Adele Perry, 135–48. Don Mills, ON: Oxford University Press, 2002.

———. "First Nations Women of Prairie Canada in the Early Reserve Years, the 1870s to the 1920s: A Preliminary Inquiry." In *Women of the First Nations: Power, Wisdom and Strength,* ed. Christine Miller and Patricia Chuchryk, with Marie Smallface Marule, Brenda Manyfingers, and Cherly Deering, 51–76. Winnipeg: University of Manitoba Press, 1996.

———. *Lost Harvests: Prairie Indian Reserve Farmers and Government Policy.* Montreal and Kingston: McGill-Queen's University Press, 1990.

———. "Man's Mission of Subjugation: The Publications of John Maclean, John McDougall and Egerton R. Young, Nineteenth-Century Methodist Missionaries in Western Canada." Master's thesis, University of Saskatchewan, 1981.

———. "The Missionaries' Indian: The Publications of John McDougall, John Maclean and Egerton Ryerson Young." *Prairie Forum* 9 (1984): 24–44.

———. "Transnational Perspectives on the History of Great Plains Women: Gender, Race, Nations, and the Forty-ninth Parallel." *American Review of Canadian Studies* 33 (Winter 2003): 565–96.

———. "The Woman's Sphere: Domestic Life at Riel House and Dalnavert." *Manitoba History* 11 (1986): 55–61.

Cashman, Anthony T. *Heritage of Service: The History of Nursing in Alberta.* Edmonton: Alberta Association of Registered Nurses, 1966.

Cavanaugh, Catherine A. "Irene Marryat Parlby: An 'Imperial Daughter' in the Canadian West, 1896–1934." In *Telling Tales: Essays in Women's History,* ed. Catherine A. Cavanaugh and Randi R. Warne, 100–122. Vancouver: UBC Press, 1990.

———. "The Limitations of the Pioneering Partnership: The Alberta Campaign for Homestead Dower, 1909–25." *Canadian Historical Review* 74 (June 1993): 198–225.

———. "'No Place for a Woman': Engendering Western Canadian Settlement." *Western Historical Quarterly* 28 (Winter 1997): 493–518.

Cavanaugh, Catherine A., and Randi R. Warne, eds. *Standing on New Ground: Women in Alberta.* Edmonton: University of Alberta Press, 1993.

———. *Telling Tales: Essays in Western Women's History.* Vancouver: UBC Press, 2000.

Cavell, Edward. *Legacy in Ice: The Vaux Family and the Canadian Alps.* Banff: Whyte Foundation, 1983.

Cebotarev, E.A. (Nora). "From Domesticity to the Public Sphere: Farm Women, 1945–86." In *A Diversity of Women: Ontario, 1945–1980*, ed. Joy Parr, 200–231. Toronto: University of Toronto Press, 1995.

Chapman, Terry L. "Sex Crimes in the West, 1890–1920." *Alberta History* 35 (Autumn 1987): 6–21.

———. "'Till Death do us Part': Wife Beating in Alberta, 1905–1920." *Alberta History* 36 (Autumn 1988): 13–22.

Chaput, Donald. "The 'Misses Nolin' of Red River." *The Beaver* (Winter 1975): 14–17.

Chartrand, Paul. "'Terms of Division': Problems of 'Outside-Naming' for Aboriginal People in Canada." *Journal of Indigenous Studies* 2 (Summer 1991): 1–22.

Choquette, Robert. *The Oblate Assault on Canada's Northwest*. Ottawa: University of Ottawa Press, 1995.

Christie, Nancy. *Engendering the State: Family, Work and Welfare in Canada*. Toronto: University of Toronto Press, 2000.

———. ed. *Households of Faith: Family, Gender, and Community in Canada, 1760–1969*. Montreal and Kingston: McGill-Queen's University Press, 2001.

Clancy-Smith, Julie Ann, and Frances Gouda, eds. *Domesticating the Empire: Race, Gender, and Family Life in French and Dutch Colonialism*. Charlottesville: University of Virginia Press, 1998.

Clark, Brian P. "The Parish and the Hearth: Women's Confraternities and the Devotional Revolution among the Irish Catholics of Toronto, 1850–1885." In *Age of Transition: Readings in Canadian Social History, 1800–1900*, ed. Norman Knowles, 357–69. Toronto: Harcourt Brace, 1998.

Clarke, Ronald W. *Men, Myths and Mountains: The Life and Times of Mountaineering*. New York: Thomas Y. Crowell, 1976.

Cohen, Marjorie Griffin. *Women's Work, Markets, and Economic Development in Nineteenth-Century Ontario*. Toronto: University of Toronto Press, 1988.

Cole, Catherine C., and Judy Larmour. *Many and Remarkable: The Story of the Alberta Women's Institutes*. Edmonton: Alberta Women's Institutes, 1997.

Cole, Douglas. *Captured Heritage: The Scramble for Northwest Coast Artifacts*. Seattle: University of Washington Press, 1985.

Cole, Douglas, and Bradley Lockner, eds. *The Journals of George M. Dawson: British Columbia, 1875–1878*. 2 vols. Vancouver: UBC Press, 1989.

Coleman, Daniel, and Donald Goellnicht. "Introduction: 'Race' into the Twenty-First Century." *Essays on Canadian Writing* 74 (Winter 2002): 1–29.

Comacchio, Cynthia R. "'A Postscript for Father': Defining a New Fatherhood in Interwar Canada." *The Canadian Historical Review* 78 (September 1997): 385–408.

———. "Bringing Up Father: Defining a Modern Canadian Fatherhood, 1900–1940." In *Family Matters: Papers in Post-Confederation Canadian Family History*, ed. Lori Chambers and Edgar-Andre Montigny, 289–308. Toronto: Canadian Scholars' Press, 1998.

———. *The Infinite Bonds of Family: Domesticity in Canada, 1850–1940*. Toronto: University of Toronto Press, 1999.

———. *"Nations are Built of Babies": Saving Ontario's Mothers and Children, 1900–1940*. Montreal and Kingston: McGill-Queen's University Press, 1993.

Comaroff, Jean and John. *Of Revelation and Revolution: Christianity, Colonialism and Consciousness in South Africa*. Vol. 1. Chicago: University of Chicago Press, 1991.

Conrad, Margaret. "'Sundays Always Make Me Think of Home': Time and Place in Canadian Women's History." In *Rethinking Canada: The Promise of Women's History*, ed. Veronica Strong-Boag and Anita Clair Fellman, 2nd ed., 97–112. Toronto: Copp Clark Pitman, 1991.

Cooper, Barbara J. "The Convent: An Option for Québécoises, 1930–1950." *Canadian Women Studies* 7 (Winter 1986): 31–34.

Cott, Nancy F. *The Grounding of Modern Feminism*. New Haven: Yale University Press, 1987.

———. *Public Vows: A History of Marriage and the Nation*. Cambridge: Harvard University Press, 2000.

Cotter, Colleen. "Claiming a Piece of the Pie: How the Language of Recipes Defines Community." *Recipes for Reading: Community Cookbooks, Stories, Histories*, ed. A. Bower, 51–71. Amherst: University of Massachusetts Press, 1997.

Coulter, Harris. *Divided Legacy*. Berkeley: North Atlantic, 1975.

Craig, Béatrice. "Families, Inheritance and Property Transmission in Rural Central Canada in the Nineteenth and Early Twentieth Centuries." In *Family Matters: Papers in Post-Confederation Canadian Family History*, ed. Lori Chambers and Edgar-Andre Montigny, 159–75. Toronto: Canadian Scholars' Press, 1998.

Creese, Gillian, and Veronica Strong-Boag, eds. *British Columbia Reconsidered: Essays on Women*. Vancouver: Press Gang Publishers, 1992.

Culbertson, Debbie. "The other vote goes to the sister." *Beaver: Exploring Canada's History* 83 (December 2002): 28–34.

Danbom, David B. "'Cast Down Your Bucket Where You Are': Professional Historians and Local History." *South Dakota History* 33 (Fall 2003): 263–73.

D'Antonio, Patricia. "Revisiting and Rewriting and Rethinking the History of Nursing." *Bulletin of the History of Medicine* 73, no. 2 (1999): 268–90.

Danylewycz, Marta. *Taking the Veil: An Alternative to Marriage, Motherhood, and Spinsterhood in Quebec, 1840–1920*. Toronto: McClelland and Stewart, 1987.

da Silva, Rachel et al. "A Brief History of Women Climbing in the Coast and Cascade Ranges." In *Leading Out: Women Climbers Reaching for the Top*, ed. da Silva, 68–107. Seattle: Seal Press, 1992.

Davies, Celia. *Rewriting Nursing History*. London: Croom Helm, 1980.

Davin, Anna. "Imperialism and Motherhood." *History Workshop Journal* 5 (1978): 9–65.

Davis, Faye. *Legal, Economic and Social Concerns of Saskatchewan Farm Women*. Saskatoon: Saskatoon Branch, Women's Legal Education Action Fund, 1989.

Dawson, C.A., and Eva R. Younge. *Pioneering in the Prairie Provinces: The Social Side of the Settlement Process*. Canadian Frontiers of Settlement, 8th vol. Toronto: Macmillan Canada, 1940.

De Brou, David, and Aileen Moffatt, eds. *"Other" Voices: Historical Essays on Saskatchewan Women*. Regina: Canadian Plains Research Center, 1995.

DeMallie, Raymond J. "Kinship: The Foundation for Native American Society." In *Studying Native America: Problems and Prospects*, ed. Russell Thorton, 306–56. Madison: University of Wisconsin Press, 1998.

de Moissac, Elizabeth, s.g.m. "La femme de l'Ouest: Leur rôle dans le histoire." Master's thesis, University of Ottawa, 1945.

———. "Les Soeurs Grises et les événements de 1869–70." La Société Canadiene d'Histoire de l'Église Catholique, *Sessions d'Étude* (1970): 215–28.

de Zwart, Mary Leah. "Home Economics Education in British Columbia 1913–1936: Through Postcolonial Eyes." Ph.D. diss., University of British Columbia, 2003.

———. "Jessie McLenaghen." In *The Homeroom: British Columbia's History of Education Web Site*, ed. Patrick A. Dunae, [online]. Nanaimo, BC: Malaspina University College, 2001: <http://www.mala.bc.ca/homeroom/Content/Topics/People/Jessie.htm> (30 May 2002).

———. "Past Roots: Annie B. Juniper." *Canadian Home Economics Journal* 48, no. 3 (1998): 101.

Dempsey, Hugh. *The Gentle Persuader: A Biography of James Gladstone Indian Senator.* Saskatoon: Western Prairie Producer, 1986.

———. *Indian Tribes of Alberta.* Calgary: Glenbow Museum, 1979.

———. *Tailfeathers: Indian Artist.* Calgary: Glenbow-Alberta Institute, 1970.

Denault, Bernard, and Benoit Levesque. *Eléments pour une sociologie des communautés religieuses au Québec.* Montreal: Les Presses de l'Université de Montréal, 1975.

Devens, Carol. *Countering-Colonization: Native American Women and Great Lakes Missions, 1630–1900.* Berkeley: University of California Press, 1992.

Dickason, Olive Patricia. *Canada's First Nations: A History of Founding Peoples from Earliest Times.* Toronto: Oxford University Press, 1997.

Dirk, Marcel M. C. *Caps, Bibs and Aprons: Memoirs of Medicine Hat General Hospital School of Nursing.* Medicine Hat: Modern Press, 1996.

———. *A Healthy Outlook: The Centennial History of the Medicine Hat Regional Hospital.* Medicine Hat: Holmes Printing, 1989.

Dobbin, L. L. *A History of the Assiniboine Indian Reserve, Sintaluta, Saskatchewan: 1877–1940.* Regina: Legislative Library, Archives Division, 1963.

Dodd, Dianne. "Advice to Parents: The Blue Books, Helen MacMurchy, M.D., and the Federal Department of Health, 1920–1934." *Canadian Bulletin of Medical History* 8, no. 2 (1991): 203–30.

Dorsch, Julie. "'You Just Did What Had to be Done': Life Histories of Four Saskatchewan 'Farmers' Wives.'" In *"Other" Voices: Historical Essays on Saskatchewan Women,* ed. David De Brou and Aileen Moffatt, 116–30. Regina: Canadian Plains Research Center, 1995.

Dranoff, Linda Silver. *Women in Canadian Law.* Toronto: Fitzhenry and Whiteside, 1977.

Dubinsky, Karen, and Lynne Marks. "Beyond Purity: A Response to Sangster," *Left History* 3 (Fall/Spring 1995/6): 205–20.

Duchaussois, P., o.m.i. *The Grey Nuns in the Far North, 1867–1917.* Toronto: McClelland and Stewart, 1919.

Dugas, G. "Établissement des Soeurs de Charité à la Rivière Rouge." *Revue Canadienne* (1890), 20–27 and (1891), 719–25.

Dumont-Johnson, Micheline. "Une perspective féministe dans l'histoire des congregations de femmes." *Études d'histoire religieuse* (1990): 29–35.

Elbert, Sarah. "Women and Farming: Changing Structures, Changing Roles." In *Women and Farming: Changing Roles, Changing Structures,* ed. Wava G. Haney and Jane B. Knowles, 245–64. Boulder and London: Westview Press, 1988.

Elias, Peter Douglas. *The Dakota of the Canadian Northwest: Lessons for Survival.* Winnipeg: University of Manitoba Press, 1988.

Emberley, Julia V. "The Bourgeois Family, Aboriginal Women, and Colonial Governance in Canada: A Study in Feminist Historical and Cultural Materialism." *Signs: Journal of Women in Culture and Society* 27, no. 1 (2001): 59–85.

Emery, George Neil. "Methodism on the Canadian Prairies, 1896–1914: The Dynamic of an Institution in a New Environment." Ph.D. diss., University of British Columbia, 1970.

Emmerich, Lisa E. "Marguerite LaFleshe Diddock, Office of Indian Affairs Field Matron." *Great Plains Quarterly* 13 (1993): 162–71.

Ens, Gerhard J. *Homeland to Hinterland: The Changing Worlds of the Red River Metis in the Nineteenth Century.* Toronto: University of Toronto Press, 1996.

Epp, Marlene, Franca Iacovetta, and Frances Swyripa, eds. *Sisters or Strangers? Immigrant, Ethnic, and Racialized Women in Canadian History.* Toronto: University of Toronto Press, 2004.

Erickson, Lesley. "At the Cultural and Religious Crossroads: Sara Riel and the Grey Nuns in the Canadian Northwest, 1848–1883." Master's thesis, University of Calgary, 1997.

———. "'A Very Garden of the Lord'? Hired Hands, Farm Women, and Sex Crime Prosecutions on the Prairies, 1914–1929." *Journal of the Canadian Historical Association*, new series 12 (2001): 115–35.

———. "The Unsettling West: Gender, Crime, and Culture on the Canadian Prairies, 1886–1940." Ph.D. diss., University of Calgary, 2003.

Etulain, Richard W. "Meeting Places, Intersections, Crossroads, and Borders: Toward a Complex Western Cultural History." *Historian* 66 (Fall 2004): 509–16.

Evans, Julie, et al. *Equal Subjects, Unequal Rights: Indigenous Peoples in British Settler Colonies, 1830–1910.* Manchester: Manchester University Press, 2003.

Ewers, John C. "Winold Reiss: His Portraits and Protégés." *Montana: The Magazine of Western History* 21 (1971): 44–55.

Fiamengo, Janice. "A Legacy of Ambivalence: Responses to Nellie McClung." In *Rethinking Canada: The Promise of Women's History*, 4th ed., ed. Veronica Strong-Boag, Mona Gleason, and Adele Perry, 149–63. Don Mills, ON: Oxford University Press, 2002.

———. "Rediscovering Our Foremothers Again: The Racial Ideas of Canada's Early Feminists, 1885–1945." *Essays on Canadian Writing* 75 (Winter 2002): 86–117.

Fink, Deborah. *Agrarian Women: Wives and Mothers in Rural Nebraska, 1880–1940.* Chapel Hill and London: University of North Carolina Press 1992.

———. *Open Country, Iowa: Rural Women, Tradition and Change.* Albany: State University of New York Press, 1986.

———. "Sidelines and Moral Capital: Women on Nebraska Farms in the 1930s." In *Women and Farming: Changing Roles, Changing Structures*, ed. Wava G. Haney and Jane B. Knowles, 55–70. Boulder and London: Westview Press, 1988.

Fink, Deborah, and Dorothy Schwieder. "Iowa Farm Women in the 1930s: A Reassessment." *Annals of Iowa* 49 (1989): 570–90.

Fiske, Jo-Anne. "By, For, or About? Shifting Directions in the Representations of Aboriginal Women." *Atlantis* 25 (Fall/Winter 2000): 11–27.

Flanagan, Thomas. *Louis "David" Riel: Prophet of the New World.* Halifax: Goodread Biographies, 1983.

————. "Louis Riel's Religious Beliefs: A Letter to Bishop Taché." *Saskatchewan History* 27 (1974): 15–28.

Flora, Cornelia Butler, and Jan L. Flora. "Structure of Agriculture and Women's Culture in the Great Plains." *Great Plains Quarterly* 8 (Fall 1988): 195–205.

Flynn, Kara. "Bridging the Gap: Women's Studies, Women's History, Gender History, and Lost Subjects." *Atlantis* 25 (Fall 2000): 130–32.

Foggo, Cheryl. "Black Faces in Unexpected Places: The Unfolding Story of Alberta's Black Pioneers." *Legacy: Alberta's Heritage Magazine* 7 (Winter 2002): 6–9.

Forget, Henriette. "Indian Women of the Western Provinces." In *Women of Canada: Their Life and Work,* compiled by the National Council of Women of Canada, 435–37. Ottawa: Government of Canada, 1900.

Foster, John E. "The Métis: The People and the Term." *Prairie Forum* 3 (March 1978): 79–90.

Foster, Henry H. "Indian and Common Law Marriages." *American Indian Law Review* 3 (1975): 83–102.

Fowke, Vernon C. *The National Policy and the Wheat Economy.* Toronto: University of Toronto Press, 1957.

————. *Rural Roads and Local Government: A Summary.* Saskatchewan Royal Commission on Agriculture and Rural Life. Regina: Queen's Printer, 1956.

Francis, Daniel. *Copying People: Photographing British Columbia's First Nations, 1860– 1940.* Saskatoon and Calgary: Fifth House, 1996.

————. *The Imaginary Indian: The Image of the Indian in Canadian Culture.* Vancouver: Arsenal Pulp Press, 1992.

Francis, Douglas R., and Howard Palmer. *The Prairie West: Historical Readings.* 2nd ed. Edmonton: Pica Pica Press, University of Alberta Press, 1992.

Francis, Douglas, Richard Jones, and Donald B. Smith. *Destinies: Canadian History since Confederation.* Toronto: Harcourt Brace, 1992.

Frankenberg, Ruth. *White Women, Race Matters: The Social Construction of Whiteness.* Minneapolis: University of Minnesota Press, 1993.

Fraser, Esther. *Wheeler.* Banff: Summerthought, 1978.

Frewen, Mary. *Catherine's Ring: A Romance of Brickwall House.* Seaview: Angel Design, 1995.

Frewen, Moreton. *Melton Mowbray and Other Memories.* London: Herbert Jenkins, 1924.

Friedberger, Mark. "The Farm Family and the Inheritance Process: Evidence from the Corn Belt, 1870–1950." *Agricultural History* 57 (October 1983): 1–13.

Friesen, Gerald. *The Canadian Prairies: A History.* Toronto: University of Toronto Press, 1987.

————. "Defining the Prairies: or, Why the Prairies Don't Exist." In *Toward Defining the Prairies: Region, Culture, and History,* ed. Robert Wardhaugh, 13–28. Winnipeg: University of Manitoba Press, 2001.

Gagan, Rosemary. *A Sensitive Independence: Canadian Methodist Missionaries in Canada and the Orient, 1881–1925.* Montreal and Kingston: McGill-Queen's University Press, 1992.

Gagnon, Anne. "The Pensionnat Assomption: Religious Nationalism in a Franco-Albertan Boarding School for Girls, 1926–1960." *Historical Studies in Education* 1 (Spring 1989): 95–117.

Gaitskell, Deborah. "At home with hegemony? Coercion and consent in African girls' education for domesticity in South Africa before 1910." In *Contesting Colonial Hegemony: State and Society in Africa and India*, ed. D. Engels and S. Marks, 110–28. London: British Academic Press, 1994.

Gerson, Carol. "Nobler Savages: Representations of Native Women in the Writings of Susanna Moodie and Catherine Parr Traill." In *Rethinking Canada: The Promise of Women's History*, 4th ed., ed. Veronica Strong-Boag, Mona Gleason, and Adele Perry, 75–86. Don Mills, ON: Oxford University Press, 2002.

Gertler, Michael, JoAnn Jaffe, and Lenore Swystun. "The Old Same Place? Gender Relations on Cooperative and Conventional Farms in Saskatchewan." *Prairie Forum* 29 (Fall 2004): 253–77.

Getty, A. L. "The Failure of the Native Church Policy of the CMS in the North-West." In *Religion and Society in the Prairie West*, ed. Richard Allen, 19–34. Regina: Canadian Plains Research Center, 1974.

Ghorayshi, Parvin. "The Indispensable Nature of Wives' Work for the Farm Family Enterprise." *Canadian Review of Sociology and Anthropology* 26 (1989): 571–95.

Gleason, Mona. *Normalizing the Ideal: Psychology, Schooling, and the Family in Postwar Canada*. Toronto: University of Toronto Press, 1999.

Glenbow Museum. *Reclaiming History: Ledger Drawings by the Assiniboine Artist Hongeeyeesa*. Calgary: Glenbow, 1993.

Gluck, Sherna Berger, and Daphne Patai. *Women's Words: The Feminist Practice of Oral History*. New York and London: Routledge, 1991.

Goode, William J. *The Celebration of Heroes: Prestige as a Social Control System*. Berkeley: University of California Press, 1978.

Gorham, Deborah. "From Bonavista to Vancouver Island: Canadian Women's History as Regional History in the 1990s." *Acadiensis* 28 (Spring 1999): 119–25.

Gosman, Robert. *The Riel and Lagimodière Families in Métis Society, 1840–1860*. Ottawa: Parks Canada, manuscript no. 171, 1977.

Gould, Ed. *All Hell for a Basement: Medicine Hat, 1883–1983*. Medicine Hat: Friesen Printers, 1981.

Goyette, Linda. "Heritage to the Next Generation: Linda Goyette Searches for Missing Stories." *Legacy: Alberta's Heritage Magazine* 7 (Winter 2002): 38–40.

Grant, John Webster. *A Profusion of Spires: Religion in Nineteenth Century Ontario*. Toronto: University of Toronto Press, 1988.

———. *Moon of Wintertime: Missionaries and the Indians of Canada in Encounter Since 1534*. Toronto: University of Toronto Press, 1984.

Grant, Julia. *Raising Baby by the Book: The Education of American Mothers*. New Haven, CT: Yale University Press, 1998.

Gray, James H. *Men against the Desert*. Saskatoon: Western Producer Prairie Books, 1980.

Green, Rayna. "The Pocahontas Perplex: The Image of Indian Women in American Culture." In *Unequal Sisters: A Multicultural Reader in U.S. Women's History*, ed. Ellen Carol DuBois and Vicki L. Ruiz, 15–21. New York: Routledge, 1990.

Greenwell, Kim. "'Picturing Civilization': Missionary Narratives on the Margins of Mimicry." *BC Studies*, no. 135 (Autumn 2002): 3–45.

Griffiths, Alison, and Gerry Wingenbach. *Mountain Climbing Guides in Canada: The Early Years*. Ottawa: Parks Canada, 1977.

Griffiths, Naomi. *The Splendid Vision: Centennial History of the National Council of Women of Canada 1893–1993*. Ottawa: Carleton University Press, 1993.

Groover Lape, Noreen. "'I Would Rather Be with My People, but Not to Live as They Live': Cultural Liminality and Double Consciousness in Sarah Winnemucca Hopkins's *Life Among the Piutes: Their Wrongs and Claims*." *American Indian Quarterly* 22 (1998): 259–79.

Gross, Stephen John. "Handing Down the Farm: Values, Strategies, and Outcomes in Inheritance Practices among Rural German Americans." *Journal of Family History* 21 (April 1996): 192–217.

Group, Thetis M., and Joan I. Roberts. *Nursing, Physician Control and the Medical Monopoly*. Bloomington and Indianapolis: Indiana University Press, 2001.

Hall, Ann M. *The Girl and the Game: A History of Women's Sport in Canada*. Peterborough, ON: Broadview Press, 2002.

Hall, Ann M., and others, eds. *Sport in Canadian Society*. Toronto: McClelland and Stewart, 1991.

Halpern, Monda. *And On That Farm He Had a Wife: Ontario Farm Women and Feminism, 1900–1970*. Montreal and Kingston: McGill-Queen's University Press, 2001.

Hansen, Peter H. "British Mountaineering, 1858–1914." Ph.D. diss., Harvard University, 1991.

———. "Partners: Guides and Sherpas in the Alps and Himalayas, 1850s–1950s." In *Voyages and Visions: Towards a Cultural History of Travel*, ed. Jas Elsner and Joan-Pau Rubies, 210–31. London: Reaktion Books, 1999.

Harkin, Michael, and Sergei Kan, eds. *Special Issue: Native American Women's Responses to Christianity, Ethnohistory* 43 (1996).

Harring, Sidney L. "Indian Law, Sovereignty and State Law." In *A Companion to American Indian History*, ed. Philip J. Deloria and Neal Salisbury, 441–59. Malden and Oxford: Blackwell, 2002.

Hart, Laurie. "Collecting and curating objects of ethnology: an ethnohistorical case study of the O. C. Edwards Collection." Master's thesis, University of Alberta, 1998.

Hawkins, Sean. "'The Woman in Question': Marriage and Identity in the Colonial Courts of Northern Ghana, 1907–1954." In *Women in African Colonial Histories*, ed. Jean Allman et al., 116–43. Bloomington and Indianapolis: Indiana University Press, 2002.

Hayward, Anne. *The Alberta Pottery Industry, 1912–1990: A Social and Economic History*. Hull: Canadian Museum of Civilization, 2002.

Heilbrun, Carolyn G. *Writing a Woman's Life*. New York and London: W. W. Norton, 1988.

Hedley, Max J. "'Normal Expectations': Rural Women without Property." *Resources for Feminist Research* 11 (March 1982): 15–17.

———. "Relations of Production of the 'Family Farm': Canadian Prairies." *Journal of Peasant Studies* 9 (October 1981): 71–85.

Heldke, Lisa. "Recipes for Theory Making." *Hypatia* 3 (1988): 15–29.

Henderson, James [Sákéj]. "First Nations' Legal Inheritances in Canada: The Mikmaq Model." *Manitoba Law Journal* 23 (1996): 1–31.

Henderson, Jennifer. *Settler Feminism and Race Making in Canada.* Toronto: University of Toronto Press, 2003.

Higham, C. L. *Noble, Wretched, and Redeemable: Protestant Missionaries to the Indians in Canada and the United States, 1820–1900.* Calgary: University of Calgary Press, 2000.

Higham, Carol L., and Robert Thacker, eds. *One West, Two Myths: A Comparative Reader.* Calgary: University of Calgary Press, 2004.

Hill, Christopher. *Lenin and the Russian Revolution.* Harmondsworth: Penguin, 1971.

Hinsley, Jr., Curtis M. *Savages and Scientists.* Washington: Smithsonian Institution Press, 1981.

Hollis, Patricia. *Women in Public: The Women's Movement, 1850–1900.* London: George Allen and Unwin, 1979.

Howard, James H. *The Canadian Sioux: Studies in the Anthropology of North American Indians.* Lincoln: University of Nebraska Press, 1984.

Howell, Colin D. *Blood, Sweat and Cheers: Sport and the Making of Modern Canada.* Toronto: University of Toronto Press, 2001.

———. "Elite Doctors and the Development of Scientific Medicine: The Halifax Medical Establishment and 19th Century Medical Professionalism." In *Health, Disease and Medicine: Essays in Canadian History*, ed. Charles G. Roland, 105–22. Toronto: The Hannah Institute for the History of Medicine, Clark Irwin, 1984.

Huel, Raymond. "The Creation of the Alpine Club of Canada: An Early Manifestation of Canadian Nationalism." *Prairie Forum* 15 (1990): 25–43.

———. *Proclaiming the Gospel to the Indians and the Métis: The Missionary Oblates of Mary Immaculate in Western Canada, 1845–1945.* Edmonton: University of Alberta Press, 1996.

Hungry Wolf, Beverly. *The Ways of My Grandmothers.* New York: Quill, 1982.

Hutson, John. "Fathers and Sons: Family Farms, Family Businesses and the Farming Industry." *Sociology* 21 (May 1987): 215–29.

Iacovetta, Franca. "Post-Modern Ethnography, Historical Materialism, and Decentring the (Male) Authorial Voice: A Feminist Conversation." *Histoire sociale/Social History* 32 (November 1999): 275–93.

———. "Recipes for Democracy? Gender, Family and Making Female Citizens in Cold War Canada." In *Rethinking Canada: The Promise of Women's History*, ed. V. Strong-Boag, M. Gleason and A. Perry, 4th ed., 299–313. Don Mills, ON: Oxford University Press, 2002.

Iacovetta, Franca, and Linda Kealey, "Women's History, Gender History and Debating Dichotomies." *Left History* 3 (Spring/Summer 1995): 221–37.

Iacovetta, Franca, and Valerie J. Korinek. "Jell-O Salads, One-Stop Shopping, and Maria the Homemaker: The Gender Politics of Food." In *Sisters or Strangers? Immigrant, Ethnic, and Racialized Women in Canadian History*, ed. Marlene Epp, Franca Iacovetta, and Franca Swyripa, 190–230. Toronto: University of Toronto Press, 2004.

Inderwick, Mary E. "A Lady and her Ranch." In *The Best from Alberta History*, ed. Hugh Dempsey, 65–77. Saskatoon: Historical Society of Alberta, 1981.

Jackel, Susan. *A Flannel Shirt and Liberty: English Emigrant Gentlewomen in the Canadian West, 1880–1914.* Vancouver: UBC Press, 1982.

Jameson, Elizabeth. "Toward a Multicultural History of Women in the Western United States." *Signs* 13 (1988): 761–91.

Jameson, Elizabeth, and Susan Armitage, eds. *The Women's West.* Norman and London: University of Oklahoma Press, 1987.

———. *Writing the Range: Race, Class, and Culture in the Women's West.* Norman and London: University of Oklahoma Press, 1997.

Jefferson, Robert. *Fifty Years on the Saskatchewan.* Vol. 1. Battleford: Canadian North-West Historical Society Publications, 1929.

Jellison, Katherine. *Entitled to Power: Farm Women and Technology, 1913–1963.* Chapel Hill and London: University of North Carolina Press, 1993.

Jensen, Joan. "'I've Worked, I'm Not Afraid of Work': Farm Women in New Mexico, 1920–1940." In *History of Women in the United States: Historical Articles on Women's Lives and Activities,* ed. Nancy F. Cott, vol. 6, *Working on the Land,* 398–423. Munich: K.G. Saur, 1993.

———. *Promise to the Land.* Albuquerque: University of New Mexico Press, 1991.

Johns, Ethel. *The Winnipeg General Hospital School of Nursing.* Winnipeg: Alumnae Association of the Winnipeg General Hospital School of Nursing, 1957.

Johnson, Allan G. *The Gender Knot: Unraveling Our Patriarchial Legacy.* Philadelphia: Temple University Press, 1997.

Johnson, Susan. "'A Memory Sweet to Soldiers': The Significance of Gender in the American West." *Western Historical Quarterly* 24 (November 1993): 495–518.

Johnston, Anna, and Alan Lawson. "Settler Colonies." In *A Companion to Postcolonial Studies,* ed. H. Schwarz and S. Ray, 360–76. Malden: Blackwell, 2000.

Jones, Chris. *Climbing in North America.* Berkeley: University of California Press, 1976.

Jones, David C. *Empire of Dust: Settling and Abandoning the Prairie Dry Belt.* Edmonton: University of Alberta Press, 1987.

Jones, David C., Roy L. J. Wilson, and Donny White. *The Weather Factory: A Pictorial History of Medicine Hat.* Saskatoon: Western Producer Prairie Books, 1988.

Jordan, Mary V. *De ta soeur, Sara Riel.* St. Boniface: Editions des Plaines, 1980.

———. *To Louis from your sister who loves you, Sara Riel.* Toronto: Griffin House, 1974.

Juniper, Annie. *Girls' Home Manual of Cookery, Home Management, Home Nursing and Laundry.* Victoria: King's Printer, 1913.

Kalmakoff, Elizabeth Ann. "Woman Suffrage in Saskatchewan." Master's thesis, University of Regina, 1993.

Kandiyoti, Deniz. "Bargaining with Patriarchy." *Gender and Society* 2 (September 1988): 274–90.

Kealey, Linda. *Enlisting Women for the Cause: Women, Labour, and the Left in Canada, 1890–1920.* Toronto: University of Toronto Press, 1998.

Kealey, Linda, and Joan Sangster, eds. *Beyond the Vote: Canadian Women and Politics.* Toronto: University of Toronto Press, 1989.

Keating, Norah C. "Legacy, Aging, and Succession in Farm Families." *Generations: Journal of the American Society on Aging* 20 (Fall 1996): 61–64.

Keet, Jean E. "The Law Reform Process, Matrimonial Property, and Farm Women: A Case Study of Saskatchewan, 1980–1986." *Canadian Journal of Women and the Law* 4 (1990): 166–89.

————. "Matrimonial Property Legislation: Are Farm Women Equal Partners?" In *The Political Economy of Agriculture in Western Canada*, ed. G.S. Basran and D.A. Hay, 175–84. Toronto: Garamond Press, 1988.

Kelcey, Barbara E., and Angela E. Davis, eds. *A Great Movement Underway: Women and the Grain Growers' Guide, 1908–1928*. Winnipeg: Manitoba Record Society, 1997.

Kelley, Ninette, and Michael Trebilcock. *Making of the Mosaic: A History of Canadian Immigration Policy*. Toronto: University of Toronto Press, 1998.

Kelm, Mary-Ellen. *Colonizing Bodies: Aboriginal Health and Healing in British Columbia 1900–1950*. Vancouver: UBC Press, 1998.

Kennedy, Jacqueline Judith. "Qu'Appelle Industrial School: 'White Rites for the Old North-West.'" Master's thesis, Institute for Canadian Studies, Carleton, 1970.

Kerber, Linda K. "Separate Spheres, Female Worlds, Woman's Place: The Rhetoric of Women's History." *Journal of American History* 75 (June 1988): 9–39.

Kidd, Bruce. *The Struggle for Canadian Sport*. Toronto: University of Toronto Press, 1996.

Kidwell, Clara Sue. "Indian Women as Cultural Mediators." *Ethnohistory* 39 (1992): 97–107.

Kinnear, Julia L. "The Professionalization of Canadian Nursing, 1924–1932: Views in the CN and CMAJ." *Canadian Bulletin of Medical History* 11, no. 1 (1994): 3–22.

Kinnear, Mary. *A Female Economy: Women's Work in a Prairie Province, 1870–1970*. Montreal and Kingston: McGill-Queen's University Press, 1998.

————. "'Do you want your daughter to marry a farmer?' Women's Work on the Farm, 1922." In *Canadian Papers in Rural History VI*, ed. Donald H. Akenson, 137–53. Garonoque: Langdale Press, 1988.

————. ed. *First Days, Fighting Days: Women in Manitoba History*. Regina: Canadian Plains Research Center, 1987.

Kirkwood, Rondalyn. "Blending Vigorous Leadership and Womanly Virtues: Edith Kathleen Russel at the University of Toronto, 1920–1952." *Canadian Bulletin of Medical History* 11, no. 1 (1994): 175–206.

Kohl, Seena B. *Working Together: Women and Family in Southwestern Saskatchewan*. Toronto: Holt, Rinehart and Winston of Canada, 1976.

Kohl, Seena B., and John W. Bennett. "Succession to Family Enterprises and the Migration of Young People in a Canadian Agricultural Community." In *The Canadian Family*, 2nd ed., ed. K. Ishwaran, 246–65. Toronto: Holt, Rinehart and Winston of Canada, 1976.

Kozak, Nadine I. "'Among the Necessities': A Social History of Communication Technology on the Canadian Prairies, 1900 to 1950." Master's thesis, Carleton University, 2000.

Kramer, Reinhold, and Tom Mitchell. *Walk Towards the Gallows: The Tragedy of Hilda Blake, Hanged 1899*. Oxford: Oxford University Press, 2002.

Kubik, Wendee. "The Study of Farm Stress and Coping: A Critical Evaluation." Master's thesis, University of Regina, 1996.

————. "Women's Contradictory Roles in the Contemporary Farm Economy." *Prairie Forum* 29 (Fall 2004): 245–52.

Kubik, Wendee, and Robert J. Moore. "Women's Diverse Roles in the Farm Economy and the Consequences for their Health, Well-being, and Quality of Life." *Prairie Forum* 27 (Spring 2002): 115–29.

Kushner, Howard I. "The Persistence of the Frontier Thesis: Gender, Myth, and Self-Destruction." *Canadian Review of American Studies* 23 (1992). Special issue, Part I, *Reinterpreting the American Experience: Women, Gender, and American Studies*: 53–82.

Lang, Sabine. *Men as Women, Women as Men: Changing Gender in Native American Cultures.* Austin: University of Texas Press, 1998.

Langford, Nanci. "Childbirth on the Canadian Prairies, 1880–1930." In *Telling Tales: Essays in Western Women's History*, ed. Catherine A. Cavanaugh and Randi R. Warne, 278–302. Vancouver: UBC Press, 2000.

Lansing, Michael. "Different Methods, Different Places: Feminist Geography and New Directions in US Western History." *Journal of Historical Geography* 29 (April 2003): 230–47.

Larson, Sylvia, Sharon Aney, and Razia Jaffer. *Women of Aspenland: Images from Central Alberta*: <http://www.albertasource.ca/aspenland/eng/index.html>

Latham, Barbara K., and Roberta J. Pazdro, eds. *Not Just Pin Money: Selected Essays on the History of Women's Work in British Columbia.* Victoria: Camosun College, 1984.

Leacock, Eleanor. "Montagnais Women and the Jesuit Program for Colonization." In *Myths of Male Dominance: Collected Articles on Women Cross-Culturally.* New York: Monthly Review Press, 1981.

Leacy, F.H. *Historical Statistics of Canada.* 2nd ed. Ottawa: Statistics Canada, 1983.

Lee, David. "The Métis Militant Rebels of 1885." In *Readings in Canadian History: Post Confederation*, 4th ed., ed. R. Douglas Francis and Donald B. Smith, 78–98. Toronto: Harcourt Brace, 1994.

Leger-Anderson, Ann. "Canadian Prairie Women's History: An Uncertain Enterprise." *Journal of the West* 37 (January 1998): 47–59.

———. "Marriage, Family, and the Co-operative Ideal in Saskatchewan: The Telfords." In *Telling Tales: Essays in Western Women's History*, ed. Catherine A. Cavanaugh and Randi R. Warne, 280–334. Vancouver: UBC Press, 2000.

Lenskyj, Helen. *Out of Bounds: Women, Sport and Sexuality.* Toronto: Women's Press, 1986.

Leonard, David, and Beverly Whalen, eds. *On the North Trail: The Treaty 8 Diary of O.C. Edwards.* Calgary: Historical Society of Alberta, 1998.

Lerner, Gerda. *The Creation of Patriarchy.* New York: Oxford University Press, 1986.

———. *Why History Matters: Life and Thought.* New York: Oxford University Press, 1997.

Lesage, Germain. *Capitale d'une Solitude.* Ottawa: Editions des Etudes Oblates, 1946.

Leslie, Anita. *Clare Sheridan.* London: Hutchinson, 1977.

———. *The Fabulous Leonard Jerome.* London: Hutchinson, 1954.

———. *Mr. Frewen of England: A Victorian Adventurer.* London: Hutchinson, 1966.

Leslie, Shane. *Long Shadows.* London: John Murray, 1966.

Leslie, Susan. *In the Western Mountains: Early Mountaineering in British Columbia.* Victoria: Aural History Program of the Provincial Archives of British Columbia, 1980.

Lévesque, Andrée. *Making and Breaking the Rules: Women in Québec, 1919–1939*, trans. Yvonne M. Klein. Toronto: McClelland and Stewart, 1994.

Levine, Philippa. *Prostitution, Race, and Politics: Policing Venereal Disease in the British Empire*. New York: Routledge, 2003.

Lewis, Norah L. "Creating the Little Machine: Child Rearing in British Columbia, 1919–1939." *BC Studies* 56 (Winter 1982–1983): 44–60.

———. ed. *Dear Editor and Friends: Letters from Rural Women of the North-West, 1900–1920*. Waterloo, Ontario: Wilfrid Laurier University Press, 1998.

Light, Beth, and Ruth Roach Pierson, eds. *No Easy Road: Women in Canada 1920s to 1960s*. Toronto: New Hogtown Press, 1990.

Lipset, S.M. *Agrarian Socialism: The Cooperative Commonwealth Federation in Saskatchewan*. Berkeley: University of California Press, [1950] 1971.

Loch-Drake, Cynthia. "Jailed Heroes and Kitchen Heroines: Class, Gender and the Medalta Potteries Strike in Postwar Alberta." Master's thesis, University of Calgary, 2001.

Loewen, Royden K. *Hidden Worlds: Revisiting the Mennonite Migrants of the 1870s*. Winnipeg: University of Manitoba Press, 2001.

Loveridge, D.M., and Barry Potyondi. *From Wood Mountain to the Whitemud: A Historical Survey of the Grasslands National Park Area*. Ottawa: Parks Canada, 1983.

Lux, Maureen K. *Medicine that Walks: Disease, Medicine, and Canadian Plains Native People, 1880–1940*. Toronto: University of Toronto Press, 2001.

MacDonald, Graham. *Where the Mountains Meet the Prairies: A History of Waterton Country*. Calgary: University of Calgary Press, 2000.

Mackenzie, John M. "The Imperial Pioneer and Hunter and the British Masculine Stereotype in Late Victorian and Edwardian Times." In *Manliness and Morality: Middle-Class Masculinities in Britain and America, 1800–1940*, ed. J. A. Mangan and James Walvin, 176–98. New York: St. Martin's Press, 1987.

Maclean, John. *Canadian Savage Folk: The Native Tribes of Canada*. Toronto: William Briggs, 1896.

———. *The Indians: Their Manners and Customs*. Toronto: William Briggs, 1907.

MacMurchy, Helen. *The Canadian Mother's Book*. Ottawa: Dominion of Canada, Department of Health, 1925.

———. *Maternal Care*. Ottawa: Department of Pensions and National Health, Canada, 1931.

———. *Mother: A Little Book for Men*. Ottawa: Dominion of Canada Department of Health, 1928.

Maggs, Christopher. "Nurse Recruitment to Four Provincial Hospitals, 1881–1921." In *Rewriting Nursing History*, ed. Celia Davies, 18–40. London: Croom Helm, 1980.

Mandelbaum, David. *The Plains Cree: An Ethnographic, Historical and Comparative Study*. Regina: Canadian Plains Research Center, 1979.

Marotz-Baden, Ramona, and Claudia Mattheis. "Daughters-in-law and Stress in Two-Generation Farm Families." *Family Relations* 43 (April 1994): 132–37.

Marotz-Baden, Ramona, and Deane Cowan. "Mothers-in-Law and Daughters-in-Law: The Effects of Proximity on Conflict and Stress." *Family Relations* 36 (October 1987): 132–37.

Marquis, Greg. "Going Public: Atlantic Canadian Academics and Popular History." *Acadiensis* 31 (Autumn 2001): 146–51.

Martin, Ralph G. *Jennie: The Life of Lady Randolph Churchill.* Vol. 2. *The Dramatic Years, 1895–1921.* Englewood Cliffs: Prentice-Hall, 1971.

Mazel, David, ed. *Mountaineering Women: Stories by Early Climbers.* College Station, TX: Texas A&M University Press, 1994.

McCallum, Margaret E. "Prairie Women and the Struggle for a Dower Law, 1905–1920." *Prairie Forum* 18 (Spring 1993): 19–33.

McCarthy, Martha. *From the Great River to the Ends of the Earth: Oblate Missions to the Dene, 1847–1921.* Edmonton: University of Alberta Press, 1995.

McClintock, Anne. *Imperial Leather: Race, Gender, and Sexuality in the Colonial Contest.* New York: Routledge, 1995.

McClintock, Walter. *Painted Tipis and Picture Writing of the Blackfoot Indians.* Los Angeles: Southwest Museum Leaflet, No. 6.

McClung, Nellie. *Clearing in the West* and *The Stream Runs Fast,* ed. Veronica Strong-Boag and Michelle Lynn Rosa. Peterborough, ON: Broadview Press, 2003.

———. *In Times like These.* Toronto: 1915.

McDougall, John. *Forest, Lake, and Prairie: Twenty years of Frontier Life in Western Canada, 1842–1902.* Toronto: Ryerson Press, 1895.

———. *In the Days of the Red River Rebellion,* ed. Susan Jackel. Edmonton: University of Alberta Press, 1983.

———. *Pathfinding on Plain and Prairie: Stirring Scenes of Life in the Canadian North-West.* Toronto: William Briggs, 1898.

McFeely, Mary Drake. *Can she bake a cherry pie? American women and the kitchen in the twentieth century.* Amherst: University of Massachusetts Press, 2000.

McLaren, Angus. *Our Own Master Race.* Toronto: McClelland and Stewart, 1990.

McLenaghen, Jessie. *Foods, Nutrition and Home Management Manual.* Victoria: King's Printer, 1931.

McManus, Sheila. "Gender(ed) Tensions In the Work and Politics of Alberta Farm Women, 1905–29." In *Telling Tales: Essays in Western Women's History,* ed. Catherine A. Cavanaugh and Randi R. Warne, 123–46. Vancouver: UBC Press, 2000.

———. "'Their own country': Race, Gender, Landscape, and Colonization around the 49th Parallel, 1862–1900." *Agricultural History* 73 (Spring 1999): 168–83.

McPherson, Kathryn. *Bedside Matters: The Transformation of Canadian Nursing, 1900–1990.* Oxford: Oxford University Press, 1996.

———. "Was the 'Frontier' Good for Women? Historical Approaches to Women and Agricultural Settlement in the Prairie West, 1870–1925." *Atlantis: A Women's Studies Journal* 25 (Fall/Winter 2000): 75–86.

McPherson, Kathryn, and Meryn Stuart. "Writing Nursing History in Canada: Issues and Approaches." *Canadian Bulletin of Medical History* 11, no. 1 (1994): 3–22.

McPherson, Kathryn, Cecilia Morgan, and Nancy Forestell, eds. *Gendered Pasts: Historical Essays in Femininity and Masculinity in Canada.* Toronto: University of Toronto Press, 1999.

McPherson, Robert S. *Sacred Land, Sacred View: Navajo Perceptions of the Four Corners Region,* Charles Redd Monographs in Western History, No. 19. Salt Lake City, Utah: Signature Books, 1992.

Memmi, Albert. *The Colonizer and the Colonized*. Boston: Beacon Press, 1965.

Mercier, Laurie. "Women's Role in Montana Agriculture." *Montana: The Magazine of Western History* 38 (Autumn 1988): 50–61.

Merriken, Ellenor Ranghild. *Looking for Country: A Norwegian Immigrant's Alberta Memoir*. Introduction by Janice Dickin. Calgary: University of Calgary Press, 1999.

Merritt, John L. *Baronets and Buffalo: The British Sportsman in the American West, 1833–1881*. Missoula: Mountain Press, 1985.

Mitchinson, Wendy. *Giving Birth in Canada, 1900–1950*. Toronto: University of Toronto Press, 2002.

———. *The Nature of Their Bodies: Women and Their Doctors in Victorian Canada*. Toronto: University of Toronto Press, 1991.

Miller, J. R. "Owen Glendower, Hotspur and Canadian Indian Policy." In *Sweet Promises: A Reader on Indian-White Relations in Canada*, ed. J. R. Miller, 323–52. Toronto: University of Toronto Press, 1991.

———. *Shingwauk's Vision: A History of Native Residential Schools*. Toronto: University of Toronto Press, 1996.

———. *Skyscrapers Hide the Heavens: A History of Indian-White Relations in Canada*. Toronto: University of Toronto Press, 1989.

Minde, Emma. *Kwayask e-ki-pe-kiskinowapahtihick = Their Example Showed Me the Way: A Cree Woman's Life Shaped by Two Cultures*, told by Emma Minde, ed., trans., with glossary by Freda Ahenakew and H.C. Wolfart. Edmonton: University of Alberta Press, 1997.

Mitchell, Estelle. *The Grey Nuns of Montreal and the Red River Settlement, 1844–1984*. Montreal: Éditions du Méridien, 1987.

Moffat, Aileen C. "Experiencing Identity: British-Canadian Women in Rural Saskatchewan, 1880–1950." Ph.D. diss., University of Manitoba, 1996.

———. "Great Women, Separate Spheres, and Diversity: Comments on Saskatchewan Women's Historiography." In *"Other" Voices: Historical Essays on Saskatchewan Women*, ed. David De Brou and Aileen Moffatt, 10–26. Regina: Canadian Plains Research Center, 1995.

Morice, Adrien-Gabriel. *Histoire de l'Église Catholique dans l'Ouest canadien (1659–1915)*. Vol. 2. St. Boniface and Montreal: Author and Granger Frères, 1921.

Morse, Bradford W. "Indian and Inuit Family Law and the Canadian Legal System." *American Indian Law Review* 8 (1980): 199–257.

Morton, Suzanne. "'To Take an Orphan': Gender and Family Roles Following the 1917 Halifax Explosion." In *Gendered Pasts: Historical Essays in Femininity and Masculinity in Canada*, ed. Kathryn McPherson, Cecilia Morgan, and Nancy M. Forestell, 106–22. Don Mills, ON: Oxford University Press, 1999.

Mossman, Mary Jane. "The Paradox of Feminist Engagement with the Law." In *Feminist Issues: Race, Class and Sexuality*, ed. Nancy Mandell. Toronto: Prentice Hall, 1995.

Mountain Horse, Mike. *My People the Bloods*. Standoff, Alberta: Glenbow-Alberta Institute and Blood Tribal Council, 1979.

Muir Edwards, Henrietta. *Legal Status of Women of Alberta*. 2nd ed. Edmonton: Attorney-General, 1921.

———. *Legal Status of Canadian Women*. Ottawa: National Council of Women of Canada, 1908.

Murphy, Lucy Eldersveld. "Public Mothers: Native American and Métis Women as Creole Mediators in the Nineteenth-Century Midwest." *Journal of Women's History* 14 (Winter 2003): 142–66.

Narayan, Uma. "Eating Cultures: Incorporation, Identity and Indian Food." *Social Identities* 1 (1995): 63–87.

Neatby, H. Blair. *The Politics of Chaos: Canada in the Thirties.* Toronto: Macmillan of Canada, 1972.

———. "The Saskatchewan Relief Commission, 1931–1934." *Saskatchewan History* 3 (Spring 1950): 41–56.

Neth, Mary. *Preserving the Family Farm: Women, Community, and the Foundations of Agribusiness in the Midwest, 1900–1940.* Baltimore and London: Johns Hopkins University Press, 1995.

Nightingale, Florence. *Notes on Nursing: What it is and What it is Not.* Philadelphia: Lippincott, [1859] 1946.

Noel, Jan, ed. *Race and Gender in the Northern Colonies.* Toronto: Canadian Scholars' Press, 2000.

Osgood, Ernest Staples. *The Day of the Cattleman.* Minneapolis: University of Minnesota Press, 1954.

Osterud, Nancy Grey. *Bonds of Community: The Lives of Farm Women in Nineteenth-Century New York.* Ithaca and London: Cornell University Press, 1991.

Owram, Doug. "The Myth of Louis Riel." *Canadian Historical Review* 63 (September 1982): 315–36.

Paisley, Fiona. *Loving Protection? Australian Feminism and Aboriginal Women's Rights 1919–1939.* Carlton South, Australia: Melbourne University Press, 2000.

Pajaczowska, C., and L. Young. "Racism, Representation, Psychoanalysis." In *Race, Culture and Difference,* ed. J. Donald and A. Rattansi, 198–219. London: Sage Publications in association with The Open University, 1992.

Palmer, Howard. *Land of the Second Chance: A History of Ethnic Groups in Southern Alberta.* Lethbridge: The Lethbridge Herald, 1972.

———. *Patterns of Prejudice: A History of Nativism in Alberta.* Toronto: McClelland Stewart, 1982.

Palmer, Howard, and Tamara Palmer. *Alberta: A New History.* Edmonton: Hurtig, 1990.

Pannekoek, Frits. *A Snug Little Flock: The Social Origins of the Riel Resistance, 1869–70.* Winnipeg: Watson and Dwyer, 1991.

Parr, Joy. "Gender History and Historical Practice." *The Canadian Historical Review* 76 (September 1995): 354–76.

Pascoe, Peggy. "Race, Gender, and Intercultural Relations: The Case of Interracial Marriage." In *Writing the Range: Race, Class, and Culture in the Women's West,* ed. Elizabeth Jameson and Susan Armitage, 69–80. Norman and London: University of Oklahoma Press, 1997.

———. "Western Women at the Cultural Crossroads." In *Trails: Toward a New Western History,* ed. Patricia Nelson Limerick, Clyde A. Milner II, and Charles E. Rankin, 40–58. Lawrence: University of Kansas Press, 1991.

Paul, Pauline. "Nursing Education Becomes Synonymous with Nursing Service." In *Prepared to Care: Nurses and Nursing in Alberta,* ed. Janet Ross-Kerr, 129–53. Edmonton: University of Alberta Press, 1998.

Payment, Diane. *"The Free People-Otipemisiwak": Batoche, Saskatchewan, 1870–1930*. Ottawa: Minister of Supply and Services, 1990.

———. *"'La vie en rose'*: Métis Women at Batoche, 1870–1920." In *Women of the First Nations: Power, Wisdom, Strength*, ed. Christine Miller and Patricia Chuchryk, 19–38. Winnipeg: University of Manitoba Press, 1996.

———. *Riel Family: Home and Lifestyle at St. Vital, 1860–1910*. Ottawa: Parks Canada, report no. 379, 1980.

———. "Une Aperçu des Relations entre les Missionaires Catholique et le Métisses pendant le Premier Siècle de Contact (1813–1918) dans l'Ouest Canadien." *Études Oblates de l'Ouest* 3 (1994): 139–58.

Pearson, John. *The Private Lives of Winston Churchill*. Toronto: Viking, 1991.

Pederson, Jane Marie. *Between Memory and Reality: Family and Community in Rural Wisconsin, 1870–1970*. Madison: University of Wisconsin Press, 1992.

Peers, Laura. "'The Guardian of All': Jesuit Missionary and Salish Perceptions of the Virgin Mary." In *Reading Beyond Words: Contexts for Native History*, ed. Jennifer S. H. Brown and Elizabeth Vibert, 284–303. Peterborough, ON: Broadview Press, 1996.

Perkin, Joan. *Victorian Women*. New York: New York University Press, 1995.

Pessen, Edward. "Status and Social Class in America." In *Making America: The Society and Culture of the United States*, ed. Luther S. Luedtke, 362–75. Chapel Hill, NC: University of North Carolina Press, 1992.

Peyer, Bernd. *The Tutor'd Mind: Indian Missionary-Writers in Antebellum America*. Amherst: University of Massachusetts Press, 1997.

Perry, Adele. "Feminism, History, and Writing British Columbia's Past." *Atlantis: A Women's Studies Journal* 25 (Fall/Winter 2000): 69–74.

———. *On the Edge of Empire: Gender, Race, and the Making of British Columbia*. Toronto: University of Toronto Press, 2001.

Pierson, Ruth Roach. *"They're Still Women After All": The Second World War and Canadian Womanhood*. Toronto: McClelland and Stewart, 1986.

Pierson, Ruth Roach, and Nupur Chaudhuri, eds. *Nation, Empire, Colony: Historicizing Gender and Race*. Bloomington: Indiana University Press, 1998.

Plane, Ann Marie. *Colonial Intimacies: Indian Marriage in Early New England*. Ithaca and London: Cornell University Press, 2000.

Poiner, Gretchen. *The Good Old Rule: Gender and Other Power Relationships in a Rural Community*. Sydney: Sydney University Press, 1990.

Prentice, Alison, and others. *Canadian Women: A History*. 2nd ed. Toronto: Harcourt Brace, 1996.

Prucha, Francis Paul, ed. *Documents of United States Indian Policy*. 2nd ed. Lincoln: University of Nebraska Press, 1975.

Rasmussen, Linda, and others. *A Harvest Yet to Reap: A History of Prairie Women*. Toronto: The Women's Press, 1976.

Rasporich, A. W. "Utopian Ideals and Community Settlements in Western Canada, 1880–1914." In *The Prairie West: Historical Readings*, ed. R. Douglas Francis and Howard Palmer, 352–77. Edmonton: University of Alberta Press, 1992.

Reichwein, PearlAnn. "Beyond Visionary Mountains: The Alpine Club of Canada and the Canadian National Park Idea, 1906 to 1969." Ph.D. diss., Carleton University, 1995.

Richardson, Sharon. "Frontier Nursing: Nursing Work and Training in Alberta, 1890–1905." *Canadian Journal of Nursing Research* 28, no. 3 (1997): 116–20.

Riley, Glenda. "The Future of Western Women's History." *Historian* (Fall 2004): 539–45.

Ramusack, Barbara N. "Cultural Missionaries, Maternal Imperialists, Feminist Allies: British Women Activists in India, 1865–1945." *Women's Studies International Forum* 13 (1990): 309–21.

Ranoa, Milagros. *Women and Decision-making in Agriculture: Barriers to Participation.* RDI Report Series 1993–2. Brandon, Manitoba: Rural Development Institute, Brandon University, 1993.

Ravenhill, A. *Alice Ravenhill: The Memoirs of an Educational Pioneer.* Toronto: Dent, 1951.

Read, Herbert. "The Philosophy of Anarchism." In *Selected Writings: Poetry and Criticism*, with a foreword by Allen Tate. London: Faber and Faber, 1963.

Research, Action and Education Centre. "Keeping Women Down on the Farm." *Resources for Feminist Research* 11 (March 1982): 12–14.

Riney-Kehrberg, Pamela. *Rooted in Dust: Surviving Drought and Depression in Southwestern Kansas.* Lawrence: University Press of Kansas, 1994.

———. ed. *Waiting on the Bounty: The Dust Bowl Diary of Mary Knackstedt Dyck.* Iowa City: University of Iowa Press, 1999.

Robertson, Valerie. "Plains Ledger Art: The Documentation of a Way of Life through the Nineteenth-Century Pictorial Account of an Unknown Assiniboine Artist." *Prairie Forum* 17 (Fall 1992): 263–74.

Rodee, Howard D. "The Stylistic Development of Plains Indian Paintings and its Relationship to Ledger Drawings." *Plains Anthropologist* 10 (November 1956): 218–32.

Roediger, David R. *Towards the Abolition of Whiteness: Essays on Race, Politics, and Working-Class History.* London: Verso, 1994.

———. *The Wages of Whiteness: Race and the Making of the American Working Class.* London & New York: Verso, 1991.

Rollings-Magnusson, Sandra. "Canada's Most Wanted: Pioneer Women on the Western Prairies." *Canadian Review of Sociology and Anthropology* 27 (May 2000): 223–38.

———. "Hidden Homesteaders: Women, the State and Patriarchy in the Saskatchewan Wheat Economy, 1870–1930." *Prairie Forum* 24 (Fall 1999): 171–83.

Roome, Patricia. "Henrietta Muir Edwards: The Journey of a Canadian Feminist." Ph.D. diss., Simon Fraser University, 1996.

Roper, Edward. *By Track and Trail: A Journey through Canada.* London: W.H. Allen and Co., 1891.

Rosaldo, Michelle Zimbalist, and Louise Lamphere. "A Theoretical Overview." In *Woman, Culture, and Society*, ed. Rosaldo and Lamphere, 17–42. Stanford: Stanford University Press, 1974.

Rosenberg, Charles E. *The Care of Strangers: The Rise of America's Hospital System.* New York: Basic Books, 1987.

Rosenfeld, Rachel Ann. *Farm Women: Work, Farm, and Family in the United States.* Chapel Hill and London: University of North Carolina Press, 1985.

Rossiter, Margaret W. *Women Scientists in America: Struggles and Strategies to 1940.* Baltimore: Johns Hopkins University Press, 1982.

Ross-Kerr, Janet C. *Prepared to Care: Nurses and Nursing in Alberta, 1859–1996.* Edmonton: University of Alberta Press, 1998.

Routledge, Karen. "Shifting Seas of Ice: The Mundays and Mount Waddington, 1926–1934." Master's thesis, Simon Fraser University, 2002.

Russell, Candyce S., and others. "Coping Strategies Associated with Intergenerational Transfer of the Family Farm," *Rural Sociology* 50 (Fall 1985): 361–76.

Rutherdale, Myra. "Revising Colonization through Gender: Anglican Missionary Women in the Pacific North-West and the Arctic, 1860–1945." *BC Studies* 104 (Winter 1994–95): 3–23.

———. *Women and the White Man's God: Gender and Race in the Canadian Mission Field*. Vancouver: UBC Press, 2002.

Rutherford, Janice. "A Foot in Each Sphere: Christine Frederick and Early Twentieth-Century Advertising." *Historian* 63, no. 1 (2000): 67–87.

Sabo, Donald F., and Joe Panepinto. "Football Ritual and the Social Reproduction of Masculinity." In *Sport, Men and the Gender Order: Critical Feminist Perspectives*, ed. Messner and Sabo, 115–26. Champaign, IL: Human Kinetics, 1990.

Sachs, Carolyn E. *Gendered Fields: Rural Women, Agriculture and Environment*. Boulder: Westview Press, 1996.

———. *The Invisible Farmers: Women in Agricultural Production*. Totowa, NJ: Rowman and Allanheld, 1983.

Said, Edward. *Orientalism: Western Conceptions of the Orient*. New York: Random House, 1978.

Salamon, Sonya. *Prairie Patrimony: Family, Farming, and Community in the Midwest*. Chapel Hill and London: University of North Carolina Press, 1992.

Sanders, Douglas. "Indian Women: A Brief History of Their Roles and Rights." *McGill Law Journal* 21, no. 4 (1975): 656.

Sandford, R. W. *The Canadian Alps: The History of Mountaineering in Canada*. Volume 1. Banff: Altitude Publishing, 1990.

Sangster, Joan. "Beyond Dichotomies: Re-Assessing Gender History and Women's History in Canada." *Left History* 3 (Spring/Summer 1995): 109–21.

———. "Reconsidering Dichotomies," *Left History* 3 (Fall/Spring 1995/6): 238–48.

———. *Regulating Girls and Women: Sexuality, Family and the Law in Ontario, 1920–1960*. Oxford: Oxford University Press, 2001.

Schwartz, Mary Ann, and B. M. Scott, eds. *Marriage and Families: Diversity and Change*. 3rd ed. Toronto: Prentice-Hall Canada, 2000.

Schwieder, Dorothy. "South Dakota Farm Women and the Great Depression." *Journal of the West*, 24 (October 1985): 6–18.

Schwieder, Dorothy, and Deborah Fink. "Plains Women: Rural Life in the 1930s." *Great Plains Quarterly* 8 (Spring 1988): 79–88.

Scott, Chic. *Pushing the Limits: The Story of Canadian Mountaineering*. Calgary: Rocky Mountain Books, 2000.

Scott, Joan. *Gender and the Politics of History*. New York: Columbia University Press, 1999.

Scowby, Christa L. "'Divine Discontent': Women, Identity, and the *Western Producer*." Master's thesis, University of Saskatchewan, 1996.

———. "'I Am A Worker, Not A Drone': Farm Women, Reproductive Work and the *Western Producer*, 1930–1939." *Saskatchewan History* 48 (Fall 1996): 3–15.

Semple, Neil. *The Lord's Dominion: The History of Canadian Methodism*. Montreal: McGill-Queen's University Press, 1996.

Shapiro, Laura. *Perfection Salad: Women and Cooking at the Turn of the Century.* New York: Farrar, Straus and Giroux, 1986.

Sheridan, Clare. *Arab Interlude.* London: Ivor Nicholson and Watson, 1936.

———. *A Turkish Kaleidoscope.* London: Duckworth, 1926.

———. *Across Europe with Satanella.* London: Duckworth, 1925.

———. *Mayfair to Moscow.* New York; Boni and Liveright, 1921.

———. *My American Diary.* New York: Boni and Liveright, 1922.

———. *Redskin Interlude.* London: Nicolson and Watson, 1938.

———. *Russian Portraits.* London: Jonathan Cape, 1921.

———. *Russian Portraits,* ed. Mark Almond. Cambridge: Ian Faulkner Publishing, 1992.

———. *To the Four Winds.* London: Andre Deutsch, 1957.

———. *West to East.* New York: Boni and Liveright, 1923.

Shoemaker, Nancy. "Kateri Tekakwitha's Tortuous Path to Sainthood." In *Negotiators of Change,* 49–71.

———. ed. *Negotiators of Change: Historical Perspectives on Native American Women.* New York: Routledge, 1995.

Shortall, Sally. "Farmwives and Power: An Empirical Study of the Power Relationships Affecting Women on Irish Farms." Ph.D. diss., National University of Ireland, 1990.

———. "Power Analysis and Farm Wives: An Empirical Study of the Power Relationships Affecting Women on Irish Farms." *Sociologia Ruralis* 32 (1992): 431–51.

———. *Women and Farming: Property and Power.* London: Macmillan Press; New York: St. Martin's Press, 1999.

Shortt, S.E.D. "'Before the Age of Miracles': The Rise, Fall, and Rebirth of General Practise in Canada, 1890–1940." In *Health, Disease and Medicine: Essays in Canadian History,* ed. Charles G. Roland, 123–52. Toronto: The Hannah Institute for the History of Medicine: Clark Irwin, 1984.

Shröder, Ingo W. "From Parkman to Postcolonial Theory: What's New in the Ethnohistory of Missions?" *Ethnohistory* 46 (1999): 809–15.

Siggins, Maggie. *Riel: A Life of Revolution.* Toronto: Harper Collins, 1994.

Silverman, Eliane Leslau. *The Last Best West: Women on the Alberta Frontier, 1880–1930.* Montreal: Eden Press: 1984.

———. "Writing Canadian Women's History, 1970–82: An Historiographical Analysis." *Canadian Historical Review* 63 (December 1982): 513–33.

Slatta, Richard W. "Taking Our Myths Seriously." *Journal of the West* 40 (2001): 3–5.

Sleeper-Smith, Susan. "Entre Catholique et Devenir Indienne: Soeur Cecelia, Une Femme Odawaise." *Recherches Amérindienne au Quebec* 32 (2002): 53–61.

———. *Indian Women and French Men: Rethinking Cultural Encounter in the Western Great Lakes.* Amherst: University of Massachusetts Press, 2001.

Slobodin, Richard. "The Subarctic Métis as Products and Agents of Cultural Contact." *Arctic Anthropology* 2 (1964): 50–55.

Smith, Cyndi. *Off the Beaten Track: Women Adventurers and Mountaineers in Western Canada.* Jasper: Coyote Books, 1989.

Smith, Erica. "'Gentlemen, This is no Ordinary Trial': Sexual Narratives and the Trial of the Reverend Corbett, Red River, 1863." in *Reading Beyond Words: Contexts for Native History,* ed. Jennifer S. H. Brown and Elizabeth Vibert, 364–80. Peterborough, ON: Broadview Press, 1996.

Smith, Helen Huntington. *The War on Powder River*. New York: McGraw-Hill, 1966.

Smith, M.G. "Alice Ravenhill: International Pioneer in Home Economics." *Illinois Teacher* 33, no. 1 (1989): 10–14.

Smith-Rosenberg, Carroll. "The Female World of Love and Ritual." *Signs* 1 (1975): 1–29.

Snell, James. "The Family and the Working-Class Elderly in the First Half of the Twentieth Century." In *Family Matters: Papers in Post-Confederation Canadian Family History*, ed. Lori Chambers and Edgar-Andre Montigny, 499–510. Toronto: Canadian Scholars' Press, 1998.

Snow, Chief John. *These Mountains Are Our Sacred Places: The Story of the Stoney Indians*. Toronto: S. Stevens, 1977.

Spalding, Philip Taft. "The Métis at Île-à-la-Crosse." Ph.D. diss., University of Washington, 1970.

Spence, Mark David. *Dispossessing the Wilderness: Indian Removal and the Making of the National Parks*. New York: Oxford University Press, 1999.

Spry, Irene. "The Métis and Mixed-bloods of Rupert's Land before 1870." In *The New Peoples: Being and Becoming Métis in North America*, ed. Jacqueline Peterson and Jennifer S. H. Brown, 98–118. Winnipeg: University of Manitoba Press, 1985.

Stanley, George F. G. *Louis Riel*. Toronto: Ryerson Press, 1963.

—. ed. *The Collected Writings of Louis Riel/Les Écrits Complets de Louis Riel*. Edmonton: University of Alberta Press, 1985.

Stanley, Timothy. "White Supremacy and the Rhetoric of Educational Indoctrination: A Canadian Case Study." In *Making Imperial Mentalities: Socialization and British Imperialism*, ed. J. Mangan, 144–62. Manchester: Manchester University Press, 1990.

Stapleford, E.W. *Report on Rural Relief Due to Drought Conditions and Crop Failures in Western Canada, 1930–1937*. Ottawa: King's Printer, 1939.

Starr, Paul. *The Social Transformation of American Medicine*. New York: Basic Books, 1982.

Stasiulis, Daiva, and Nira Yuval-Davis, eds. *Unsettling Settler Societies: Articulations of Gender, Race, Ethnicity, and Class*. London: Sage, 1995.

Stevenson, Winona. "The Journals and Voices of a Church of England Native Catechist: Askenootow (Charles Pratt), 1851–1884." In *Reading Beyond Words: Contexts for Native History*, ed. Jennifer S. H. Brown and Elizabeth Vibert, 304–29. Peterborough, ON: Broadview Press, 1996.

Stølen, Kristi Anne. "The Gentle Exercise of Male Power in Rural Argentina." *Identities: Global Studies in Culture and Power* 2 (April 1996): 385–406.

Stoler, Ann Laura. *Carnal Knowledge and Imperial Power: Race and the Intimate in Colonial Rule*. Berkeley: University of California Press, 2002.

—. "Tense and Tender Ties: The Politics of Comparison in North American History and (Post)Colonial Studies." *Journal of American History* 88 (December 2001): 829–64.

Strang, J., and J. Toomre. "Alexis Soyer and the Irish Famine." In *The Great Famine and the Irish Diaspora in America*, ed. A. Gribben, 66–84. Amherst: University of Massachusetts Press, 1999.

Strange, Carolyn. *Toronto's Girl Problem: The Perils and Pleasures of the City, 1880–1930*. Toronto: University of Toronto Press, 1995.

Strange, Kathleen. "'I Hadn't Believed That There Was So Much Pain in the World.'"
In *No Easy Road: Women in Canada, 1920s to 1960s*, ed. Beth Light and Ruth
Roach Pierson, 180–83. Toronto: New Hogtown Press, 1990.

Strathy, Kerrie A. *Legacy: A History of Saskatchewan Homemakers' Clubs and Women's
Institutes, 1911–1988*. Saskatoon: Saskatchewan Women's Institute, 1988.

——. "Saskatchewan Women's Institutes: The Rural Women's University,
1911–1986." Master's thesis, University of Saskatchewan, 1987.

Street, Margaret. *Watch-Fires on the Mountains: The Life and Writing of Ethel Johns*.
Toronto: University of Toronto Press, 1973.

Strong-Boag, Veronica. "Making a Difference: The History of Canada's Nurses."
Canadian Bulletin of Medical History 8 (1991): 231–48.

——. *The New Day Recalled: Lives of Girls and Women in English Canada,
1919–1939*. Markham: Penguin, 1988.

——. "Pulling in Double Harness or Hauling a Double Load." In *The Prairie West:
Historical Readings*, 2nd ed., ed. R. Douglas Francis and Howard Palmer,
401–23. Edmonton: Pica Pica Press, 1992.

Strong-Boag, Veronica, and Carol Gerson. *Paddling Her Own Canoe: The Times and
Texts of E. Pauline Johnson, Tekahienwake*. Toronto: University of Toronto
Press, 2000.

Strong-Boag, Veronica, and others, eds. *Painting the Maple: Essays on Race, Gender
and the Construction of Canada*. Vancouver: UBC Press, 1998.

Strong-Boag, Veronica, and Michelle Lynn Rosa. "Introduction: 'Some Small Legacy
of Truth.'" In *Nellie McClung: The Complete Autobiography; Clearing in the
West and The Streams Runs Fast*, ed. Veronica Strong-Boag and Michelle
Lynn Rosa. Peterborough, ON: Broadview Press, 2003.

Sundberg, Sara Brooks. "A Female Frontier: Manitoba Farm Women in 1922." *Prairie
Forum* 16 (Fall 1991): 185–204.

——. "Farm Women on the Canadian Frontier: The Helpmate Image." In *Farm
Women on the Prairie Frontier: A Sourcebook for Canada and the United
States*, ed. Carol Fairbanks and Sara Brooks Sundberg, 71–90. Metuchen,
NJ: Scarecrow Press, 1983.

Sutherland, Neil. *Children in English-Canadian Society: Framing the Twentieth
Century Consensus*, 2nd ed. Waterloo: Wilfrid Laurier University Press, 2000.

Swystun, Lenore. "Women in Farming: A Social Economy of Multi-Family and
Single Family Farms in Saskatchewan." Master's thesis, University of
Saskatchewan, 1996.

Sylvester, Kenneth Michael. *The Limits of Rural Capitalism: Family, Culture, and
Markets in Montcalm, Manitoba, 1870–1940*. Toronto: University of Toronto
Press, 2001.

Symes, David G. "Bridging the Generations: Succession and Inheritance in a
Changing World," *Sociologia Ruralis* 30 (1990): 287–89.

Szasz, Margaret Connell, ed. *Between Indian and White Worlds: The Cultural Broker*.
Norman: University of Oklahoma Press, 1994.

Tanner, John. *A Narrative of the Captivity and Adventures of John Tanner during Thirty
Years Residence Among the Indians in the Interior of North America*. Prepared
for the press by Edwin James. Minneapolis: Ross and Haines, [1830] 1956.

Taylor, Betty. *Clare Sheridan*. Hastings: 1984.

Taylor, Janet Edgar, Joan E. Norris, and Wayne H. Howard. "Succession Patterns of Farmer and Successor in Canadian Farm Families." *Rural Sociology* 63 (December 1998): 553–73.

Taylor, Jeffery. *Fashioning Farmers: Ideology, Agricultural Knowledge and the Manitoba Farm Movement, 1890–1925*. Regina: Canadian Plains Research Center, 1994.

Thomas L.G. "Privileged Settlers." In *Ranchers' Legacy: Alberta Essays*, ed. Patrick A. Dunae, 159–62. Edmonton: University of Alberta Press, 1986.

Thomas, Nicholas. *Colonialism's Culture: Anthropology, Travel and Government*. Princeton: Princeton University Press, 1994.

Thompson, E. P. *The Making of the English Working Class*. London: Penguin, 1968.

Thompson, John Herd. *Forging the Prairie West*. Toronto: Oxford University Press, 1998.

Thompson, John Herd, with Allen Seager. *Canada 1922–1939: Decades of Discord*. Toronto: McClelland and Stewart, 1985.

Tobias, John L. "Protection, Civilization, Assimilation: An Outline History of Canada's Indian Policy." In *The Prairie West: Historical Readings*, ed. R. Douglas Francis and Howard Palmer, 207–24. Edmonton: University of Alberta Press, 1992.

Tomkins, George S. *A Common Countenance: Stability and Change in the Canadian Curriculum*. Scarborough, ON: Prentice-Hall, 1986.

Treaty 7 Elders and Tribal Council, and others. *The True Spirit and Original Intent of Treaty 7*. Montreal: McGill-Queen's University Press, 1996.

Turner, Victor. *The Ritual Process: Structure and Anti-Structure*. Ithaca: Cornell University Press, 1969.

Twiss, Fannie. *The Rural School Luncheon*. Regina: King's Printer, 1916.

Unsworth, Walt. *Hold the Heights: The Foundations of Mountaineering*. Seattle: The Mountaineers, 1994.

Usher, Jean. "Apostles and Aborigines: The Social Theory of the Church Missionary Society." In *Prophets, Priests, and Prodigals: Reading in Canadian Religious History, 1608 to the Present*, ed. Mark G. McGowan and David Marshall, 15–43. Toronto: McGraw Hill, 1992.

Valverde, Mariana. "'When the Mother of the Race is Free': Race, Reproduction, and Sexuality in First-Wave Feminism." In *Gender Conflicts: New Essay in Women's History*, ed. Franca Iacovetta and Mariana Valverde, 3–26. Toronto: University of Toronto Press, 1992.

Van de Vorst, Carolina. "A History of Farm Women's Work in Manitoba." Master's thesis, University of Manitoba, 1988.

Van Kirk, Sylvia. *"Many Tender Ties": Women in Fur Trade Society in Western Canada, 1670–1870*. Winnipeg: Watson and Dwyer, 1980.

———. "What If Mama is an Indian?: The Cultural Ambivalence of the Alexander Ross Family." In *The Developing West: Essays on Canadian History in Honour of Lewis H. Thomas*, ed. John E. Foster, 123–36. Edmonton: University of Alberta, 1983.

Vein, Rossel. "La Correspondance de Sara Riel." *Écrits de Canada français* 22 (1966): 243–76.

Vickers, Jill McCalla. "Feminist Approaches to Women in Politics." In *Beyond the Vote: Canadian Women and Politics*, ed. Linda Kealy and Joan Sangster, 16–36. Toronto: University of Toronto Press, 1989.

Voyageur, Cora. "They Called Her Chief: A Tribute to Fort MacKay's Indomitable Leader Dorothy McDonald." *Legacy: Alberta's Heritage Magazine* 7 (Winter 2002): 14–17.

Voyce, Malcolm. "Testamentary Freedom, Patriarchy and Inheritance of the Family Farm in Australia." *Sociologia Ruralis* 34 (1994): 71–83.

Waiser, Bill. "Introduction: Place, Process, and the New Prairie Realities." *Canadian Historical Review* 84 (December 2003): 509–17.

Ward, Michael P., James S. Milledge, and John B. West. *High Altitude Medicine and Physiology*. 3rd ed. New York: Oxford University Press, 2000.

Ward, W. Peter. *White Canada Forever: Popular Attitudes and Public Policy Toward Orientals in British Columbia*. 2nd ed. Montreal: McGill-Queen's University Press, 1990.

Ware, Vron. *Beyond the Pale: White Women, Racism and History*. London: Verso, 1992.

Warner, Marina. *Alone of All Her Sex: The Myth and the Cult of the Virgin Mary*. London: Picador, 1990.

Watkins, Bari. "Woman's World in Nineteenth-Century America." *American Quarterly* 31 (Spring 1979): 116–27.

Waudo, Judith. "Home Economics in Kenya: Challenges and Perspectives." *Curriculum Technology Quarterly* 12 (2002): <http://www.ascd.org/publications/ctq/2002fall/toc.html> (14 January 2004)

West, John B. *High Life: A History of High-Altitude Physiology and Medicine*. New York: Oxford University Press, 1998.

Whatmore, Sarah. *Farming Women: Gender, Work and Family Enterprise*. London: Macmillan, 1991.

White, Hayden. *Tropics of Discourse: Essays in Cultural Criticism*. Baltimore: Johns Hopkins University Press, 1978.

White, Pamela Margaret. "Restructuring the Domestic Sphere – Prairie Indian Women on Reserves: Image, Ideology and State Policy, 1880–1930." Ph.D. diss., McGill University, 1987.

White, Richard, and John M. Findlay, eds. *Power and Place in the North American West*. Seattle and London: Centre for the Study of the Pacific Northwest and University of Washington Press, 1999.

Whitehead, Margaret. "A Useful Christian Woman: First Nations Women and Protestant Missionary Work in British Columbia." *Atlantis* 18 (1992–93): 142–66.

Williams, Carol J. *Framing the West: Race, Gender, and the Photographic Frontier in the Pacific Northwest*. Oxford: Oxford University Press, 2003.

Wrobel, David M. "Introduction: What on Earth Has Happened to the New Western History?" *Historian* 66 (Fall 2004): 437–42.

Yee, Shirley J. "Gender Ideology and Black Women as Community-Builders in Ontario, 1850–1870." In *Rethinking Canada: The Promise of Women's History*, 4 ed., ed. Veronica Strong-Boag, Mona Gleason, and Adele Perry, 87–102. Don Mills, ON: Oxford University Press, 2002.

Young, Egerton R. *By Canoe and Dog Train Among the Cree and Saulteaux Indians*. London: Hazell, Watson, and Viney, 1890.

———. *Children of the Forest: A Story of Indian Love*. Toronto: Musson, 1902.

———. *Indian Life in the Great North-West*. Toronto: Musson, Led., 1902.

———. *Oowikapun: Or How the Gospel Reached the Nelson River Indians.* New York: Eaton and Mains, 1896.

———. *When the Blackfeet Went South: And Other Stories.* London: Wyman and Sons, n.d.

Young, Jennifer J. "Farm Women of Alberta: Their Perceptions of Their Health and Work." Master's thesis, University of Alberta, 1997.

Young, Kevin, and Philip White. "Sport, Physical Danger, and Injury: The Experiences of Elite Women Athletes." *Journal of Sport and Social Issues* 19 (February 1995): 45–61.

Young, Kevin, Philip White, and William McTeer. "Body Talk: Male Athletes Reflect on Sport, Injury and Pain," *Sociology of Sport Journal* 11 (June 1994): 175–94.

Zaharia, *Sikotan* Floram and *Makai'sto* Leo Fox. *Kitomahkitapiiminnooniksi: Stories from Our Elders.* Vol. 1. Edmonton: Donahue House, 1995.

Zemon Davis, Natalie. "Iroquois Women, European Women." In *Women, "Race," and Writing in the Early Modern Period*, ed. Margo Hendricks and Patricia Parker, 243–58. New York: Routledge, 1994.

Zimmer, Ronald P. "Early Oblate Attempts for Indian and Métis Priests in Canada." *Études Oblates* (October-December 1973): 276–91.

Zlotkin, Norman. "Judicial Recognition of Aboriginal Customary Law in Canada: Selected Marriage and Adoption Cases." *Canadian Native Law Reporter* 4 (1984): 1–17.

index

www.ingramcontent.com/pod-product-compliance
Lightning Source LLC
Chambersburg PA
CBHW050623280326
41932CB00015B/2500